CAPITAL DRAWINGS

CAPITAL DRAWINGS

———

Architectural Designs for Washington, D.C.,
from the Library of Congress

EDITED BY C. FORD PEATROSS

With the assistance of Pamela Scott, Diane Tepfer, and Leslie Freudenheim

THE JOHNS HOPKINS UNIVERSITY PRESS · BALTIMORE

IN ASSOCIATION WITH THE LIBRARY OF CONGRESS · WASHINGTON, D.C.

This book and the Washingtoniana Project in the Prints and Photographs Division of the Library of Congress from which it developed were made possible by generous grants from the Morris and Gwendolyn Cafritz Foundation.

9   8   7   6   5   4   3   2   1

The Johns Hopkins University Press
2715 North Charles Street
Baltimore, Maryland 21218-4363

www.press.jhu.edu

Frontispiece: Thomas U. Walter, architect. "Interior View, Library of Congress," United States Capitol, Washington, D.C. Perspective. Ink and watercolor on paper. 1852. ADE-UNIT 2592, no. 1, B size. LC-USZC4-3777.

Library of Congress Cataloging-in-Publication Data

Capital drawings : architectural designs for Washington, D.C., from the Library of Congress / edited by C. Ford Peatross.

    p. cm.

    From the Washingtoniana II project of the Prints and Photographs Division of the Library of Congress.

    Includes bibliographical references and index.

    ISBN 0-8018-7232-4 (hardcover : alk. paper)

    1. Architectural drawing—Washington (D.C.) 2. Library of Congress. Prints and Photographs Division. 3. Architecture—Washington (D.C.) —Designs and plans. 4. Washington (D.C.)— Buildings, structures, etc. I. Peatross, C. Ford. II. Library of Congress. Prints and Photographs Division.

    NA2695.U6L533 2005

    720'.22'2753—dc22   2004025490

A catalog record for this book is available from the British Library.

CONTENTS

Foreword by James H. Billington … vii

Preface … viii

Chapter One
WASHINGTON, D.C.
From L'Enfant's Dream to Edge City
C. FORD PEATROSS … I

Chapter Two
THE UNITED STATES CAPITOL
Icon of the Republic
DAMIE STILLMAN … 59

Chapter Three
THE WHITE HOUSE
Seat of the Presidency
WILLIAM SEALE … 87

Chapter Four
BUILDING FOR BUSINESS
Commercial Architecture in Metropolitan Washington
RICHARD LONGSTRETH … 109

Chapter Five
TWENTIETH-CENTURY HOUSING
Single-Family Residences, Apartment Buildings, and Planned Communities
GWENDOLYN WRIGHT … 151

Chapter Six
THE VIETNAM VETERANS MEMORIAL
Grateful Memory, Lost Bravado
PAMELA SCOTT … 173

COLOR PLATES … 181

Acknowledgments … 219

Appendix A. Ordering Reproductions and Exploring the Architecture, Design, and Engineering Collections … 220

Appendix B. Architects, Designers, and Engineers: A List of Online Resources … 222

Notes … 231

Essay on Sources … 244

List of Contributors … 245

Index … 246

FOREWORD

Since the founding of the Republic, the ongoing process of designing and building its capital has been at the center rather than the periphery of the development of American architecture, design, and engineering. Early on, George Washington and Thomas Jefferson recognized the expressive power as well as the practical necessity of the capital's buildings and monuments, enlisting the best talent available for their design. Since its establishment as the seat of government in 1800, Washington, D.C., has grown to be the centerpiece of a sprawling metropolitan region, serving as a testing ground for new building types and technologies and as the locus of the search for a national identity in the design arts.

From its earliest days, pictorial materials have had an important place in the Library of Congress, the oldest national cultural institution in the United States. Its founder, Thomas Jefferson, was an avid collector and user of architectural, design, and engineering books and textbooks, drawings, and engravings. It is therefore appropriate that among its vast collections, the Library of Congress has millions of books, manuscripts, prints, photographs, and original design and record drawings that tell us about the development and achievements of the professions of architecture, design, and engineering, especially in the United States. These represent a significant proportion of the more than 127 million items held by the library, over 14 million of which are housed in its Prints and Photographs Division.

Washington, D.C., did not arise in a day, and one of the richest of these groups of documents tells the story of its planning, growth, and influence. In 1790 in Philadelphia, Congress approved the Federal District, as Washington was first known. The Residence Act fixed its location on the Potomac River, and ten square miles of territory were donated by Maryland and Virginia. Over the course of two centuries, the physical fabric of Washington, D.C., evolved, and the nation's capital and its designers served as catalysts and models for the entire country.

This volume is to serve as a portal and a guidebook for the newly available documents that tell this story and to encourage their use and exploration. It also is intended to celebrate the completion of an ambitious, decade-long project that has seen more than forty thousand drawings, prints, and photographs in the library's Prints and Photographs Division conserved, properly housed, cataloged, and made available for the first time at the library and worldwide through more than three thousand electronic records in the Prints and Photographs Online Catalog (www.loc.gov/rr/print/).

Each of these "capital drawings" reflects some aspect, large or small, of the lives, history, aspirations, and values of its creators and sponsors—the famous and the obscure. More than that, each provides a lens through which we can examine the history and development of a city and nation through the buildings, monuments, and public and private spaces that have given them physical form and symbolic meaning. They represent the creative energy and technical knowledge of over five hundred architects, designers, and engineers. The essays in this volume demonstrate the potential of these materials for further study and research and have been written by a distinguished group of scholars, who plumb their depths.

None of this would have been possible without the generous support of the Morris and Gwendolyn Cafritz Foundation, which has supported all of this work and this publication.

We invite you to visit the Library of Congress when you are in Washington, D.C., and to make use of our award-winning Web site from your home, school, or office. The site, www.loc.gov, has become one of the most popular locations on the Internet for a wide range of users, from individuals to schoolchildren, to scholars and professionals in many fields and it receives more than three billion hits a year.

Through it, or more directly through the online catalog of our Prints and Photographs Division, you can enjoy almost instantaneous access to the records and online images for all of the drawings illustrated in this volume as well as for many thousands more.

James H. Billington
Librarian of Congress

PREFACE

As this preface was being written, the Mars Rover exploration vehicles *Spirit* and *Opportunity* were focusing the attention of the entire world on two relatively small areas of that vast planet, attempting through local observations to understand more about its character and potential for further exploration. This book attempts something not dissimilar, through the analysis and selection of a relatively small number of examples from a huge, almost unexplored archive—itself but a tiny crater within the universal holdings of the Library of Congress—to encourage the research, study, and further dissemination of tens of thousands of graphic documents detailing the evolution, history, and fundamental physical characteristics of the "capital of the free world."

The Library of Congress began in 1800 as a small legislative research library and has become the largest library in the world, with more than 127 million items, including more than 18 million books, 12 million photographs, 5 million maps, and 54 million manuscripts. Yet, relatively few students of American architecture, design, and engineering are aware of the full size, range, and research potential of the holdings of the Library of Congress and its Prints and Photographs Division, even though they have provided one of the principal locations for the study of these subjects since early in the nineteenth century. Nowhere in the general descriptions of holdings, or even in the name of the Prints and Photographs Division, will users see the category "drawings" listed, a situation this volume attempts in part to ameliorate.

Among the greatest strengths of the collection is material concerning the development of Washington, D.C., and, over the course of two centuries, its greater metropolitan area. This material is of seminal importance to researchers studying the arts, architecture, landscape architecture, urban and suburban development, historic preservation, industrial and interior design, the decorative arts, sculpture, American studies, and engineering history, among other related fields of inquiry. It has great strength in holdings representing both the private and the public design sectors and the productive synapses that occur between them. Furthermore, it follows the historical development of the professions of architecture, engi-

neering, urban and landscape design; of graphic representation; of building technologies and the vagaries of politics, economics, and taste.

This volume thus is intended for a wide and varied audience and to serve as an introduction and gateway to a vast body of newly available information. It stands quite modestly at the head of more than three thousand detailed electronic catalog records representing more than forty thousand drawings, prints, photographs, and related research materials for the projects and executed works of over five hundred architects, designers, engineers, and landscape architects, spanning two centuries. This publication, its associated electronic resources, and the rich and largely unplumbed archive that they represent offer the possibility to enlarge substantially, even to revise, our understanding and appreciation of the roles of the arts of design and engineering in the creation of Washington, D.C., and of its place in the history of our nation and the world.

Each illustration is intended not only to make a point but also to provide an invitation to explore further and go deeper, to mine the rich new veins of the graphic goldmine for which this publication presents but a core sample. Dozens and hundreds and thousands of related documents await the discovery and inspection of the interested public, design professionals, architectural historians, and scholars in many fields and, perhaps most of all, K–12 students and their teachers, who can use this archive to learn more about the meaning and variety of American history and the significance of its built environment. It offers to improve their critical abilities and to enhance and enlarge their sense of stewardship of this great heritage.

Most conspicuously, it provides a forum for a number of distinguished scholars to share their expertise and to expand our awareness and understanding of the usefulness and significance for study and analysis of a wide range of document types. Their essays discuss and their illustrations have been chosen to emphasize this richness and diversity. They include design and presentation drawings for some of our nation's most important buildings, monuments, and memorials, such as the U.S. Capitol, the White House, and the Vietnam Veterans Memorial; for the anonymous but important structures of everyday life such as group housing and small commercial establishments; and for ambitious projects of all types that were never built, for which these documents often provide the only remaining evidence. Their symbolic and functional purposes range from defining the core of our national identity and accommodating its activities and rituals to selling real estate and hamburgers, the alpha and omega of human civilization. Not infrequently, these drawings are works of art, evidence of the highest levels of human creativity. Seen together with associated specifications, correspondence, site plans, photographs, and promotional materials, they explain the often arduous process of funding, decision making, design, and construction. They inform, inspire, and, on occasion, even dismay.

Throughout this volume, readers may be surprised when they happen upon buildings, structures, or projects located outside of the Washington, D.C., metropolitan area, including works designed, built, or sponsored by government agencies both here and abroad; works by architects, designers, and engineers who were based here for all or part of their careers but who often carried on extensive practices elsewhere; and designs deposited in the Library of Congress to secure their copyrights, all of which are included. A few examples have also been chosen to emphasize the richness of related collections both in the Prints and Photographs Division and other custodial divisions of the Library of Congress, such as the Geography and Map Division.

Chapter 1 has as its focus the Washington that could have been but for various reasons was not. It is overarching, beginning with the various proposals for the U.S. Capitol and moving through the late twentieth century. It brings together the subjects covered in the subsequent essays, but also includes many building purposes, technologies, and typologies represented in the library's collections but which could not be fitted within this single volume: additional monuments and memorials, a national university and church, theaters, recreational structures, museums, bridges, urban and landscape designs, private homes and a retreat, an embassy, office residences, and the Supreme Court and Library of Congress.

In chapter 2, on the U.S. Capitol, the depth and breadth of the library's holdings are demonstrated. It points to related materials, providing a sweeping and highly informed overview of the complex evolution of this nation's "principal edifice" over two centuries. Chapter 3 is comparable in scope and provides an authoritative analysis tracing the development of one of the world's most conspicuous and recognizable residences, from President's House to Executive Mansion to White House. It identifies and explains many of the key figures and moments in that process. Washington's remarkably innovative and central position in the design and construction of the nation's commercial buildings since the late nineteenth century is examined in detail in chapter 4, which notably investigates a wide range of document types, emphasizing their role in both facilitating and subsequently interpreting the buildings they represent. In chapter 5, an expert reexamination of twentieth-century housing reveals that the Washington, D.C., area rose above the norm at critical times in history; it sometimes provided valuable models but often it followed the middle of the road. Chapter 6 incisively explicates the complicated process, from competition to completion, that resulted in Maya Lin's Vietnam Veterans Memorial. That memorial reinvigorated the appreciation of memorials as a building type, leading to the current level of public interest in the development and in the selection of a design for the World Trade Center memorial, guided in part by Lin, who served on its jury. In all of these essays, the significance for future research of both the library's holdings and related holdings in other institutions are examined and assessed.

Additional tools are also provided for researchers including directions for exploring the collections of the Prints and Photographs Division and for ordering reproductions; a list of the online resources for architects, designers, and engineers; an essay on sources; and an index.

Originally, the plan was for this volume to be much larger and to be modeled on the guidebook to the photographic holdings of the Prints and Photographs Division edited by Kathleen Collins and published in 1989 at the conclusion of the Washingtoniana I

Project, which made more than three hundred fifty thousand Washington-related images available to the public. What intervened was the enormous growth and possibilities offered by the library's Web site and on-line catalog. That dispelled what was envisioned as a Government Printing Office publication, possibly comprising two volumes, including nearly three thousand catalog entries, many additional illustrations, a number of additional essays, and more than five hundred biographical entries for the creators of the drawings or projects represented and led to this much more streamlined, attractive, and widely available version published in cooperation with the Johns Hopkins University Press.

Today the catalog entries and illustrations are far more easily searchable and available through electronic means via the Internet and the library's and the Prints and Photographs Division's Web sites, where the additional essays and biographical entries will join them. Included among these will be essays by Hélène Lipstadt, James M. Goode, Pamela Scott, and Frances Brousseau and hundreds of biographical entries prepared by Pamela Scott, Leslie Freudenheim, Diane Tepfer, James O'Gorman, Jeffrey Cohen, Denys Peter Myers, Charles M. Harris, Thomas Somma, Barbara Wolanin, and William Allen.

Again, we thank the Morris and Gwendolyn Cafritz Foundation for making all of this possible, in addition to all of the staff and friends referred to in the acknowledgments section of this volume. May this volume provide new models; inspire, assist, and encourage renewed exploration; and foster a deeper understanding and appreciation of both the "capital" and the "drawings" that tell its story, which is also the story of this nation and its people.

Note on Dimensions of Documents

Illustration captions do not provide specific dimensions for items. The call number itself provides size information for most items. In some instances, the online record for the document gives its exact dimensions.

The following table provides the approximate range of dimensions, although the size of the item can be smaller than the range given because of the size of its housing (mat or folder).

AA size	11″ × 14″
A size	14″ × 18″
B size	14″ × 18″ to 20″ × 24″
C size	20″ × 24″ to 22″ × 28″
D size	22″ × 28″ to 28″ × 40″
E size	29″ × 40″ to 35″ × 48″
F size	35″ × 48″ to 46″ × 75″
FF	40″ × 60″
F Lot	10½″ × 15½″
G Lot	10″ × 12″ to 15″ × 18″
H Lot	15″ × 18″ to 22″ × 40″

CHAPTER ONE

WASHINGTON, D.C.

——

From L'Enfant's Dream to Edge City

C. FORD PEATROSS

E. Savage pinx. et sculp.

George Washington Esq.ʳ

PRESIDENT of the UNITED STATES of AMERICA.

From the Original Portrait Painted at the request of the Corporation of the University of Cambridge in Massachusetts

Published June 25 1793, by E. Savage, N.º 54 Newman Street

THE FEDERAL CITY began as a vision of the founding fathers, in particular George Washington and Thomas Jefferson. Located near the fall line and at the juncture of the Potomac and Anacostia rivers, it has always been a place where ambitious dreams and good intentions have come up against political, fiscal, and physical realities—its human dimensions seeming to mirror its geography. Washington, D.C., has served as a proving ground for some of the best ideas and talent and for some of the worst that the nation has had to offer. As the seat of the U.S. government, its agencies, elected representatives, and the representatives of foreign governments, the city has grown in size, in influence, and in power. It has become a focal point and, for many Americans and citizens of the world, a mecca. Washington is a crucible for testing current concerns and issues: its institutions are barometers that measure change and influence in the lifestyles, health, economic and social well-being, patterns of settlement, technological achievements, and commonly and uncommonly held beliefs, attitudes, values, and tastes of the American people. Its public spaces, buildings, and monuments have provided the stage for our great national events; for our shared debates, protests, celebrations; and for acts of mourning and remembrance.

The authors of the chapters that follow have written mostly about the Washington that was built, whose elements were proposed and achieved, discussed, debated, funded, and constructed. But this essay explores, to a greater extent, the other Washington, the city known only as its creators imagined it. This Washington is preserved in the documents through which architects, designers, engineers, and city planners conceived and presented it. Extant works continue to draw our attention through their physical presence. Lost or destroyed buildings and structures are remembered through the prints, photographs, and publications that have recorded and disseminated their images and descriptions locally and, for the more famous, nationally and internationally.

Unbuilt projects, however, exist as graphic and intellectual exercises, no matter how earnest or frivolous, small or grand, possible or impossible. Most were recorded, if at all, only in publications, and many of those publications were not widely circulated. The majority of projects remain little known or totally unknown, even to experts.[1] A great privilege of those who work with architectural and design archives is experiencing these works that might have been. It is possible to envision them as built, to imagine not just how they might have changed the appearance of the city but, more broadly, how they might have affected the everyday lives of residents and visitors, the function of its institutions, and the course of its history.

The unrealized plans for a city can be intriguing, accomplished, and even absurd. As products of their creators' imaginations, these unbuilt plans continue to inspire and delight and sometimes to baffle and dismay. Always they cause us to think more actively about the hopes, intentions, and possibilities they represented. An awareness of what might have been can inform and improve the decisions and actions of both patrons and designers, now and in the future. Had these projects become realities, the metropolitan Washington of today—that segment of an almost continuous urban strip extending from Richmond to Baltimore and steadily expanding to the east and west—would not, to varying degrees, have been the same.[2]

Place Your Bets

Design proposals are always a gamble. Rarely are the aspirations for the future of a project more forcefully conveyed than when its image is associated with its proponents, whether client or designer. In no place is the joint identity and destiny of the dreamer and the dream more demonstrable than in those rare portraits that show both. The following portraits show the bettors with their architectural "hands" placed on the table, so to speak, for their success to be judged for all time. In Edward Savage's 1793 engraved portrait of George Washington (FIG. 1.1), the artist modified his earlier life portrait of 1789 to show the president holding the plan for the new city of Washington, which he had commissioned two years earlier from Peter (Pierre) Charles L'Enfant, in the latter's prescient words, to "lay the Foundation of a city which is to become the Capital of this vast Empire . . . drawn on such a scale as to leave room for

FIG. 1.1. Edward Savage, artist. "George Washington Esq. President of the United States of America, from the Original Portrait Painted at the request of the Corporation of the University of Cambridge in Massachusetts." In this version, the president is shown holding the proposed plan for the new city of Washington. Drawn, engraved, and published by E. Savage, no. 54, Newman Street [London]. Mezzotint. 1793. PGA-Savage, B size. LC-USZ62-16586.

that aggrandisement & embellishment which the increase of the wealth of the Nation will permit it to pursue at any period however remote."[3] After two centuries in the making, their common dream is generally recognized as the basis of one of the great city plans of all time.

Nathaniel Owings, a founding partner of the famous architectural firm of Skidmore, Owings & Merrill (SOM), was appointed by President Kennedy in 1962 to head his Advisory Council on Pennsylvania Avenue for the purpose of developing a master plan to guide the revitalization of the avenue and the city's core. In a portrait by Vincent Perez (FIG. 1.2), Owings is shown in front of an image of the resulting plan of 1964 as if it had become a reality. The 1964 plan incorporated many excellent features, including returning the Mall largely to pedestrian use, which have been carried out, and Owings's personal and political skills were as critical to this process as his design talents. One of the principal features of the plan, shown at the middle left in the portrait, was a vast "National Square" at the Fifteenth Street terminus of Pennsylvania Avenue, its center marked by a gargantuan fountain from which were to radiate paving patterns inspired by Michelangelo's Piazza di Campidoglio in Rome, and peppered by Lilliputian figures attempting to traverse it. Well-intentioned but ill-conceived, the square would have required the demolition of one of the city's livelier areas, including the Hotel Washington and the Willard Hotel, culminating in a Pennsylvania Avenue newly lined with blocks of stultifyingly uniform buildings based on an SOM prototype (ADE-UNIT 2198, no. 1, photo).

Opening the vista from the Capitol to the southern portico of the Treasury Department would have been in accord with L'Enfant's principles of reciprocal views, but ever since President Andrew Jackson made the unfortunate decision to locate the Treasury Building in a position that would block the view of the White House, the reciprocity has been not between two major branches of the government, as intended, but between the legislative branch and the monetary department of the executive branch, a relationship not without irony.

However pleasant the fountain may have been, and L'Enfant had proposed grand fountains for five of the city's squares, each with "constant spout of water,"[4] it would not have prevented the wilting of tourists in the summer heat, and it is not clear how the National Square's pedestrian nature would have comported with the traffic pouring up and down the avenue. Its depiction serves to remind us that not all designs, or their elements, are equal, and to be prudent in how we allow ourselves to be portrayed.[5]

Good Beginnings

We have begun our journey by showing President Washington holding L'Enfant's great plan or, rather, the print made from Andrew Ellicott's version of that plan, engraved in Philadelphia by Thackara and Vallance in 1792, which was probably sent to the artist in London.[6] The sampling of design drawings for the major buildings and structures that embellished this plan begins with designs for the most important of them all—the U.S. Capitol. Of the many architects who were called on to produce designs for the Capitol, Stephen (Étienne Sulpice) Hallet and B. Henry Latrobe are the most interesting. Among all the unexecuted designs produced, certain drawings stand out as the most exceptional in terms of both their power and the large and small ways they might have changed history.

Pamela Scott has observed that in more than one of Hallet's designs for the Capitol, staircases were to provide access to the cupola crowning the dome; this "belvedere" would have provided visitors with a sweeping view of the city, of the Potomac River and its Eastern Branch (the Anacostia River), and of the countryside beyond the Capitol (fig 1.3). Even today, only the privileged few who make the unfriendly ascent to the top of the present cast-iron dome; those venturing to the top of the Washington Monument for a cramped and solitary, not even periscopic, view through its pigeonhole openings; and those arriving or departing from the local airport enjoy anything resembling what Hallet envisioned. Had this overall view been regularly available to the public, to lawmakers, and to the city's designers, the development

Vincent Perez

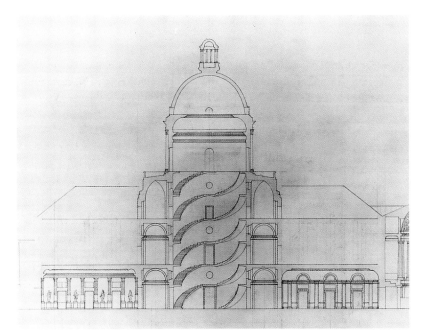

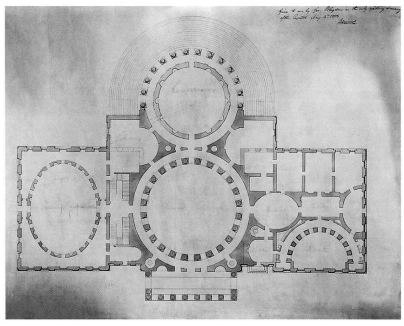

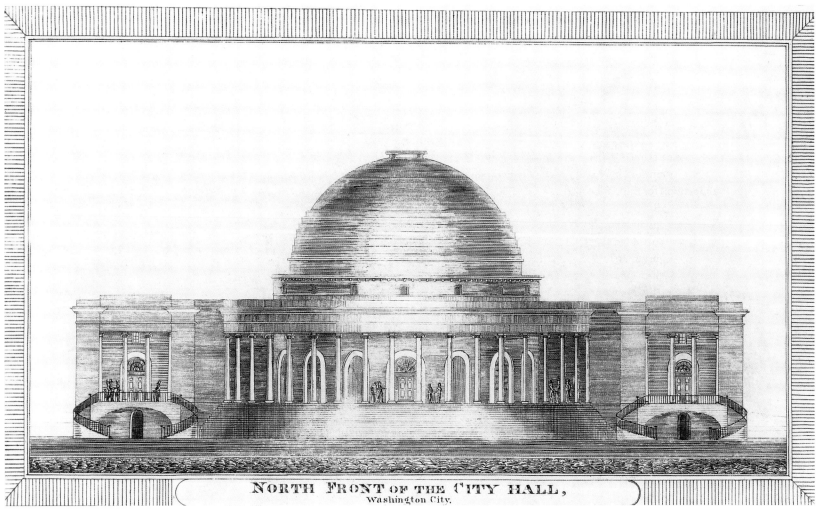

NORTH FRONT OF THE CITY HALL,
Washington City.

and appearance of the Capitol's grounds and surrounding structures, the Mall, and the city itself might have been considerably different.

William Thornton's proposal of the later 1790s to modify his winning design for the Capitol to include a high dome mounted above an open colonnade would have provided an even more spectacular vantage point, with vistas from its gallery framed by allegorical statues (PLATE 1.1). Or, had George Hadfield's City Hall of 1820 been completed to include its great dome (FIG. 1.4), the views of and between the two structures would have been among the city's principal pleasures.[7]

Thornton's high dome would have faced the Mall, surmounting the western extension of the Capitol originally intended to house the Conference Room, a principal chamber of the Capitol called for in the 1792 competition and never completed. The room remains prominent in the plan for the Capitol of William Thornton, received by Latrobe as "the only existing drawing of the Capitol" in 1803 (FIG. 1.5), but Latrobe does not show it on his own plans for the Capitol after 1806 (FIG. 2.12). Its semicircular projection on the Capitol's west front continued to appear, however, on plans of Washington even beyond that made by Nicholas King in 1818.

As projected by Stephen Hallet in his final or "E" scheme, submitted in March 1793, after the design competition for the Capitol had officially closed, the Conference Room would have been one of the most magnificent public chambers in all of the Americas. Nobly proportioned and detailed in the French classical tradition, its character and quality are revealed in Hallet's beautiful sectional drawing, which only came to light when the Library of Congress acquired it in 1976 (PLATE 1.2). A freestanding Ionic colonnade supports the Pantheon-inspired dome, lit by an oculus, in an auditorium situated above a vaulted ground-floor chamber. Although the full range of the intended purposes of the Conference Room and its antechambers are unclear, and a subject suitable for further investigation, its existence necessarily would have had profound effects on how the government functioned.

First, it would have provided a great ceremonial space for important addresses and joint sessions of the House and Senate. Second, as its name implied, it would have provided a neutral area between the two houses for discussion, mediation, and negotiation, functions that instead became relegated to a number of smaller rooms and lobbies. Third, it might have provided a presence in the Capitol, and even offices in its antechambers, for the nation's chief executive. Any or all of these factors might have significantly influenced the historical development of the young nation and its form of government, continuing to this day. Architecture does matter.

A Spark of Genius

Despite the superb publications during the past quarter century devoted to the work of Latrobe, the range and quality of his contributions deserve to be more widely known and appreciated. He was one of the great geniuses, not just of American architecture but also of the period in general. By example through his works and magnificent drawings and through his training of the next generation of American architects and engineers, he set the course and standards for the future development of those professions in this country. At the federal level, no less discerning a figure than Thomas Jefferson chose Latrobe in 1803 as the first official architect, not just for the Capitol but for the United States, knowing full well that there would be a price to pay in terms of mediating the consequences of the architect's genius and temperament with the nation's elected representatives.[8]

A book could be devoted to an exploration of Latrobe's unbuilt projects alone, but a few in particular would have made Washington, D.C., a different place had they been built: his Washington Monument of 1800; the first Library of Congress, 1806–9; the National University of 1815; and the Marine Asylum of 1812–16. In addition, a few favorite examples of his unbuilt domestic buildings intended for Washington and neighboring Virginia, still exceptional for their beauty, elegance, imagination, innovative features, and appropriateness to site and climate, all of which seem remarkably modern almost two centuries later, are discussed here.

FIG. 1.3 (*opposite, left*). Stephen Hallet, architect. Rotunda stairway, scheme "D," U.S. Capitol, Washington, D.C. Longitudinal section, "D3-Section of Plan D1." Ink, graphite, wash, and watercolor on paper. 1793. ADE-UNIT 2460, no. 3, E size. LC-USZ62-63154.

FIG. 1.4 (*opposite, right*). William Thornton, architect. U.S. Capitol, Washington, D.C. Plan. Graphite, ink, and watercolor on paper. 1797–1800. ADE-UNIT 2470, no. 2, C size. LC-USZ62-13238.

FIG. 1.5. George Hadfield, architect. Washington City Hall, North Front. New Jersey, South Carolina, and Virginia Avenues, S.E., Washington, D.C. Elevation. Engraving. n.d. PGA-Anon, AA size-North. LC-USZ62-26746.

Latrobe's proposal for the first Library of Congress was included in the plan for the Capitol presented to Jefferson in 1806 and had been fully developed by 1808 (PLATE 1.3; FIG. 1.6). It would have provided Washington with one of its most beautiful rooms and launched the young nation's first cultural institution in grand style. Combining a Roman barrel vault and apsidal plan with Egyptian Revival detailing, in style the design recalled the great library at Alexandria, Egypt. Entering from the handsome vestibule opposite the Senate chamber, visitors would have stepped down into a chamber overlooking the Mall, with a hemicycle screened by Egyptian columns to the left, beneath a gallery of colonnettes modeled after bundles of papyrus, and illuminated from the right by a great lunette window, defined by the curve of the vaulted ceiling rising more than forty feet above. Sadly, it would have been short lived—and undoubtedly lost when the British burned the Capitol in 1814. Would that its magnificence, and the thought of being remembered as the figure who destroyed the "second" Alexandrian library, had given Admiral Cockburn pause before he had his men set their torches. Even as late as the 1980s, constructing Latrobe's library was being considered, a proposal that still has merit.

Latrobe apparently did not develop his 1815 design for a national university beyond the tantalizing plan that survives in the Library of Congress's Geography and Map Division (FIG. 1.7). It is little remembered, except by scholars; yet, its merits were considerable and its presence would forever have changed the form and the fortunes of the Mall, whose center it would have occupied just east of the President's Park (now known as the Ellipse), from Fifteenth to Thirteenth Streets. Its west front was dominated by a great, domed central entrance pavilion and observatory with a portico overlooking the canal, a large basin at the mouth of the Potomac, and the river itself. The central pavilion and its portico projected into and across the Fifteenth Street axis, making the structure highly visible from three directions: the President's House on the north, the river, and the southern approach to the Mall.[9] To the east, its buildings formed an open quadrangle with a portico on its cen-

tral axis facing a domed university church, looking toward the Capitol and situated in the middle of a circular intersection with Thirteenth Street, like a jewel in its mount.

Drawn at the time Latrobe was advising Jefferson on the design of the future University of Virginia, the quadrangle shares the unusual feature of having the professors' houses as pavilions between ranges of lodging rooms for the students. Its proximity, and that of its faculty and students, to the Capitol was likely to have exerted a substantial effect on the intellectual dynamics of the city and the government, perhaps making the early capital a center of academic as well as political life. The Mall and the Smithsonian Institution and its various parts would have, no doubt, developed quite differently with a national university already in place, and a different form and location would have been suggested for any Washington monument.

Almost at the same time, between 1812 and 1816, Latrobe developed more fully his designs for a nearby "marine hospital," authorized by Congress in 1811, to be built a few blocks southeast of the Capitol, between North Carolina and South Carolina Avenues, facing west to New Jersey Avenue and its visual axis to the Capitol's east portico. Included are section and elevation drawings that provide a more complete image of his intentions (FIG. 1.8). Like the university, it had central and flanking wings that defined a quadrangle, which featured a formal garden. A monumental Greek Doric portico opened onto a great domed hall that served as vestibule for a church on one side and a refectory on the other, which again would have been among the most noble chambers in the city or even the nation. Imagine looking from a Latrobe-designed Capitol out New Jersey Avenue to his Marine Asylum and Hospital, northwest out Pennsylvania Avenue to a President's House with the additions of his north and south porticoes, and east (fireproof repository; ADE-UNIT 2563, no. 1) and west extensions, and westward from his propylaeum entrance to the Capitol, across a Mall embellished with his canal and picturesque landscaping, to his university church framed by his national university.

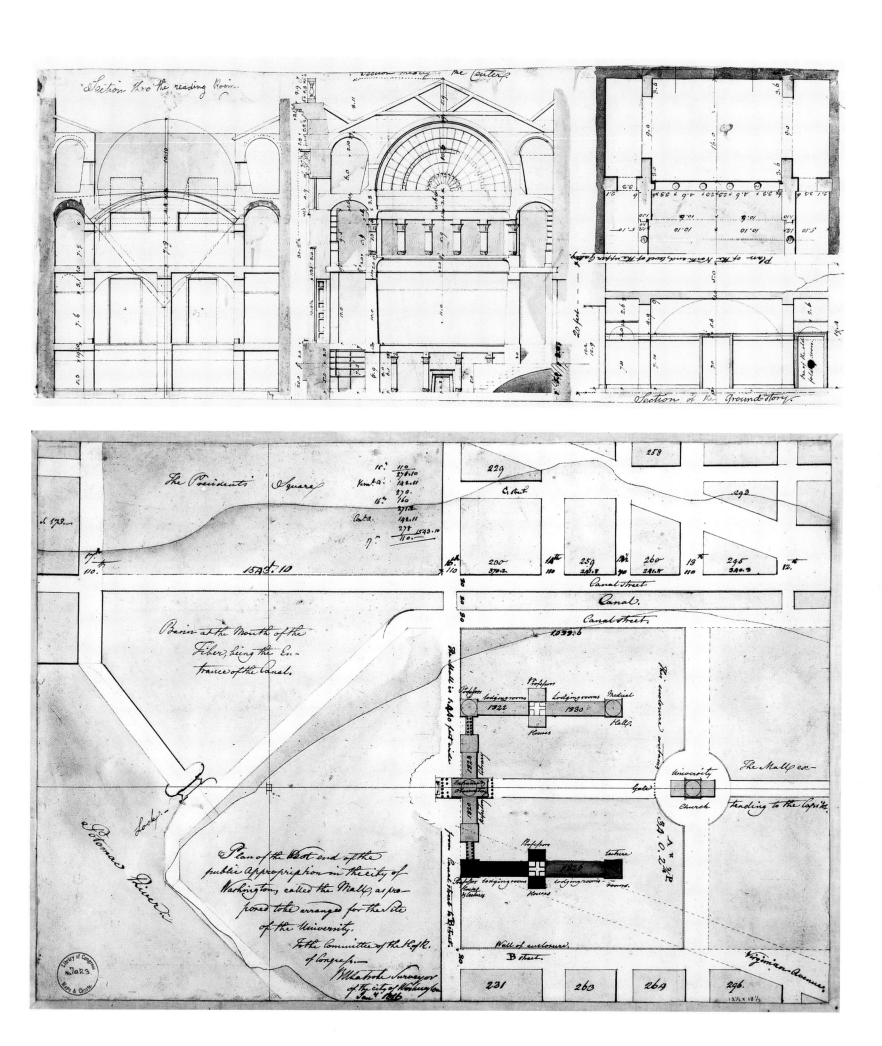

Section thro the reading Room.

Section thro the Center.

Plan of the Work and level of the upper Gallery

Section of the Ground Story.

20 feet

The Presidents' Square

Basin at the Mouth of the Tiber, being the Entrance of the Canal.

Canal street.
Canal.
Canal street.

University
Church

The Mall extending to the Capitol.

Gate

Potomac River.

Lock

Plan of the West end of the public Appropriation in the City of Washington, called the Mall, as proposed to be arranged for the Site of the University.

To the Committee of the H. of R. of Congress

B. H. Latrobe Surveyor of the City of Washington
Jan'y 1816

Professors Lodging rooms
Medical Hall

Professors Houses

Library

Professors lodging rooms
Professors Houses

Lecture rooms

Wall of enclosure.
B street.

258
229
292
230
259
260
295
231
263
264
296.

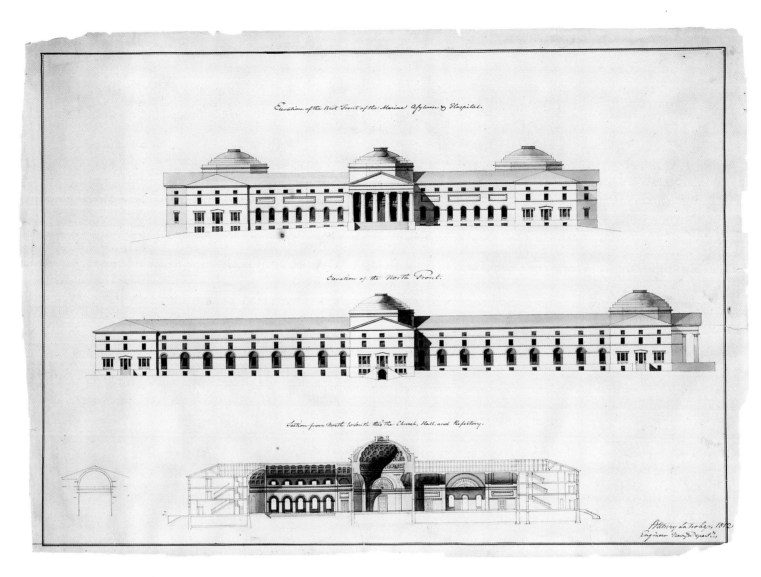

Elevation of the West Front of the Marine Asylum & Hospital.

Elevation of the North Front.

Section from North to South thro' the Church, Hall, and Refectory.

B Henry Latrobe, 1812
Engineer Navy Yard.

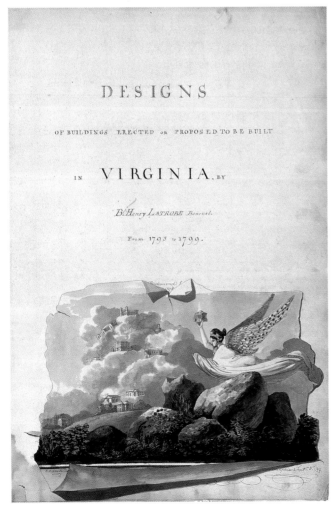

DESIGNS

OF BUILDINGS ERECTED OR PROPOSED TO BE BUILT

IN VIRGINIA, BY

B. Henry LATROBE Boneval.

From 1795 to 1799.

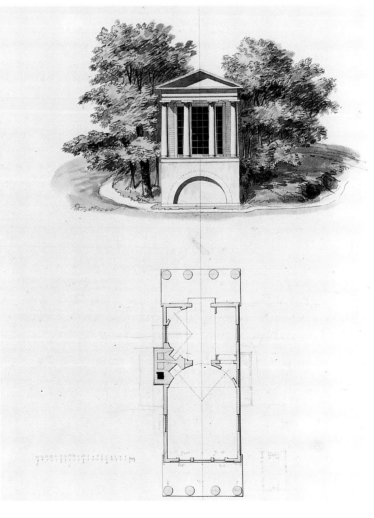

Before any of these projects, however, Latrobe had recorded his earliest American designs in an album of drawings entitled *Designs of Buildings Erected or Proposed to Be Built in Virginia . . . from 1795 to 1799* (ADE-Unit 2886, no. 2, C size. LC-USZC4-19), which, had it been published (also still a possibility), would today be among the most famous American architectural books. For its frontispiece, drawn in Philadelphia in 1799, Latrobe conceived a remarkable trompe l'oeil conceit—his unbuilt Virginia projects of the 1790s suspended in an ether of the best architectural intentions (FIG. 1.9, *left*). Of his built projects in America, the winged figure of genius (more specifically, the "architect's imagination") holds aloft a model of the Bank of Pennsylvania, whose construction he was currently supervising. Two projects he executed in Virginia, the Pennock House in Norfolk and the Harvie House in Richmond, rest on terra firma.[10]

In this album is a design for a small, temple-form retreat beautifully situated in a grove of trees beside a limpid stream (FIG. 1.9, *right*). One excuse for including this drawing here is a weak one: that its alcove bed is nearly a contemporary of one Thomas Jefferson had built in his chambers at Monticello. In truth, among all those in the library's collections, this project has long been one of the author's favorites, and he could not resist sharing it with others. It is a rare form for America, with elements of neoclassicism, picturesque garden planning, and the garden folly combined to produce an idyllic sanctuary, a hermitage intended for thought, for writing, or for communing with nature that a Jefferson, a Thoreau, a Tolstoy, a Shaw, or a Faulkner might relish. Build it, someone, and invite the author for a weekend.[11]

A more ambitious, unrealized rural villa by Latrobe to which he would also readily accept an invitation can be seen in the design conceived for Clifton near Richmond (ADE-Unit 2560, no. 2, B size. LC-USZC4-52), but which began as the preliminary design for Riverside, near Bladensburg, Maryland, now a suburb north and east of Washington. Latrobe's clients for Riverside, Henri Joseph Stier and his family, had fled Napoleon from their native Antwerp, bringing with them a magnificent collection of paintings. Beautifully proportioned and detailed, the de-

sign enjoys many of the finest attributes of English country house architecture, situated to enjoy a sweeping river vista, well adapted for the American climate with wide eaves, large, walkout windows, sheltering piazzas, and clusters of shade trees on its southern exposure, inviting cool breezes inside. The cupola would have provided additional ventilation and light to a two-story entrance rotunda and, in the Riverside plan of 1801, the gallery conceived for the display of the Stiers' works of art. In this rendering and in an accompanying plan, the house and its picturesque garden, with sinuous paths, are seductively rendered, although apparently not enough to get it built exactly as designed at either site.[12]

House Proud, or Residential Rivalries

Latrobe and William Thornton became bitter architectural rivals and, in addition to their work on the new building for the U.S. Capitol, each vied to provide the new Federal City with its finest private residence. It is useful and informative to compare their most sophisticated schemes, unrealized in the case of Latrobe and only in part in the case of Thornton. Elegant and innovative in their plans and features, neoclassical in inspiration, republican in simplicity, these two residences borrowed features from the new Capitol, including interior and exterior domed rotundas. Had they been completed as designed, they would have established a new standard of taste, provided a jump-start for the Greek Revival in America, and today be widely recognized as two of the most significant buildings of the Federal period.[13]

For a town house in the new "Foedera[l] City," Latrobe contemplated a more urban and sophisticated cousin of his contemporary but obviously suburban Riverside and Clifton (PLATE 1.5). It is represented among the unrealized cloud-born perspectives in his volume of designs for houses in Virginia (PLATE 1.4). The intended client was John Tayloe III, the scion of a wealthy and influential Virginia family. No stranger to architectural ambitions, Tayloe was born in 1771 in the handsome Palladian house completed by his father in 1758 at the family seat, Mount Airy plantation, in Richmond County. Educated abroad at Eton and Cambridge, Tayloe returned to Virginia at the age of twenty to manage a vast inheritance. In 1792, he married Ann Ogle of Annapolis and Belair plantation in Prince George's County, Maryland, whose family was as prominent in her state as Tayloe's was in his. Her father and grandfather had both served as governor of Maryland, the latter for three terms.

Before the removal of the federal government to its new seat in 1800, in an attempt to secure a commission from the young couple, probably between 1796 and 1797, Latrobe produced a beautiful and highly detailed series of drawings, depicting a house for them down to the smallest details, including the books on the shelves in the library and the silver on the sideboard in the dining room. Shown here are Latrobe's watercolor renderings for the south or principal elevation and an unusual "exploded view" for the dining room. The first (PLATE 1.4) shows a highly planar and linear façade with graduated, simple window openings punctuating a stuccoed wall surface intended to eliminate the more conventional and distracting patterns of brickwork. This treatment provides emphasis to the horizontal bands of highly figured Aquia stone string courses and cornices that organize and snugly corset the entire composition, including the flanking, neatly domed pavilions and a severe but noble Delian portico, creating a tense and attractive architectural package, alive with compressed energy.

Latrobe provided the Tayloes with an unusual drawing (PLATE 1.5) that allowed them to imagine an elegant dining room ready to welcome guests. Grouped around the floor plan are wall elevations (one a section, as well), which they could fold up in their mind's-eye and project themselves into, as if it were a room in a doll's house. At one end, a large tripartite window offers a garden view, framed by verdigris-colored walls that provide a background for an impressive display of paintings, with portraits of distinguished Tayloe and Ogle ancestors taking pride of place. Ornate mirrored sconces shimmer above and draw attention to sideboards laden and glimmering with the family silver, including examples of the latest and most fashionable neoclassical styles. As on the exterior, here an encompassing horizontal dado rail binds and disciplines the ensemble, defining the upper level of both the sideboards and the unconventionally low fireplace opening, which is flanked by classical maidens.

The exact site in the city for which Latrobe's project was intended is unknown, but it was not the irregular site Tayloe purchased in 1797. For that property William Thornton soon prepared preliminary sketches (ADE-UNIT 2581), including a few of the features that Tayloe had admired in Latrobe's scheme. They were the basis for the distinguished but less ambitious town house erected according to Thornton's designs of 1799–1801 and known today as the Octagon.[14] Thornton's Octagon was innovative in plan but less so in its outward appearance.

Far more adventurous, and more directly comparable to Latrobe's Tayloe project, were Thornton's later designs for a commanding site in nearby Georgetown, today known as Tudor Place. The home of the Peter family for almost two centuries and now a museum, Tudor Place as completed embodied a compromise, incorporating an existing wing and avoiding some of the bolder and more elaborate elements proposed by Thornton. Thornton's elite and well-connected clients were Robert Peter, a wealthy tobacco exporter, and his wife, Martha Parke Custis, the daughter of Martha Washington's son from her first marriage, John Parke Custis. Soon after the Peters acquired the property in 1805, Thornton produced a series of studies and renderings for them. The grandest, and perhaps the furthest from what was actually built, is shown here (PLATE 1.6).

As an example of international neoclassicism, this elegant lemon yellow casino, its domed rotunda set like a jewel into a façade of arched niches containing pedestals with sculptures of antique maidens, all beneath a shallow, hipped roof, would have been equally at home as a folly reflecting in the lake of a Repton landscape, terminating an allée in a French *jardin du plaisir*, ornamenting the grounds of a Prussian *Schloss*, or welcoming a tzarina's summer party on the banks of the Neva—as in its proposed site overlooking the raw and sprawling outlines of the capital of a new nation.

Monumental Ideas

William Thornton had produced a series of proposals for monuments to George Washington even during his lifetime, including *tempiettos* bearing marked similarities to the Tudor Place portico just illustrated (ADE-UNIT 2466). Following Washington's death in 1799, Latrobe was among those who prepared designs in 1800 for a monument in his honor (FIG. 1.10; ADE-UNIT 2545, no. 2, B size). Supported by a spreading, stepped podium, its lower, cubic mass, with battered walls and coved cornice in the Egyptian style, was punctuated on four sides by in-antis porticoes with archaic Greek Doric columns proportioned like those he used in the first Supreme Court Chamber in the Capitol. On the interior, triangular murals showing scenes from Washington's life were to have filled the inward-slanting faces of the finely stepped pyramidal roof. Simple, powerful, and forthright, it would have set a standard for monumental architecture in America that was not to be realized until the twentieth century and is a worthy ancestor to John Russell Pope's pyramidal studies for the Lincoln Memorial, completed over a century later.[15]

In 1837 the prominent publisher Peter Force, then mayor of Washington and an officer of the Washington National Monument Society, further distinguished himself as an amateur of architecture by putting forth a design for a monument to George Washington (FIG. 1.11). A massive, truncated pyramid housing a smaller one in its interior volumes, it recalls Latrobe's proposal in form but crudely and with the type of gigantism that long has appealed to the American psyche. Its vast scale is indicated by the antlike figures at its base, implying that its footprint would have obliterated the Mall rather than graced it. If it took a half-century to complete Robert Mills's accepted design for the monument (and then only in part), then we can assume that, lacking a pharoah, Force's project would still be abuilding. Most intriguing was its interior space, a great, vaguely bottle-shaped, graduated void lit by a single oculus at the summit.

FIG. 1.10. B. Henry Latrobe. Proposed Washington Monument, Washington, D.C. Perspective. Graphite, ink, and watercolor on paper. Ca. 1799–1800. ADE-UNIT 2545, no. 1, B size. LC-USZ62-14342. Latrobe Papers C69.

Force, whose collection of Americana provided a foundation for the holdings of the Library of Congress, could not have known of the French architect Étienne-Louis Boullée's various designs of the 1780s for gargantuan conical and pyramidal structures, some truncated and, like his proposed cenotaph to honor Sir Isaac Newton, with its great spherical void, intended to have vast interior chambers that continue to define for us the eighteenth-century concept of the sublime. These grandiose projects remain, nonetheless, distant, if unequal, cousins.[16]

The Library of Congress's Washingtoniana project brought to light a previously unknown and more complete version of Robert Mills's development of his winning design for the Washington Monument, circa 1847, representing his final intentions and executed by his son-in-law, the lithographer Charles Fenderich (PGA Fenderich, C size, no. 243).[17] It reminds us that the Washington Monument is an unfinished project, lacking Mills's great pantheon and museum at its base intended to honor George Washington and the founders and heroes of the young republic. The lone 555-foot obelisk finally was completed in 1884 with a modified apex by Lieutenant Colonel Thomas Lincoln Casey of the Army Corps of Engineers (ADE-UNIT 2518, no. 2) but remains a fractional element of the original intended design. In part because of this, a substantial proportion of those visiting Washington today understand it to be a monument representing the city rather than the man.

The potential glories of both Mills's modified design for the Washington Monument of 1851 and Andrew Jackson Downing's 1851 design for the public grounds, stretching from the White House to the Capitol, are represented best in a magnificent and extremely rare color lithograph published by Benjamin Franklin Smith in 1852 (PLATE 1.7).[18] A bird's-eye perspective, it lays forth a vision of a fully funded, immaculately groomed, dreamlike Washington-to-be fueled by the imaginations of artist, architect, and landscape designer. The folks at Disney Imagineering could not have done it better. The Tiber Canal, described as "fetid" during most of its history, before being filled in to create Constitution Avenue, is here rendered as a magnet for commerce and pleasure-

seekers. The latter, indeed, are seen everywhere, singly, in groups and families, on boats, in carriages, and on foot and horseback, sailing on the Tiber, riding and strolling through Downing's picturesque plan, crossing two new bridges across the canal, conversing, and gazing and pointing from the roof and parapet walkway of Mills's pantheon. The columns of the latter appear to be Egyptian inspired but, in fact, represent Mills's development of the Indian corn columns in the Capitol designed by his master, Latrobe, as an appropriately American architectural order, with bundled corn rather than papyrus stalks making up the shafts, replacing the earlier Greek Doric order that shows in most representations of his Pantheon. Silvery jets of water pulse from fountains south of the White House and at the east end of the Mall, where one sees the Capitol, flanked on the right by the new Smithsonian Institution and on the left by George Hadfield's City Hall, with its dome miraculously realized. Rising above the skyline from left to right, the massive and gleaming white forms of Mills's Treasury Department, Patent Office, and Post Office buildings further proclaim his role in setting the new scale and form of a monumental federal city.[19]

Continuing in a different direction, if one follows the axis of Downing's suspension bridge up Fifteenth Street to the entrance of the President's Park at the end of Pennsylvania Avenue, a monumental gateway that he proposed as an entrance to the public grounds can also be seen completed but as a small and blurry detail. A wood engraving illustrating an article on Washington and Downing's planned improvements, published in *Harper's New Monthly Magazine* in 1852, describes its intended scale and character on the model of a Roman triumphal arch (FIG. 1.13). L'Enfant had conceived some sort of monumental gateway framing the approach to the Capitol at the opposite end of Pennsylvania Avenue, and there have been a number of subsequent proposals for Washington's own Marble Arch or Arc de Triomphe, during the past two centuries, all to no avail. Downing recognized that the intermediate scale of such structures, larger than sculptural monuments but smaller than most buildings, allows flexibility in their placement and makes them useful tools in relieving often

SKETCH of a DESIGN for Washington's Monument
by
Peter Force
1837

monotonous streetscapes, defining and punctuating intersections and entrances, and framing views. They guide the visitor, are the delight of view painters and photographers, and provide the vantage points that postcards are made of.[20]

Between the time that construction on the Washington Monument was halted in 1855 and its completion in 1884, dozens of ambitious proposals to alter its design were put forward, mostly by architects and mostly architectural in nature. In the 1870s, Vinnie Ream Hoxie proposed a remarkable alternative to these that treated the unfinished monument as a pedestal for a gigantic full-length sculptural representation of George Washington (FIG. 1.12). It allowed no conjecture concerning the subject of the monument, and its effect, if built, would have been indelible. At age eighteen, the precocious sculptor had received the commission for the full-length statue portrait of Abraham Lincoln that stands in the Capitol Rotunda. In 1875 she won the competition for the Admiral David Farragut Monument in Farragut Square, selected over Randolph Rogers and Olin Levi Warner. That she was a woman working in nineteenth-century Washington only made Hoxie's achievements as a sculptor even more remarkable. She produced designs for a number of large-scale projects for sculptural monuments for the city of Washington, many quite handsome and accomplished. Her talents are not, however, displayed to their best advantage in this proposal, whose lack of success is likely to inspire relief rather than regret.[21]

One may say the same about all of architect H. R. Searle's various designs for completing the Washington Monument. One, which he deposited for copyright in 1877, both invites and defies description (FIG. 1.14). It appears to draw on the architectural traditions of various civilizations, ranging from the Egyptian, and possibly the Babylonian and Persian, to Mayan, without bringing credit to any of them. His attempts to enliven the monument's shaft with horizontal and vertical courses and moldings and a flared capital result in making it appear more like an industrial-scale smokestack in search of a factory than anything to do with the memory of the nation's first president. Of the many Egyptian-inspired

FIG. 1.12. Vinnie Ream Hoxie, sculptor. Proposed "Design for the Washington Monument," Washington, D.C. Perspective. Photographic print of drawing. Ca. 1870–78. ADE-UNIT 2582, no. 1, C size (Photo). LC-USZ62-113998.

monuments proposed for Washington—we have already seen examples by Latrobe, Force, Mills, and Searle—none besides Mills's obelisk were built.[22]

Another to add to the "things-probably-best-not-built" list is oddly endearing and perhaps the most distinctively Egyptian of all, if anything can be more Egyptian than a pyramid: J. Goldsborough Bruff's 1873 proposal for the *Grand National Monumental Sphinx, Guarding Our Liberties* (FIG. 1.15). To have been executed in granite "in the Egyptian style of the finest era of their arts," it is perhaps alone among American monumental designs in its attempt to transform this particular Pharaonic form into a symbol of republican virtues. Its inscription would have read: "An emblem of keen, far-sightedness, energy, strength, valor, and immortality." As with so many of these schemes, the facts surrounding its history and even its intended location are murky.

For many years a draftsman in the Office of the Supervising Architect of the Treasury Department,

FIG. 1.13 (*opposite*). Andrew Jackson Downing, architect. "Entrance to the Public Grounds," Washington, D.C. Perspective view. Engraving. *Harper's New Monthly Magazine* 6 (December 1852), 5. LOT 2472. Digital ID: cph 3c29020.

Bruff was a prolific and imaginative designer, primarily of decorative details, who was also known for his drawings of the California Gold Rush.[23] Bruff's archive was a 1986 gift to what they still referred to as the "Congressional Library," by his great-granddaughters, Mary Procter Keyser and Thelma G. Procter, who had proudly guarded their own liberties by participating in the suffragist movement, marching in 1913 along Pennsylvania Avenue to the Capitol to demand an amendment to the U.S. Constitution to enfranchise women.

Imperial Aspirations

The third quarter of the nineteenth century saw the design development and construction of a vast and grand new building for the Library of Congress, designed to serve not only as a great research institution but also as a conspicuous symbol of the young nation's seriousness of purpose, of its cultural and scientific achievements, and of the importance it placed on the free dissemination of knowledge and information. It was to Washington, D.C., what Gar-

nier's Opera was to the Paris of the Second Empire.

From the time of the original design competition in 1873 until the library's completion in early 1897, the process produced hundreds of design drawings and thousands of working drawings. More than thirty architects and firms participated, representing a wide range of training and experience from the United States and abroad. Although the firm formed by John Smithmeyer and Paul Pelz in 1873 won the initial competition and ultimately produced an accepted design in 1886, additional proposals were requested or invited through the mid-1880s.[24]

Awarded second prize among the first submissions, in 1873, was a design by Adolph E. Melander, a Swedish architect briefly based in Boston. He chose to express the culturally ambitious scale of the proposed library by including a grand perspective for a vast, vaulted, skylit hall with elaborately painted ceilings and each bay defined by pedestals supporting a small army of classical statuary. In Melander's library, visitors were clearly intended to be impressed, if not downright intimidated, by these devices. A diminutive President Ulysses S. Grant is seen

FIG. 1.14 (*opposite*). H. R. Searle, architect. Proposed design for the completion of the Washington Monument, Washington, D.C. Perspective. Photographic print of drawing. Ca. 1877. LOT 4386-33 (Washington). LC-USZ62-4055.

FIG. 1.15. J. Goldsborough Bruff, designer. Proposed "Design for a Grand National Monumental Sphinx." Elevation. Graphite and ink on paper. 1873. ADE-UNIT 1930, no. 12, B size. LC-USZ62-113975.

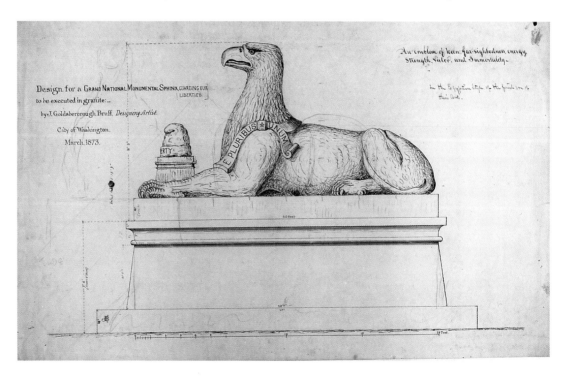

PROPOSED CONGRESSIONAL LIBRARY, WASHINGTON, D.C

employing these architectural resources to full effect, receiving representatives of the Ottoman Empire with whom he was then in the process of renegotiating a treaty, one of whom holds his hand ready on his saber, made anxious perhaps as much by artistic excess as by diplomatic challenges (PLATE 1.8).

The design put forward in 1880 by Alexander R. Esty, a native of Massachusetts who had worked in the Boston office of Gridley J. F. Bryant, was unlike any other (FIG. 1.16). Esty had made a specialty of church architecture in New England, work that was later admired by Ralph Adams Cram as an embodiment of the principles of Gothic architecture revived in England by Sir George Gilbert Scott, G. E. Street, and William Butterfield. Dropped like an exposition building onto an unlandscaped site with a cavernous maw of an entrance, it gives the unlikely appearance of a walled Gothic fortress that has defied its vertical and asymmetrical tendencies and managed to pull itself into quadrangular order for the protection of the treasures in the great octagonal reading room at its core. The spreading buttresses of the latter, which actually were intended to divide it into fireproof sections, give the outward appearance of its being tied down, wanting to rise up from its earthly bondage, like Gulliver. Had it been built, a new version of the

Gothic style might have been born: the horizontal.[25]

Smithmeyer & Pelz's precompetition proposals (before 1873), winning submission (1873), and final accepted design (1886), by contrast, were all inspired by Italian Renaissance models, as seen through a Teutonic rather than an Anglo-American lens. The former (FIG. 1.17) featured an entrance defined by yet another attempt to provide Washington with a triumphal arch and crowned, like the entrance portico of Mills's Washington Monument, with a quadriga (charioteer and four horses). As part of a façade that might have been composed for Dresden or Vienna by Gottfried Semper, the entrance was flanked by arcades in part inspired by one of the key monuments of Italian Renaissance architecture, Filippo Brunelleschi's Foundling Hospital in Florence of 1419, providing visitors and scholars with a welcome shelter in which to stroll or sit and reflect while gazing toward the Capitol building, opposite. It is signed "Schmidtmeier & Pelz," demonstrating that both the architects and their building were still in the process of becoming American.

In 1875 the firm was asked to provide an alternative design for the library in the Victorian Gothic style (FIG. 1.18) for the Judiciary Square site where the Pension Building, now the National Building Museum, ultimately was completed in 1887. In style it recalls many

FIG. 1.16 (*opposite, top*). Alexander R. Esty, architect. "Committee of Experts" design proposal for the Library of Congress ("Congressional Library"), Washington, D.C. Perspective. Ink on paper. 1880–1881. ADE-UNIT 2450, no. 3, D size. LC-USZ62-59059.

FIG. 1.17 (*opposite, bottom*). Schmidtmeier [*sic*] & Pelz, architects. Precompetition design for the Library of Congress, Washington, D.C. Elevation. Graphite, ink, and wash on paper. 1873. ADE-UNIT 2440, no. 3, C size. LC-USZ62-94550.

FIG. 1.18. J. L. Smithmeyer & Co., architects. P. J. Pelz, J. L. Smithmeyer, delineator. Victorian Gothic Design for the Library of Congress at Judiciary Square, Washington, D.C. Perspective. Ink and wash on paper. Ca. 1875. ADE-UNIT 2445, no. 19, F size. LC-USZ62-116878.

of the schemes submitted in the British Law Courts competition and Sir George Gilbert Scott's St. Pancras Station of the 1860s, and is similar in plan and scale, and roughly contemporary with London's Natural History Museum (1866–81) by Alfred Waterhouse, Paris's Hôtel de Ville (1874–82) by Ballu and Deperthes, and most significantly, the preliminary schemes for Vienna's neo-Gothic Neue Rathaus (1872–83) by Friedrich Schmidt, in Smithmeyer's hometown. Pelz's rendering bristles with energetic and intelligently developed ornament appropriated from medieval cloth halls and Venetian palaces, passed through both Ruskinian and Germanic sieves, and applied on an institutional scale to a quadrangular building mass, punctuated centrally and at its corners by large pavilions and towers. The exterior is far livelier and more interesting than that finally completed in 1897 and deserves to be better known.[26]

Over the River

Before construction was begun in 1926 on McKim, Mead and White's Memorial Bridge, the connection between Washington, D.C., and Arlington Memorial Cemetery had been the subject of numerous design proposals. Begun as a military cemetery during the Civil War on the appropriated site of the Custis-Lee Mansion, on the Virginia side of the Potomac River, the cemetery was located within the original plan of the District of Columbia but on land that had been ceded back to Virginia in 1846. Following the establishment of the cemetery, it became a site for numerous events requiring officials and residents from the city to make their way across the Potomac, usually by way of the old Aqueduct Bridge from Georgetown. It was inevitable that a bridge offering a more direct route and designed more in keeping with the memorial and ceremonial purposes of the cemetery, be proposed.

Among the most interesting are different schemes for ceremonial bridges across the Potomac River proposed by Smithmeyer & Pelz in 1887, which were inspired by their earlier studies for the Library of Congress. The first (FIG. 1.19) recalls their precompetition design for the library with its pair of stepped triumphal arches, again crowned with quadrigas, framing a central draw span and connected to steel arch spans sprung between additional large masonry piers. The second design (FIG. 1.20), modeled on the same plan but strikingly different in style, was intended to be in honor of General Ulysses S. Grant and featured artfully composed, turreted towers combining elements of the German Rundbogenstil and the American Richardsonian Romanesque. The bridge's towers have marked similarities to Richardson's recently completed hospital in Buffalo, New York, and would have echoed Smithmeyer & Pelz's Romanesque Revival design for Georgetown University's Healy Hall, which also had been developed from their rejected designs for the Library of Congress.[27]

Executive Development

Chapter 3 discusses the library's small but rich and fascinating trove of drawings representing the various nineteenth-century proposals for the improvement and expansion of the building complex L'Enfant initially identified as the "President's Palace," by Latrobe as the "President's House," by Thomas U. Walter as the "Executive Mansion," and by the American public, for most of the twentieth century, as the White House. Frederick D. Owen's plan of 1890 (FIG. 1.21), *An Adaptation of the Suggestions of Mrs. Harrison for the Extension of the Executive Mansion*, would have transformed it into a combination museum and botanical garden, with wings for art galleries and social and state functions connected to the original structure by statuary halls. The first lady's plans would have framed an interior courtyard with an illuminated "allegorical fountain," closed on the south by a huge greenhouse for orchids, water and palm gardens, and "cataracts" within and without.

Although Mrs. Harrison's "suggestions" may at first consideration appear immodest, they paled compared with those promulgated just a few years later by Mary Foote (Mrs. John Brooks) Henderson, wife of a Missouri senator and the grand dame and chief promoter of Sixteenth Street as the "Avenue of the Presidents." To this effect, she commissioned elaborate houses for embassies up and down the boulevard, but for the choicest site, across from her own estate,

"MEMORIAL BRIDGE,,
FROM WASHINGTON, D.C. TO ARLINGTON, VA.

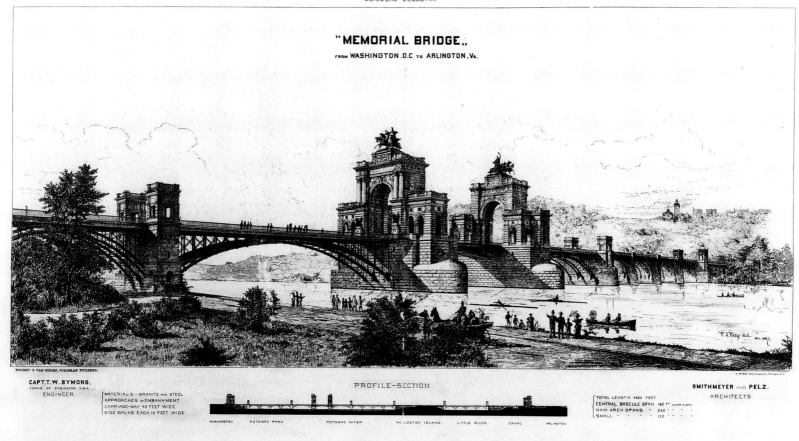

WRIGHT & VAN BUREN, CORCORAN BUILDING.

CAPT. T. W. SYMONS,
CORPS OF ENGINEERS U.S.A.
ENGINEER.

MATERIALS--GRANITE AND STEEL
APPROACHES IN EMBANKMENT
CARRIAGE-WAY 40 FEET WIDE
SIDE WALKS EACH 10 FEET WIDE

PROFILE-SECTION

WASHINGTON   POTOMAC PARK   POTOMAC RIVER   ANALOSTON ISLAND   LITTLE RIVER   CANAL   ARLINGTON

TOTAL LENGTH 4650 FEET
CENTRAL BASCULE SPAN 160 FT CLEAR WIDTH
MAIN ARCH SPANS   240 " "
SMALL "   120 " "

SMITHMEYER AND PELZ.
ARCHITECTS

PROPOSED "MEMORIAL BRIDGE,, IN HONOR
OF
GENERAL, U.S. GRANT.
FROM WASHINGTON, D.C. TO ARLINGTON, VA.

WRIGHT & VAN BUREN, CORCORAN BUILDING.

CAPT. T. W. SYMONS
CORPS OF ENGINEERS U.S.A.
ENGINEER.

MATERIALS--GRANITE AND STEEL.
APPROACHES IN EMBANKMENT
CARRIAGE-WAY, 40 FEET WIDE
SIDE-WALKS, EACH, 10 FEET WIDE.

PROFILE-SECTION.

WASHINGTON   POTOMAC PARK.   POTOMAC RIVER.   ANALOSTON ISLAND.   LITTLE RIVER.   CANAL.   ARLINGTON.

TOTAL LENGTH . 4650 FEET.
CENTRAL BASCULE SPAN, 160 FT CLEAR WIDTH.
MAIN ARCH SPANS   240 " "
SMALL "   SPANS   120 " "

SMITHMEYER AND PELZ.
ARCHITECTS.

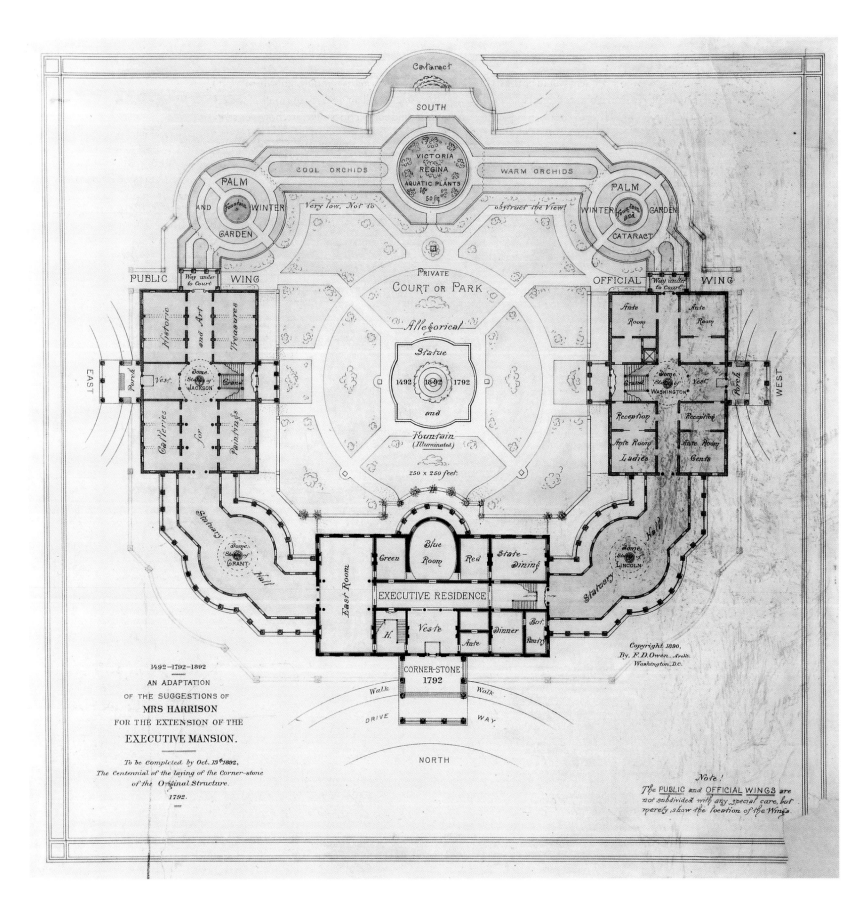

Cataract

SOUTH

COOL ORCHIDS

VICTORIA
REGINA
AQUATIC PLANTS
is
50 ft

WARM ORCHIDS

PALM
AND
WINTER
GARDEN

Fountain

Way under to Court

PUBLIC WING

Very low, Not to

obstruct the View!

PALM
WINTER
GARDEN
Fountain and
CATARACT

OFFICIAL WING

Way under to Court

PRIVATE
COURT or PARK

Allegorical

EAST

Historic and Art Treasures

Vest.

Dome. Statue of JACKSON

Grand

Statue
1492 1892 1792

and

Fountain
(Illuminated)

250 x 250 feet.

Ante Room

Ante Room

Grand

Dome. Statue of WASHINGTON

Vest.

Porch

WEST

Galleries for Paintings

Reception

Reception

Ante Room
Ladies

Ante Room
Gents

Statuary Hall

Dome. Statue of GRANT

Blue Room

Green

Red

State-Dining

Dome. Statue of LINCOLN

Statuary Hall

East Room

EXECUTIVE RESIDENCE

H.

Veste

Ante

Dinner

But.
Pantry

CORNER-STONE
1792

1492–1792–1892

AN ADAPTATION
OF THE SUGGESTIONS OF
MRS HARRISON
FOR THE EXTENSION OF THE
EXECUTIVE MANSION.

To be Completed by Oct. 13th 1892,
The Centennial of the laying of the Corner-stone
of the Original Structure.
1792.

Walk

DRIVE

Walk

WAY

NORTH

Copyright 1890,
By, F. D. Owen, Archt.
Washington, D.C.

Note!
The PUBLIC and OFFICIAL WINGS are
not subdivided with any special care, but
merely show the location of the Wings.

she felt that the only proper resident would be the nation's chief executive. Paul Pelz, the principal designer for the firm of Smithmeyer & Pelz, produced a number of independent works. In 1898 Mrs. Henderson commissioned him to provide designs for a new, more suitable, and immensely more expansive executive residence. Its scale and characteristics were palatial, even imperial, in concept and perhaps more at home in Vienna, Berlin, or perhaps Newport than in Washington (FIGS. 1.22, 3.22). One can imagine the chill winds sweeping across or the sweltering heat radiating up from its great staircases and terraces in Washington's winters and summers. Presumably, the two visitors who have just alighted from their carriage in Jules Crow's rendering have allowed an additional half-hour to make their ascent, and to recover from it, before their appointment.

Had it been carried out, Mary Foote Henderson's replacement White House would have immediately and forever changed the nature of the presidency, not likely for the better. The ceremonies, receptions, dinners, balls, and other grand events that the structure would have hosted so grandly, and which would have furnished excellent grist for the mills of society columnists and social critics alike, are, however, sadly missed. The shady groves, splashing fountains, and sparkling cascade of Meridian Hill Park, built instead on the site between 1912 and 1936, remain a far wiser solution. Henderson's vision was not to be, and her own house, popularly known as "Henderson's Castle," succumbed to the wrecking ball in 1949.[28]

Grand Plans

Following L'Enfant and Downing, and before the McMillan Commission plan of 1901–2, the most ambitious scheme for the replanning of Washington focused on the area extending to the Potomac west of the President's Grounds, or Ellipse. Dubbed the "National Galleries of History and Art," the vast museum complex to be located there was intended to serve as "a great systematic educational institution." The site stretched from the principal entrances on Seventeenth Street, south of the present site of the

FIG. 1.21 (*opposite*). Frederick D. Owen, architect. "An Adaptation of the Suggestions of Mrs. Harrison for the Extension of the Executive Mansion," Washington, D.C. Site plan. Graphite, ink, and watercolor on paper. Ca. 1890. ADE-UNIT 2838, no. 1, D size. LC-USZ62-114211. LC-USZC4-1857.

FIG. 1.22. Paul J. Pelz, architect. Jules T. Crow, delineator. "Proposed Executive Mansion," Meridian Hill, Washington, D.C. Perspective. Ink on paper. 1898. ADE-UNIT 2802, no. 2, F size. LC-USZ62-105250.

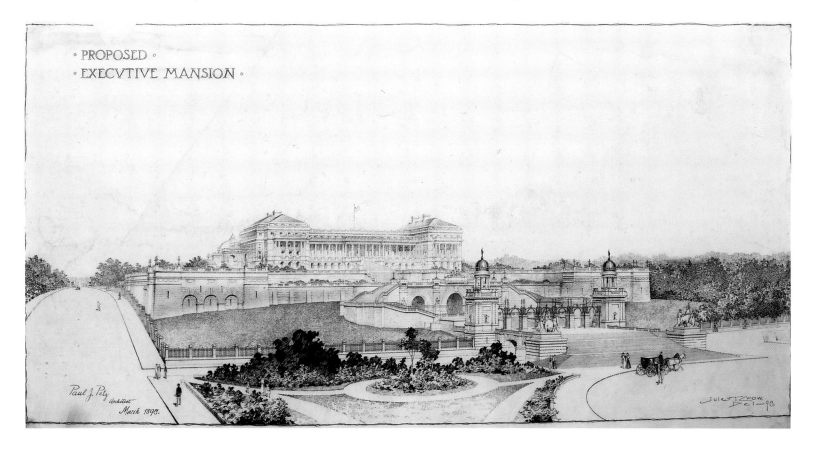

· PROPOSED ·
· EXECVTIVE MANSION ·

Paul J. Pelz Architect
March 1898.

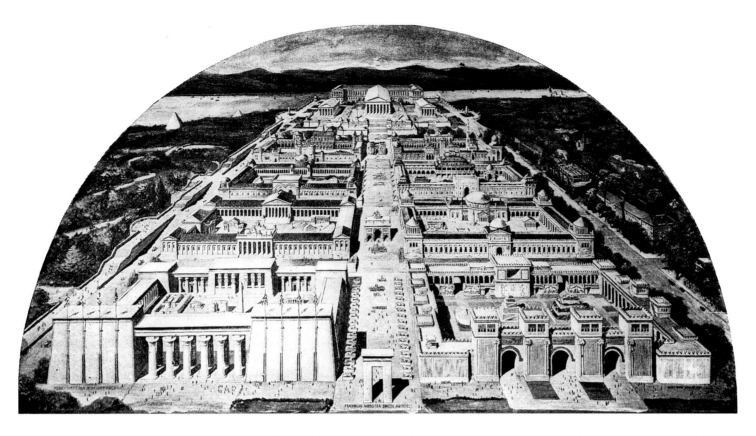

Corcoran Gallery of Art, its spine a wide central processional avenue punctuated by historical gateways and, yet again, a triumphal arch. At its western terminus, a Memorial Temple of the Presidents of the United States, a replica of the Parthenon enlarged by half, would have crowned the elevated site of the old Naval Observatory, overlooking the Mall and the Potomac River, creating a sort of Presidential Parnassus, recalling in both style and purpose the pantheon Mills intended as the base of the Washington Monument. Flanking the central avenue, courtyards were to represent eight of the world's great civilizations or epochs: Egyptian, Assyrian, Greek, Roman, Byzantine, Medieval, Saracenic, and East Indian.

The scheme was the brainchild of a figure who has been largely and unjustifiably forgotten: Franklin Webster Smith. Smith convinced the esteemed James Renwick to contribute his architectural services for the initial plan (FIG. 1.24) of 1890, one of his last works prior to his death in 1895, the original drawing for which came to the Library of Congress from his descendant, Jean Hewitt, in 1991. A half-century earlier, Robert Dale Owen, like Smith, had selected the precocious Renwick (still in his twenties) to visualize his own architectural visions for Washington and of a national architectural style, with the winning competition entry for the original

building of the Smithsonian Institution, now known as the Castle.

After Renwick, Smith enlisted the talents of a wide range of the city's and the nation's architects, including his firm, Renwick, Aspinwall, and Russell, a young Bertram Goodhue, Paul Pelz, and Henry Ives Cobb, among others, and a perspective view published in 1900 (FIG. 1.23) shows substantial changes from the Renwick plan. To further promote his scheme, in 1898 Smith erected a prototype Hall of the Ancients with Egyptian and Roman elements at 1312 New York Avenue, N.W., where it stood until 1926. To be built in concrete rather than plaster, the initial concept for the National Galleries of History and Art presaged even the World's Columbian Exposition. Both high-minded and somewhat hokey, it would have provided a permanent Dreamland for Little Nemo to explore. [29]

Smith's various proposals were prophetic, if not successful. He spent years petitioning Congress and others to enlist support in acquiring the site and building the National Galleries and for numerous other projects for the "aggrandizement" of Washington, ranging from a new axial avenue from the Capitol to the White House, south of Pennsylvania Avenue, cutting through today's Federal Triangle, to a new administration building for St. Elizabeths Asylum, described as an architectural "expression of cheerfulness" intended to contribute to the health and well-being of the inmates.[30] Smith's architecture sought not only to improve and inform but to heal. His ideas, designs, and enthusiasms were presented in a rather chaotic and ever-changing (and today rare) series of promotional pamphlets and publications from the 1890s onward, and they foreshadowed in form and function the McMillan commission plan of 1901–2 (FIGS. 1.25, 1.26), the early schemes for the Lincoln Memorial and Memorial Bridge, the axial redevelopment of the Mall as a matrix for the building of theme museums, and the eventual redevelopment of Lafayette Square, Sixteenth Street, and Pennsylvania Avenue. In sum, they predicted and perhaps influenced much of the evolution of Washington's core in the twentieth century. Unfortunately for Smith, he lacked sufficient erudition and influence, and his dreams, in addition to being highly idiosyncratic, were underfinanced and proved too bold and sweeping—and perhaps a little silly—for their time.

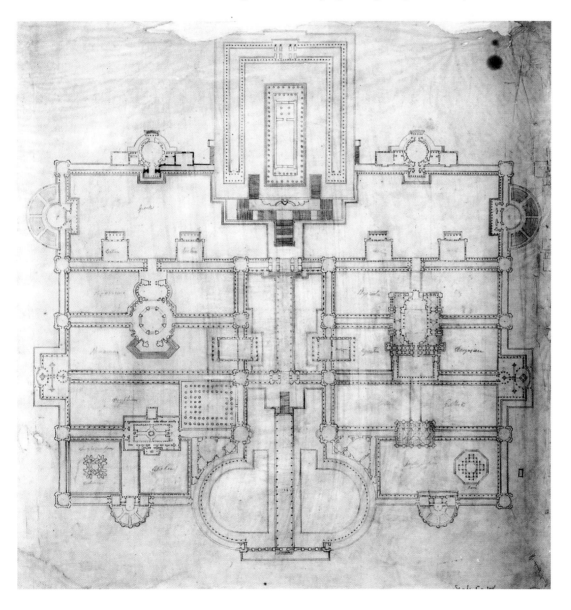

FIG. 1.24. Renwick, Aspinwall and Russell, architects, for Franklin Webster Smith. Proposed National Gallery of History and Art, between 17th and 26th Streets and B (now Constitution Avenue) and F Streets, N.W., Washington, D.C. Site plan. Graphite on linen. 1890. ADE-UNIT 2791, no. 1, E size. LC-USZ62-114213.

Fit for a King

Students of Washington are so thoroughly inculcated regarding the importance and influence of the McMillan Plan that many neglect to study its features critically. It is necessary to look at the drawings with a fresh eye from time to time in order to remind ourselves that, although much was proposed, much was never realized. The original drawings hang today in the offices of the Commission of Fine Arts, serving to inspire and sometimes to intimidate those presenting new projects for Washington's architectural development, but copies of them have been made widely available since they were first exhibited (FIGS. 1.25, 1.26). They show, for example, that the extensive formal landscaping planned for the area surrounding the Washington Monument was never carried out.

Multiple terraces and fountains were to have been arranged in an elaborate grid extending in all directions from the base of the monument, a sort of Ver-

sailles for the masses. A handsome pleasure ground with many advantages, it nevertheless would have obstructed and perhaps obviated the massive gatherings of celebration and protest that have made that area so important in the nation's history during the last century. A wide and unobstructed greensward has served us well, and it is curious that the recently completed World II Memorial can be seen as a partial realization of the elements intended by the McMillan Plan, which for many reasons, both good and bad, never went forward.

In contrast to the great open terraces proposed for Pelz's Executive Residence and for the Mall in the McMillan Plan, we can contemplate the more modest, bosky, and elegant proposal for a memorial fountain developed by the sculptor Paul Bartlett and architect Glenn Brown between 1915 and the early 1920s (PLATE 1.9). The carefully colored photograph of the presentation rendering from Bartlett's papers presents us with a scene inspired by Fragonard but with dapper Washingtonians strolling and relaxing rather than courtiers with swings. Commissioned in the fall of 1915 by the American Society of Civil Engineers to be erected in Washington, D.C., it was intended to honor Alfred Noble, the engineer who had built the tunnels under the Hudson River for the Pennsylvania Railroad.

Historian Thomas Somma has determined that the Alfred Noble Memorial Fountain, or "Fountain of the Engineers," was never completed, an apparent casualty of the uncertain fiscal climate in America following the end of the Great War.[31] Brown designed the architectural features and the bowl, and Bartlett was responsible for the large, seated male figures. Photographs accompanying this and photographs of other drawings show that a full-scale plaster mockup was built on the site (ADE-UNIT 2188). The fountain's shaded benches looked onto jets of water burbling into a large basin and would have offered a refreshing, welcome respite from Washington's blistering summers, a cool darkness not inappropriate for honoring Noble's tunneling prowess.

If Henderson had a dream, then it can be said that publisher John Brisben Walker had a fantasy, because his project for a Rocky Mountain castle as a summer

FIG. 1.25 (opposite, top). Senate Park Commission. F. L. V. Hoppin, artist. "The Future Washington," Washington, D.C. Bird's-eye perspective. Printed from a contemporary glass-plate photographic negative of the original drawing published by the Detroit Photographic Company. 1902. LC-D4-33482. Also represented in a print in LOT 4386-12. LC-USZ62-77379.

FIG. 1.26 (opposite, bottom). Senate Park Commission. Charles Graham, artist. Washington Monument Grounds, "The Future Washington," Washington, D.C. Bird's-eye perspective. Printed from a contemporary glass-plate photographic negative of the original drawing published by the Detroit Photographic Company. 1902. LC-D4-17434.

FIG. 1.27. J. J. B. Benedict, architect. "Sketch for the Summer Residence for the Presidents of the United States, Mount Falcon (near Morrison, Colorado), Rocky Mountains," for John Brisben Walker. Photomechanical copy of drawing. 1911. LOT 8092, G size. LC-USZ62-129024.

residence for the president of the United States (FIG. 1.27) was akin to the architectural extravagances of Bavaria's King Ludwig II. Walker, editor of *Cosmopolitan Magazine*, commissioned Denver architect J. J. B. Benedict to conjure up his dream, like Mrs. Henderson, near his own home on Mount Falcon, in Morrison, Colorado. Jules Jacques Benois Benedict studied at the École des Beaux-Arts for four years in the 1890s and worked in the Chicago office of Frost and Granger and the New York office of Carrère & Hastings before settling in Denver in 1909. Had it been completed, perched on a promontory like Neuschwanstein, its direct inspiration, this summer residence would have brought the president, his family, and certain governmental functions closer to the geographic center of the expanded nation for at least a part of the year. Both the fresh air and the photo opportunities would have been marvelous. Instead, in 1918, a destructive and perhaps providential lightning strike brought its construction, never resumed, to a halt.[32]

Some of the twentieth century's most notable mountain retreats were, however, designed for the pleasure of some of its least respected figures: William Randolph Hearst's San Simeon, parodied as Xanadu by Orson Welles in *Citizen Kane*, and Adolf Hitler's Berghof, captured affectionately for all time in the Führer's own home movies before it was blasted away by American bombers. However tempting, it is probably best that the presidents of the United States did not join this exclusive club; Owen's and Pelz's elaborate schemes for executive residences are made to look almost democratic by comparison.

The Wright Stuff

Whereas most readers of this volume probably have at least a passing acquaintance with the names of a number of the architects mentioned thus far, one name that is known to more Americans than any other, and justifiably so, is Frank Lloyd Wright. If they were asked, however, what projects Wright proposed either for the federal government or for the city of Washington during a career that spanned more than seven decades, most would fail to produce an answer.

In fact, Wright produced four projects. Two were for the federal government: a design for a U.S. embassy in Tokyo in 1914 and the "Cloverleaf" scheme for Federal Defense Housing in 1942 (ADE-UNIT 2449). Private developers commissioned two other projects in the 1920s and in 1940.

The first of the privately commissioned projects was for an automobile objective, a gigantic spiraling tourist attraction crowning Sugarloaf Mountain, meant to rise distinctively above the rolling foothills between Washington and Baltimore. The second was a mixed-use, multiple-tower development incorporating a hotel, apartments, shops, a theater, and parking, a structure that would have redefined the northwest quadrant of the city. It was known as the Crystal Heights project (FIG. 1.35; ADE-UNIT 2451). All of these projects drew on Wright's best talents and principles of design. Had they been built as planned, today these would be among his most famous works and the subjects of international study and admiration. Sadly for all us, none of them were to be.

Wright's plan for a U.S. embassy proposed for Tokyo (FIG. 1.28) and deposited for copyright in the Library of Congress in 1914, is the least known of the four; it is contemporary with his early designs for Tokyo's Imperial Hotel (ca. 1913–22) and worthy of comparison to it. Like the huge residence projected for farm-machinery heir Harold C. McCormick on the bluffs of Lake Michigan in 1907, the embassy employed a rigorously symmetrical plan unprecedented in Wright's domestic projects of the period. Nevertheless, it brings together the broad spreading roofs, terraced courtyards, horizontal fenestration, and other compositional elements that characterized his early Prairie Houses and the 1914 design for his own house and studio at Taliesin, near Spring Green, Wisconsin. This he does here, however, on a scale even more extensive than for his most ambitious private residences.

The articulation of the embassy's central pavilion appears to have close cousins in the Avery Coonley House (1906–8) in Riverside, Illinois, and Wright's design for the Como Orchards Summer Colony (1909–10) in Darby, Montana. Understandably and probably quite self-consciously, the design for the embassy

UNITED STATES EMBASSY BUILDINGS TOKIO JAPAN
FRANK LLOYD WRIGHT ARCHITECT CHICAGO ILLINOIS U·S·A

SCALE ONE SIXTEENTH INCH TO ONE FOOT
NOTE "FOR PRIVATE CIRCULATION ONLY" USE PROHIBITED WITHOUT PERMISSION

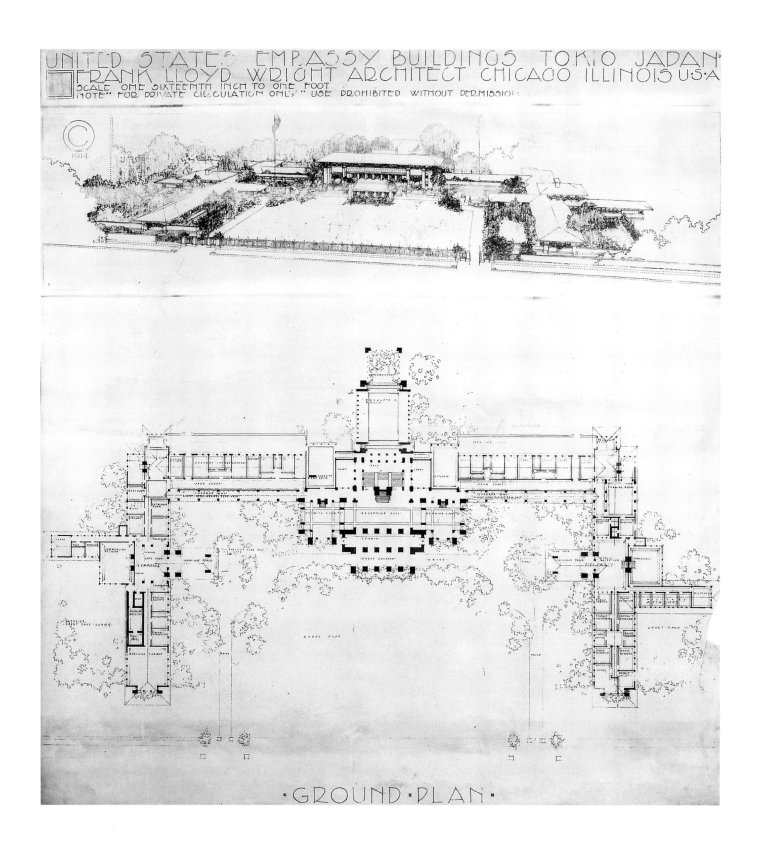

© 1914

·GROUND·PLAN·

BOSTON PEACE JUBILEE ✦ NAVAL TOWER
- THE TOWER OF A THOUSAND COLUMNS -

is much more "American" than Wright's scheme for Tokyo's Imperial Hotel (1914–23), but the two share the idea of lower wings branching out from a central pavilion to define landscaped courtyards. Oh, that Wright's design had been built as an executive residence, rather than an embassy, and in Washington, D.C., rather than in Tokyo, and on the Meridian Hill Park site slated for Pelz's presidential palace![33]

Higher and Higher

Three years later, we find the self-consciously horizontal replaced by the absurdly vertical in the Boston Peace Jubilee Naval Tower, or the "Tower of a Thousand Columns," designed by J. H. Harper, a Washington, D.C., engineer, and copyrighted in 1917 (FIG. 1.29). Harper's Boston tower proposal represents a sort of Jack-and-the-Beanstalk metamorphosis of elements of the east front, rotunda, and dome of the U.S. Capitol into a column of more than twenty stories, telescoped above a pedimented entrance portico, and truncated just above the Corinthian peristyle at its summit to provide what appears to be an ominously tiny landing platform (with an off-center wind direction indicator) to serve the most intrepid of aviators. Closer inspection shows that the volutes of the massive column's capital are actually parts of four huge harps, which we pray (to preserve the sanity of the citizens of Boston) are not activated by the wind, to make it a sort of "singing" tower. The plan depicts a forest of concentrically arranged columns resembling a connect-the-dots puzzle until one observes the ramping "auto entrances" and "auto exits" that explain the base to be a huge parking garage. Its use of a triumphal column and neoclassical architectural forms to celebrate early twentieth-century technological advances in land and air travel as much as the end of a great war, appear anachronistic, until one begins to inventory the pyramids, obelisks, and sphinxes put forward for the nation's capital.

Comparably driven by America's burgeoning new automobile culture was Frank Lloyd Wright's project for an "automobile objective," intended for a mountaintop approximately thirty miles northeast of Washington (PLATE 1.10). In 1924 Gordon Strong, a wealthy Chicago lawyer and real-estate speculator, commissioned Wright to come up with an "impressive," "beautiful," and "enduring" structure and site plan (together incorporating parking facilities for more than 1,200 automobiles) that would attract automobile tourists, including day-trippers from Washington and Baltimore, to his property at Sugarloaf Mountain, straddling the line between Montgomery and Frederick counties in Maryland.

An ancient monadnock isolated by glacial activity, Sugarloaf enjoyed panoramic views of the surrounding countryside and of the piedmont ranges to the west. And for it, Wright envisioned a great spiraling, ramping structure that automobilists could enjoy from their cars while driving up and down it. They also could park, picnic, and explore the grounds, various viewing platforms around and on top of the structure, fountains, and a waterfall. Inside Wright proposed shops, restaurants, and, variously, a dance hall, a theater, a great planetarium, and a gallery with aquariums and natural history exhibits. The presentation drawings produced for the project are ravishing, done in colored pencil on Japanese and tracing paper.

This rendering, presented to the Library of Congress by Donald D. Walker in 1986, is one of the few to show a great vertical mass projecting from the spiral, anchoring a mooring mast for airships and, indeed, the entire composition. A biplane soars to the right and hundreds of pleasure-seekers stroll about the structure and through a Japanese-inspired and framed landscape, some carrying brightly colored parasols, as in a Ukiyo-e woodcut by Hiroshige, Hokusai, or Kunisada. Far more daring, ambitious, and costly than anything the client had in mind, it was never built, but it did provide the seed for one of Wright's most famous buildings, New York's Guggenheim Museum (1943–59), where the spiral was to be inside, rather than out.[34]

I Remember Mama

Equally bold and massive was Joseph W. Geddes's astonishing proposal of the late 1920s for a Mothers' Memorial for Washington, D.C. Only a National Photo Company photograph of his perspec-

FIG. 1.29. J. H. Harper, engineer. "Boston Peace, Jubilee Naval Tower, the Tower of a Thousand Columns," Boston, Massachusetts. Plan and elevation. Photographic print of drawing. 1916–1917. ADE-UNIT 2027, Photo size. LC-USZ62-113954.

tive drawing survives (FIG. 1.30); it is not known what became of Geddes after 1930. The project probably relates to proposals made in February 1923 by Congressman John W. Langley, chairman of the House Committee on Public Buildings and Grounds, for "an acropolis at Massachusetts Avenue and W Street, N.W., containing a conservatory of music and a temple of tribute to motherhood," putting its location near Observatory Circle and the current vice-presidential mansion, near the grounds of the National Cathedral. Mother's Day had been established by Congress in 1913; this was not the first monumental scheme put forward, but certainly the most ambitious.

Trained in Glasgow and London, Geddes worked in Scotland and England before immigrating to the United States in 1920, where he worked for five years in the New York office of Warren & Wetmore, architects of New York's Grand Central Station. In 1924 he was employed on the restoration of Colonial Williamsburg, sponsored by John D. Rockefeller Jr., who, at the same time, was supporting the construction of New York's Riverside Church, another project of comparable scale.

Geddes's drawing for a monument celebrating motherhood features a massive, stepped tower, framed on four corners by commemorative columns. Its multiple-staged platforms were to be ascended by a central monumental stairway of daunting proportions. Rodin-like sculptural representations of motherhood, presumably in all its manifestations, were placed at the cheekblocks, in the center of the stairway (recalling sculptor Daniel Chester French's *Alma Mater* on the steps of the Columbia University's Low Memorial Library) at the bases and summits of the columns, above the multiple entrances, and on vertical niches. The tower shows the influence of New York's setback skyscrapers, churches, and synagogues of the 1920s, and evokes the image of the surviving pier of a great suspension bridge. The entire composition shares the scale and gravity characteristic of the post–World War I projects of the American Battle Monuments Commission. Dour and brooding, it would be completely at home in the eternal twilight of Batman's Gotham City, as imagined by Tim

Burton. One would not be surprised to find a searchlight projecting the bat signal in the sky to the left and, inside, a Wayne family chapel, an entire apse dedicated to Sigmund Freud, and a busy trauma center for visitors of all ages.[35]

The Commission of Fine Arts has no record that the Geddes Memorial even reached the review stage, which is a shame. Otherwise we would have comments from the members, like those accorded a rival scheme in 1925.[36]

Looking East

Cass Gilbert, one of the original members of the Commission of Fine Arts, serving from 1910 to 1916, had proved his own considerable architectural skills in a number of major commissions. The 1901 design for the U.S. Customs House in New York (now the National Museum of the American Indian; ADE-UNIT 2548, no. 1, A size) took his career out of Minnesota and launched him as a figure of national importance, a position secured forever with the completion of the critically acclaimed Woolworth Building, the world's tallest, in 1913 (ADE 11, Gilbert, no. 45, A size).[37] At its opening, President Woodrow Wilson pushed a button in Washington that illuminated more than five thousand windows in the 793-foot tower.

In Washington, D.C., Cass Gilbert is best known for his much-admired building for the U.S. Supreme Court, completed in 1935, in which he established the architectural identity of that institution. Few realize that it is not on the site he preferred. In a brilliant sketch of 1927 from his papers in the Library of Congress (FIG. 1.31), Gilbert shows his proposal to place the new building on a direct axis several blocks to the east of the Capitol, rather than in its present location. His plan shows he is fully aware of the major axis running from Lincoln Park at east of the Capitol to the Washington and Lincoln Memorials and Memorial Bridge at the other end of the Mall. His Beaux-Arts training led him also to appreciate and exploit the possibilities offered by Washington's system of radial avenues, which connected the city's nodes both visually and symbolically

FIG. 1.30. Joseph W. Geddes, architect. "Mothers Memorial," Washington, D.C. Perspective. Printed from a contemporary glass-plate photographic negative of the original drawing published by the National Photo Company. Ca. 1926–1930. LOT 4386-33 (reference print). LC-F82-951.

MOTHERS MEMORIAL
WASHINGTON D.C.
- JOSEPH W. GEDDES - A.I.A. ARCHITECT -

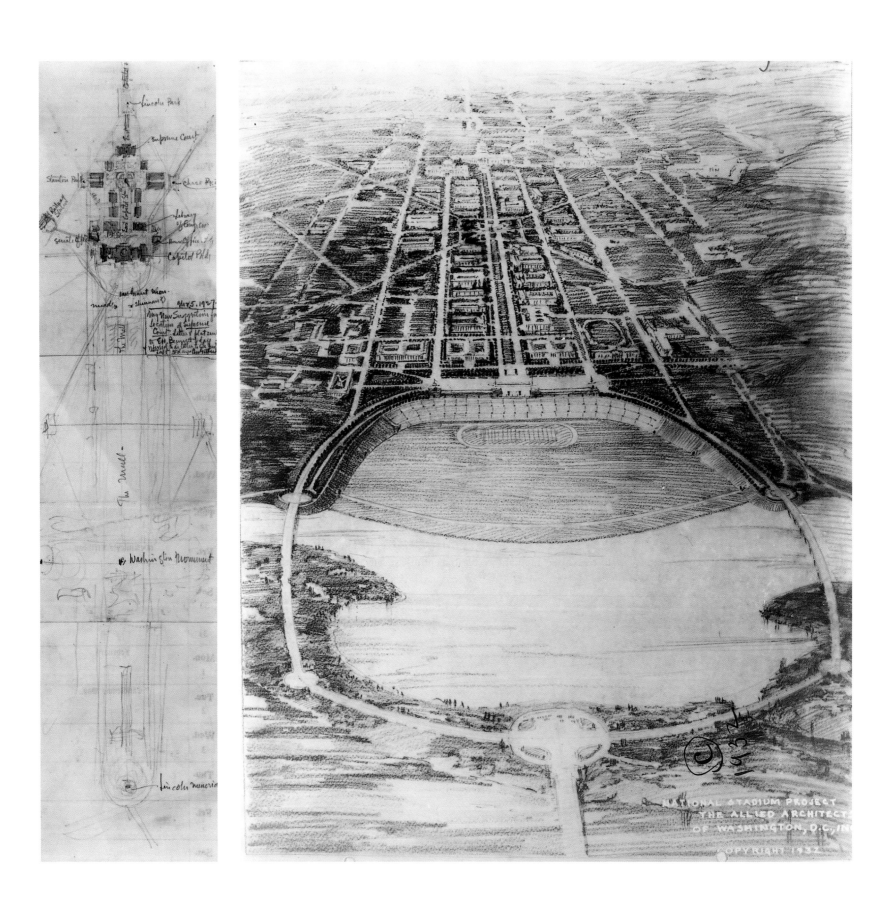

NATIONAL STADIUM PROJECT
THE ALLIED ARCHITECTS
OF WASHINGTON, D.C., INC
COPYRIGHT 1932

according to L'Enfant's original principles, here reinforced by the precepts of the McMillan Plan. Gilbert's proposal for the site would have provided a more suitably scaled and articulated setting for the Supreme Court.

Of course, Gilbert provided an excellent solution for the irregular site he ultimately was given across First Street, northeast of the Capitol and flanking the Library of Congress, but the site he first proposed would have expressed more demonstrably the constitutional and functional distinctions between the judicial and legislative branches of government. Today, the Supreme Court remains but one of many structures in a campus of legislative branch buildings surrounding the Capitol, rather than the more centrally, conspicuously, properly, and effectively mounted gem it might have been.[38]

Five years later, in 1932, further consideration was given to the development of the East Capitol Street axis in a proposal copyrighted by the Allied Architects of Washington, D.C., for a National Stadium Project. The bird's-eye perspective (FIG. 1.32), probably drawn by Tax Evermann, shows not only a sports facility on the river directly east of the Capitol, over three decades before the construction of Robert F. Kennedy (RFK) Stadium on the same site, but also the development of the entire length of East Capitol Street. The latter was to be widened and receive a central, landscaped, tree-lined median flanked by Beaux-Arts structures clearly intended for institutional and governmental uses, altering dramatically the primarily residential character of the area that continues to this day.

Organized by Horace W. Peaslee about 1925, the Allied Architects was a loose confederation of prominent local architects formed to secure large-scale commissions from the government and the private sector. The alliance was modeled on a comparable organization formed in Los Angeles by G. E. Bergstrom, later architect of the Pentagon, in 1919. The principals of the Washington enterprise were Louis Justement, Gilbert LaCoste Rodier, Frank Upman, and Nathan C. Wyeth, and their most significant commission was the Longworth House Office Building, for which they first submitted designs in 1925. By 1929 there were thirty-four members, "organized to act in an advisory capacity and to give service on buildings in the National Capital of a monumental character designed for public or semipublic use."[39] The Allied Architects disbanded in 1949.

On the Edge

The term "Edge City" was introduced by *Washington Post* correspondent Joel Garreau in his groundbreaking 1991 publication, *Edge City: Life on the New Frontier.* Garreau details the profound shift during the previous two decades of human life, jobs, and other activities to suburban areas that increasingly were becoming the principal centers of population, employment, commerce, and recreation, supplanting their former role as largely residential areas for commuters.[40]

In many ways, Washington's transformation into an Edge City can be said to have really taken off with the career of Arthur B. Heaton, a member of the Allied Architects and one of the area's most prolific and versatile designers during the first half of the twentieth century.[41] The Library of Congress's Heaton Archive, donated by architect Leon Chatelain III, includes representation of most of his work after about 1910, through to the late 1940s, and is remarkable for the quality of its drawings and the range of building types and materials represented. Heaton enthusiastically embraced the new age of the automobile and the demands it made on architecture, understanding its needs and exploiting its possibilities. He produced some of the earliest and most thoughtful examples of "drive-in" architecture in the country.[42] A small portfolio of examples has been chosen to represent the variety and quality of his work and its inventiveness.

Heaton's office produced projects primarily for the District of Columbia but also for Chevy Chase and the adjacent and expanding suburbs in Virginia and Maryland, including that crucible of urban experimentation, Greenbelt. An avid motorist, Heaton even entered a 1932 competition for a new automobile license plate for the District of Columbia (ADE-UNIT 944). Frank Lyon, a developer in Arlington, Virginia, for whom the current Lyon Park and Lyon Village neighborhoods are

FIG. 1.31 (*opposite, left*). Cass Gilbert, architect. "My New Suggestion for Location of [U.S.] Supreme Court," East Capitol Street, Washington, D.C. Site plan. Graphite and on paper. 1927. ADE-UNIT 2552, no. 1, B size. LC-USZ62-116850.

FIG. 1.32 (*opposite, right*). Allied Architects of Washington, D.C. Tax Evermann, delineator. "National Stadium Project," East Capitol Street, Washington, D.C. Bird's-eye perspective. Photographic print of drawing. 1932. ADE-UNIT 2040, no. 6, Photo size. LC-USZ62-113962.

named, recognized Heaton's talents and made good use of them. To study one of Heaton's proposals (later partially realized) for the development of what remains a major intersection on Lee Highway, one of the principal arteries leading west from Washington into Virginia (FIG. 1.33), is like looking into a crystal ball for the seed of what becomes, over a quarter of a century later, Tysons Corner, featured in Garreau's discussion of Washington as an "Edge City."[43]

Heaton's proposal is all the more telling when one recognizes that it is also intended for the intersection of the right-of-way for the Washington and Old Dominion Railroad, which in the 1980s was transformed into Interstate 66. Here, in the mid-1930s, most of the elements of automobile-driven design are already in place or incubating: major and minor roadways, entrances and exits accommodating turning radiuses, an "inn" with garages for its clients, a "park & shop center" with multiple stores, a restaurant, and a swimming pool, all surrounded by parking, parking, parking. L'Enfant's, Latrobe's, Downing's and the McMillan Commission's principles of planning, including both formal and picturesque landscaping elements, have been absorbed and translated into a new idiom, and the *machine* (here the automobile) now governs the *park*.[44]

Keeping Up Appearances

While the Washington area could embrace with ease modern developments in transportation and commercial architecture, it remained extremely conservative in the outward face given to its domestic architecture, preferring various historical styles. Drawing mostly on Georgian, Federal, and other early American vocabularies for inspiration, it included, nevertheless, a respectable dose of the medieval, ranging from Gothic to Tudor. Mediterranean, Italianate, and, especially in the 1920s, Spanish motifs, also enjoyed spurts of popularity. As we will see later, the conspicuously modern house was exceptional, even in the post–World War II era, and has all but vanished today.

George N. Ray was a facile draftsman who had learned his trade from Clarke Waggaman, who provided the upper echelons of Washington society with elegant townhouses and mansions before his untimely death in the flu epidemic of 1919. Ray continued in this tradition and expanded the firm's production of elegant commercial buildings until the Great Depression, including occasional work for clients as far away as Massachusetts and Kansas, often producing many alternative design schemes for them to choose from.[45]

One of the author's favorite Ray sketches was done in 1927 for a house for George H. Kennedy in Worcester, Massachusetts (PLATE 1.11). It shows the degree to which a capable architect of the period could appropriate and translate a wide range of historical motifs for an American lifestyle. Inventive half-timber decoration defines the story above a handsome entrance and a conspicuously flanking garage door, all framing a huge window bay proclaiming an interior "great room," that fixture of today's McMansions. The comfy domain of a pre-dot-com, neo-Tudor arriviste, the Kennedy design conjures up the image of a house that Snow White might have purchased after she signed her contract with Disney, and got her first Duesenberg. One can almost hear the muffled "Hi-Ho's" audible from the party gathered around its cheerfully blazing fireplace, which appears to be placing its neatly thatched roof at some risk.

For those with a stricter housing budget, Luther Reason Ray, an architect without a license, provided a more modest alternative (FIG. 1.34). A conventional one-and-a-half-story, three-bedroom, one-and-a-half-bath, central hall plan home, with attached garage, hides behind a vaguely medieval exterior. A massive chimney anchors a flurry of gables and roof pitches, its brickwork growing out of more expensive stonework that is concentrated on the front for maximum visibility. It strives, with the inclusion of two small leaded-glass windows, to conjure up an image of antiquity, of a building centuries rather than months in the making. A model by no means particular to Washington, D.C., it and its multiple variations were happily chosen by countless Americans in the 1920s and 1930s, and built from north to south and east to west, in towns and cities small and large and even in decidedly rural locations.[46]

FIG. 1.33. Arthur B. Heaton, architect. Lyon Village Development for Frank Lyon, Lee Highway at Woodmont Avenue, Clarendon, Arlington County, Virginia. Site plan. Graphite and colored pencil on paper. 1934–1937. ADE-UNIT 588, no. 3, C size. LC-USZ62-114035.

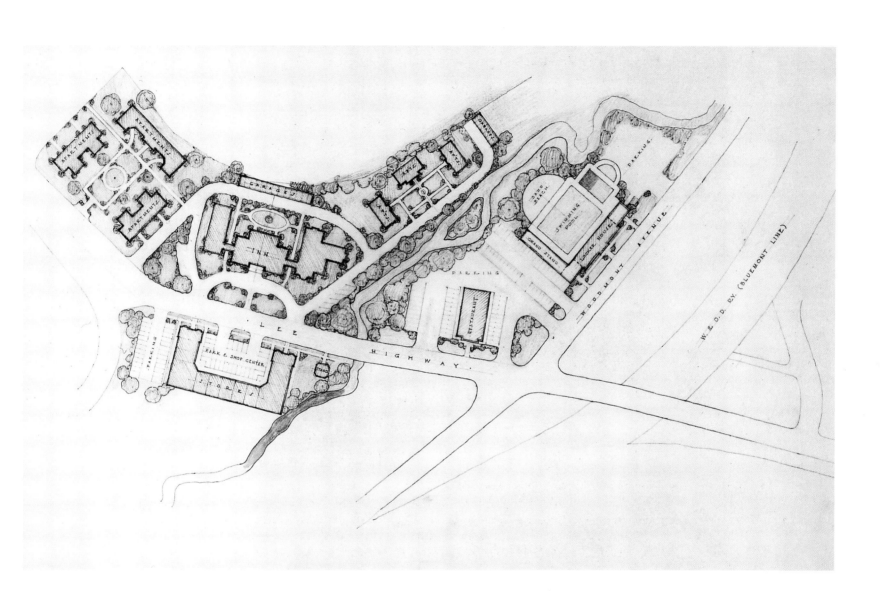

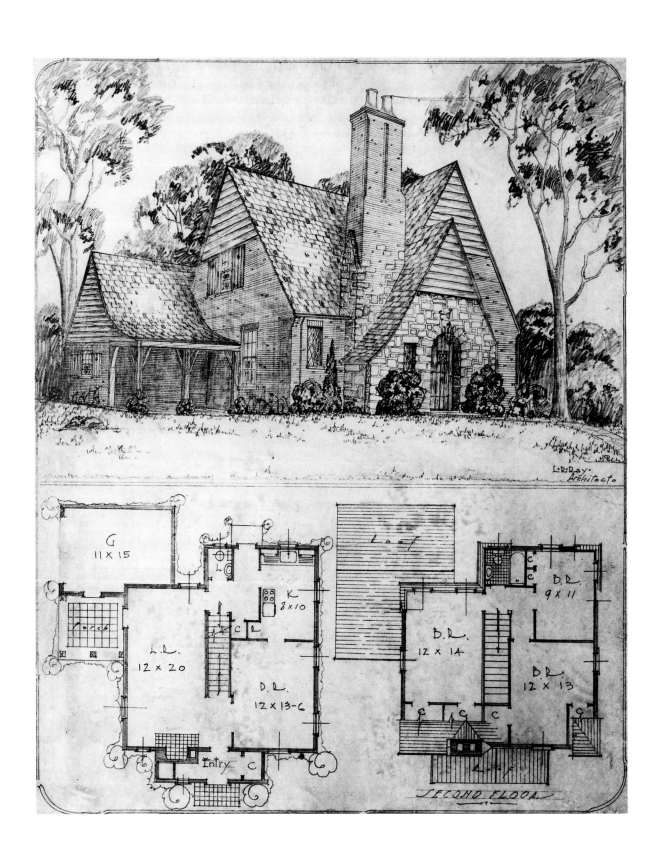

L.R.Day.
Architects

G
11 X 15

Porch

K
8x10

L.R.
12 x 20

D.R.
12 x 13-6

C

Entry   C

Roof

B.R.
9 X 11

B.R.
12 x 14

B.R.
12 x 13

C   C   C

SECOND FLOOR

One of the considerable architectural challenges offered by the new automobile suburbs was the need for conveniently placed filling and service stations, but their commercial nature and appearance presented a quandary in terms of zoning and property values. To make them more acceptable, architects like Heaton dressed them in mantles of similar cloth, making them almost indistinguishable from houses in the adjacent neighborhoods. In 1933 he produced a series of sketches for a handsome stone station for the American Oil Company in the Norman style on a carefully landscaped site (ADE-UNIT 975, ADE-UNIT 1511).

Everything Shiny and New

Heaton was equally at home in designing up-to-date commercial buildings using new materials such as chromium, aluminum, Vitrolite, and structural porcelain enamel, which allowed gleaming, permanent exterior wall finishes in a wide palette of colors previously unavailable, impractical, or unaffordable. That these new products substantially extended the possibilities for the designers of small commercial buildings from the 1920s onward is evident in a wide range of projects by both Heaton and Luther Ray, whose archive in the Library of Congress is also filled with projects for what we now refer to as the "commercial vernacular." As the twentieth century developed, these ubiquitous and ephemeral, often boldly imaginative and just as often banal, buildings have populated and defined our downtowns, main streets, suburbs, highways, and emergent commercial "strips" in increasing numbers. Distinctively American, they offered one of the few laboratories for architectural experimentation during the Great Depression, when most non-government-subsidized construction ground to a halt. Washington, as it geared up for the New Deal and then World War II, was exceptional both for its continued building activity during the period and the opportunities that it offered to local architects.[47]

Of all of Heaton's projects, his versatility as a master of the commercial vernacular is perhaps best, and most enjoyably, displayed in the remarkably varied series of sketches for the local Blue Bell System

Hamburger Restaurants of the mid-1930s. His search for a distinctive visual identity for Blue Bells was intended to result in an immediately recognizable iconic building, a device already proven in the White Castle chain, of which 115 examples had been opened by 1931, following the probable invention of the hamburger-on-a-bun by J. Walter Anderson of Wichita, in 1916.

From elegantly composed Moderne and Deco/Regency (PLATES 1.12 to 1.14) pavilions, which, except for their prominent "Hamburger 5¢" signage, could as easily have served an upscale jeweler, parfumerie, or beauty salon as a fast-food restaurant, they range in appearance from checkerboard fronts owing a debt to Josef Hoffman and the Viennese Sezession Movement (ADE-UNIT 721, no. 2, A size), to a self-consciously Spartan, flat-roofed simplicity derivative of the then current International Style (PLATE 1.15). One even more proletarian design, not shown here, proclaimed "FOOD FOR ALL" in large letters across its façade (ADE-UNIT 721, no. 1, A size).

Luther Reason Ray was not a professionally trained architect but an entrepreneur and an amateur who sometimes used that title and who produced a much wider range of designs than the Tudor cottage already seen (FIG. 1.34) His naiveté as a draftsman is evident in many of his renderings but so are his native design skills and commercial acumen. In his Blue Moon (PLATE 1.16), probably a café or bar, the ground story of an existing building is to receive a seductive makeover in lilac-tinted Vitrolite with boldly curvaceous windows in thin frames of chrome, all intended to shimmer and pulse at night under the neon sign above, drawing customers through its double doors like helpless moths.

It is doubtful that the Blue Moon enjoyed an interior as exotic as that projected for Washington's Madrillon Restaurant, actually more a cabaret, which included a stage for performers (PLATE 1.17). Here the designer was the artist Winold Reiss, who also was one of New York City's leading commercial designers of the 1920s and 1930s. Trained at Munich's Royal Academy of Fine Arts and School of Applied Arts, after completing his daringly modern Restaurant Crillon in 1919, Reiss was commissioned to design the interiors

FIG. 1.34. Luther R. Ray, architect. Unidentified house. Perspective and plans. Graphite and colored pencil on illustration board. Ca. 1930s. ADE-UNIT 2745, no. 9, A size. LC-USZ62-129025.

CRYSTAL HEIGHTS WASHINGTON D C FRANK LLOYD WRIGHT

of dozens of the finest restaurants, clubs, and hotels in New York, Chicago, and Los Angeles. His sketch for the Madrillon, one of more than two hundred drawings given to the Library of Congress by Tjark and Renate Reiss, attests to the bold use of color for which he was famous. In the 1920s, Reiss was the consultant chosen to develop the colors, promotional materials, and innovative architectural and interior design uses for DuPont's new synthetic upholstery material, Fabrikoid, and surfacing material, Muralart, the commercial cousins of what are best known today as Naugahyde and Formica. These new materials allowed rich colors to be used in durable, easily maintained finishes on interiors, to cover walls, tables, or built-in and freestanding furniture and fixtures. The banquettes in the Madrillon were probably to have been upholstered in Fabrikoid and the tabletops and possibly the lower wall surfaces finished in Muralart.[48]

Luther Ray's most notable work was in yet another new material exploited in commercial buildings: structural porcelain enamel. At age fourteen, he had apprenticed in a structural steel, boiler, and sheet metal shop where he gained experience in drafting, estimating, and writing specifications. By 1937 he had founded the Structural Porcelain Enamel Company, which served as a distributor and promoter of building tiles and similar materials manufactured by the Toledo Porcelain Enamel Company, the Wolverine Porcelain Enamel Company, and Kaiser Aluminum and Chemical Sales, Inc. Ray developed and adapted porcelain enamel architectural panels and tiles to clad the walls and roofs of various businesses.

The green and white tile panels and green tile roofs of his diminutive Little Tavern restaurants, for example, still glisten at a number of locations in the District, Maryland, and Virginia, although under new names. Ray's archive also reveals his involvement with the orange tile roofs that made Howard Johnson's restaurants so distinctive from the late 1930s onward. His clients included A&P supermarkets, automobile sales agencies, and automotive service stations. A number of more specialized establishments are represented, like the rifle range clad in red, blue, and yellow porcelain enamel tiles, depicted in one of his crude perspective drawings, which also

served as the preliminary layout or key drawing for estimating the costs of and guiding installation (PLATE 1.18). In contrast, from the early 1930s, his *Scheme Showing Vitrolite Treatment on Theater Front* for Washington's Circle Theatre demonstrates that he was equally at home in producing rather sophisticated designs that employed structural-glass cladding (PLATE 1.19).

The Latest and the Greatest

Frank Lloyd Wright's Crystal Heights development of 1940, which he intended to occupy the site of today's Washington Hilton and the adjacent property down to Florida Avenue, would have changed the character of that part of the city (FIG. 1.35). It was the idea of an enlightened and adventurous developer, Roy S. Thurman, who went on to hire the architect William Lescaze to design one of the city's first modern buildings, the Longfellow Building (1940–41), at the intersection of Connecticut Avenue and M Street, N.W. Thurman had secured options on a magnificent, undeveloped parcel of land, conveniently and dramatically situated on an elevation that enjoyed a commanding, panoramic view of the city. He then enlisted Wright as the architect and put together the financing for his project.

Wright brought to Thurman's project a number of elements from his earlier, more famous scheme for New York's St. Mark's-in-the-Bouwerie Towers (1927–31), in particular the idea of multiple residential towers cantilevered from central service cores. The structural system of these towers allowed for the elimination of exterior bearing walls and made free-flowing and geometrically inventive interior spaces and the expansive use of windows possible. Other elements were taken from his San Marcos-in-the-Desert Resort project (1928–29) of the same period, including a drive-through entrance and interior columns employing cast glass blocks.

Wright's aerial perspective shows that his white marble and patinated bronze towers were to have been clustered, as in his Chicago grouped-tower project of 1930, here around a garden intended to preserve a venerable and locally famous oak tree. Balconies hovered

FIG. 1.35. Frank Lloyd Wright, architect. Proposed "Crystal Heights" apartment house and hotel development for Roy S. Thurman, Connecticut and Florida Avenue, N.W., Washington, D.C. Bird's-eye perspective. Colored pencil and ink on diazoprint. 1940. ADE-UNIT 2451, no. 2, E size. LC-USZC4-9543.

above a vast parking structure meant to serve the entire complex and, echoing the plans of L'Enfant and Downing, great fountains pulsed into the air, sparkling before a sweeping view of the city and the Mall. Lines of automobiles surround the structure, move in and out at various points, and array themselves along the perimeter of its multilayered parking deck like busy insects carefully tending their hive.

But what a hive! Wright's interior, filled with crystalline columns illuminated from within, was to have included shops, restaurants, a huge cabaret and bar, and a motion picture palace whose exterior and thrusting diagonal signpost were to have dominated the intersection of Connecticut and Florida Avenues. B. Henry Latrobe's project of 1800 for "a theater, assembly room, and a hotel" (ADE-UNIT 2885) in Richmond, Virginia, would have been the young nation's first mixed-used development, and Crystal Heights stands, or would have stood, as a worthy successor.

Not unexpectedly, Washington's design establishment welcomed Thurman and Wright's project with folded rather than open arms, and Wright took an eager and vocal part in the battle for its approval, waged in the popular press and documented in materials that accompany the drawings donated to the Library of Congress by Thurman in 1989. By the time the required modifications had been made—principally the lowering of the highest tower—and it looked as if the project just might pass muster, Thurman's options and financing had expired, depriving us all of an architectural masterpiece that certainly would continue to rival or surpass anything in town.[49]

Klaatu barada nikto

As modest as Wright's Crystal Heights was expansive, Charles M. Goodman's 1939 design study for modular, metal housing is rendered in his distinctive style (FIG. 1.36), a masterly use of graphite washes to emphasize the streamlined surfaces introduced by America's industrial designers for automobiles, trains, airplanes, and commercial products in the 1930s. One could imagine Klaatu, the extraterrestrial emissary played by Michael Rennie, or Gort, his sleekly metal-

FIG. 1.36. Charles M. Goodman, architect. Proposal for modular housing, Washington, D.C. Bird's-eye perspective. Graphite. 1939. LC-USZ62-129026.

lic robot in the 1951 Robert Wise film *The Day the Earth Stood Still*, comfortably retiring to this space-age retreat between takes for some rest or lubrication.

Trained at Chicago's Armour Institute of Technology, later the Illinois Institute of Technology (IIT), in 1935 Goodman arrived in Washington where his talents as a designer were quickly recognized in the Office of the Supervising Architect of the Treasury Department. Soon the young architect was producing schemes for post offices and other federal buildings in various parts of the country, introducing his own formulas for monumental modernism. Contemporary to his modular metal housing, he designed the U.S. Government Building for the New York World's Fair of 1939–40 and a few years later was instrumental in the much-admired design for Washington's National Airport. His work after World War II continued to be innovative, original, and highly influential both in the Washington area and beyond. His landmark Hollin Hills residential development in Fairfax County, Virginia, provided one of the finest models for postwar domestic architecture. It was followed by commissions from National Homes of Lafayette, Indiana, one of the nation's leading manufacturers of prefabricated buildings, and from Alcoa Aluminum, for the Alcoa Research Houses of the late 1950s.[50]

From the 1950s through the early 1980s, Goodman remained at the forefront in the development of a whole new range of building types, including many of those that helped to create and define Washington and its burgeoning suburbs inside and outside of the Beltway. They include experimental, prefabricated, military, subsidized, and high-rise housing; residential subdivisions and new towns, such as Reston, Virginia; schools and universities; shopping centers; corporate and trade association headquarters; and research, office, medical, and industrial parks. Goodman's archive was a recent gift to the Library of Congress from his wife, Dorothy S. Goodman, and thus was not a part of the Washingtoniana Project or available to the other authors but is included here with a few other recent acquisitions to demonstrate the ongoing growth of the collections and to underscore the value of making them equally accessible for research and study.

Filling Station , Shopping Center, Hollin Hills, Fairfax County, Va = Chas. M. Goodman Associates , Architects & Engineers • 814 18th St, N.W. Washington, D.C.

Residence for Mr. & Mrs. Fredrick B. Lee , Arlington Co., Va • Chas. M. Goodman , Associates , Architects & Engineers , Washington , D.C. • June 4, 1951

Glazed Expressions

At the age of seventy-one, our friend Arthur B. Heaton was still meeting design challenges head on—especially if they involved one of his favorite subjects, the automobile service station. In his 1946 drawing for a Sinclair station, he is working in Luther Ray's preferred idiom, structural porcelain enamel, but leaving Ray at the starting gate in the agility with which he develops sophisticated and elegant alternative plans and elevations, one of which is represented here (PLATE 1.20), sited on an irregular lot. The station boasts a sales area with a fully glazed, semicircular bay window that invites customers to inspect the merchandise on display and allows the staff a clear view from the inside. The sales area leads to the service bays and the men's restroom, whereas the women's restroom, unlike the men's, is entered from the outside, defining and defending a male sanctum that presumably is of no interest—and possibly even offensive—to members of the opposite sex during this period in the evolution of American automobile culture. The neatly landscaped exterior is defined by horizontal courses of porcelain enamel tiles in the distinctive Sinclair livery of green and white, wrapping around the streamlined pavilion formed by the circular bay, which rises above and anchors the entire composition.

Heaton's station is made to appear almost stodgy, however, by comparison to the Miesian pavilion that Charles Goodman proposed only three years later, in 1949, for his innovative and influential Hollin Hills development in Washington's Virginia suburbs (FIG. 1.37). The thinnest possible slab of a roof hovers above walls and supports that have been pared to a minimum, supporting signage that is bold but also carefully edited: "Gas." Exterior and interior visibility is at a maximum, revealing the latest in modern furniture and shelves, cantilevered from the rear wall and an interior support. These reinforce the structure's "clean" lines and message. In the evening, the spot lighting would have rendered the glass walls all but invisible, and the white ceiling and illuminated signs would have floated against the night sky above a warm, glowing interior.

The Horizontal Fifties

A similar aesthetic is seen in Goodman's 1951 design for a residence for Mr. and Mrs. Fredrick Lee in Arlington, Virginia, where again the roof and walls are refined to their basic elements, opening the interior of the house to nature (FIG. 1.38). It is as avant-garde as any house in America at the time, whether by Philip Johnson, Marcel Breuer, Charles and Ray Eames, Eero Saarinen, Ralph Rapson, Paul Rudolph, or Frank Lloyd Wright. More than that, it is inviting, even seductive, drawing the viewer inside and making him or her want to be there, to stay there, and, with luck, to live there.

An insistent horizontality ties the house elegantly to the landscape but is by no means oppressive, relieved by the gentle vertical thrusts of massive stone chimney walls that counterbalance each other on opposing axes, standing as comforting totems, identifying the separate pavilions and carrying messages of warmth and security. The open feeling of the interior spaces is achieved with minimal supports and by the use of carefully articulated floor-to-ceiling and clerestory window units that were to become a Goodman signature, and which he designed to be prefabricated, a lifelong interest.

It is difficult to imagine that Goodman's Lee House could have a contemporary, neoclassical parallel until one looks at the 1954 proposal for a National Hall (FIG. 1.39) by Eggers & Higgins, the successor firm to John Russell Pope, architects of the National Archives (1935), the National Gallery of Art (1936–40), and the Jefferson Memorial (1939–43). The National Hall is supremely horizontal, with blank walls stretched like taffy from its central pavilion, as if Promethean draft horses were pulling in opposite directions, drawing out its wings that, if released, might rebound with a resounding "thwop" were they not made of marble. There the similarities end, however, for the National Hall is as likely to hover, and be as transparent, as a stone quarry.

The pavilion is capped by a vestigial stepped pyramid recalling both Latrobe's proposal for the Washington Monument (FIG. 1.10; ADE-UNIT 2545, no. 2, B size) and Pope's for the Lincoln

FIG. 1.37. Charles M. Goodman Associates, architects. Proposal for "Filling station, Shopping center, Hollin Hills, Fairfax County, Va." Perspective. Graphite on trace. 1949. LC-USZ62-129027.

FIG. 1.38. Charles M. Goodman Associates, architects. "Residence for Mr. & Mrs. Fredrick Lee, Arlington County, Va." Perspective. Graphite on trace. 1951. LC-USZ62-129028.

FIG. 1.39. Eggers & Higgins, architects. Proposal for "National Hall," Independence Avenue and the Mall, between 4th and 7th Streets, S.W., Washington, D.C. Perspective. Photographic print of original drawing by Peter A. Juley & Son. 1954. ADE-UNIT 2896, no. 2, C size (photo). LC-USZ62-129030.

FIG. 1.40. Harbeson, Hough, Livingston & Larson, architects. Proposed alterations, West front, U.S. Capitol, Washington, D.C. Elevation. Diazoprint. 1963. ADE-UNIT 2386, no. 4, D size. LC-USZ62-114172.

Memorial, except that it supports something that looks to be a globe, a rather blatant emblem of the nation's greatly expanded international presence following World War II. The hall was to be located on the Mall opposite the now widely admired National Gallery of Art, completed by the same firm in 1941 following sketches made by Pope between 1935 and 1937, just before his death. It demonstrates just how wrong the formulas that were so successful in one building could go in another, as in a bad movie sequel.

Sadie Pope successfully prevented her husband's successors from using their own names in completing the Jefferson Memorial after his death, and she just may have been on to something. In fairness, Otto R. Eggers was a brilliant designer and renderer who served as Pope's right hand for almost thirty years, becoming so adept at his brand of elegant neoclassicism that one might say he was, like Minerva, born fully formed out of Jupiter's head. In attacking the design for the National Gallery of Art as retardataire, the dean of the Harvard School of Design and proponent of the International Style, Joseph Hudnut, awarded John Russell Pope the sobriquet, "the Last of the Romans." As Hudnut more than implied, even the gods make mistakes.[51]

Had either the National Hall or Eggers & Higgins's 1951 proposal for a national theater (ADE-UNIT 1949, no. 1, Photo) been carried out, they are likely to have "fixed" Washington's need for a large-scale facility for the performing arts. There would have been no need for the John F. Kennedy Center, completed in 1971, and more to the city's benefit. American quarrymen would also have been very pleased; Italy donated the marble for the Kennedy Center, whereas these earlier projects almost certainly would have resulted in huge stone orders from domestic sources.

Nothing historical was sacrosanct in postwar Washington. In the late 1940s and early 1950s, the White House and the House and Senate chambers in the Capitol were gutted and furnished with new, banal interiors. The Capitol became the subject of numerous proposals for enlargement, including the successful campaign of 1958–62 to extend

its east front thirty-two feet. Demonstrative of the ruling aesthetic of the time—and of the impulse to homogenize and regularize the historic—was the 1963 proposal for the Capitol's west front elicited from Harbeson, Hough, Livingston & Larson (H2L2) of Philadelphia by J. George Stewart, Architect of the Capitol, to corral Bulfinch's central and Walters's flanking pavilions within a continuous Corinthian palisade (FIG. 1.40). Their presentation drawing goes even further, completely visually suppressing the existing vertical elements flanking the Capitol's dome by means of a sort of graphic flat top that struggles to dissipate the energetic and dramatic massing so carefully composed by its creators and apparently so disturbing to their successors. The drawing masks and emasculates the building's baroque qualities in a manner that is both coolly elegant and dishonest. It is to architecture what a stretch limo is to automobile design. Longer sometimes is no more than that.[52]

New Cities

In the 1930s the federal government had provided a major proving ground for the design and construction of entirely new satellite cities: Greenbelt, Maryland, in the Washington, D.C., suburbs, and Radburn, New Jersey. By the middle 1960s, the construction of more than seventy-five "new towns" was under way in the United States, and the Washington metropolitan area was again a focal point. This time around, however, the activity was funded primarily by the private sector, producing the new towns of Reston, Virginia, developed by Robert E. Simon (hence the name) and Columbia, in Howard County, Maryland, where James W. Rouse provided the guiding hand. These entrepreneurs sought out both local and national architectural talent for their ambitious schemes, some of which did not make it past the drafting board.

Perhaps the most original and interesting of the latter was Paul Rudolph's design for an entirely new and complete city for thirty thousand inhabitants: Stafford Harbor, Virginia. It was to be located on an almost five thousand–acre waterfront site

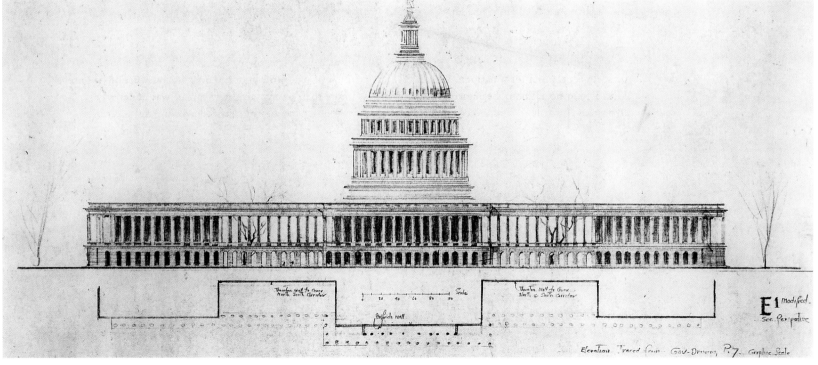

FIG. 1.41. Paul Rudolph, architect-planner. Makoto Miki, chief assistant on drawings. Chambers & Conrad, Inc., land planner. Calvin B. Burns, mechanical engineer. Chord Development Corporation, owner. Ridge clusters, Stafford Harbor, Stafford County, Virginia. Bird's-eye perspective. Print from cronar negative from original drawing. 1966. Bequest of Paul Rudolph, 1997. Digital file. LC-DIG-ppmsca-03482.

on the Potomac River in Stafford County, Virginia, thirty-eight miles south of Washington, past George Washington's Mount Vernon on the way to the Chesapeake Bay. In the mid-1960s, its location was viewed as "central," not just to metropolitan Washington, but "between Philadelphia and Richmond." The original scheme proposed for the site could not have been more different than Rudolph's. It was to have been a sort of residential Disneyland, made up of separate theme villages with names like "Amsterdam" and "Marseille," each governed by its own architectural style, ranging from Italian to Polynesian. The mind reels.

In the spirit of Frank Lloyd Wright, Rudolph embraced, took inspiration from, and both exploited and preserved the natural features of the site, imposing on it his own bold and highly original architectural vocabulary and his notions of a somewhat revised domestic and civic order. In the 1940s, Rudolph, an architectural wunderkind, had studied under Gropius at Harvard, and in the 1950s, he made a huge splash with his innovative and elegant Florida buildings. In 1958, at the age of forty, Rudolph was made chairman of Yale's School of Architecture and given the commission for its new building.

Rudolph's collaborator on the Stafford Harbor project was Makoto Miki, who assisted in the preparation of the remarkable series of renderings, just two of which are shown here (FIGS. 1.41, 1.42). They depict an architecture that self-consciously makes use of only one-fifth of the available site and that reinforces the natural topography by placing major groups of buildings along the ridges and harbor, leaving the intervening valleys free. The ridge clusters share common spines traversed by service roadways that connect and pass under and through the structures, connecting directly with their internal garages. The stepped clusters also enjoy unobstructed views across the undeveloped valleys and to the harbor and Potomac River beyond.

By contrast, the harbor itself has an artificial, almost baroque, shoreline, with a large marina to accommodate 750 boats, a "botel," a hotel, shops, and businesses. The town's center, the focus of the inner curve of the harbor, is marked by grand, urbanistic

gestures. Its obelisk and circular amphitheater are appropriated classical forms, which by now have acquired an American identity and lineage, traceable from the nearby Washington Monument and Capitol dome, reinterpreted in Wallace K. Harrison's Trylon and Perisphere, housing Norman Bel Geddes's General Motors Democracity at the 1939–40 New York World's Fair (itself marking the sesquicentennial of George Washington's presidential inauguration), and more recently, in the Marin County Civic Center by Frank Lloyd Wright and Taliesin Associates of 1957–63. Stafford Harbor was planned to grow to include eleven thousand terrace and multiple-family housing units, four thousand freestanding units, a kindergarten and schools, a golf course, a stadium and sports hall, tennis courts, and swimming pools. A recent bequest to the Library of Congress, Paul Rudolph's entire archive, representing his work over five decades, includes thousands of his remarkable drawings. This contribution provides another example of ongoing acquisitions that have enormous potential for future research, but which were not available to the other authors and are not yet completely available to researchers.[53]

Missing the Pont

Washington's waterfront sites have been the objects of numerous proposals from L'Enfant's time onward. Sadly, most of these, especially the more lively ones, have been unsuccessful. Chloethiel Woodard Smith, an awarding-winning and highly respected member of the Washington architectural community, produced master plans for two waterfront towns: Auverne, in Queens County, New York, and La Clede Town, in St. Louis, Missouri. She designed waterfront townhouses for Reston, Virginia. A key figure in launching and guiding the massive projects associated with the renewal of Washington's southwest waterfront from the early 1950s onward, she was responsible for a number of its major elements: Capitol Park, five high-rise structures and four hundred townhouses with landscape design by Dan Kiley; and the more upscale 6.3-acre Harbour Square section, with 447 apartments.[54]

It is unfortunate that the most unusual and dramatic part of her master plan for this area was not completed in some form: the Channel Waterfront Bridge, also dubbed the Ponte Vecchio, after the famous bridge in Florence, Italy, which inspired it (FIG. 1.43). Varying in width and two-thirds of a mile in length, it would have provided a pedestrian and commercial link between the city's redeveloped Southwest area, leading from Harbour Square across the Washington Channel, to Hains Point in East Potomac Park and the site proposed for a new National Aquarium (PLATE 1.21). With exterior and interior walkways on three levels leading to more than one hundred shops and restaurants enjoying views across the water to the Jefferson Memorial and the Mall, its concept was superior to its rather stolid appearance.

Appearance aside, Smith's bridge would have become one of the city's major attractions, a magnet for residents from here and beyond, enlivening an area that still only partially realizes the potential of its waterfront location as a shared civic asset. Every grand exposition has the recreational equivalent of a midway, and monumental Washington has many of the qualities of the former. However, there is something in the human spirit that allows it to absorb just so many abstract concepts, high-minded ideals, and historical images before it requires a remedial dose, however temporary and fleeting, of the amusing and, perhaps, to a certain degree, the vulgar.

Something Fishy

Washington's "Ponte Vecchio," as described, was to connect to a new National Fisheries Center and Aquarium, authorized by congressional act in 1962, and to have been situated on Hains Point, a spit of man-made land in East Potomac Park opposite Washington's Southwest waterfront. Kevin Roche John Dinkeloo and Associates, successor firm to Eero Saarinen and Associates, which had just completed Washington's acclaimed Dulles International Airport, developed their designs for the aquarium from 1965 to 1967 in collaboration with the office of Charles and Ray Eames. The Eames Office was commissioned to develop the related exhibitions,

graphics, films, and other materials (ADE-UNIT 2805; ADE-UNIT 2806; ADE-UNIT 2810), including a 1967 film and 1969 booklet detailing their proposals. Charles Eames and Eero Saarinen had formed a fast friendship while at Michigan's Cranbrook Academy, and they worked together on a number of projects over the years, from the Case Study Houses of the 1940s to Dulles Airport.

Following Saarinen's untimely death in 1961, Kevin Roche continued to collaborate with the Eames Office on the IBM Pavilion for the 1963–64 New York World's Fair and, beginning in 1965, on the aquarium project. Almost exactly contemporary is Roche's acclaimed headquarters building for the Ford Foundation, on Forty-second Street in New York City (1963–68), whose focal point is a twelve-story vertical conservatory. Although the funds for construction had been appropriated, the aquarium project was canceled by the Nixon administration, following the departure of Secretary of the Interior Walter J. Hickel, its chief proponent.[55]

The aquarium proposed by Roche and Dinkeloo and the Eames Office was markedly different in concept and mission from its replacement, the National Aquarium that opened in Baltimore, Maryland, in 1981. The mandate of the first was as a center of scientific research, displaying aquatic life for "educational, recreational, cultural, and scientific purposes," with the conservation of natural resources as the underlying concept of its exhibits. Science is not mentioned in the mission statement of the Baltimore Aquarium, whereas one of its goals is "to contribute substantially to the economic development of the region."

Some of these differences are revealed in the layered, mixed-media, cutaway perspective presentation piece for the earlier aquarium proposal (PLATE 1.21). The perspective, based on an axonometric drawing by Glen Fleck of the Eames Office, was a part of Ray Eames's 1988 bequest to the Library of Congress and makes use of what, in the 1960s, were the latest techniques of graphic representation. Elevated on a two-hundred-foot-square podium, a one-hundred-foot-high curved, crystalline greenhouse dominates the composition. It was to have sheltered a variety of natural habitats and to have included fish, animals,

FIG. 1.42. Paul Rudolph, architect-planner. Makoto Miki, chief assistant on drawings. Chambers & Conrad, Inc., land planner. Calvin B. Burns, mechanical engineer. Chord Development Corporation, owner. Harbor, city center, plaza, and amphitheater, Stafford Harbor, Stafford County, Virginia. Bird's-eye perspective. Print from cronar negative from original drawing. 1966. Bequest of Paul Rudolph, 1997. Digital file. LC-DIG-ppmsca-03481.

birds, reptiles, insects, and growing plants, representing a freshwater Everglades, a brackish mangrove swamp, and saltwater intertidal zones.

The purpose of the greenhouse was not solely functional. Prominent on Washington's skyline, adjacent to the Jefferson Memorial, in clear view from approaching bridges and the Mall, the "ecological greenhouse" was to have been a prominent landmark and, at night, a glowing "symbol and reminder of our increasing national concern for the natural environment." Its outdoor terrace was to have been home to a beaver pond and freshwater stream, a cattail marsh, a sphagnum bog, an aviary, and a children's aquarium. Inside one could have observed the environmental dynamics of a trout stream, a coral reef, and exhibitions with ecological themes, including endangered species and those that survive in "extreme" environments. An information center and theater would have helped orient and educate visitors, and exhibition tanks would have displayed live aquatic specimens, in re-creations of their natural habitats where possible. The proposed National Fisheries Center and Aquarium also was to house a library, available to both the public and staff, and a major research center.

Basically, the proposed aquarium was about observing, studying, respecting, maintaining, and preserving the natural environment—and aquatic resources. To build it today, on a location that is still

available, would be not duplicative but useful. Its mission, rather than having been met, has grown more meaningful and relevant during the past three decades, and its interpretive, research, and outreach functions could now take full advantage of the intervening revolution in electronic media. With a voice clearer and more distinct than any other presented here, this project asks to be given a second chance.[56]

Axes to Grind

The creators of the proposed aquarium determinedly oriented its plan to have two of its four sides serve as diagonal axes, stretching like arms, linking it both visually and symbolically in two directions: northeast toward the U.S. Capitol and northwest toward the Jefferson and Lincoln memorials and Washington Monument.

In 1981 the largest design competition in American history was held for the development of a site adjacent to the Lincoln Memorial, which had been approved in 1980 for a Vietnam Veterans Memorial. This national competition, organized by Paul Spreiregen, resulted in a unanimous decision by the jurors to choose a design submitted by Maya Lin, a Yale undergraduate architecture student at the time. The rest is history and is treated more fully in chapter 6. In plan a V-shape, Lin's design featured two axial arms

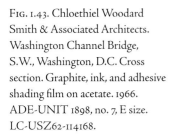

FIG. 1.43. Chloethiel Woodard Smith & Associated Architects. Washington Channel Bridge, S.W., Washington, D.C. Cross section. Graphite, ink, and adhesive shading film on acetate. 1966. ADE-UNIT 1898, no. 7, E size. LC-USZ62-114168.

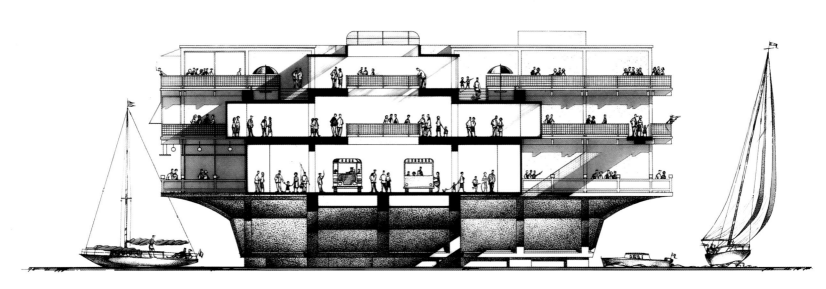

reaching out from an apex, as in the aquarium plan just discussed, but in this case toward the Capitol and the Lincoln Memorial. As built, it demonstrates the power of that simple idea.

At Jan Scruggs's behest, beginning in 1984, the papers of the Vietnam Veterans Memorial Fund, including photographs and drawings representing the more than 1,400 competition entries, were donated to the Library of Congress. These documents constitute a remarkable catalog of American architectural ideas, training, and practice in the late twentieth century, from the most urbane and abstract to the most personal, direct, and visceral.

One of the latter is by an anonymous entrant (PLATE 1.22). It requires minimal description; the image of a monumental helmet, its oculus a bullet hole, with an equally monumental dog tag for the inscription of the names of the more than fifty-seven thousand fallen and missing in action (required by the competition guidelines), says it all. Like Peter Force's design for the Washington Monument, at first glance it amazes and perhaps amuses, not unlike a sculpture by Claes Oldenberg, where a mundane object is enlarged to heroic proportions. These impressions quickly dissipate as, with some embarrassment, one remembers the messenger and absorbs the message.

Over time, perhaps the least developed of the major axes that L'Enfant designed for the city has been that stretching southwest from the Capitol along Maryland Avenue. It stands in stark contrast to its dominant twin, Pennsylania Avenue, today fully fleshed out along its diagonal course from the Capitol to the Treasury Department and White House, framing the north side of the Mall and the Federal Triangle. The McMillan Plan of 1901–2 tried to correct this imbalance, proposing to provide Maryland Avenue with a suitable terminus. At its juncture with the axis running south from the White House and past the Washington Monument would be placed a group of memorial buildings to national heroes.

Cass Gilbert's 1927 study for a new location for the Supreme Court had already attempted to reinvigorate the bilateral symmetry to the south of the Mall and along Maryland Avenue. Even as late as 1963, Paul Rudolph proposed that the Supreme Court be relocated to form a southwestern terminus for Maryland Avenue and an entrance to the city, on the axis of Fourteenth Street, and over existing bridges at that location. A monumental Madison Memorial Gateway was to frame Maryland Avenue at its Capitol end, and a balancing FDR Memorial Gateway was to be at the head of Pennsylvania Avenue, recalling L'Enfant's proposal for similar framing elements.[57]

From 1982 to 1989, in a series of design charettes involving students, architects, and landscape architects, many of the basic principles and proposals incorporated in the L'Enfant, McMillan, and subsequent plans for the city were considered, together with entirely new approaches and needs, in analyzing several key sites, squares, and intersections in central Washington, D.C. Under the academic leadership of Gregory Hunt and Iris Miller, who donated what came to be known as the Urban Design Charrettes Collection to the Library of Congress in 1991, the process produced more than six hundred drawings now housed in the library's Geography and Map Division both because of their size and their relationship to the plan of Washington. The term "charette" (or charrette) originated in nineteenth-century Paris, at the French École des Beaux-Arts, where students rushed to complete their examination drawings in time to place them on the charette, or cart that was pushed around to gather them. It has evolved to mean any intense effort to solve a design problem within a rigid time period, by professional architects, landscape architects, and urban planners.[58]

Each of the Washington Urban Design Charrettes was organized around the problems and potential of a particular site. In 1984, the Portal Site charette dealt with the area where the Fourteenth Street vehicular and rail bridges converge with the axis of Maryland Avenue and its visual link to the Capitol, recognizing the negative and positive characteristics of the site as "urban leftover" and "urban gateway." Portal team leaders came from New York, Berkeley, Philadelphia, and Albuquerque. They included Ulrich Franzen, Donlyn Lyndon, Antoine Predock, Peter Roland, Susanna Torre, Laurie Olin, and Gerald Allen.

The team, led by Olin and Allen, produced plan and

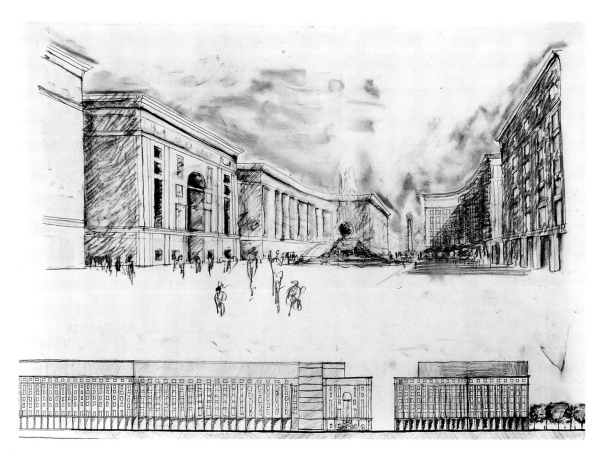

FIG. 1.44. Laurie Olin and Gerald Allen, "Portal" Team A, architects. Looking toward the Capitol across a pedestrian plaza on the diagonal axis of Maryland Avenue, S.W., proposed design for Portals Site, between the 14th and 12th Streets and the Southwest Expressway, S.W., Washington, D.C. Perspective. Crayon and fluid and color markers on paper. 1984. Geography and Map Division, Urban Design Seminar/Charrettes Collection, 1984.1, A22:ov.

perspective sketches (FIGS. 1.44, 1.45), details from a single sheet measuring more than fifteen feet in length. They illustrate the team's proposal to develop a pedestrian plaza that rejoices in the visual assets of the Maryland Avenue axis and reinforces it, punctuating the view toward the Capitol dome with a fountain and monumental column. Buildings with common cornice and base course lines, but otherwise articulated with considerable variety and intelligence, frame both the plaza and the views from it in various directions. The plan of the plaza is given spatial and visual variety by the incorporation of irregular doglegs, which recall those recommended for the same purposes by both L'Enfant and Rudolph, here one internal and the other external. The external dogleg leads to a pedestrian bridge providing access to the Washington Channel waterfront across the expressway.

In contrast to the 1964 National Square proposal by Nathaniel Owings and Skidmore, Owings &

Merrill, with which it shares a great fountain, the portal site proposal enjoys a more human scale and is fitted out with sheltering arcades and umbrellas that offer an escape from the hot sun or a sudden shower. These and the other documents in the Urban Design Charettes collection are filled with the kind of careful consideration of the design principles, both good and bad, that have served Washington during the past two centuries. They suggest the potential these (potential) principles hold for the future.

In the Swim of Things

One cannot, however, conclude this excursion with an example of the best of the traditional. It is often said that bold and innovative projects are not appropriate to the character and purpose of Washington, D.C. In fact, even if not fully realized, such projects are what have made Washington the success

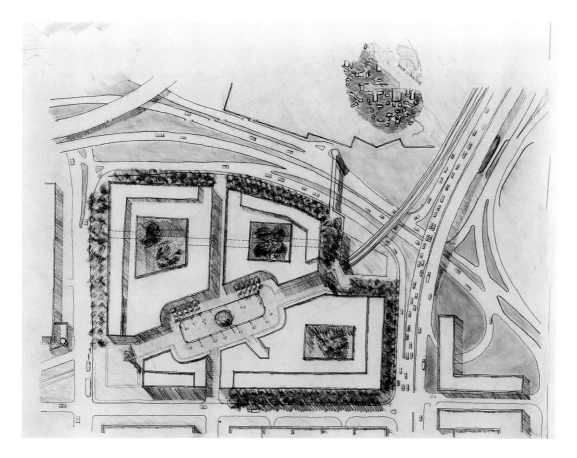

that it is, from L'Enfant and Latrobe onward. Of course, we have seen projects of all kinds that both should and should not have been built. The proposals for them continue to keep the debate lively, as it should be, and the participants on their toes.

Between 1989 and 1991, Doug Michels, then styling himself "world architect" and working with Jim Allegro, developed a remarkable proposal for a site on Massachusetts Avenue near the Mall, Union Station, the Smithsonian, and "within easy reach" of the U. S. Capitol (PLATE 1.23; ADE-UNIT 1983). Conceived as a four-hundred-room luxury hotel, with its Dolphin Museum, first-class restaurant, health spa, convention facilities, ballroom, and parking facilities, Dolphin America was to serve as an "aquatic retreat for mind, body, and spirit," its evocative exterior in curving forms of white marble and blue mirror glass. As the dramatic sectional rendering shows and the architect's press release explains, its interior, "sparkling

with water and iridescent with light," was defined by the dynamic, curving forms of a "Power Dome," a "Cathedral of Water" intended to join the ranks of Washington's other monuments as a "timeless symbol of free world thinking and supercreative ideas," and tanks where bottlenose dolphins, intended to "create a vibrant atmosphere of energy and imagination," would leap and splash. Dolphin America was to serve, under one roof, the combined purposes of a Marriott, Sea World, Woods Hole, Aspen, Esalen, Main Chance Spa, and the holodeck of the starship *Enterprise*. Like Bruff's Grand National Monumental Sphinx, the dolphins were seen as symbols, this time of "freedom, salvation, and rebirth . . . intriguing and mystical figures in legend and life."

Like Latrobe's University Church, Dolphin America was to have brought its message within sight of the Capitol; and, like the National Aquarium, it would have been educational as well as enjoyable, fostering interaction between species, and celebrating popular culture, scientific research, and human creativity.

Michels, educated at Yale, remains best known for the now iconic Cadillac Ranch, near Amarillo, Texas—ten great-finned Cadillacs half-buried in a row in an open field and at the same angle—executed in the early 1970s when he was a member of an avant-garde group of architects known as the Ant Farm. He cofounded the Dolphin Embassy, an Australian-based research group that designed the *Oceania* sea craft as a laboratory for the study of human-dolphin communication. In the 1980s, while he was a Loeb Fellow at Harvard, Michels conceived Project Bluestar, a space station with a team of dolphin astronauts. His untimely demise in a climbing accident in Australia in 2003 cut short a brilliant career.[59]

Rather than being pragmatic, Dolphin America clearly falls into the category of visionary architecture. It proposes new solutions for newly defined human needs, in the process conjuring up either entirely new forms or unprecedented uses for existing ones. In the same way that Frank Lloyd Wright's projected automobile objective for Gordon Strong of 1925 responded to America's obsession with driving, and William Douden's Hotel Dewey (ADE-UNIT 2020), proposed in 1928, responded to a perceived need to provide Washingtonians with a combination swimming pool and motion picture theater, Michels's Dolphin America reflects and magnifies the concerns of the time. It is an architectural response to the contemporary mania surrounding dolphins, a convergence of increasing concern for the natural environment, and a fascination with the possibilities of contact and communication with other species.

The Vision Thing

The design, promotion, and making of even the most pragmatic and predictable building projects, as with so many creative pursuits, operate in a realm rife with economic and professional uncertainties. For every successfully completed work, there are competitions lost, bubbles burst, workers and contractors who fail to produce or do so badly, technology that fails, patrons and clients who bail, change their minds, or do not pay, even with modest schemes. The possibilities for such failures can increase exponentially with the scale, cost, and boldness of a project. For the architects, designers, and engineers with the imagination, skill, knowledge, and chutzpah to produce them, such "visionary" projects are the ultimate expression of risk.

George Washington and Nathaniel Owings did not hesitate to stamp their images and stake their reputations on their bold and daring visions for a future Washington. Such schemes are not for the shy or retiring; they are tightrope acts and wagers requiring the highest skills and confidence. Yet, there is some element of "vision" in every project presented here, and to the extent that each of them embodies a spark of imagination or kernel of wisdom that may inspire and inform others, they are legacies from their creators that demand to be preserved and made available, so that we may learn from and delight in them for generations to come.

There should be no expiration date on many of these ideas, and in time a number of these visions may descend from the clouds and become realities, as in Latrobe's fanciful drawing of Virginia buildings. Perhaps his beautiful rustic retreat or the glorious aquarium envisioned by Roche and Dinkeloo and the Eames Office will be built for a few or many to enjoy. The path to reality can be arduous and that to quality even more daunting, but we should all be guided and encouraged by the words that Thomas Jefferson offered to his good friend James Madison in 1785 concerning his enthusiasm for architecture:

But how is a taste in this beautiful art to be formed in our countrymen, unless we avail ourselves of every occasion when public buildings are to be erected, of presenting to them models for their study and imitation? . . . [more important is] the comfort of laying out the public money for something honourable, the satisfaction of seeing an object and proof of national good taste, and the regret and mortification of erecting a monument of our barbarism which will be loaded with execrations as long as it shall endure . . . You see I am an enthusiast on the subject of the arts. But it is an enthusiasm of which I am not ashamed, as its object is to improve the taste of my countrymen, to increase their reputation, to reconcile them to the rest of the world, and procure them its praise.[60]

CHAPTER TWO

THE UNITED STATES CAPITOL

———

Icon of the Republic

DAMIE STILLMAN

THE CENTRAL EDIFICE of the American government and the most famous building in the country, the U.S. Capitol has had an extremely complicated history. Well represented in the collections of the Library of Congress, it figures prominently in the story of American architecture both of the 1790s and the first quarter of the nineteenth century and of the 1850s and 1860s, as well as in the engineering exploits of that later epoch. As the home of the legislative branch and the seat of government since 1800, it has become the symbol of the nation, with its tall cast-iron dome not only dominating Washington but also epitomizing the country for Americans and the world.

Dramatically involved in the design and erection of this major structure were three of our first four presidents, along with a number of later ones; a host of architects; and a veritable army of craftsmen, artists, and engineers. Stephen Hallet and William Thornton in the 1790s, B. Henry Latrobe and Charles Bulfinch in the first quarter of the nineteenth century, Thomas U. Walter and Montgomery Meigs in the 1850s and 1860s, Frederick Law Olmsted in the last quarter of the nineteenth century, and Alfred Easton Poor in the mid-twentieth century all made significant design contributions and/or supervised construction. But a great many others have left drawings for the building, made proposals for its enlargement, or supervised work on it.

Its genesis lay in the compromise effected to fund the national debt in return for the location of the capital of the new nation on the banks of the Potomac, embodied in "An Act for establishing the temporary and permanent seat of the Government of the United States," passed by Congress on July 16, 1790. Even earlier, on September 11, 1789, Peter (Pierre) Charles L'Enfant, hearing of a scheme in Congress "to lay the foundation of a Federal City which is to become the Capital of this vast Empire," wrote to George Washington, inaugurated five months earlier as the first president of the United States, of "my ambition and the desire I have . . . to share in the undertaking."[1] And at the end of November 1790, Secretary of State Thomas Jefferson noted in a memorandum the following points that would be crucial in the development of the building to house Con-

gress: (1) two squares of the new city should be allocated for the Capitol; (2) "The Commissioners should have some taste in architecture, because they may have to decide between different plans. / They will, however, be subject to the President's direction in every point"; and (3) "The plan for the public buildings is to be approved by the President. / The Commissioners will no doubt submit different ones formed by themselves, or obtained from ingenious architects. Should it be thought proper to excite emulation by a premium for the best, the expense is authorized, as an incident to that of the Buildings."[2]

In January 1791 the president appointed the first commissioners, and in March Jefferson requested L'Enfant to go to the area to make "drawings of the particular grounds most likely to be approved for the site of the Federal town and buildings"[3] and subsequently to design the public edifices. During that time, Jefferson both made a design of his own for the legislative center based on the Pantheon and told L'Enfant of his views on such a building: "Whenever it is proposed to prepare plans for the Capitol, I should prefer the adoption of some one of the models of antiquity, which have had the approbation of thousands of years."[4] Much later, in 1812, after a good part of the Capitol had been erected, Jefferson elaborated to Latrobe on this particular theme, emphasizing even more his commitment to the classical ideal as eminently appropriate for the architecture of democracy by referring to the Capitol as "the first temple dedicated to the sovereignty of the people, embellishing with Athenian taste the course of a nation looking far beyond the range of Athenian destinies."[5]

The nature of L'Enfant's design for the Capitol is somewhat uncertain, as is the question of how complete a design he created, but there are strong indications about the general shape he had in mind. Given Jefferson's clear statement to L'Enfant on his preference for a design based on an ancient prototype, we should not be surprised that the architect was interested in seeing Jefferson's design for the Virginia State Capitol in the summer of 1791.[6] Despite this inquiry and a few months of work, no extant designs for the Capitol by L'Enfant are known. And, as late as March 8, 1792, Jefferson wrote one of the commis-

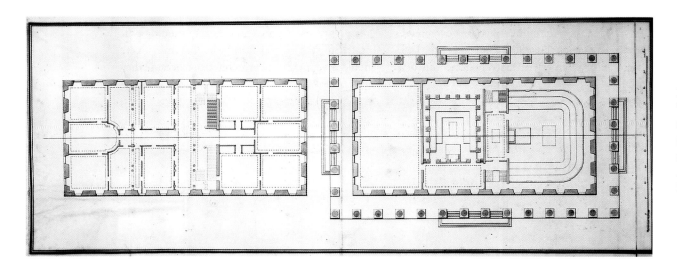

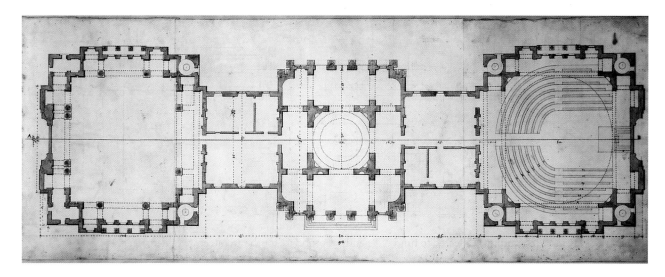

sioners, Thomas Johnson, that "Majʳ. Lenfant had no plans prepared for the Capitol or government house. he said he had them in his head."[7] Still, he was reputed to have been showing them to John Trumbull in Philadelphia two weeks earlier,[8] and his instructions to his assistant Isaac Roberdeau in December 1791 included digging of the foundation, which should presuppose at least a plan.[9]

In fact, it seems likely that the basic scheme of L'Enfant's Capitol design was indicated on his plan of the city, published early in 1792. Here, he would appear to be combining a rectangular temple format with the cylindrical Pantheon, the latter projecting on the west front as a semicircular exedra. The presence of this ba-

sic shape in both Thornton's winning design of a year later and the last scheme of his principal competitor, Hallet, would suggest perhaps that Washington or the commissioners, who would have been delighted if the resulting plan should echo that on the published city map, had recommended this idea to both men.

However, because no definite designs were forthcoming from L'Enfant and because his high-handed manner culminated in his refusal to acknowledge the authority of the commissioners, he was dismissed by Jefferson on February 27, 1792. Two weeks later, advertisements for a competition for the design of the Capitol and President's House appeared in various papers, with a deadline of July 15, 1792. Specifying the kinds of rooms required and their sizes, as well as the types of drawings, these advertisements elicited a substantial number of entries, most of which are preserved at the Maryland Historical Society, although Hallet's is in the Library of Congress. Extant drawings include those of Samuel McIntire and Samuel Dobie, along with designs by a variety of builders and amateurs; and records indicate that others were submitted which have not survived.[10]

After the deadline, none was selected, though there were features of two of them, those of Hallet and Judge George Turner, which induced the commissioners to ask them to revise their submissions in the hope that a satisfactory design would emerge. Of Turner's, we know very little, except that Washington apparently liked the dome and "Pilastrade,"[11] although Charles M. Harris believes that the designs generally considered to be Thornton's early scheme, created on Tortola and preserved at the American Architectural Foundation, are really those of Turner.[12]

Of Hallet's, however, we have not only the competition entry but also a whole series of revisions. Apparently, sometime in 1791, Hallet had shown Jefferson a design, subsequently referred to as his "fancy piece" (scheme B; ADE-UNIT 2458; PLATE 2.1), composed of three units, the central one set back, colonnaded, and topped by a dome on a high arcaded drum derived from Louis Le Vau's College des Quatres Nations in Paris of 1662–74.[13] Presumably inspired by Jefferson's preference for a Capitol based on an antique model, Hallet actually submitted to the competition a totally different design—one for a peripteral temple—which he elaborated through designs submitted in August 1792 (scheme A; ADE-UNIT 2457; FIG. 2.1).[14]

Asked by the commissioners either to enlarge the competition design or to develop a design based on the "fancy piece," which he had shown Jefferson the year before, apparently so that they would have a design available when prospective purchasers came to the first sale of lots for the new city on October 8, Hallet acceded to the latter request. The result was scheme C (ADE-UNIT 2459), which in basic format is a revision of scheme B. In terms of plan (FIG. 2.2), the three principal units were made more discrete, with the two wings changed from rectangles to squares and the center elongated into a transverse rectangle projecting to both east and west and joined by links to the wings. In the elevation (PLATE 2.2), the central unit featured a more powerful version of the Doric order, the wings now sprouted square domes, and all of the sculptural decoration was eliminated, with only thirteen emblematic stars inserted in the portico's entablature. The commissioners were still not satisfied, for as they wrote Jefferson on October 14:

The plan which he has exhibited, and which was drawn by our directions, after his fancy piece, does not meet altogether with our approbation, nor does it appear to be agreeable to his own taste, and judgment. We have therefore desired him to make any departure from it, he may approve of, in this future plan, consulting the President & your self on the subject. We have not a doubt of his possessing the highest merits in his line; as everything he has exhibited, those not approved of, has still evinced more taste, and practical skill, than has appeared in any of the numerous ones with which we have been favored.[15]

While Hallet worked on a further revision, which he eventually submitted in late January 1794, Thornton, who had written from the West Indian island of Tortola in July, asking permission to submit a design late, had arrived in Philadelphia and, after consulting Turner and again asking the commissioners if he could still submit a design, was working on a "new plan more suited to the situation."[16]

On January 28, 1793, Hallet showed Washington his fourth design (scheme D; ADE-UNIT 2460; PLATE 2.3), which further extended the central block, returned the wings to transverse rectangles but eliminated their pediments and domes, transformed the order to Ionic, reintroduced sculptural ornamentation, and altered the portico and dome. During this meeting, Washington may have suggested as a model Jacques-Gabriel Soufflot's design for the church of Ste. Geneviève (1755–80) in Paris, transformed into the French Panthéon after the Revolution.

By this point, however, Washington had already seen or was to see the next day Thornton's new design, which was to be, in fact, his first submission; and, as Jefferson wrote one of the commissioners on February 1, "Doctor Thornton's plan . . . has so captivated the eyes and judgment of all as to leave no doubt you

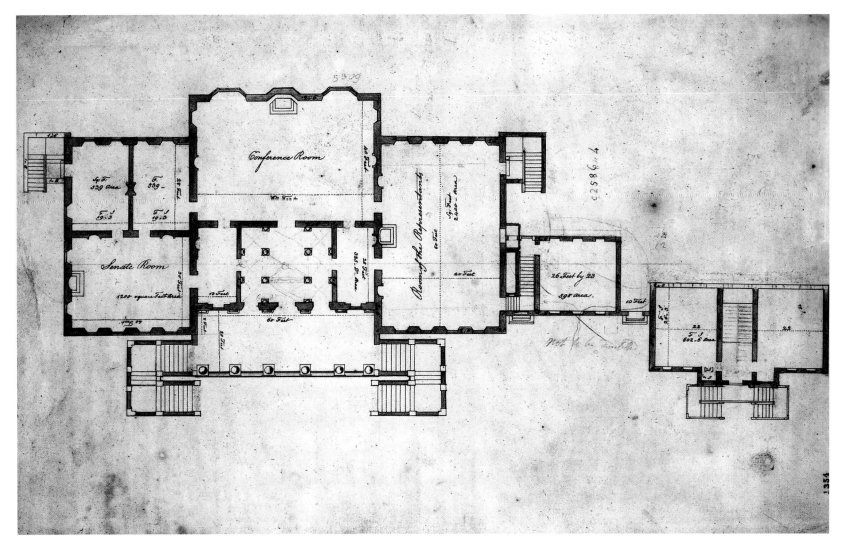

FIG. 2.3. William Thornton, architect. Tortola scheme, U.S. Capitol, Washington, D.C. Plan. Ink, graphite, wash, and watercolor on paper. 1792. ADE-UNIT 2468, no. 1, B size. LC-USZ62-37140.

will prefer it . . . It is simple, noble, beautiful, excellently distributed, and moderate in size."[17] This design, which does not appear to survive, was apparently quite different from the scheme he had devised on Tortola and which he had brought with him to Philadelphia in the fall of 1792. Although Harris believes that those drawings that are generally considered Thornton's Tortola scheme are actually Turner's submission, with the plans possibly copied by Thornton, almost all other students of the subject have seen the plans in the Library of Congress (ADE-UNIT 2469, ADE-UNIT 2468; FIG. 2.3) and the elevation drawings in the American Architectural Foundation (AAF) as either Thornton's first conception or an early revision. The Tortola drawings, if indeed, that is what the drawings at the AAF are, illustrate a tripartite composition of a central block with giant portico, joined by one-story links to two-story wings, the east front

inspired by Colen Campbell's English country house at Wanstead, in Essex, of ca. 1714–20 but the west front characterized by three canted projections. An alternate version includes a large semicircular projection on the west front, together with similar exedrae on the north and south.

Exactly what Thornton submitted to the commissioners in the winter of 1793 is uncertain, but its east front would appear to resemble the engraving published on the Robert King Jr. map of Washington of 1818 (FIG. 2.4), possibly, however, with curved exedrae on the north and south end, as well as on the west front. This would make it quite close to the east front drawing (PLATE 2.4), made by Thornton subsequently, ca. 1795–97, though with some minor differences. Its plan, however, would appear to have been closer to the Tortola scheme, though incorporating between the central circular rotunda and the conference room on

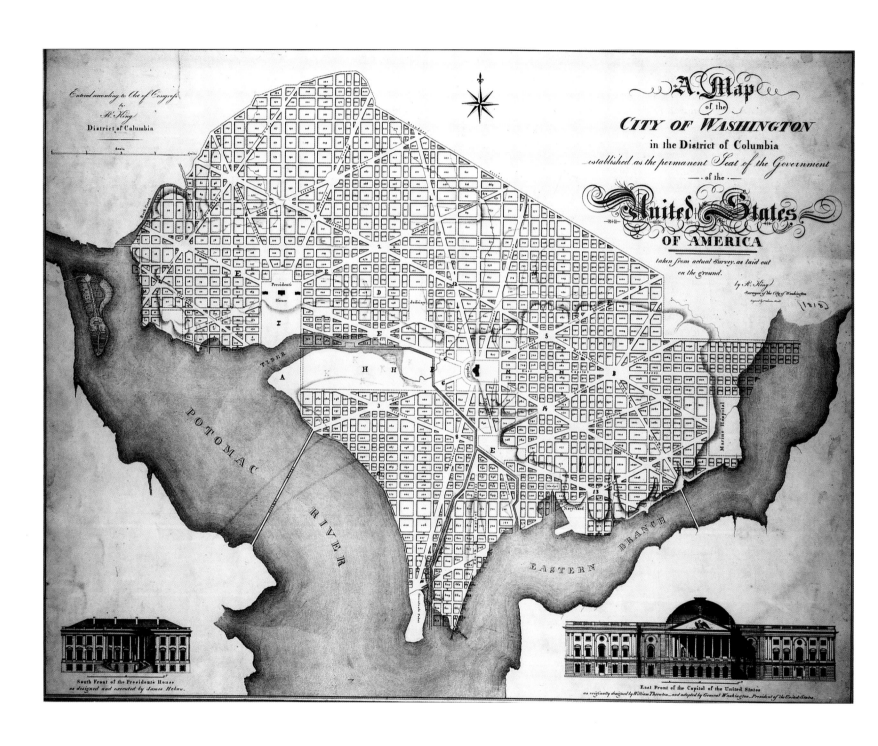

A Map
of the
CITY OF WASHINGTON
in the District of Columbia
established as the permanent Seat of the Government
of the
United States
OF AMERICA

taken from actual Survey, as laid out
on the ground.

by R. King
Surveyor of the City of Washington

[1818]

Entered according to Act of Congress
by
R. King
District of Columbia

POTOMAC RIVER

TIBER

EASTERN BRANCH

Presidents House

Marine Hospital

South Front of the Presidents House
as designed and executed by James Hoban.

East Front of the Capitol of the United States
as originally designed by William Thornton, and adopted by General Washington, President of the United States.

the west with its projecting exedra an "executive apartment" dear to Washington's heart.

Hallet, meanwhile, was preparing a final design (scheme E; ADE-UNIT 2461), which, as he told Jefferson on March 15, 1793, was the first that reflected his own ideas, rather than those suggested by others.[18] Like Thornton's, it featured a conference room projecting on the west front (PLATE 2.5), though in this case a French neoclassical rotunda with tiered seating rather than a square room with a semicircular exedra. Hallet's drawings, beautifully rendered, show the House of Representatives in the south wing and the Senate in the north (FIG. 2.5), as executed, rather than reversed, as is the case, apparently, on the Thornton design, along with dramatic exterior and interior treatments. Although the commissioners evidently saw some parts of this submission but not all, and Washington (and they?) received Hallet's written description sent to Jefferson on March 15, they had already decided to award the prize to Thornton, which they did officially on April 5, 1793.[19] Certain similarities between the two final designs, as noted above, suggest that Hallet may have seen Thornton's design and possibly altered his conception, at least in terms of such facets of the elevation as the

penciled level of the wings and the pedimented windows topped by square ones above that. Similarities in general plan, but not in specifics, however, suggest both Thornton and Hallet may have been shown either some sketch by L'Enfant or, more likely, the plan of the Capitol included on L'Enfant's city plan, with the idea either expressed or implied that it would be desirable were the adopted design to resemble the outline shown on this map. This would explain the presence of the dramatic western projection in both designs and testify either to Washington's enjoyment of that L'Enfant feature or the commissioners' desire that the map used for selling lots might be accepted as authoritative because it reflected the general contour of the Capitol.

Having awarded the prize to Thornton, who was a physician not a trained architect, the commissioners then appointed Hallet to evaluate Thornton's design and to estimate its cost and report "on the great points of practicability time and expense."[20] He and James Hoban, who had won the competition for the President's House, not only found "irregularity & impracticability of several parts of the plan—the enormous expence, the length of time necessary to accomplish the building,"[21] but Hallet also seems

FIG. 2.4 (*opposite*). Robert King, Surveyor of the City of Washington. "A Map of the City of Washington in the District of Columbia established as the permanent Seat of the Government of the United States of America." Engraving. 1818. Geography and Map Division. LC-USZ62-15171.

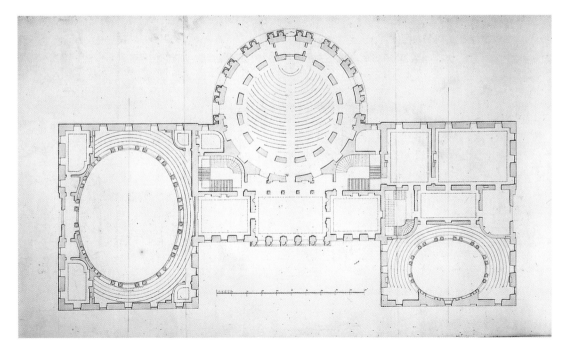

FIG. 2.5. Stephen Hallet, architect. "Principal floor," scheme "E," U.S. Capitol, Washington, D.C. Plan. Ink, wash, and watercolor on paper. March 1793. ADE-UNIT 2461, no. 3, E size. LC-USZ62-37079.

to have interpreted his assignment as a commission to correct and to improve Thornton's scheme, as is exemplified in his drawings (ADE-UNIT 2461, nos. 4 and 2), where he appears to have introduced a good part of his own final plan. Washington directed Jefferson to hold a conference to consider Hallet's objections to the Thornton design; and on July 15 this was held, attended by Jefferson, Thornton, Hallet, Hoban, Samuel Blodgett, Thomas Carstairs, and William Williams, the last two an architect and a master mason suggested by Thornton. In general, it was agreed by the consultants that Hallet's conference plan was "Dr. Thornton's plan, rendered into practicable form" and "a work of great merit," though its central recession on the east was disliked.[22] It was upon this plan, though with the recession still under discussion, that the foundation was begun and the cornerstone laid on September 18, 1793, with the inscription "James Hoban and Stephen Hallette, architects." A week later Hoban was appointed superintendent with Hallet his assistant.

Between then and June 1794, Hallet was revising the plans as work progressed, two versions being exemplified by ADE-UNIT 2461, nos. 5 and 6. Because he would neither turn over the drawings to the commissioners nor acknowledge Hoban as the superintendent, Hallet was fired on June 28, 1794, maintaining that he had never meant to introduce anything of Thornton's plan, despite the commissioners' intentions that he only make Thornton's design more practicable. During this time or within the next few years, Thornton seems to have created drawings combining his premiated design with some of the changes Hallet had, in fact, made, resulting in a series of drawings (ADE-UNIT 2470) that were formerly thought to be connected with the winning competition entry. The most significant features of these drawings, some of which were given to Latrobe after he took over as architect, were the colonnaded rotunda in the center behind the east front portico and the circular conference room beyond it dramatically projecting from the west front (FIG. 2.6). This last space is shown on the elevation for that façade (see PLATE 1.1) as a semicircle surrounded by a giant Corinthian colonnade topped by statues,

above which was a large open Corinthian colonnade crowned by a full hemispherical dome, akin to the dome shown over the east front. There are other drawings related to this west front design, especially ADE-UNIT 2470, no. 1 (FIG. 2.7) and one in the White House labeled "First design of the Capitol," and it may be that the domed, two-tiered, colonnaded conception should be associated with a scheme to turn the space originally allocated to the conference room into a memorial-cum-mausoleum for Washington, after his death in 1799, though Thornton also referred to it as a "Temple of Virtue" and a "Temple of fame."[23]

Hoban temporarily continued to be in charge of the work on the Capitol until October 1, 1795, when the Englishman George Hadfield officially began work as the architect, having been suggested by Trumbull and offered the job by mail. His tenure lasted until late May or early June 1798, when he, too, was fired, to be succeeded again by Hoban, who was responsible for completing the north wing for the reception of Congress in December 1800. On November 22 of that year, Congress took possession, with the north wing largely complete, foundations laid for the south wing, and some foundations in the center. Two drawings in the Maryland Historical Society may represent Hadfield's scheme to eliminate the basement and add an attic, but they and the guilloche belt course actually executed may be the only visual evidence of his work on the Capitol.[24]

Between 1801 and 1803, the principal work on the building was the construction of a temporary elliptical chamber for the House of Representatives in the south wing, with Hoban in charge; but on March 15, 1803, President Jefferson appointed Latrobe "Surveyor of the public buildings," and for the next fourteen years, with a crucial four-year interruption between 1811 and 1815, Latrobe was in command, erecting a new south wing, completely revamping the existing north wing, and planning the central block, in the process creating a series of extremely impressive neoclassical spaces. During both campaigns, he had to contend with a variety of difficulties, including slow appropriations by Congress, sniping from Thornton in the earlier work, and controversy with Samuel Lane, the Commissioner of Public Buildings, to

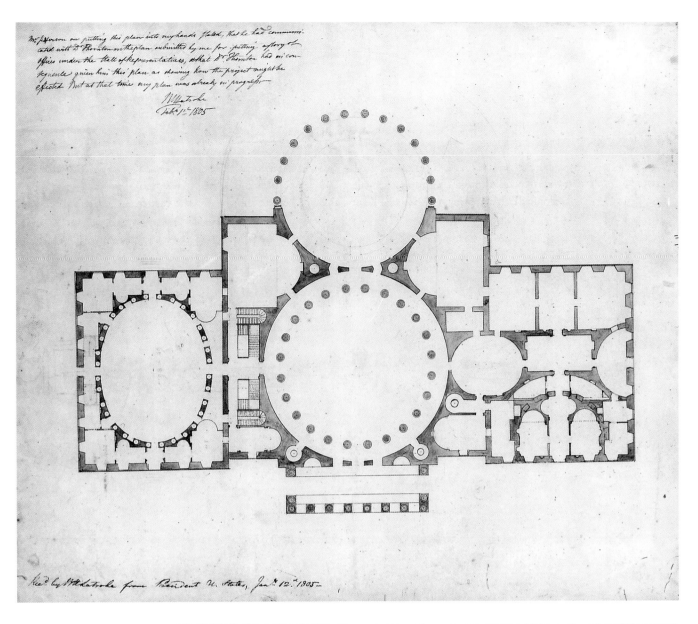

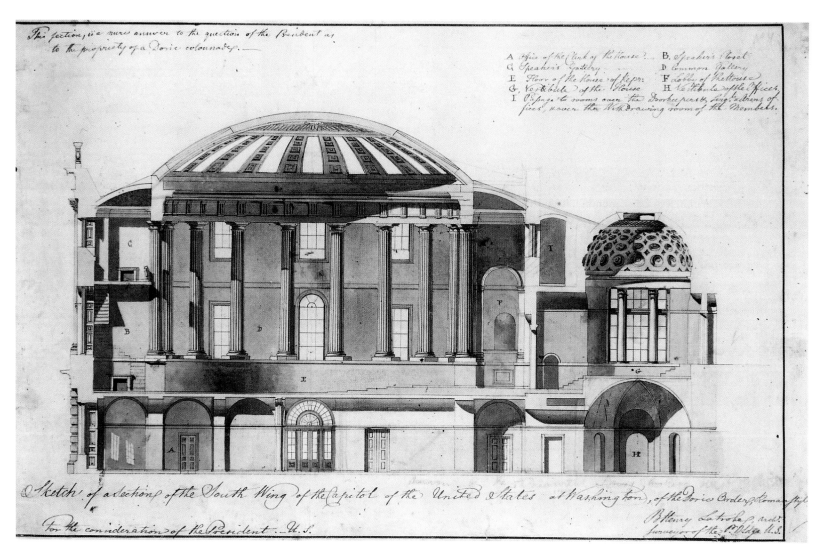

This section, is a mere answer to the question of the President as to the propriety of a Doric colonnade.—

A Office of the Clerk of the House   B Speaker's Closet
C Speaker's Gallery   D Common Gallery
E Floor of the House of Repr.   F Lobby of the House
G Vestibule of the House   H Vestibule of the Offices
I Passage to rooms over the Doorkeepers &c, Eng: & rooms of offices, & over the Withdrawing room of the Members.

Sketch of a Section of the South Wing of the Capitol of the United States at Washington, of the Doric Order, Roman Style

For the consideration of the President. U.S.

B Henry Latrobe archt.
Surveyor of the Pub: Bldgs. U.S.

whom he was responsible from April 1816 to his resignation late in 1817.[25]

Within less than a month, Latrobe had prepared a report to Jefferson "on the State of the public Buildings in this City," and during the next eight years, he completed his first campaign of work on the Capitol. This included building the south wing, including rebuilding what had been started but in inferior construction, employing Thornton's design, as on the north wing for the exterior, but building the House of Representatives Chamber as a rectangle with two apsed ends, rather than as an oval; rebuilding the interior of the north wing after dry rot had been found, creating the Supreme Court Chamber in the original Senate space, but only one story tall, and creating a new Senate Chamber above; rebuilding the Senate stairway in an oval space and creating also in the north wing the Library of Congress; and redesigning, though not executing, the east and west central fronts, both with porticoes, the former with a pediment and monumental stairs, the latter with a straight unpedimented portico, preceded by a propylaeum, eliminating on paper the curved west center that had been a dominant feature of Thornton's premiated design and Hallet's redesign. All of this that was built—essentially the south wing and the interior of the north wing—was executed with great professional skill, using fireproof masonry vaulting to a substantial extent.

The work of this first campaign is represented by a large number of drawings in the Library of Congress, and there are others in the collection of the Architect of the Capitol. Ranging from working drawings to extremely elegant finished renderings, the Library of Congress drawings illustrate beautifully Latrobe's ability as designer and as engineer. We can, for example, see him struggling with the redesign of the Hall of Representatives, both in plan and section, the latter tellingly illustrated by drawings of 1804 (FIGS. 2.8, 2.9), studying the lines of the sun, as he employed, at Jefferson's insistence, the vaulting scheme of the Halle au Blé in Paris much admired by the president, rather than the side-lit cupola associated with Sir John Soane in England, which Latrobe himself much preferred and, in fact, showed on his exterior perspective of 1806 (FIG. 2.10). There are also studies for the Supreme Court Chamber, for example, ADE-UNIT 2462, no. 36, B size, of 1808 and ADE-UNIT 2462, no. 37, C size, of 1809, where he created vaults strong enough to support the Senate Chamber above it but which his chief assistant John Lenthall in his absence erected in a different fashion, resulting in the collapse of the vaults and Lenthall's tragic death.

FIG. 2.8 (*opposite, top*). B. Henry Latrobe, architect. "Sketch of a Section of the South Wing of the Capitol of the United States at Washington, of the Doric Order, Roman style." Graphite, ink, wash, and watercolor on paper. 1804. ADE-UNIT 2462, no. 14, C size. LC-USZ62-13247.

FIG. 2.9 (*opposite, bottom*). B. Henry Latrobe, architect. South Wing, U.S. Capitol, Washington, D.C. Section. Graphite, ink, wash, and watercolor on paper. 1804–1805. ADE-UNIT 2462, no. 18, C size. LC-USZ62-94653.

FIG. 2.10. B. Henry Latrobe, architect. "To Thomas Jefferson, Pres., U.S.," east and north fronts, U.S. Capitol, Washington, D.C. Perspective presentation drawing. Ink, wash, and watercolor on paper. 1806. ADE-UNIT 2462, no. 13, D size. LC-USZ62-37197.

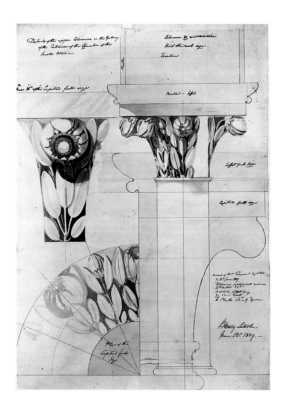

rating the dramatic western exedra (FIG. 2.12), reflecting those he had received, a ground-floor plan of 1806 (FIG. 2.13), which shows the shapes planned for many spaces, including the Supreme Court Chamber, elliptical stair hall with cruciform stairs, dramatic central rotunda, and a host of others, as well as how they would be supported.

On July 1, 1811, with the north and south wings completed but the center still unbuilt, Latrobe retired as Surveyor of Public Buildings and, at about the same time, Congress halted appropriations, the latter precipitated by preparations for war with Britain. During that war, the War of 1812, the British on August 24, 1814, in retaliation for the American sacking of York (now Toronto), burned the Capitol. The result was disastrous. Although the walls remained standing, much of the interior was damaged or destroyed. A drawing by Latrobe of the wreckage in the House of Representatives, ADE-UNIT 2462, no. 19, C size, for example, attests to the devastation, as does the record drawing of 1814 by George Munger, rediscovered and acquired by the Library in 2001 (PLATE 2.8).[26]

Through various intermediaries, Latrobe sought the commission to repair the damage and rebuild the Capitol, and on May 16, 1815, the three commissioners appointed by President Madison the previous February announced that Latrobe had been rehired. For the next two-and-a-half years, he was responsible for replacing his original work with a newly designed House of Representatives, this time in a semicircular shape and topped by his preferred low, broad cupola with windows on its sides; a somewhat altered Senate Chamber (with a similar cupola and a complex double half-dome), its vestibule, and a flanking rotunda with a ring of columns bearing tobacco-leaf capitals and a new staircase; and designs for a new and newly positioned Library of Congress in an extended west front, along with a host of redesigned elements.

Again, these and other changes are represented by an important group of drawings in the collection, supplemented by others in that of the Architect of the Capitol. Among those in the Library of Congress are such drawings for the House of Representatives as east-west and north-south sections of the south

Among the drawings of details is that of 1809 for the magnolia capitals in the upper gallery of the Senate entrance (FIG. 2.11), one of a series of unusual orders invented by Latrobe, the corncob capitals in the present entrance vestibule of the north wing being perhaps the most famous. Equally innovative was the Egyptian decoration planned for the Library of Congress on the west side of the north wing, which also featured a dramatic semicircular end (ADE-UNIT 2462, no. 33, D size, and ADE-UNIT 2462, no. 34, C size; FIG. 1.6, PLATE 1.3).

In addition to the perspective of the east front of 1806, which shows the grand stairway ultimately erected by Bulfinch, the low saucer dome over the rotunda, and the side-lit cupolas that Latrobe wanted over the House and Senate chambers, there are such exterior elevations as those of 1811 for the west and south fronts (PLATES 2.6, 2.7) illustrating his proposed Doric entranceway framed by guard houses that would have provided a dramatic western approach to the building. And there are a whole series of plans ranging from a site plan of ca. 1803–6 still incorpo-

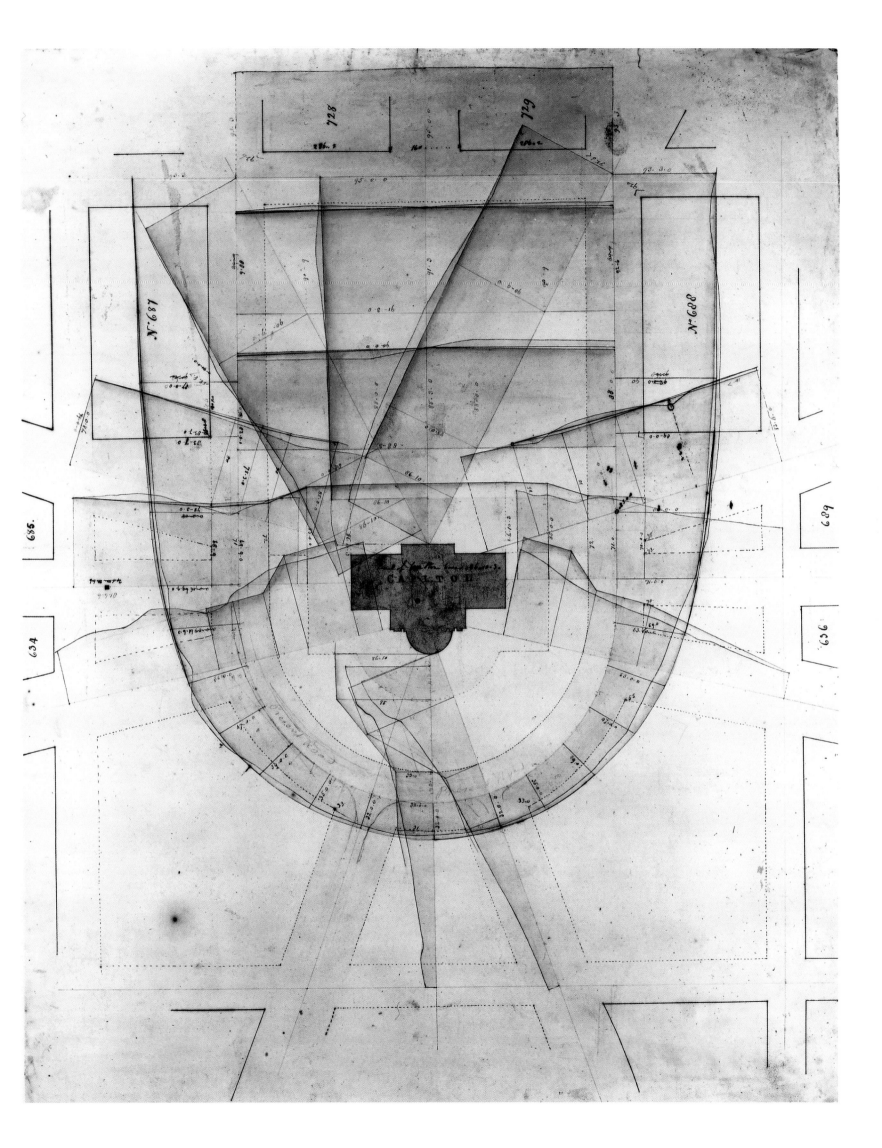

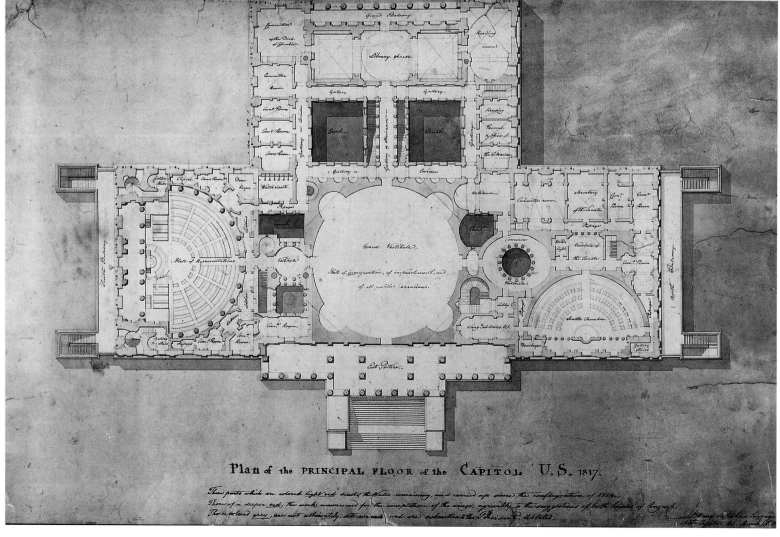

Plan of the PRINCIPAL FLOOR of the CAPITOL U.S. 1817.

wing delineated by Latrobe's son (ADE-UNIT 2463, nos. 6 and 8, D size), and details of the curved north colonnade and the dome and elevations of the walls with their pilasters, panels, and chimney pieces (ADE-UNIT 2463, nos. 10 and 9, D size; ADE-UNIT 2463, no. 11, C size). For the north wing, there are a comparable north-south section that includes, as well, ideas for the central rotunda and the crypt beneath it (ADE-UNIT 2463, no. 18, D size) and other more limited sections that feature the two-level half-dome of the Senate Chamber, with the lower ovals filtering the eastern sunlight's entry into the space (ADE-UNIT 2463, no. 20, B size). A series of plans for the rebuilding are ADE-UNIT 2463, nos. 1–3 and 5, and ADE-UNIT 2463, nos. 14–16, D size, with the second numbered of these (FIG. 2.14), for the principal floor, dated March 18, 1817, effectively showing not only the various new reconstructed spaces but the planned east portico, rotunda (labeled "General

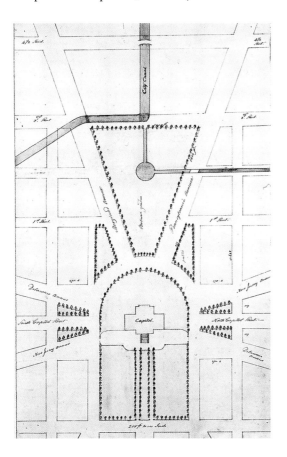

Vestibule—Hall of inauguration, of impeachment, and of all public occasions"), and west central extension for the Library of Congress.

Unwilling to contend further with Lane, Latrobe submitted his resignation on November 20, 1817, and it was accepted four days later. At first, it was thought that "it will require perhaps two persons to supply his place," and both John McComb Jr. and Charles Bulfinch were unofficially approached;[27] but, in the end, Bulfinch alone was appointed to the post on January 8, 1818, remaining until June 27, 1829, when he resigned, the initial phase of the Capitol largely complete.

To Bulfinch are due the completion of work on the north and south wings, especially finishing the House of Representatives Chamber; the execution of the central section with its great domed rotunda above a dramatic crypt, the east front with its grand staircase, and the west front with the Library of Congress behind it; and gate piers, railings, and landscaping. In most of this, he was expected to follow Latrobe's designs and to a substantial extent he did, though he left his mark in a number of places, especially in the rotunda, the heightened dome, the Library of Congress, and the west front.

There are drawings for all of this in the Library of Congress collection, though apparently none elsewhere. Among them are a copy of the ground plan inherited from Latrobe (ADE-UNIT 2474, no. 1), site and landscaping plans (FIG. 2.15), and various floor plans and details thereof (ADE-UNIT 2473, no. 1, B size; ADE-UNIT 2473, no. 2, D size; ADE-UNIT 2474, no. 14, A size; ADE-UNIT 2474, nos. 1, 2, 4, and 6, D size; ADE-UNIT 2474, nos. 5, 11, 15, and 16, C size; and ADE-UNIT 2474, no. 3, E size); a design for the ceiling of the House of Representatives (FIG. 2.16) and revisions of the entrance (ADE-UNIT 2474, no. 17, D size; and ADE-UNIT 2474, nos. 5, 14, and 13, C size), the last inscribed "Vestibule of the South wing with plan of proposed improvements" (FIG. 2.17); designs for the exterior dome (ADE-UNIT 2474, nos. 8 and 9, C size; FIG. 2.18), which was executed in wood; and a section of the rotunda (ADE-UNIT 2474, no. 7, B size). In this last (PLATE 2.9) are shown the powerful unfluted Doric columns and the vaults of the crypt; the walls of the rotunda proper with

FIG. 2.13 (opposite, top). B. Henry Latrobe, architect. "Ground Story," U.S. Capitol, Washington, D.C. Plan. Graphite, ink, and watercolor on paper. 1806. ADE-UNIT 2462, no. 2, D size. LC-USZ62-37081.

FIG. 2.14 (opposite, bottom). B. Henry Latrobe, Surveyor of the Capitol. "Plan of the Principal Floor of the Capitol, U.S.," Washington, D.C. Plan. Ink, watercolor, graphite, and wash on paper. 1817. ADE-UNIT 2463, no. 2, D size. LC-USZ62-11125.

FIG. 2.15. Charles Bulfinch, architect. Site and landscaping plan, U.S. Capitol, Botanic Garden, and City Canal, Washington, D.C. Ink, watercolor, and wash on paper. Ca. 1820–1825. ADE-UNIT 2473, no. 1, B size. LC-USZ62-33552.

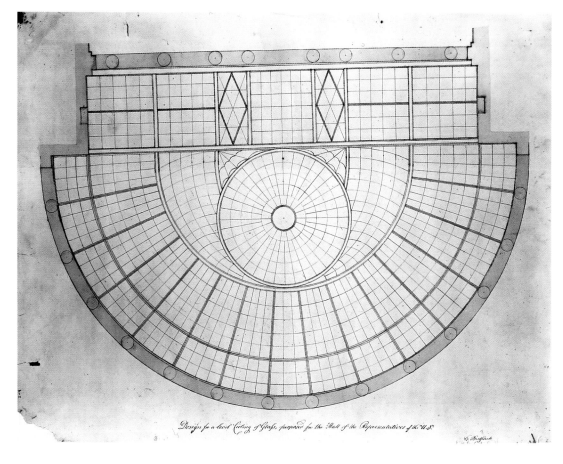

Design for a level Cieling of Glass, purposed for the Hall of the Representatives of the U.S.

FIG. 2.16. Charles Bulfinch, architect. "Design for a level Cieling [*sic*] of Glass, proposed for the Hall of the Representatives," U.S. Capitol, Washington, D.C. Reflected plan. Ink, watercolor, and wash on paper. Ca. 1818–1822. ADE-UNIT 2474, no. 17, D size. LC-USZ62-37109.

FIG. 2.17 (*opposite*). Charles Bulfinch, architect. "Vestibule of South Wing, with plan of proposed improvements," U.S. Capitol, Washington, D.C. Plan. Ink, watercolor, and graphite on paper. Ca. 1818–1822. ADE-UNIT 2474, no. 13, C size. LC-USZ62-37107.

pilasters, historical paintings, inset panels (one with an eagle atop bundled fasces), and a frieze with laurel wreaths; and the square-coffered dome with oculus.

Plans of the various floors of the Capitol (FIG. 2.19) as completed by Bulfinch are recorded in drawings of ca. 1832–34 by A. J. Davis and in an engraving of the plan of the ceilings (FIG. 2.20) in the collection (ADE-UNIT 2464). The east front can be seen in Davis's watercolor of 1834 (PLATE 2.10) and John Plumbe's ca. 1846 photograph, and the west front, in August Kohlner's engraving of 1839 and John Rubens Smith's watercolor drawing of 1828 (PLATE 2.11), all also in the collection. The House of Representatives Chamber is perhaps best pictured in the painting by Samuel F. B. Morse of 1821 in the Corcoran Gallery of Art.

For the next twenty years after completion of the Capitol by Bulfinch, no new construction was undertaken, although designs for its enlargement began to appear. In 1836 Robert Mills was appointed "Architect of New Buildings (Treasury and Patent Office)" and also put in charge of maintenance and changes at the Capitol. In 1844 and 1846, he made designs for alterations to the House of Representatives Chamber and the east front; and in 1850 he designed extensions that would have enlarged the Capitol through new wings for the House and Senate south and north of the existing building, a western hemicycle, and a much taller dome. No drawings for these elements exist in the Library of Congress, but some do in the collection of the Architect of the Capitol.[28]

It seems to have been this set that was submitted to the Senate, along with estimates and a statement, on May 1, 1850. Encouraged by the dramatic increase in the number of Senators and Representatives and dreadful acoustics in the House Chamber, the Senate Committee on Public Buildings recommended

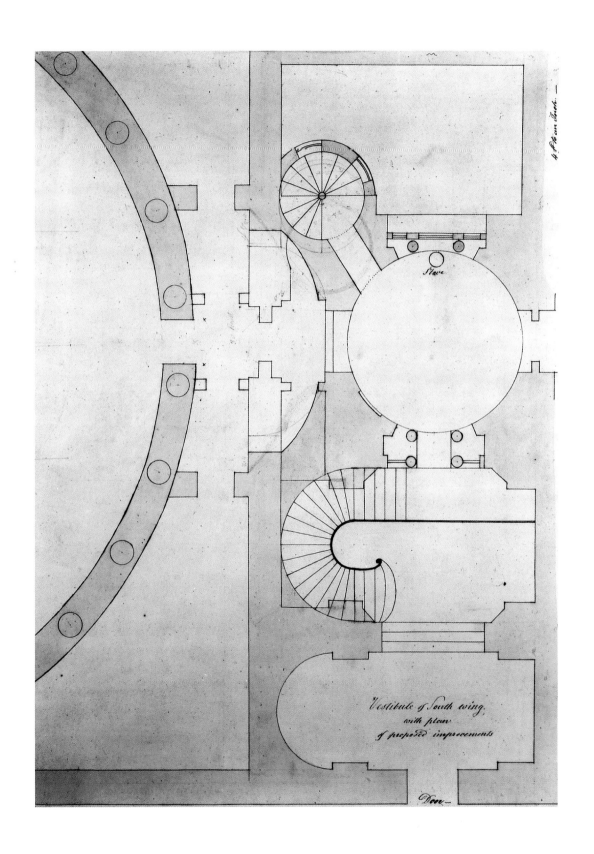

Vestibule of South wing.
with plan
of proposed improvements

FIG. 2.18. Charles Bulfinch, architect. Study "No. 2" for dome, U.S. Capitol, Washington, D.C. Elevation. Ink, wash, and graphite on paper. Ca. 1820–1822. ADE-UNIT 2474, no. 9, C size. LC-USZ62-33562.

FIG. 2.19 (*opposite, top*). B. Henry Latrobe and Charles Bulfinch, architects. Alexander Jackson Davis, del. Principal floor, U.S. Capitol, Washington, D.C. Measured drawing, plan. Ink, wash, and watercolor on paper. Ca. 1832–34. ADE-UNIT 2464, no. 4, C size. LC-USZ62-63158.

FIG. 2.20 (*opposite, bottom*). B. Henry Latrobe and Charles Bulfinch, architects. Alexander Jackson Davis, delineator. I[thiel]. Town & A. J. Davis, publisher. "Plan of the Ceilings," U.S. Capitol, Washington, D.C. Measured drawing, reflected plan. Engraving. Ca. 1834. ADE-UNIT 2464, no. 5, C size. LC-USZ62-133434.

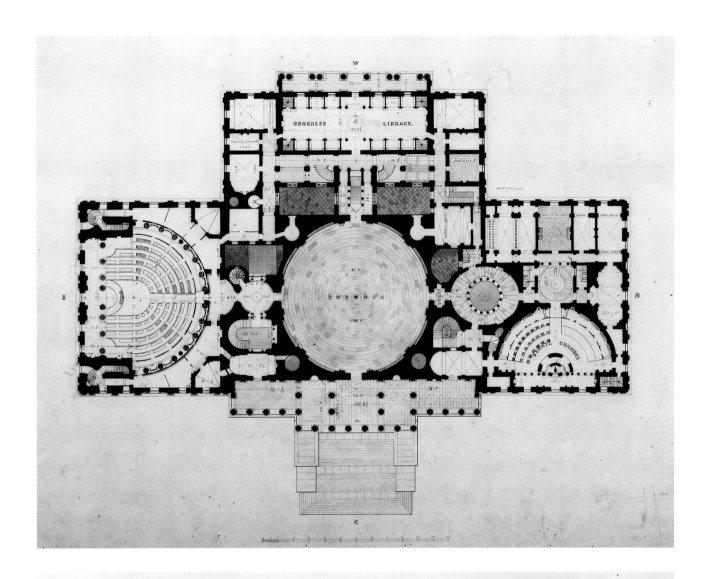

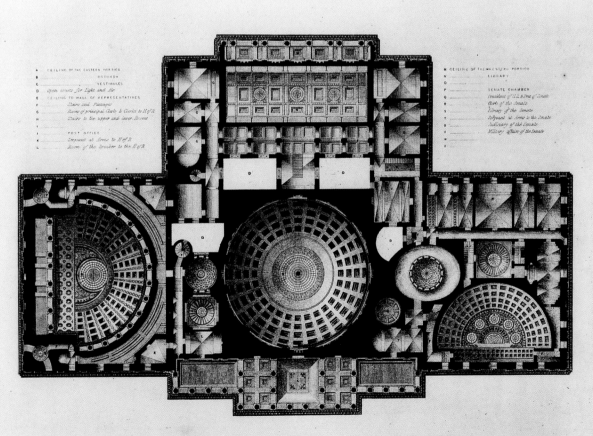

adoption of these designs; but on September 25, the Senate, instead of approving this recommendation, authorized a competition. Five days later, Congress appropriated $100,000 for an extension.

Advertised in Washington newspapers in early October, the competition provided for two alternate approaches—a separate building east and independent of the existing Capitol or extensions to its north and south. When the competition closed on December 1, 1850, four designs were selected for final study; and two months later, on February 8, 1851, Mills was either asked to create a plan combining features of those four designs or, in fact, had already done so. This, however, came to naught, for in the spring, President Millard Fillmore appointed Thomas U. Walter "Architect of the United States Capitol Extension," and on June 11, he took the oath of office. The cornerstone was laid, appropriately enough, on July 4, 1851.

The extension, which consisted of two marble wings connected to the original buildings by corridors, it being Fillmore's wish "not to mar the harmony and beauty of the present structure,"[29] was finally completed in 1868; but by that time, two other additions had also been accomplished: a new dome and the replacement of the Library of Congress behind the west front. A fire on December 24, 1851, completely destroyed the library and necessitated that addition. A month later, Walter had submitted plans for its replacement with a new, all-iron structure within the existing stone walls. Money was appropriated in March 1852, work began in April, and the project was completed in August 1853 (see frontispiece).[30]

As construction progressed on the extension, it became apparent to Walter and others that the existing dome would be much too small for the greatly enlarged length of the Capitol, and, in addition, its wooden structure posed the continuous threat of fire, as demonstrated in the burning of the Library of Congress. Therefore, in 1854, he created a revised design for the building with a tall, cast-iron dome, and on March 3, 1855, Congress appropriated $100,000 to replace the old dome with a new one of cast iron in conformity with Walter's proposal.

Work advanced rapidly on the extension, except for a nine-month hiatus in 1861–62 caused by the Civil War.

The new House of Representatives Chamber opened at the end of 1857, and the new Senate Chamber, in January 1859. The bronze cast of Thomas Crawford's statue of Freedom (photographs of maquettes: ADE-UNIT 2759; FIGS. 2.21, 2.22) was placed atop the dome on December 2, 1863, and the interior dome painting of Constantino Brumidi's *Apotheosis of Washington* was revealed in January 1866. The last portico of the extension (but not the sculpture) was completed on November 1, 1867; and the final balustrade was installed (against Walter's advice) in 1868.[31]

In addition to Walter, significant contributions to this work were made by Montgomery Meigs and August Schoenborn, as well as by the iron foundries, especially Janes, Beebe & Co. (later Janes, Fowler, Kirtland & Co.; ADE-UNIT 2593). Meigs, a captain in the Army Corps of Engineers, was appointed Superintendent of the Capitol Extension on April 4, 1853, a month after control of the work had been transferred from the Interior to the War Department. Meigs saw himself not only as an engineer but also as Walter's supervisor; he and Walter had a variety of controversies, although, in general, the work progressed well. It seems to have been Meigs who suggested two crucial changes in the wings: the exterior addition of porticoes and the movement of the legislative chambers from the western halves of the wings to their centers to be surrounded by corridors and committee rooms. He was also apparently responsible for the heating and ventilating systems, the iron roofs of the wings, the placing of the exterior columns of the dome on brackets, and the encouragement of much of the ornamentation in the form of painting and sculpture, including the appointments of Constantino Brumidi for the former and Thomas Crawford for the latter.[32] Drawings and photographs connected with Brumidi's work are in LOT 13061 and ADE-UNIT 2893.

Schoenborn, trained in Germany and Walter's chief draftsman and assistant from 1851 to the completion of the work and beyond, long after Walter left the Capitol, claimed in his memoirs of 1895 and 1898 that he was responsible for most of the drawings and many of the ideas: "I can truly say, that I made all the original drawings of the work, including all plans,

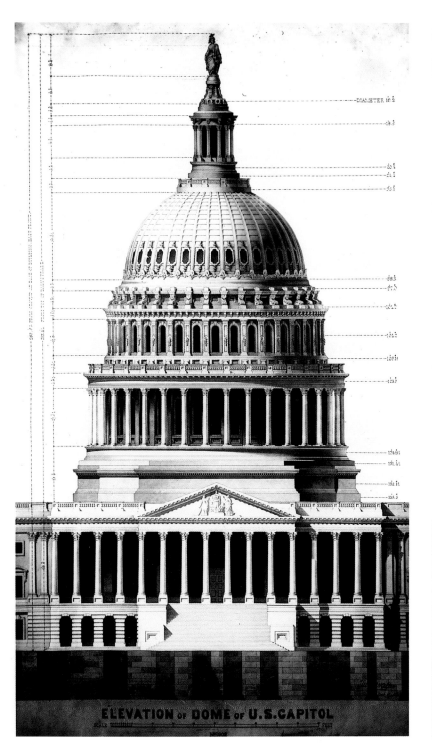

ELEVATION of DOME of U.S.CAPITOL

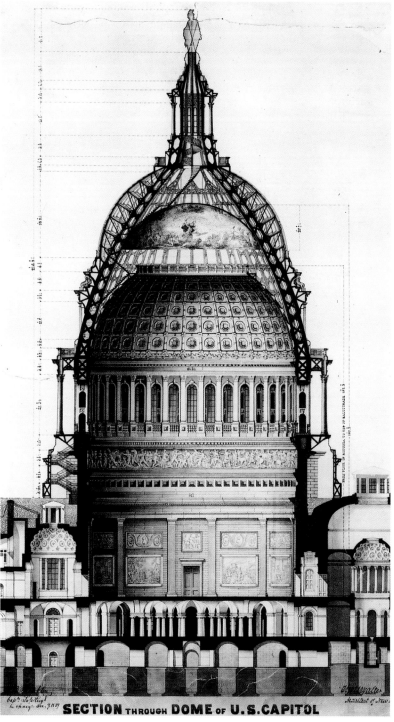

SECTION through DOME of U.S.CAPITOL

sections, details, all architectural ornamentation and enrichment, Column-Capitals and even working drawings. The other draughtsmen, who were employed being merely copyists."[33] In terms of design, he specifically declared responsibility for the iron library and its roof and the structure, but not the exterior, of the dome: "The construction of the Dome I claim as my design, which was adopted against several other skeems by Walter and Sonnemann. I also studied out all the working drawings for this construction and invented and designed all ornaments in—and outside of the Dome including full sized details."[34]

At the same time, Schoenborn paid great tribute to Walter as an architect, a draftsman, a watercolorist, and "My dear Friend," as well as the specific designer of the exterior of the dome.[35] A careful reading of Schoenborn's words in context and an understanding of the roles of architects and draftsmen in such a situation suggest that, although Schoenborn's role was highly significant, the organizing and guiding hand was that of Walter, who remains, of course, the real architect. The conception of the two wings linked to the original building by corridors and the exterior of the dome are certainly Walter's contribution, even though, as with any architect with an office staff, many of the details and even design suggestions are those of people working for him.

For this project, there are two drawings in the collections of the Library of Congress, plus four others, bequeathed to the Library of Congress by Ida Walter in 1914 and now in the custody of the Architect of the Capitol's office. Included in the first group is a beautiful perspective (ADE-UNIT 2592, no. 1, B size) of the Library of Congress, the iron room that was not only among the earliest such in the United States but which earned encomiums galore. The other, dated June 19, 1862, includes details of iron doors (ADE-UNIT 2595, no.1, D size; FIG. 2.27). In the other group, all of which bear dates of 1859, are an exterior elevation (FIG. 2.23) and a cross-section (FIG. 2.24) of the central section, including both the dome and part of the original building beneath; a more detailed section through the dome; and a detail of the cupola and statue of Freedom (Walter, nos. 1902, 1901, 1926, and 1925, respectively). In addition to this last

group, there are 1,480 other drawings by Walter and his office in the collection of the Architect of the Capitol, with smaller quantities at the Athenaeum of Philadelphia, the Winterthur Museum, the American Architectural Foundation, and a private collection.[36] The Library of Congress also has 115 salted paper photographic prints (ADE-UNIT 2895) of drawings in the Architect of the Capitol's collection, ranging from plans of foundations and elevations of the façades (FIG. 2.25) to details of ornaments and construction (FIGS. 2.26, 2.27).

By 1859, the rivalry and difficulties between Walter and Meigs came to a head with Meigs's arguments with his superior, the Secretary of War, who, with the concurrence of President Pierce, relieved Meigs of his connection with the Capitol on November 1, replacing him with Captain William B. Franklin. Walter himself, as a result of a disagreement with the Secretary of the Interior, whose department had resumed authority over the work, resigned on May 26, 1865. Three months later, on August 30, his former assistant, Edward Clark, was appointed to succeed him, remaining in office until 1902.

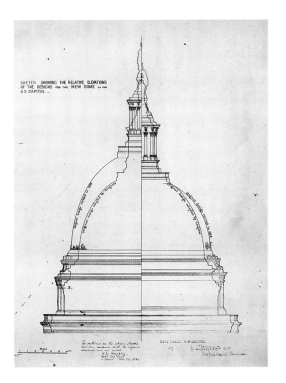

FIG. 2.25. William B. Franklin, Captain, Engineers, in charge. Thomas U. Walter, architect. "Sketch Showing the Relative Elevations of the Designs for the New Dome of the U.S. Capitol," Washington, D.C. 1860. Salted paper photographic print of drawing. ADE-UNIT 2895, no. 9, A size. LC-USZ62-114027.

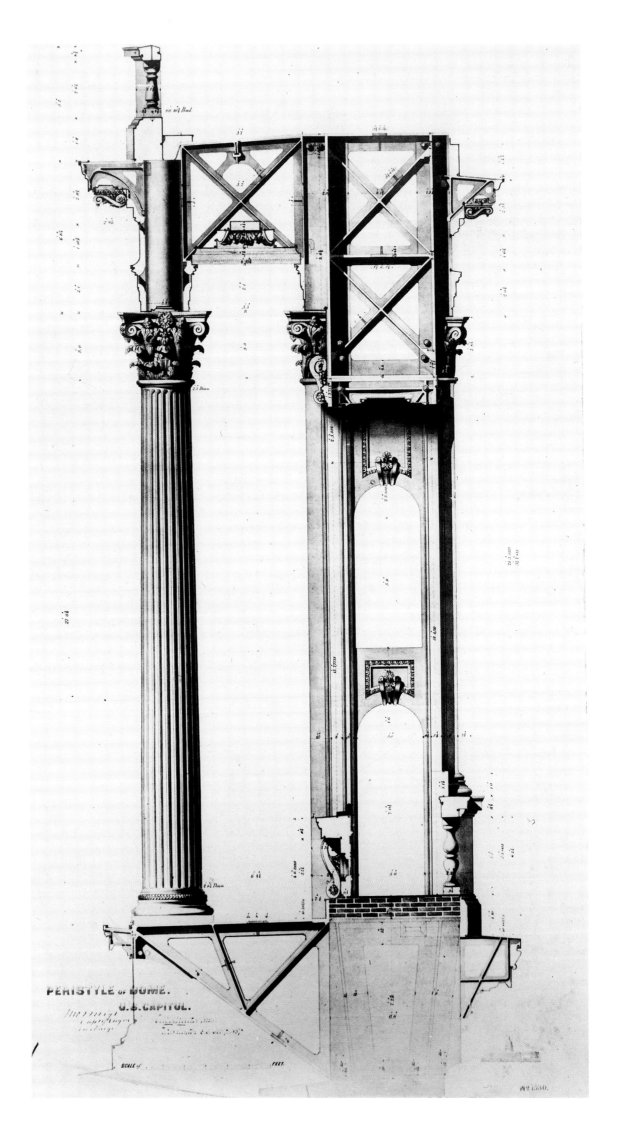

Fig. 2.26. Montgomery C. Meigs,
Captain, Engineers, in charge.
Thomas U. Walter, architect.
"Peristyle of Dome," U.S. Capitol,
Washington, D.C. Elevation
and section. 1857. Salted paper
photographic print of drawing.
ADE-UNIT 2895, no. 42, A size.
LC-USZ62-114139.

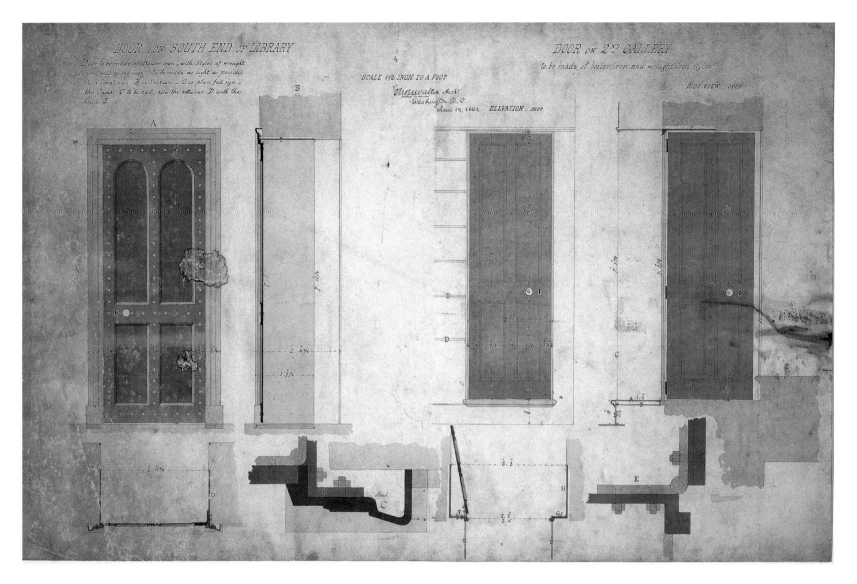

DOOR FOR SOUTH END OF LIBRARY

DOOR ON 2ᴺᴰ GALLERY

Before he left office, Walter had proposed extensions to the east and west fronts, apparently to increase the mass under the dome and thereby visually strengthen the central section in comparison with the wings, but the designs do not survive.[37] Walter apparently again proposed such extensions in 1875; and in 1880 Congress asked Clark, Alexander R. Esty, and John L. Smithmeyer to examine the possibility of either extending the Capitol or erecting a new building for a new Library of Congress. They all recommended the latter but suggested that the east front could be extended to improve the accommodations and functioning of Congress. No drawings for this proposed enlargement seem to be extant, but some engravings and a description are. These engravings, conceived by Smithmeyer and his partner Paul Pelz, indicate not only an extension of the east-central section, essen-

tially reproducing the original, but the erection of wings with towers between this projection and the existing Senate and House wings.[38]

While the various schemes for enlargement of the Capitol were under consideration, Frederick Law Olmsted was appointed in 1874 to work on landscaping. Eventually, he was responsible for replanning the north, south, and west grounds, including the stone terraces, which were executed in 1886–91, with Thomas Wisedell designing that part of the work.

In the early twentieth century, two major architectural firms were involved with planning for the Capitol. About 1900–1908, but especially in 1904, Carrère and Hastings, in association with Elliott Woods, the Architect of the Capitol from 1902 to 1923, proposed still another extension to the east front, again

FIG. 2.27. Thomas U. Walter, architect. Iron doors, Library of Congress, U.S. Capitol, Washington, D.C. Plans, elevations, and details. Ink and watercolor on paper. 1862. ADE-UNIT 2595, no.1, D size. LC-USZC4-3793.

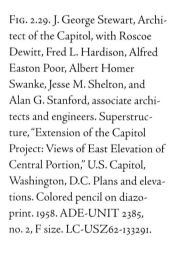

unexecuted; and ca. 1908 D. H. Burnham was involved with the designing of exterior plazas.[39] No drawings for these projects between the completion of the north and south extensions and the dome in 1868 and the mid-1950s exist in the Library of Congress, but more than 8,500 are preserved in the collection of the Architect of the Capitol, including those from the offices of Clark, Olmsted, Carrère and Hastings, and Burnham.

Finally, after the unsuccessful efforts of scores of architects to enlarge the Capitol to east or west, an eastern extension of the central section was undertaken from 1958 to 1964, following the design of Alfred Easton Poor (ADE-UNIT 2385; FIG. 2.28). Originally suggested by Walter exactly one hundred years before the completion by Poor, supported by Schoenborn in his memoirs of the 1890s, and proposed by a variety of others, this was finally carried out under the auspices of Architect of the Capitol George Stewart and the firm of DeWitt, Poor, and Shelton due to congressional pressure for additional accommodation and a desire to provide a visual base for the edge of the dome. As a result, the center of the east front was extended approximately thirty-two feet and reproduced in marble. From this project, the Library of Congress has a large photostat labeled "Extension of the Capitol Project: Views of East Elevation of Central Portion," with the portico picked out by hand in red, along with details of the north and south returns and connections, a plan of the portico, photographs, and some documents (ADE-UNIT 2385; FIG. 2.29). Approximately 1,500 drawings are preserved by the Architect of the Capitol.

As that project was nearing completion, Poor designed in 1963–65 restorations of the old Supreme Court and Senate Chambers, with the work actually

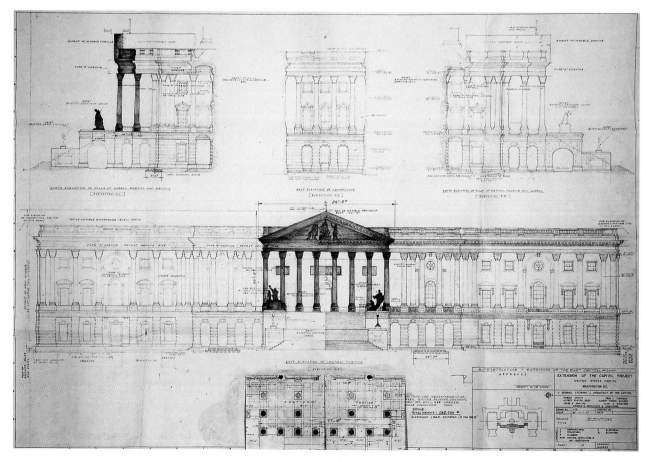

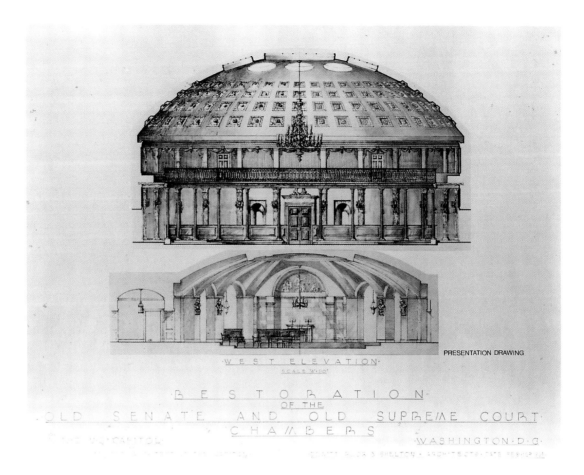

PRESENTATION DRAWING

·W E S T · E L E V A T I O N·

·R E S T O R A T I O N·
OF THE
·OLD   S E N A T E   A N D   O L D   S U P R E M E   C O U R T·
C H A M B E R S ·WASHINGTON·D·G·

carried out in 1972–75 and 1972–76, respectively (Lot 13047). For this, the Library of Congress has one original drawing of a cast-iron stove for the old Senate Chamber, designed in September 1975 and revised in December and again in January 1976 (ADE-UNIT 2388, no. 2, A size); photostats of two alternate designs for chandeliers for the old Supreme Court Chamber, dated 1973 (ADE-UNIT 2389); and an album on the restoration (LOT 13047; FIG. 2.30).

Even before the completion of the eastern extension, Poor also designed an extension of the central section to the west. Various alternatives were suggested before June 13, 1963, when these were sent from Harbeson, Hough, Livingston & Larson to Poor (ADE-UNIT 2386). Other drawings are dated 1966, and in March 1978, a "Report and Recommendations for the Extension of the West Central Front of the United States Capitol" was prepared by Poor and his firm, Poor, Swanke, Hayden, Connell and Robert (ADE-UNIT 2384).[40] None of this, preserved in the collection of the Library of Congress, was, of course, executed; instead, the original west front designed and built by Bulfinch was restored between 1983 and 1987. Approximately four hundred drawings for Poor's abortive west-front proposal are in the collection of the Architect of the Capitol. In the 1990s, interior courtyards behind the west front were filled in with designs by Hugh Newell Jacobsen, with the drawings in the Architect of the Capitol's collection.

After two centuries of competition, controversy, design, modification, and execution, the Capitol stands not only as the symbol and legislative center of the United States but as a major demonstration of the history, glories, and difficulties of American architecture. Much of this is captured in the rich collection of drawings preserved in the Library of Congress.[41]

CHAPTER THREE

THE WHITE HOUSE

——

Seat of the Presidency

WILLIAM SEALE

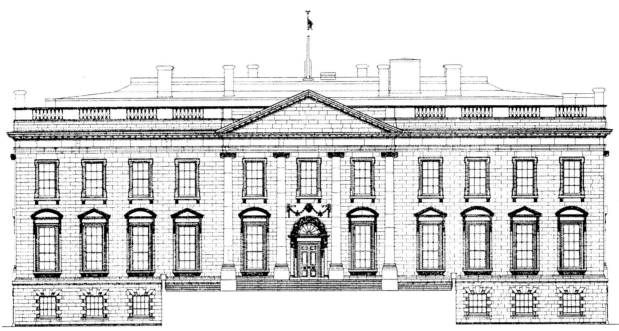

ELEVATION THROUGH AREAWAY   FRONT COLONNADE REMOVED

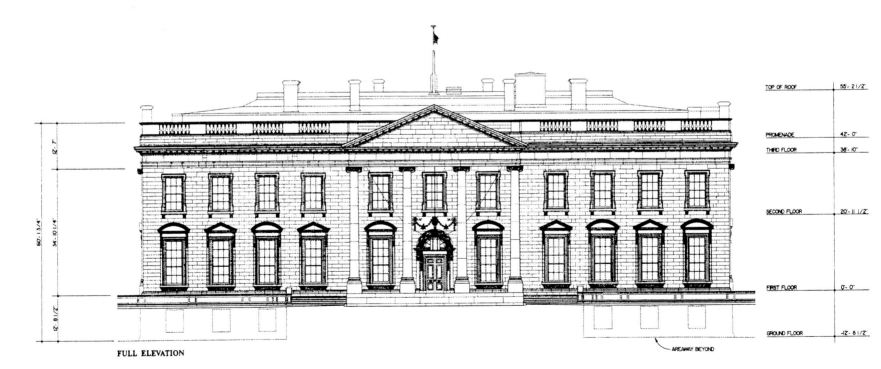

FULL ELEVATION

TOP OF ROOF   55'- 2 1/2"

PROMENADE   42'- 0"
THIRD FLOOR   38'- 10"

SECOND FLOOR   20'- 11 1/2"

FIRST FLOOR   0'- 0"

GROUND FLOOR   -12'- 8 1/2"

AREAWAY BEYOND

SURVIVING DESIGN and construction drawings made during the two-hundred-year history of the White House number remarkably few. In general, they have survived by accident or were kept without much thought given to their use or value with the files of various federal offices charged with the maintenance of the presidential residence. Architectural changes in the White House always take place in a hurry. At times they have not been accompanied by detailed drawings or even sketches. Even when they exist, little importance had been attached to them before the last two decades when something of a scramble ensued in sweeping up the scattered leaves. Interest in the history of the White House, generated largely by the public programs of the private, nonprofit White House Historical Association, have raised the general importance of all historical documentation about the house, including architectural drawings.

The earliest surviving drawing for the house, an as-built plan of the main floor and an unrealized section, both drawn on a single sheet by James Hoban (1762–1831), is not in official collections but in Thomas Jefferson's personal papers at the Massachusetts Historical Society. Likewise, Hoban's well-known elevation, probably made in the autumn of 1793, which shows the final modification of the competition project, has descended in the personal papers of B. Henry Latrobe (1764–1820), through his son, and is owned by the Maryland Historical Society. Hoban's personal and professional papers were apparently destroyed in a fire at his house in 1833 two years after his death.[1]

Interest in the architectural history of the White House originated in the years 1889–1902 with Colonel Theodore Bingham (1858–1934) of the Army Corps of Engineers, who was in charge of Washington's public buildings and grounds from 1897 to 1903.[2] Bingham sought a historical context to serve as a design basis for large additions he proposed to the White House. He assembled papers and such drawings as were available in the Office of the Commissioner of Public Buildings. For further inspiration, Bingham ordered tracings, now lost, of additions made to Leinster House, Dublin, between 1896 and 1905. This had been Hoban's model for the White House.[3]

Bingham was followed by the architectural historian Fiske Kimball who published an article, "Genesis of the White House," in the February 1918 issue of *Century Magazine*, on Hoban's design sources for the White House. Yet these efforts produced no cohesive collection of White House architectural materials. Although some interest was maintained in the architecture of the White House following Kimball's publication, it was not high. When President Harry S. Truman undertook to rebuild the house within its old walls between 1948 and 1952, no coherent body of historical material was available and the result was a virtually new interior. Such a radical rebuilding was primarily seen as necessary for security. Assembly of historical materials about the White House, including architectural drawings, or copies of them, began during the administration of John F. Kennedy, between 1961 and 1963, and continued under the encouragement and patronage of presidents and wives since then, notably Mrs. Richard M. Nixon. The result has been a great awareness of the importance of the White House as an American architectural as well as presidential icon.[4]

Today the researcher begins with an inquiry at the Office of the Curator of the White House for a general overview of what architectural drawings are available and where they are located. In addition, the White House liaison office of the National Park Service maintains files of twentieth-century drawings, as well as a large catalog that gives the location of historical drawings, prints, and photographs. Between 1988 and 1992, the Historic American Buildings Survey made detailed measured drawings and photographs of the White House as it stood in the period of its two hundredth anniversary. Forty-one of these drawings, together with 602 large-format photographs, are housed in the Prints and Photographs Division and are available for researchers there and through the Library's Web site (HABS DC-17; HABS DC, WASH,134–; FIGS. 3.1, 3.2). The Geography and Map Division has a sketch for the White House grounds by Jefferson done about 1804 that shows a layout of driveways, built and maintained until the 1850s (FIG. 3.3).[5]

The largest collection of written materials (it also includes some sketches and drawings) on the White

FIG. 3.1. Historic American Buildings Survey. Brian F. Pedersen, Timothy A. Buehner, Hugh D. Hughes, delineators. North Elevation, the White House, 1600 Pennsylvania Avenue, N.W., Washington, D.C. Elevations. Ink on polyester film. 1988–1992. Digital file of HABS DC-37, sheet 30 of 85.

House, dating from 1791 until 1933, is in Record Group 42, Records of the Office of Public Buildings and Public Parks of the National Capitol, in the National Archives. Architectural drawings, made mostly in the late nineteenth and early twentieth centuries, are found in the Cartographic and Architectural Branch (RG 42) at the National Archives. Like the collection at the Library of Congress, the inventory is spotty, but field notebooks and surveys done before about 1840 are particularly useful.

It is well for the researcher to be aware of the major changes the White House underwent during its history that might have generated architectural drawings. Eighteenth- and nineteenth-century transformations include the period of original construction (1792–1800); the addition of the east and west fire-proof wings, for which construction began after July 1, 1805; reconstruction after the 1814 fire; the addition of the south portico (1824) and that on the north (1829–1830); and the addition of a conglomeration of greenhouses between 1857 and about 1890.

Twentieth-century remodeling and additions were initiated by Theodore Roosevelt, who built the first executive office in the West Wing in 1902, called at the onset "temporary." Further changes include the expansion of the West Wing and building of the first Oval Office in 1909, rebuilding and expansion of the attic of the White House itself in 1927, a reconstruction of the burned-out West Wing in 1930 and major expansion in 1934, which included building the present Oval Office. Expansion of the East Wing and building of the bomb shelter began after the beginning of

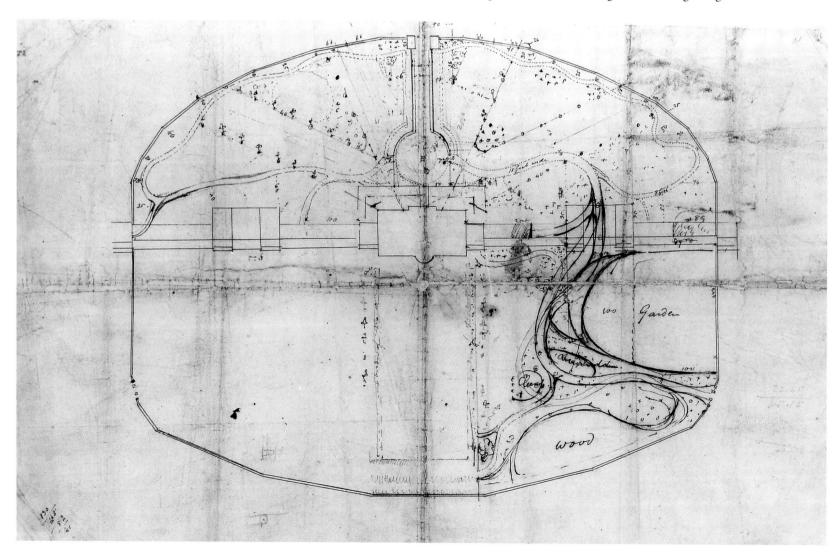

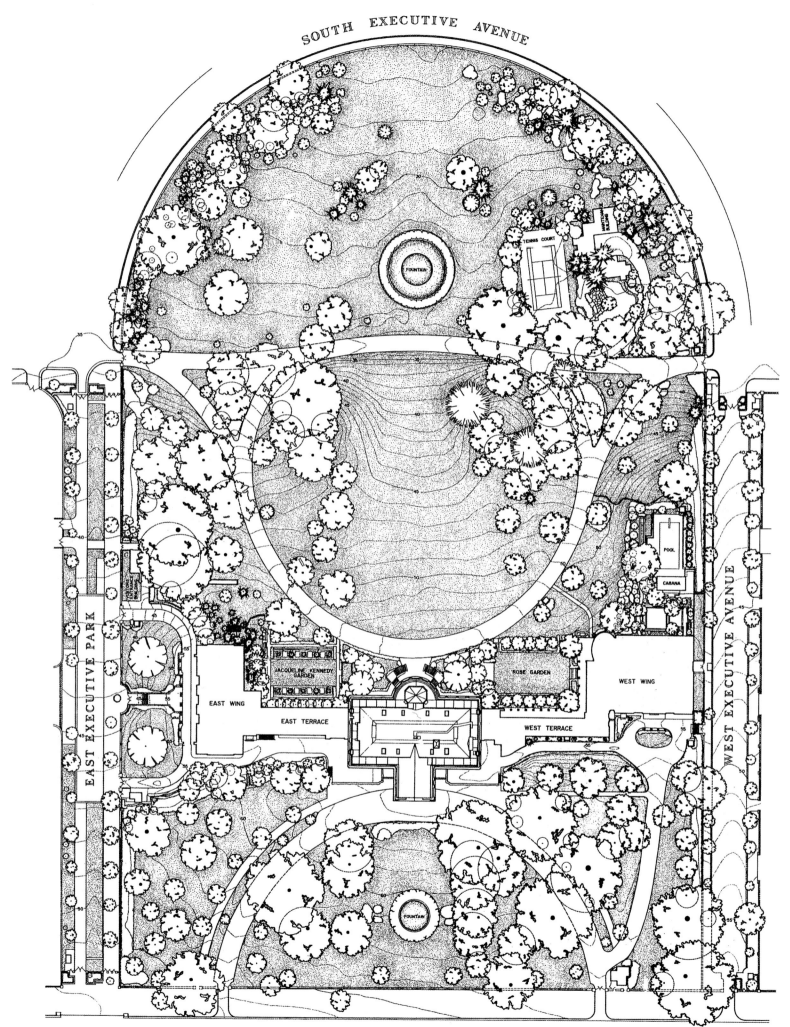

SOUTH EXECUTIVE AVENUE

FOUNTAIN

TENNIS COURT

POOL

CABANA

EAST EXECUTIVE PARK

WEST EXECUTIVE AVENUE

JACQUELINE KENNEDY GARDEN

ROSE GARDEN

WEST WING

EAST WING

EAST TERRACE

WEST TERRACE

FOUNTAIN

PENNSYLVANIA AVENUE

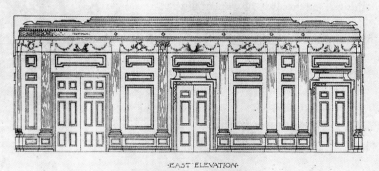

·EAST·ELEVATION·

·NORTH·ELEVATION·

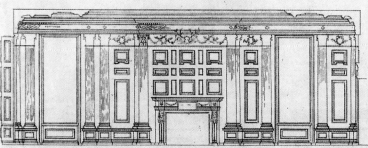

·WEST·ELEVATION·

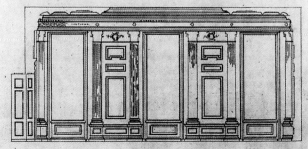

·SOVTH·ELEVATION·

STATE·DINING·ROOM·
PRESIDENT'S·HOVSE·
SCALE ½IN=1FT·

McKIM·MEAD·&·WHITE·
ARCHITECTS·
160·5TH·AVE·N·Y·C·

DRAWING·NO·310·(REVISED)
MADE July 30, 1902
BY

World War II, construction of the "Truman balcony" in 1947, and finally, the gutting and reconstruction of the house between 1948 and 1952.[6]

Of these periods, significant detailed drawings exist only for the work carried out during Roosevelt's and Truman's administrations. Tracings of drawings by McKim, Mead & White of New York, architects of the 1902 renovation, are in the New-York Historical Society. A smaller number of drawings and blueprints are owned by the Avery Architectural Archives, Columbia University, and a few are in the Library of Congress (FIGS. 3.4, 3.5). President Truman's rebuilding was planned and supervised by Lorenzo S. Winslow, a government architect who had long been associated with the White House. Complete drawings for this work are part of the archive of the White House liaison, National Park Service; Winslow's diaries are in the Office of the Curator of the White House.

Photographs are the greatest resource for the study of most periods of the architectural history of the White House. Field notes, sketches, descriptions, even old prints and some architectural drawings, must be compared to study the White House before about 1850. After that one cannot proceed without a familiarity with the White House in the camera's eye. The first known photographs of the White House were taken in 1846, a view of the south front by John Plumbe (FIG. 3.6), and of President James K. Polk and his cabinet in the State Dining Room, almost certainly by Plumbe.[7] Extensive photographic coverage of the house inside and out was first made in 1867.[8] Photographs together with written records provide the best evidence of the character of numerous changes to the White House.

The drawings of the White House in the Prints and Photographs Division are an excellent small collection that emphasizes the early years. Some are revealing on their own, while others supplement drawings or historical information housed in other institutions or elsewhere in the Library of Congress. The earliest is a set of five construction drawings (LOT 13057) in ink and watercolor wash on rough paper for an arched platform that bridged a deep areaway in front of the north entrance. President Jefferson commissioned B. Henry Latrobe to produce them in 1807–1808, while Latrobe as surveyor of public buildings worked on completing the Capitol. Latrobe's drawings include two plans and three sections; he proposed a relatively narrow stone floor to the porch supported by a groin vault below and parapet railings on the sides to terminate in heavy piers flanking nine broad steps. Through all the trials and changes the White House underwent, Latrobe's north steps, including the substructure, survive as part of the wider-floored portico commenced by Hoban in 1829.

In 1803 Latrobe drew the first record (FIG. 3.7) we have of a president's use of the White House when he recorded the principal floor of the house as Jefferson used it. In this, a narrow wooden bridge—predecessor of the later vault—spans the north areaway and on the south an apparently uncovered balcony of wood is built to what we know as the Blue Room, with stairs hugging the wall for the approximately fifteen feet to the ground.[9]

The drawing shows that Jefferson had created a span of rooms for his use, beginning with the oval drawing room, where he received foreign ambassadors, the adjacent antechamber we call the Red Room, and the "library" or office and cabinet room that was to be under all subsequent administrations as the State Dining Room. The East Room was as yet unfinished, and there was no grand stairway. Latrobe was to design the original grand stairs, and they are shown here as he reversed them from Hoban's original—to give vistas from the cross hall to the already proposed east and west wings.

James Madison continued Latrobe's services as surveyor of public buildings and already in the months between Madison's election in November 1808 and his occupancy of the White House on March 4, 1809, Latrobe was fast at work planning the redecoration of a portion of the state interiors. Two drawings—although they are only a sampling—are the best example of what he accomplished. In creating a three-room suite for entertainment, including the oval parlor and the two rooms to the west of it, he apparently gave the Madisons a sumptuous setting for their weekly receptions. Political urgency fueled the expenditure

FIG. 3.4. McKim, Mead & White, architects. Jules Guérin, delineator. H. C. Merrill, engraver. "The South Portico and the New Wings as Seen from the White House Grounds," the White House, Washington, D.C. Perspective. Halftone plate. 1902. LC-USZ62-114077.

FIG. 3.5. McKim, Mead & White, architects. "State Dining Room, President's House," Washington, D.C. Elevations. Diazoprint. 1902. ADE-UNIT 2402, no. 12, E size. LC-USZ62-114249.

because Madison devised social occasions that would help raise support by bringing key politicians under friendly terms to meet with him. One drawing (PLATE 3.1) for a "looking glass frame" presumably for over the mantel in the oval parlor, now the Blue Room, is in high British taste of the time, which is ironic, considering that Madison's frequent guests were the bold "war hawks." Latrobe designed a tall plate mirror in a marbleized frame, all crowned by a heavy cornice decorated with a row of gilded palmettes and a lambrequin, probably fabric, spangled with gilded balls that may have surrounded the room as a decorative border or cornice. The second drawing (in the Maryland Historical Society) shows fashionable English-style "Grecian" furniture emblazoned with the Union shield L'Enfant had first used in Federal Hall.

The collection also houses three of Latrobe's most famous drawings, projects for improvements to the White House, two elevations, highly finished with figures, and a plan, not dated but apparently a set with the other two, which are dated. It is the dates that are problematic. The elevation (PLATE 3.2) from the east is dated 1807, while that of the south is dated 1817 (PLATE 3.3,) but the architect notes that it is redrawn

from an earlier drawing of 1807. Whether the dates are inaccurate is uncertain. Was this a project for Jefferson, made so late in the president's administration, or did Latrobe do this for Madison to see, at some point in his later career in Washington, after the war? Hoban was already assigned to rebuilding the White House exactly as it had been, only it was to have porticoes on the north and south.

For political reasons, Madison wanted a different reconstruction: the phoenix was to rise because it had been a symbol of endurance. Such a remodeling as that proposed in the plan (FIG. 3.8), if actually carried out in 1807, would have involved major demolition by Jefferson, who was to leave office not long after and would have needed to move out. The plan seen as a project for the rebuilding of the burned-out shell makes more sense historically, even though the reconstruction was well along by 1817.

There was a small controversy at the time about who had designed the porticoes, with Hoban claiming them as part of the original plan. Textual sources from Jefferson's time that mention the porticoes have not yet been found, although there is in Jefferson's papers a sketch, by him or someone else, showing a

FIG. 3.6 (*opposite*). John Plumbe, photographer. South front, President's House, Washington, D.C. Half plate daguerreotype. Ca. 1846. DAG no. 1231. LC-USZC62-112293. *Below*, B. Henry Latrobe, architect. "Flank of the Stone Stairs to the President's House, North Entrance, looking West," Washington, D.C. Elevation. Ink, watercolor, and graphite on paper. 1808. LOT 13057, p. 2. LC-USZC4-60.

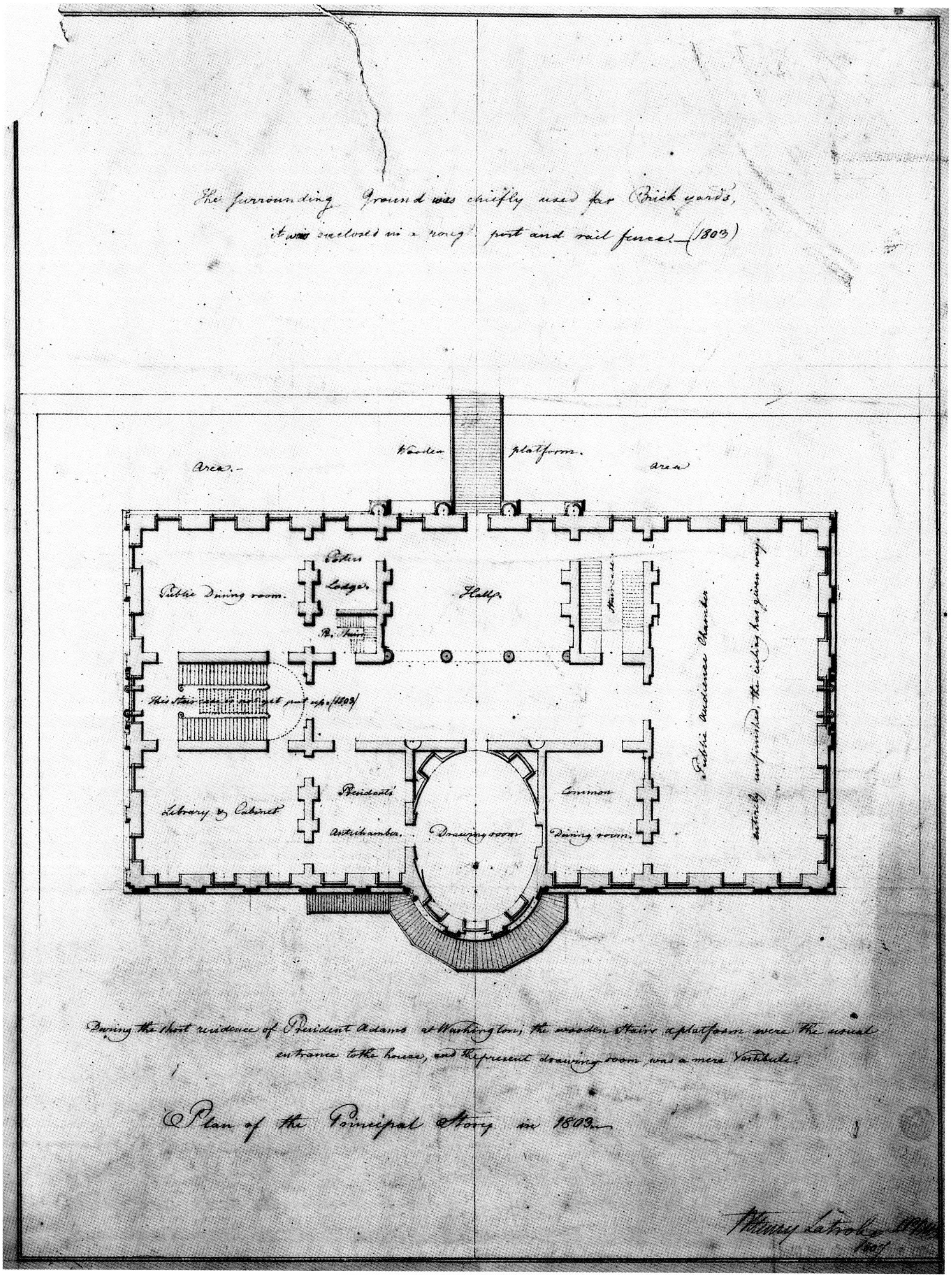

FIG. 3.7. B. Henry Latrobe, architect. "Plan of the Principal Story in 1803, during the short residence of President Adams . . . ," President's House, Washington, D.C. Plan. Ink, watercolor, graphite on paper. 1807. ADE-UNIT 2464, no. 1, B size. LC-USZ62-10794.

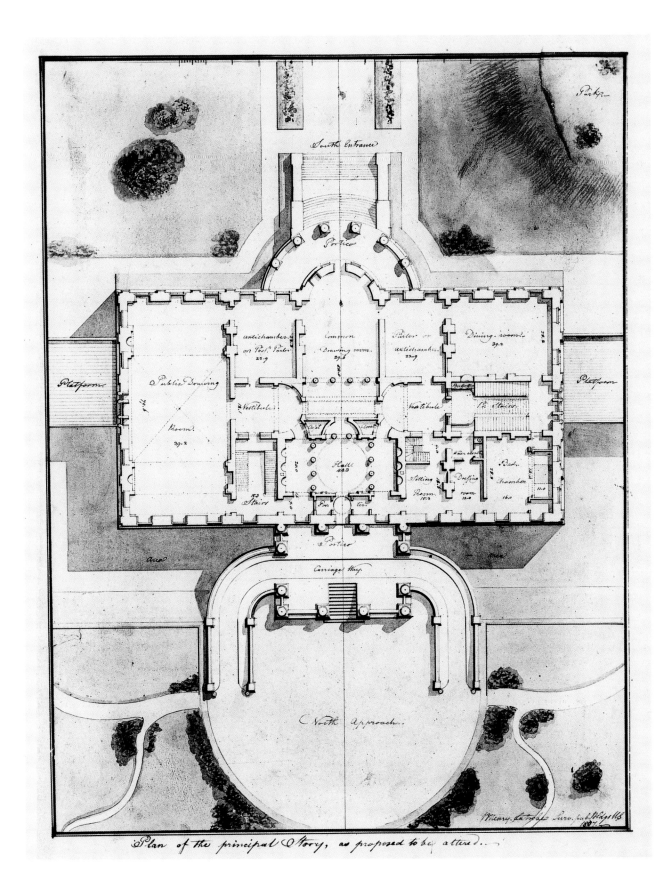

Fig. 3.8. B. Henry Latrobe, architect. "Plan of the Principal Story, as proposed to be altered," President's House, Washington, D.C. Plan. Ink, watercolor on paper. 1807–1817. ADE-UNIT 2464, no. 2, B size. LC-USZ62-10795.

Fig. 3.9. Variously attributed to B. Henry Latrobe, George Blagden, et. al. President's House, Washington, D.C. Measured drawing, plan. Graphite on paper. Ca. 1805–1820. ADE-UNIT 1125, no. 1, A size. LC-USZ62-121257.

Fig. 3.10. Attributed to William Thornton, architect. South front and wings, White House, Washington, D.C. Plan. Ink, watercolor on paper. N.d. ADE-UNIT 2465, no. 1, A size. LC-USZ62-37199.

colonnade around the bow of the White House. Those built and standing today were designed by Hoban. If these drawings are indeed dated to 1807, the idea was probably Latrobe's. Jefferson (or someone) has drawn what looks like tentative column bases in a semicircular plan on the south front in a drawing of the plan of the White House in the Maryland Historical Society. The plan, never realized, nor mentioned in written documents of either time, takes an outdated, barnlike arrangement of rooms and converts them into an elegant interior of the English sort, with antechambers, screens of columns, and water closets. To have executed this would have involved a drastic reconstruction of the central interior of the White House, certainly an odd ambition for a busy president with only about a year left in office. Built or not, this is surely the most sophisticated concept for a great house that exists among early American drawings. Professors Patrick Snadon and Michael Fazio have suggested that the drawings might be no more than an exercise by Latrobe to interest Jefferson. The issue of why they came up in 1817 has, as yet, no answers.[10]

The Prints and Photographs Division has custody of two other early, graphic curiosities relating to the White House. One is an undated plan with partial ground measurements for the President's House (FIG. 3.9). Undoubtedly a record drawing made to provide information for some building project at the White House, the sketch could have been made by nearly anyone taking dimensions on site. Latrobe is of course a possibility; George Blagden, the stonemason, is another. One can even relate it in style to Jefferson's architectural schematics. Whoever made the drawing seemed to record clearly the wings as built, indicating that their full length is not included; obviously, the call for the drawing did not require measuring the entire wings. In that the north areaway bridge designed by Latrobe is drawn, it is likely that the document postdates its construction in 1807. The reason for the play of half-circles on the south, an apparent attempt to track freehand the outlines of the southward bow, is unknown. One guess is that this drawing is a fragment from a series of similar drawings made before or during the reconstruction of the house after the War of 1812.

The other is a small ink drawing showing the south view of the White House and wings to the east and west, screened by plantings of Lombardy poplar trees (FIG. 3.10), attributed by Charles M. Harris to William Thornton.[11] Thornton openly mocked the wings built by Latrobe to Jefferson's design. (Latrobe also mocked the design, but quietly.) It is possible that this was some sort of project outlined by Thornton for detached wings between the public offices to the sides, perhaps made in discussion with Jefferson while Jefferson was making plans. It is possible it was some idea for rectifying the narrowness of the house on its site. Any such attribution concerning this mysterious drawing is, however, purely speculative.

Three drawings (ADE-UNIT 2503), all for the north portico, by Charles Bulfinch are of historical importance in the collection. These are in part tracings, or they come from the tracings that Bulfinch made of Hoban's original White House drawings. When it was decided to build the north portico in 1828 at the time of Andrew Jackson's election, the Committee of Public Buildings dispatched Bulfinch to find the "original plans." At Hoban's house, Hoban and Bulfinch took down the drawings "old and worn from use," which had been hung in frames, and Bulfinch made tracings. These drawings are presumably part of what was traced that day, and they are all that is left of the drawings used in building the portico. One is a north elevation (FIG. 3.11); the other two are plans of the north porch (ADE-UNIT 2503, nos. 2 and 3, A size; FIG. 3.12). They show several options for avoiding blocking light to the basement kitchen. The drawings are particularly rare because the originals from which they were made were presumably lost when Hoban's house burned in 1833.[12]

Certainly the most provocative drawings in the collection are those by Thomas U. Walter, which were made when extensive remodeling was ordered by Franklin Pierce at the beginning of his administration in 1853 (ADE-UNIT 2594). Included in the objectives were a better heating system, some additional plumbing, and an updating with Rococo Revival touches of the interior decorations, which had not been changed in any major way since James K. Polk's administration (1845–1849). Walter redesigned

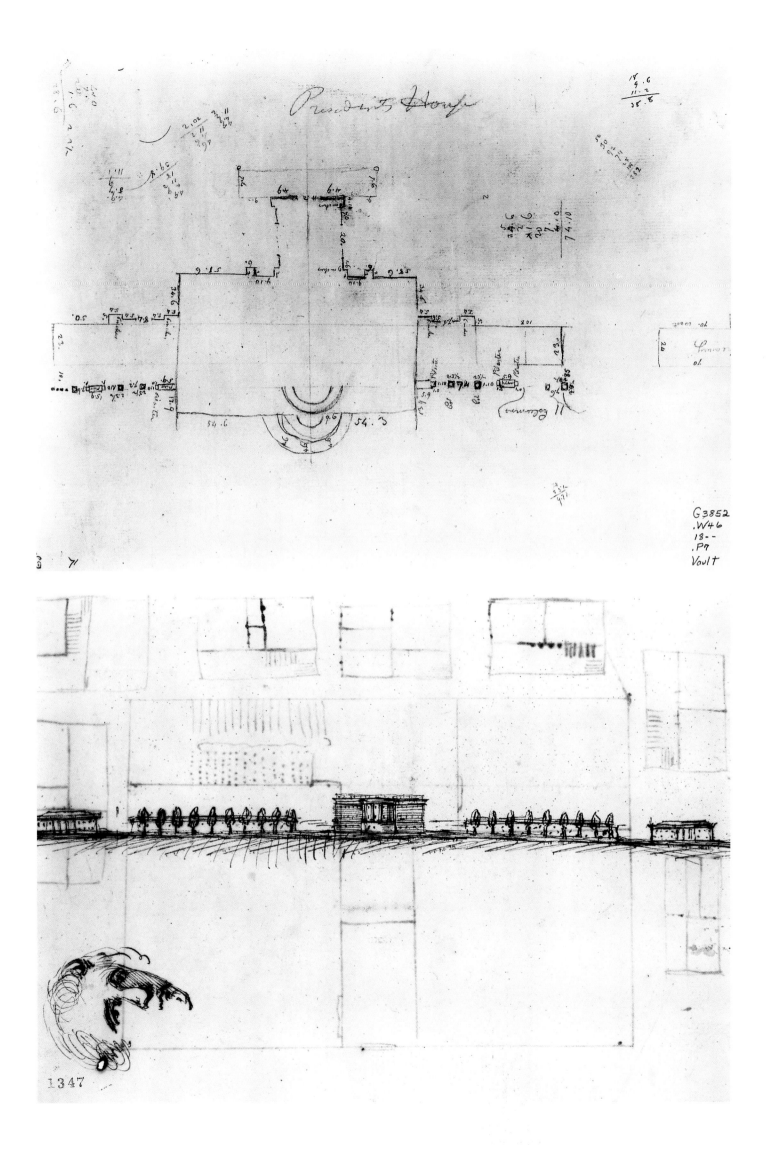

Presidents House

1347

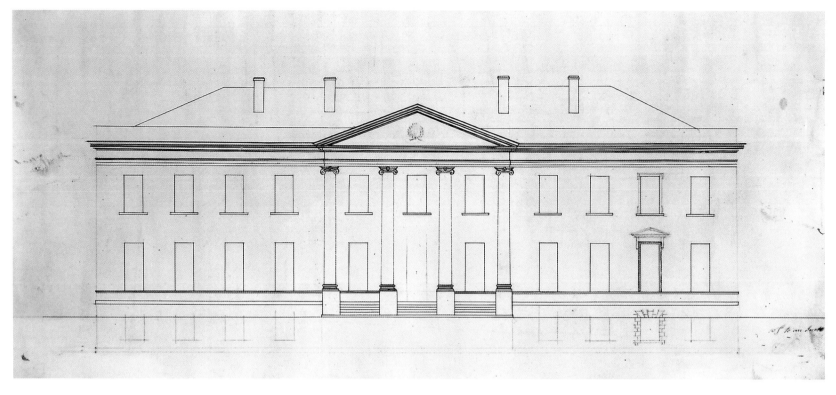

FIG. 3.11. Charles Bulfinch, after James Hoban, architects. North front, White House, Washington, D.C. Elevation. Ink, graphite on paper. 1828. ADE-UNIT 2503, no. 1, C size. LC-USZ62-133603.

the wooden screen of windows and French doors that had crossed the entrance hall since 1837, replacing it with a screen of iron. Three projects are shown in Walter's drawings; the one accepted was the simplest, and in 1883 it would be fitted with Tiffany's stained glass, removed by McKim in 1902 (FIG. 3.13). Two other interior drawings show a storm entrance for the north door (FIG. 3.14) and a revised archway in the transverse hall that led to the East Room (FIG. 3.15), both schemes executed in the remodeling of 1853–1854. Two Walter elevations of the house show it as Pierce knew it (FIGS. 3.16, 3.17).

Of greater interest—and confusion—are the plans for the main floor, second floor, and basement (FIGS. 3.18–3.20). These were drawn to describe proposed heating systems with hot water and hot air, but in doing so, they also show the configuration of the house in 1853. They are difficult to interpret because, although Walter has shown alterations that we can identify, nothing is labeled as new or existing. For example, in his plan, he removes the old grand staircase on the west entirely, replacing it

with an ordinary stair of two ranges and a landing. This we know was never done, no matter the practical advantage of closing the great open well created by Jefferson's stairs.

Walter also projected a second inside stair, beneath the office stair on the north, giving access to the basement from that point. This was never done, although the convenience to the president's messengers for moving in and out unseen can be easily imagined.

The seven plans are thus at once a treasure and a frustration, but they are the best and earliest we have for the private and service parts of the house. One supposes that Walter's rendering of the smaller of the two basement kitchens (one for banquets, the other a family kitchen) is correct, with its bake oven built into the masonry walls and a base for an early iron range. Because he had been making proposals for the kitchen, he would have certainly included more modern equipment. Comparisons to inventories clarify some of the mysteries, but alas, not all, and the drawings must be seen as conjectural in any historical analysis until perhaps a labeled set turns up.

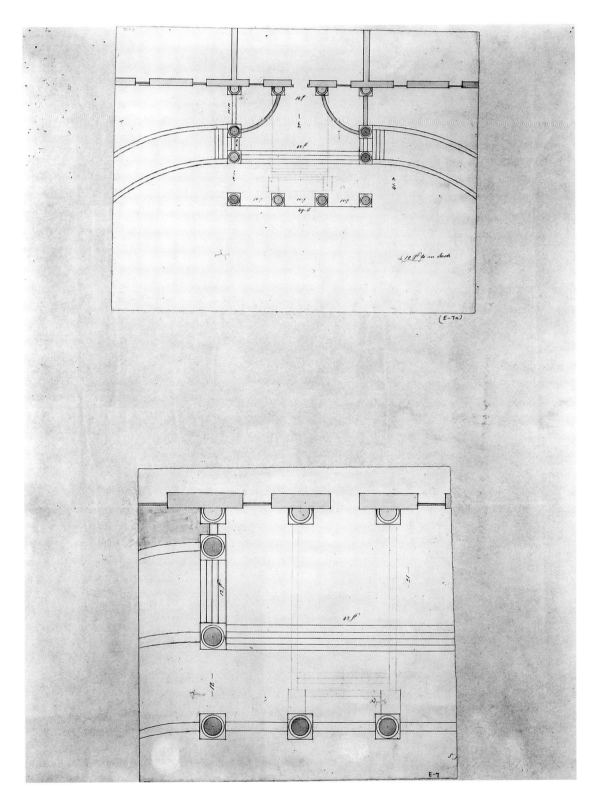

FIG. 3.12. Charles Bulfinch, after James Hoban, architects. Portico and driveway, President's House, Washington, D.C. Plan. Ink, watercolor on paper. 1828. ADE-UNIT 2503, no. 2, A size. LC-USZ62-37101.

The engineer Frederick D. Owen, a civilian employee of the U.S. Army and a friend of Mrs. Benjamin (Caroline) Harrison, delineated her plans for expanding the White House in the 1890s. The original of Owen's ambitious plan is in this collection (see FIG. 1.21), as are photographs of the accompanying drawings (FIG. 3.21). He proposed extensive aboveground additions, including vast southward wings, linked east and west by a long conservatory and thus creating a quadrangle with the historic house,. Tabled for lack of adequate support in Congress, the plans lost their chief patron when Caroline Harrison died in 1891.

The Army Corps of Engineers kept the idea alive, however, and Colonel Theodore Bingham, commissioner of public buildings, added Owen to his staff in the early 1890s and kept him busy for a full decade making plans and revising plans for expanding the White House. Substantial additions were seen as the only solution because efforts to demolish the house or move the president elsewhere had been unpopular and continually rebuffed by Congress. By 1900, with reluctant approval from President William McKinley, Bingham had refined his plan; it faintly echoed additions made to Leinster House in Dublin,

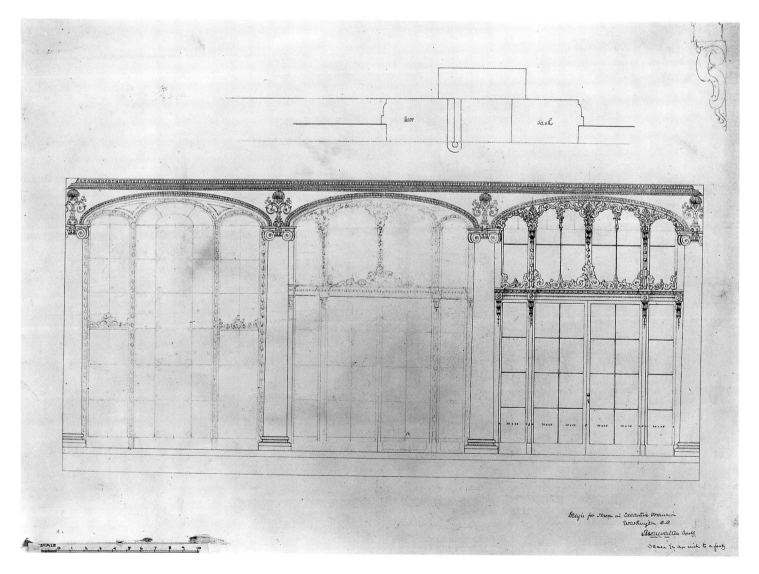

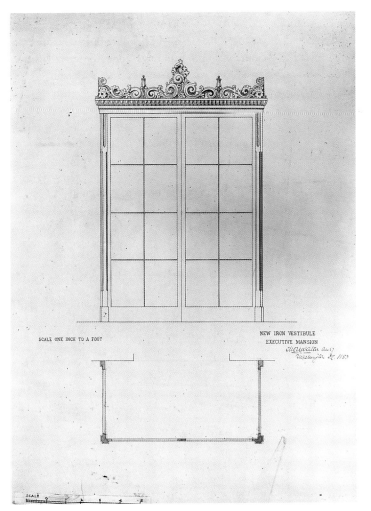

SCALE ONE INCH TO A FOOT

NEW IRON VESTIBULE
EXECUTIVE MANSION

SCALE

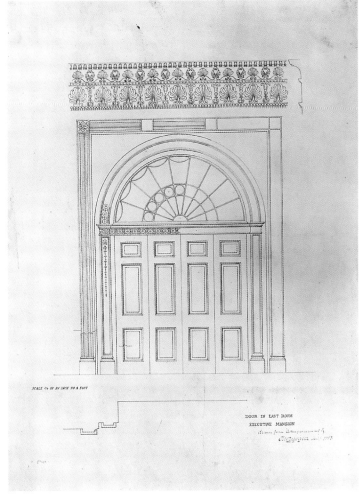

SCALE 3/4 OF AN INCH TO A FOOT

DOOR IN EAST ROOM
EXECUTIVE MANSION

Hoban's original model for the White House. Owen's plans for this, together with a plan for Leinster House, which was expanded at about that time, are in the Cartographic and Architectural Archives branch of the National Archives and exist in more detail than those for the earlier scheme.

The effort to build a new White House, or to improve the original, won adherents beyond official circles. Especially after 1893, when Washington received its first ambassador, and the city took on a polish in official society that it had not known before, various interested citizens became embarrassed over the tattiness of the town. One such person, Mrs. John Brooks Henderson, at her own expense commissioned a number of Beaux-Arts–style mansions for

use as embassies. In 1898 she retained Paul Pelz, architect of the just completed Library of Congress, to design a new executive residence. It was to be located on Meridian Hill about two miles above the White House on its Sixteenth Street axis.

Pelz produced a full presentation of the proposed mansion and published it in bound folio-size books. Two of his perspectives for the mansion (FIGS. 1.22, 3.22), really a palace atop broad terraces, show fountains playing and a vastness of scale that reminds one of L'Enfant and Washington and their original plans for the city. Copies of the complete publication of the 1898 plan are found in the Prints and Photographs Division (LOT 13040), the Office of the Curator of the White House, and the library of the University of San Diego.

FIG. 3.14 (*top left*). Thomas U. Walter, architect. "New Iron Vestibule, Executive Mansion," Washington, D.C. Elevation and plan. Ink, graphite, watercolor on paper. 1853. ADE-UNIT 2594, no. 11, D size. LC-USZ62-69791.

FIG. 3.15 (*top right*). Thomas U. Walter, architect. "Door in East Room, Executive Mansion," Washington, D.C. Elevation and plan. Ink, graphite on paper. 1853. ADE-UNIT 2594, no. 10, D size. LC-USZ62-69789.

SCALE 10 FEET TO AN INCH   NORTH ELEVATION

EXECUTIVE MANSION
DRAWN FROM ADMEASUREMENTS BY
Chetuvata
Architect of Public Buildings. 1853

SCALE 10 FEET TO AN INCH   SOUTH ELEVATION

EXECUTIVE MANSION
DRAWN FROM ADMEASUREMENTS BY
Chetuvata
Arch.t Pub. buildings 1853

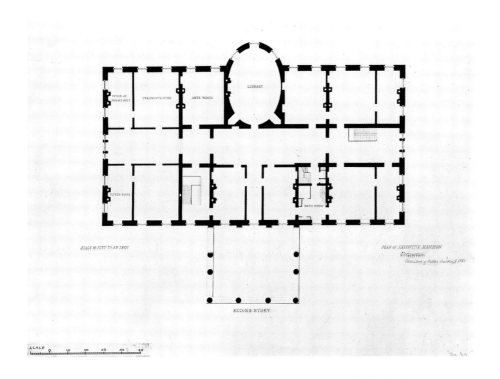

SECOND STORY

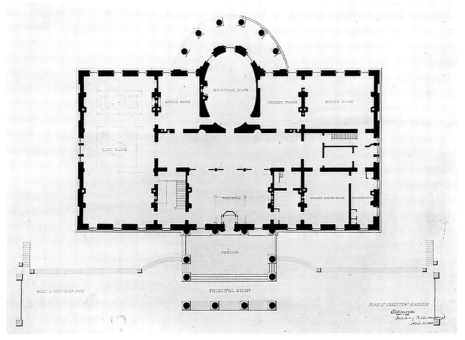

PRINCIPAL STORY

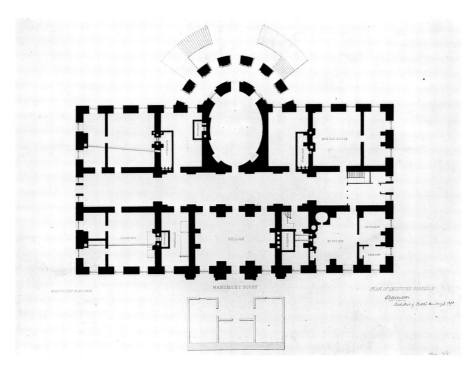

BASEMENT STORY

FIG. 3.16 (*opposite, top*). Thomas U. Walter, architect. "North elevation, Executive Mansion," Washington, D.C. Measured drawing. Ink, colored ink, watercolor on paper. 1853. ADE-UNIT 2594, no. 7, D size. LC-USZ62-114195.

FIG. 3.17 (*opposite, bottom*). Thomas U. Walter, architect. "South elevation, Executive Mansion," Washington, D.C. Measured drawing. Ink, colored ink, watercolor on paper. 1853. ADE-UNIT 2594, no. 8, D size. LC-USZ62-133824.

FIG. 3.18 (*left, top*). Thomas U. Walter, architect. "Second Story, Plan of Executive Mansion," Washington, D.C. Plan. Ink, colored ink, watercolor on paper. 1853. ADE-UNIT 2594, no. 6, D size. LC-USZ62-69787.

FIG. 3.19 (*left, center*). Thomas U. Walter, architect. "Principal Story, Plan of Executive Mansion," Washington, D.C. Plans. Ink, colored ink, watercolor, and graphite on paper. 1853. ADE-UNIT 2594, no. 5, D size. LC-USZ62-69786.

FIG. 3.20 (*left, bottom*). Thomas U. Walter, architect. "Basement Story, Plan of Executive Mansion," Washington, D.C. Plans. Ink, colored ink, watercolor on paper. 1853. Whether the underground storage rooms were built at this time is not known, but similar facilities were there fifty ears later. ADE-UNIT 2594, no. 3, D size. LC-USZ62-69788.

· VIEW · FROM · THE · SOUTH ·
· OF · THE · RESIDENCE · WINGS ·
· CONSERVATORY · AND · COURT ·

Official Wing

WEST

National Win

EAST

F. D. Owen
Archt.

· PROPOSED ·
· EXECUTIVE MANSION ·

Paul J. Pelz
Architect
Feb. 1898

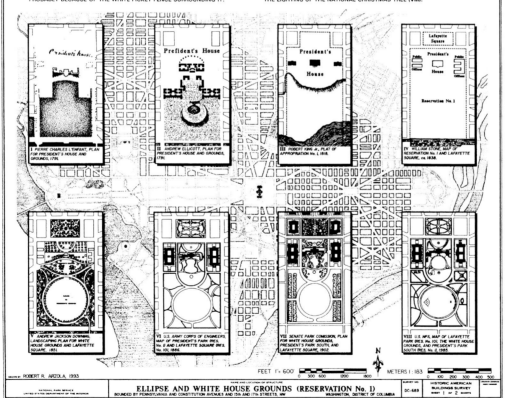

DEVELOPMENT OF APPROPRIATION No.1

VIEW OF THE NORTH FACADE OF THE WHITE HOUSE WITH THE DEPARTMENTS OF STATE AND THE TREASURY ON THE LEFT AND THE DEPARTMENTS OF WAR AND THE NAVY ON THE RIGHT. BASED ON A WATERCOLOR BY BARONESS HYDE DE NEUVILLE, 1820.

THE RECTANGULAR EXPANSE BOUNDED BY FIFTEENTH, SEVENTEENTH, AND H STREETS AND CONSTITUTION AVENUE WAS ORIGINALLY "RESERVED" FOR THE "PRESIDENT'S PALACE" ON PIERRE L'ENFANT'S 1791 PLAN FOR THE CITY OF WASHINGTON (I). ON ANDREW ELLICOTT'S PLAN OF 1792, CITY SQUARE NOS. 167 AND 221 WERE CARVED OUT OF THE NORTH CORNERS OF THE SPACE TO BE SOLD FOR PRIVATE DEVELOPMENT (II). THE REMAINDER WAS PURCHASED BY THE GOVERNMENT AS "APPROPRIATION NO. 1," ONE OF SEVENTEEN RESERVATIONS SET ASIDE FOR PUBLIC BUILDINGS. GEORGE WASHINGTON RECOMMENDED CONSTRUCTING FEDERAL OFFICES IN THE APPROPRIATION, AND BY 1800 THE WHITE HOUSE WAS FLANKED BY THE TREASURY BUILDING ON THE EAST AND THE WAR DEPARTMENT ON THE WEST--ALL BURNED BY THE BRITISH IN 1814. THE STRUCTURES WERE REBUILT, BUT THE SURROUNDING GROUNDS REMAINED LARGELY UNIMPROVED. BEFORE THE CITY CANAL WAS CONSTRUCTED IN THE 1830s, THE TIBER CREEK FLOWED THROUGH PART OF THE RESERVATION AND FREQUENTLY FLOODED THE LOW LAND SOUTH OF THE WHITE HOUSE, WHICH WAS USED AS A COW PASTURE AND DUMPING GROUNDS (III). IN THE 1820s, A SEGMENT TO THE NORTH WAS SEPARATED FROM THE WHITE HOUSE GROUNDS BY AN EXTENSION OF PENNSYLVANIA AVENUE, AND IT WAS LANDSCAPED AS A PUBLIC PARK NAMED IN HONOR OF GENERAL LAFAYETTE (IV). IN AN EFFORT TO BEAUTIFY THE FEDERAL LAND IN 1851, RENOWNED LANDSCAPE DESIGNER ANDREW JACKSON DOWNING PROPOSED PICTURESQUE PLANTINGS AND MEANDERING PATHS IN LAFAYETTE PARK AND AN ELLIPTICAL LAWN IN THE SWAMPY GROUND SOUTH OF THE WHITE HOUSE, BUT HIS DEATH IN 1852 AND THE OUTBREAK OF THE CIVIL WAR HALTED IMPLEMENTATION (V). DURING THE WAR, TROOPS CAMPED IN LAFAYETTE PARK, REPUTEDLY HANGING LAUNDRY ON THE ANDREW JACKSON STATUE. CATTLE AND HORSES WERE CORRALLED IN THE REGION SOUTH OF THE WHITE HOUSE CALLED THE "WHITE LOT" PROBABLY BECAUSE OF THE WHITE PICKET FENCE SURROUNDING IT.

WIDESPREAD POST-WAR PUBLIC-WORKS PROJECTS INCLUDED THE CONVERSION OF THE NOXIOUS CANAL INTO A ROADWAY, WITH MUCH OF THE DREDGED MUCK USED TO GRADE THE WHITE LOT. ADDITIONAL FILL WAS SUPPLIED BY 1871 EXCAVATIONS FOR THE IMMENSE STATE, WAR, AND NAVY BUILDING THAT REPLACED THE WAR DEPARTMENT. BY THE 1880s THE WHITE LOT--THEN CALLED THE PRESIDENT'S PARK--AND LAFAYETTE PARK, WERE FULLY GRADED AND PLANTED BY THE U.S. ARMY CORPS OF ENGINEERS AND FEATURED LANDSCAPES SIMILAR TO DOWNING'S DESIGNS (VI). WHILE LAFAYETTE PARK BECAME A POPULAR RESORT FOR INFLUENTIAL WASHINGTONIANS LIVING NEARBY, THE ELLIPSE WAS USED FOR BAND CONCERTS, RELIGIOUS REVIVALS, CIVIL WAR REUNIONS, AND BY CYCLISTS WHO RACED AROUND ITS PERIMETER. THE 1901 McMILLAN SENATE PARK COMMISSION PLAN PROPOSED A MORE FORMAL DESIGN FOR PRESIDENT'S PARK AND A BEAUX ARTS OFFICE COMPLEX SURROUNDING LAFAYETTE PARK (VII). ITS ONLY REAL IMPACT, HOWEVER, WAS ON THE LAYOUT FOR LAFAYETTE PARK IMPLEMENTED BY WORKS PROGRESS ADMINISTRATION LABORERS DURING THE DEPRESSION. AS WASHINGTON'S DOWNTOWN BECAME INCREASINGLY COMMERCIAL AND CONGESTED IN THE TWENTIETH CENTURY, THE PARKS SURROUNDING THE WHITE HOUSE PROVIDED WELCOME GREEN SPACE AMID THE ACRES OF CONCRETE AND ASPHALT. THE ELLIPSE WAS EQUIPPED FOR SPORTS, INCLUDING ARCHERY, BASEBALL, CROQUET, AND TENNIS IN THE 1920s, BUT SINCE THE 1960s THE PARKS NEAR THE EXECUTIVE MANSION HAVE ALSO BECOME PLACES TO EXERCISE FIRST AMENDMENT RIGHTS THROUGH PROTESTS AND DEMONSTRATIONS. NOW ADMINISTERED BY THE NATIONAL PARK SERVICE, LAFAYETTE PARK, THE WHITE HOUSE GROUNDS, AND PRESIDENT'S PARK SOUTH ARE DOTTED WITH COMMEMORATIVE STATUES, FOUNTAINS, AND PLANTINGS; THEY REMAIN SITES FOR RECREATION AND CEREMONY, SUCH AS ANNUAL EASTER-EGG ROLLS AND THE LIGHTING OF THE NATIONAL CHRISTMAS TREE (VIII).

FIG. 3.21 (*opposite, top*). F. D. Owen, architect. "View from the South of the Residence Wings, Conservatory and Court, An Adaptation of the Suggestions of Mrs. Harrison for the Extension of the Executive Mansion," Washington, D.C. Perspective. 1891–1901. Photographic print. ADE-UNIT 2838, no. 10 (Photo). LC-USZ62-3767.

FIG. 3.22 (*opposite, bottom*). Paul J. Pelz, architect. Jules T. Crow, delineator. "Proposed Executive Mansion," Meridian Hill, Washington, D.C. Perspective. Ink on paper. 1898. ADE-UNIT 2802, no. 1, F size. LC-USZ62-105251.

FIG. 3.23. Historic American Buildings Survey. Robert R. Arzola, delineator. Development of Appropriation No. 1, Ellipse and White House Grounds (Reservation no. 1), bounded by Pennsylvania and Constitution Avenues and 15th and 17th Streets, N.W., Washington, D.C. Plans and perspective. Ink on polyester film. 1993. Digital file of HABS DC-689, sheet 1 of 2.

FIG. 3.24. Waddy. B. Wood, architect. "President's [Inaugural] reviewing stand" for Franklin D. Roosevelt, Washington, D.C. Graphite and watercolor on illustration board. 1940. ADE-UNIT 1115, no. 1, D size. LC-USZC4-3723.

Donald H. Drayer's design for a new closet for President Lyndon B. Johnson (ADE-UNIT 1228, no. 1, F size) was made in 1965 and, except for the large set of drawings made between 1988 and 1992 by the Historic American Buildings Survey, is the most recent drawing for the White House in the Prints and Photographs Division. Drayer's design is typical of the kind of voluminous drawings found in the architect's office of the White House liaison at the National Park Service. Most of those are restricted by the Secret Service for security reasons.

Drawings for minor renovations for the White House appear almost monthly. In the past, they were seldom seen as important and were thrown out, but since the renovations in 1952, and especially since the early 1960s, more attention has been paid to the preservation of all drawings of the White House. In addition to the practical need for every-day reference, such drawings are now recognized as part of the ongoing historical documentation of the house and are very carefully maintained. Drayer's drawing for a closet has a place among others for fence repairs, new doors, replaced mantels, and walkways, to name but a few; it is a link in the chain that chronicles the design and building history of the White House.

Finally, for a broader context, the scholar is advised to consult a variety of documents in the custody of the Prints and Photographs Division that record the design and appearance of the buildings and grounds directly adjacent to the White House or that represent extensions of its purpose and serve as symbols of the executive branch of government. These can range from the contemporary illustrations of Andrew Jackson Downing's plans for the President's Park of the early 1850s and the documentary drawings of the same area made by the Historic American Buildings Survey, showing its development over the next century and a half (FIG. 3.23), to Waddy B. Wood's 1940 design for President Franklin D. Roosevelt's inaugural reviewing stand (FIG. 3.24) and the designs for the airborne and rail extensions of the executive mansion: Raymond Loewy's 1962 design for the original Air Force One (LC-USZC4-11490), "designed with President Kennedy's collaboration in the oval room of the White House in three meetings in the spring of 1962," and Drayer's 1964 design for the "Lady Bird Special" train (ADE-UNIT 1406).

CHAPTER FOUR

BUILDING FOR BUSINESS

——

Commercial Architecture in Metropolitan Washington

RICHARD LONGSTRETH

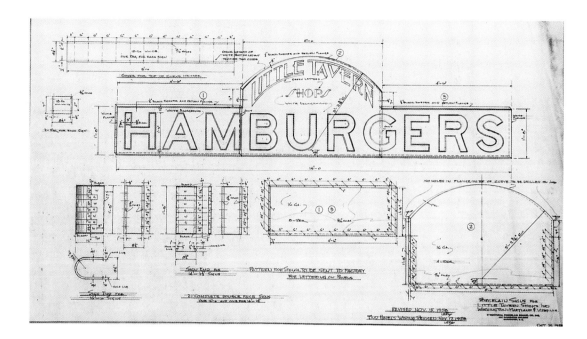

FIG. 4.1. Luther R. Ray, architect. Structural Porcelain Enamel Co., Inc. "Porcelain Signs for Little Tavern Shops, Inc., Washington, Maryland & Virginia." Elevation and details. Graphite on paper. 1958. ADE-UNIT 2821, no. 1, D size. LC-USZ62-133469.

FIG. 4.2 (*opposite, top*). George N. Ray, architect. Business building for the Lambert Tree Estate, 1000 Connecticut Avenue, N.W., Washington, D.C. Field notes. Measured drawing, first-floor plan. Graphite on letterpress graph paper. 1927. ADE-UNIT 282, no. 9, A size. LC-USZ62-114001.

FIG. 4.3 (*opposite, bottom*). George N. Ray, architect. Stores and a restaurant, "proposed building on the Austrian Embassy site," Connecticut Avenue and Eighteenth Street, N.W., Washington, D.C. Diagrammatic layout. Plans. Graphite on paper. 1920s. ADE-Unit 77, no. 1, recto, A size. LC-USZ62-114008.

THE DRAWINGS of Washington-area commercial architecture form an unusual lot.[1] With a few exceptions, this material does not encompass those types that have been the most frequently studied: tall office buildings, department stores, or the headquarters of major financial institutions and other companies. The architects represented do not loom large among those who have been national leaders in the commercial sphere. Indeed, until recently, important commissions for commercial buildings no less than for governmental ones in the nation's capital often have gone to architectural firms based in other cities.[2] Furthermore, Washington, D.C., has seldom been an incubator of major new developments in commercial design. By 1910 one can find an increasing number of examples that reflect the tendencies then most current in the field, but the pervasive pattern was to emulate standards set in cities such as New York and Chicago.[3]

Rather than documenting seminal work, the designs for commercial buildings included in the Library of Congress collection are of value for their representative attributes, affording a rich array of examples from the mainstream. This material is the product of more than a half-dozen architectural firms and covers nearly a century of practice. The great bulk of material, however, falls within a fifty-year period—between 1910 and 1960—and is the product of offices headed by Clarke Waggaman and George Ray, Arthur Heaton, Luther Ray (who was no relation to George), and Donald Drayer. Much less survives from the

office of Alfred Mullett and its successor, A. B. Mullett & Company, headed by his sons and from the office of Waddy Wood. Only small fragments are on file for yet others. In each case, the content differs in time span, types of buildings and locations, and the scope of material. Although each component has particular interest, the collection also should be considered in its entirety. Together this assemblage provides a diverse and often quite detailed account of methods used in the creation of commercial buildings as they have evolved over a considerable period of time.

As a whole, this material contains a wealth of information on both design and building, from Mullett's relatively sophisticated structural system for a tall office building of the mid-1880s (ADE-UNIT 40; FIG. 4.14) to Drayer's economic and expedient one for a shopping center of the mid-1950s (FIGS. 4.39–4.42). There are many kinds of documents that are seldom saved, such as full-sized details by Heaton (ADE-UNIT 484, ADE-UNIT 526) or the diagrammatic plans for porcelain enamel signs by Luther Ray (FIG. 4.1), in addition to those kinds most often seen, such as presentation drawings (PLATE 4.1). Of all the architects represented, George Ray left the richest record of his day-to-day activities.[4] There are numerous documents from the first stages of a commission, including field notes on buildings to be remodeled, lists of required spaces, and diagrammatic layouts (FIGS. 4.2, 4.3). For exterior elevations, there are quick sketches made to record ideas, rough and

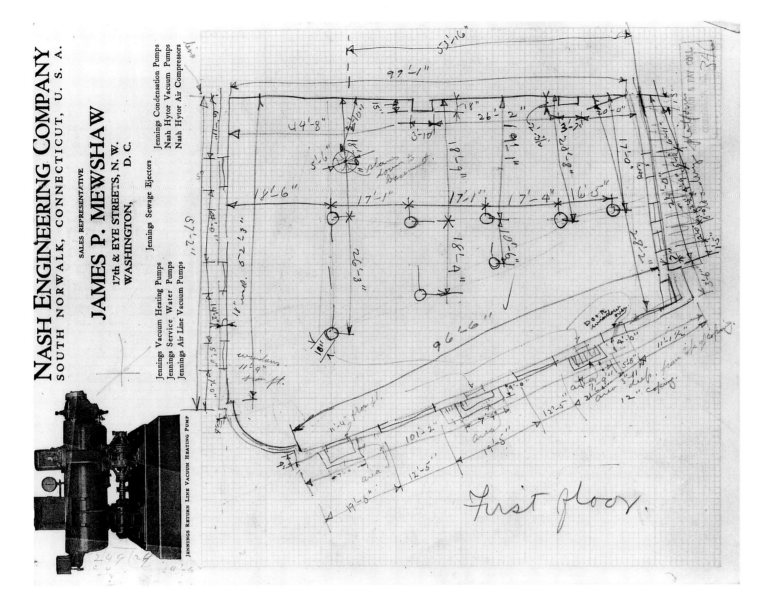

First floor.

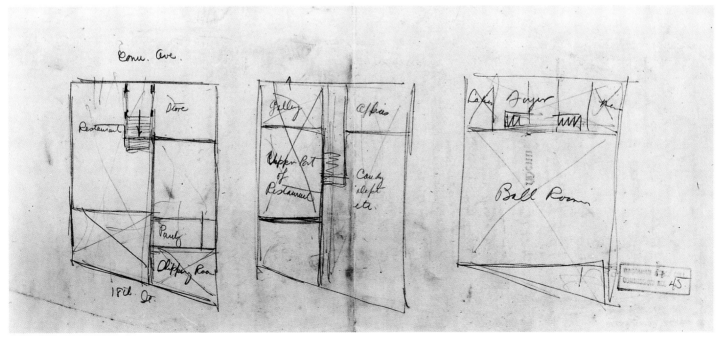

FIG. 4.4 (*right*). George N. Ray, architect. Stores, and a restaurant, "proposed building on the Austrian Embassy site," Connecticut Avenue and Eighteenth Street, N.W., Washington, D.C. Rough compositional study. Plans. Graphite on paper. 1920s. ADE-Unit 77, no. 4, C size. LC-USZ62-114101.

FIG. 4.5 (*bottom left*). Waggaman & Ray, architects. "The B. F. Saul Company." 15th Street, N.W., Washington, D.C. Facade study. Graphite and colored pencil. 1923. ADE-UNIT 272, no. 27, C size. LC-USZ62-116906.

FIG. 4.6 (*bottom center*). Waggaman & Ray, architects. "The B. F. Saul Company," 15th Street, N.W., Washington, D.C. Facade study. Graphite and colored pencil. 1923. ADE-UNIT 272, no. 25, C size. LC-USZ62-114144.

FIG. 4.7 (*bottom right*). Waggaman & Ray, architects. "The B. F. Saul Company," 15th Street, N.W., Washington, D.C. Facade study. Graphite and colored pencil. 1923. ADE-UNIT 272, no. 18, C size. LC-USZ62-116905.

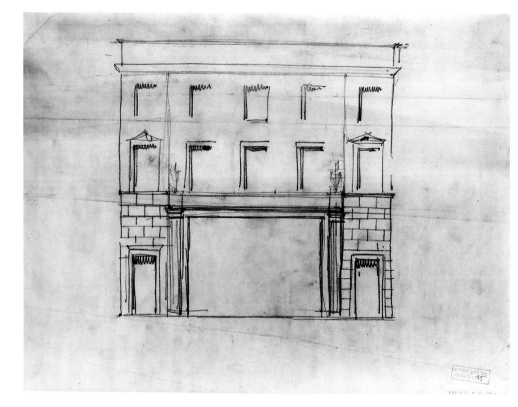

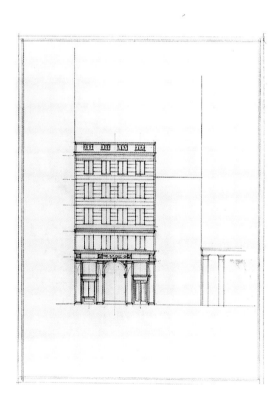

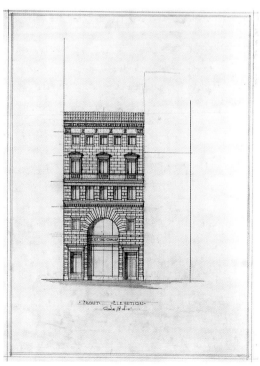

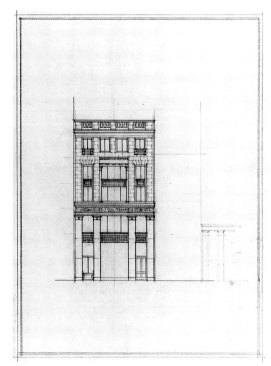

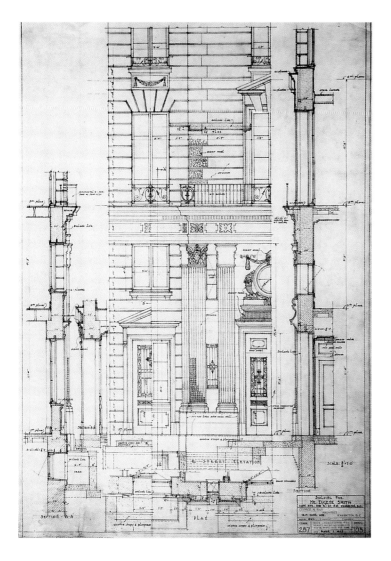

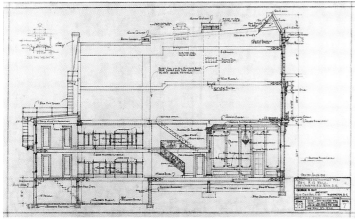

detailed compositional studies, and even meticulous examinations of numerous alternative treatments (FIGS. 4.4–4.7). Preliminary drawings survive for sectional details of both the building fabric (ADE-UNIT 248, no. 25) and finishes and for furniture layout. Finally, a substantial range of drawings underscore the intricacies that could be bestowed on even the design of small buildings of the early twentieth century (FIGS. 4.8, 4.9).

Such evidence should allay resurgent arguments that drawing from historical sources and relying upon standard compositional arrangements constitute an excuse for designing quickly, with little thought. This material should also remind people that the power and endurance of a design lie not just with its basic qualities; in the final analysis, it is the details that distinguish the product, irrespective of its vocabulary.

The collection further yields no small amount of insight into the development of building types, including some for which documentation such as can be found here is extremely rare. The motel is a good case in point.[5] Although he almost never designed work outside the elite quarters of Washington, George Ray did prepare a prototypical scheme for a chain of "tourist homes" in 1925 (FIG. 4.10). The complex is not only large for that time (twenty-nine units) but includes the unorthodox feature of a garage in the center of each cabin. Fifteen years later, Heaton made studies for a complex that reflects motel planning at its most genteel, with fourteen cabins and garages connected by a covered walk set around a landscaped court (FIG. 4.11). Drayer's motel was common when it was drawn in 1952: orderly, respectable, relatively commodious, and without the slightest pretension (FIG. 4.12). A project done by him only six years later, however, reflects the rapid emergence of large and elaborate complexes that assume an increasing number of hotel attributes (FIG. 4.13). Finally, one of Drayer's last projects is a hotel connected to an office building by a three-deck parking garage but situated, like its motel predecessors, along a major artery, well removed from the city center.

Perhaps the collection's greatest value lies in the urbanistic realm. The contents include a wide spectrum

FIG. 4.8. George N. Ray, architect. "Building for Mr. Eugene Smith," 1700 Connecticut Avenue and R Street, N.W., Washington, D.C. Final working drawing, R Street facade. Plan, elevation, and sections. 1925. ADE-UNIT 217, no. 24, E size. LC-USZ62-133471.

FIG. 4.9. George N. Ray, architect. "Alterations and additions" to a store building with a beauty shop and apartments above for Mrs. F. G. Wall, 1714 Connecticut Avenue, N.W., Washington, D.C. Final working drawing. Section and details. Graphite on linen. 1926. ADE-UNIT 230, no. 57, D size. LC-USZ62-116858.

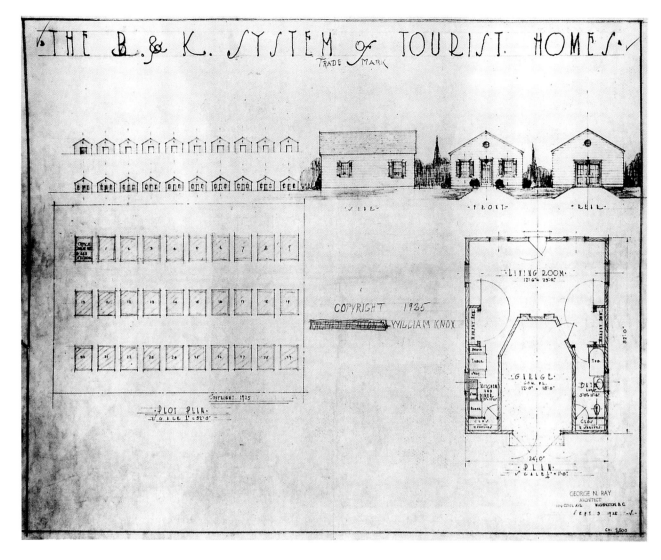

FIG. 4.10 (*right, top*). George N. Ray, architect. "The B. & K. System of Tourist Homes." Plans and elevations. Photostat. Ca. 1925. Unknown if building realized. ADE-UNIT 2028, no. 1, A size. LC-USZ62-114070.

FIG. 4.11 (*right, bottom*). Arthur B. Heaton, architect. "Colony Lodge (Motel)," near Washington, D.C. Site and floor plans and elevations. Graphite on tracing paper. 1940. Unknown if building realized. ADE-UNIT 819, no. 5, C size. LC-USZ62-116841.

FIG. 4.12 (*opposite, top*). Donald Hudson Drayer, architect. Motel for L. S. Hutchison and C. W. Sydnor, Route 15, near Leesburg, Virginia. Plan and elevations. Graphite on paper. 1952. ADE-UNIT 1197, no. 1, D size. LC-USZ62-133468.

FIG. 4.13 (*opposite, bottom*). Donald Hudson Drayer, architect. "Proposed Calvert Motor Hotel," U.S. Route 1 and Guilford Drive, College Park, Maryland. Site plan, plans, and bird's-eye perspective. Graphite on tracing paper. 1958. Project. ADE-UNIT 1317, no. 2, C size. LC-USZ62-114122.

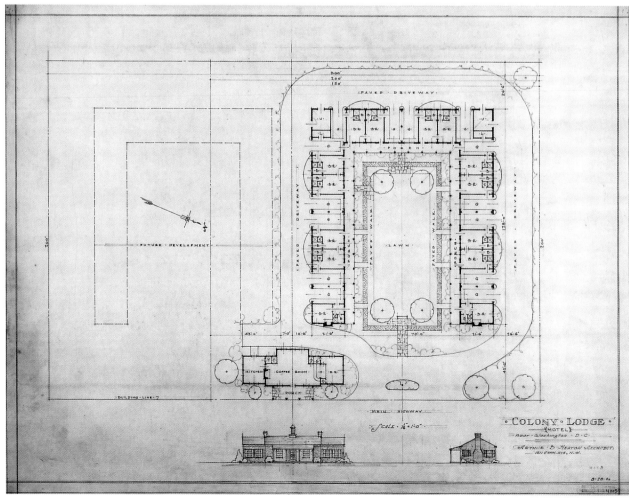

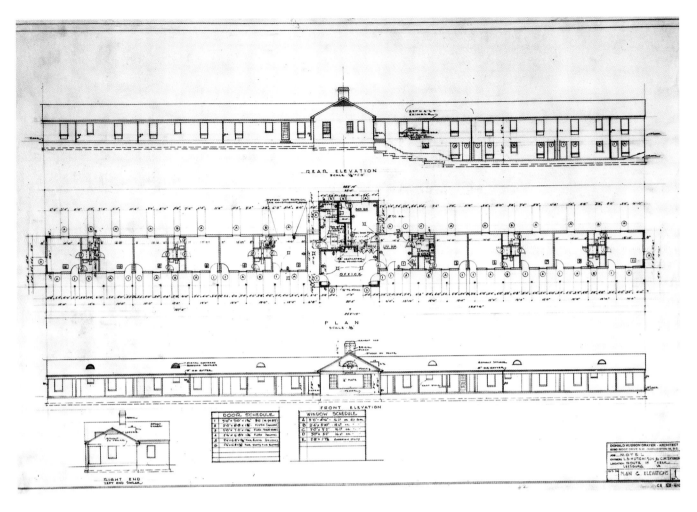

REAR ELEVATION
SCALE 1/8"=1'0"

PLAN
SCALE 1/8"

FRONT ELEVATION

RIGHT END
LEFT END SIMILAR

DOOR SCHEDULE

WINDOW SCHEDULE

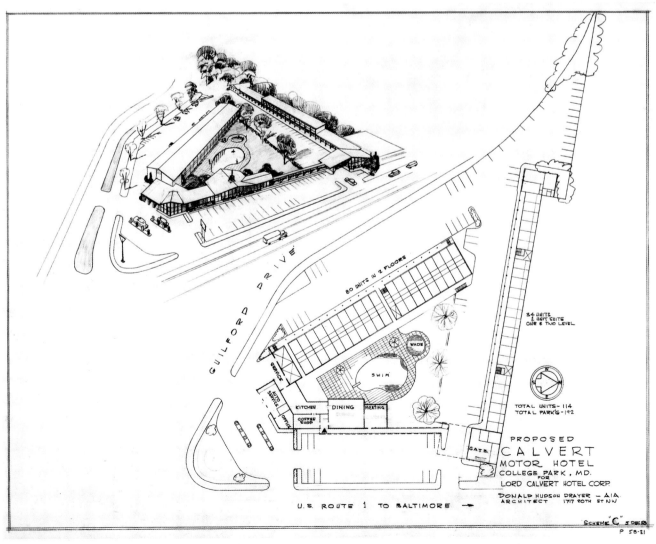

GUILFORD DRIVE

80 UNITS IN 2 FLOORS

34 UNITS
1 UNIT SUITE
ONE & TWO LEVEL

WADE

SWIM

SERVICE

AUTO SERVICE

KITCHEN   DINING   MEETING

COFFEE SHOP

OFFICE

GATE

TOTAL UNITS - 114
TOTAL PARK'G - 192

U.S. ROUTE 1 TO BALTIMORE →

PROPOSED
CALVERT
MOTOR HOTEL
COLLEGE PARK, MD.
FOR
LORD CALVERT HOTEL CORP.

DONALD HUDSON DRAYER - AIA
ARCHITECT   1717 20TH ST N.W.

SCHEME "C" IDEA

P 58-31

of types—most of them modest in size, in use, and often in appearance—that comprise a significant portion of twentieth-century metropolitan fabric. Many examples represent national patterns in building development and design; others are key contributors to the qualities associated with a singular place. Although most of this material has been long ignored or dismissed, of little more than local interest, it is precisely such documentation that needs to be examined with greater care if we are to understand the city and its outlying areas and the definitive role architecture plays in its character and form. Here, beyond the grand master plans and major landmarks, lies work that collectively is at least as important to creating the distinctive features of the urban landscape, including the framework for its complex multitude of functions. This essay is written as a prolegomenon to suggest some of the many ways in which the collection provides a source for inquiry.[6]

Large Buildings in the Urban Core

Washington's commercial center did not include a strong, single concentration of business development as many other cities experienced during major periods of expansion between the mid-nineteenth and mid-twentieth centuries.[7] Even when some similar or mutually reinforcing functions located in proximity to one another, others of the same kind would be established some distance away. This dual pattern was evident from the start in the construction of tall office buildings. The eight-story "tower" designed by Mullett for the Baltimore *Sun* (1885–1887) to house that newspaper's Washington bureau at 1317 F Street, N.W., lay apart from what was then the commercial core to the south along Pennsylvania Avenue and to the east along Seventh Street (FIG. 4.14).[8] Soon thereafter the facility was rivaled by the eight-story Atlantic Building (1887–1888) and the nine-story headquarters of the Washington Loan and Trust Company (1890–1891) on F Street four blocks to the east. The first sequels of a more ambitious nature were constructed at the beginning of the next decade on sites still further afield. The Evening Star Building (1899–1900) rose along the Pennsylvania

Avenue corridor at Eleventh Street, while the Bond (1900–1901) and Colorado (1902–1903) buildings were situated in an entirely new area for such work, Fourteenth Street at New York Avenue and at G Street, respectively.[9]

The most intensive campaign of commercial development yet to occur in Washington began several years later, in 1906, and continued for just under a decade. However, almost no work of consequence was undertaken during this period along Pennsylvania Avenue or Seventh Street and only a few major new projects were located on F Street. Instead, the blocks of Fourteenth and Fifteenth Streets between F and H became the principal focus of activity. Spearheaded by enterprises such as Wood, Donn & Deming's monumental Union Trust Company Building (1906–1907) (ADE-UNIT 481, no. 2; FIG. 4.15), this area became known as the core of a new business district that would rival the best current work in the governmental sector along the Mall and also match in sophistication, if not in size, the skyscraper centers of the largest U.S. cities.[10]

At the same time, equally sizable office buildings were being erected outside this emerging quarter: at the northern fringes of the older area (e.g., Eighth and G, Ninth and New York) and at the West End, the corridor along Pennsylvania Avenue west of the White House (e.g., Seventeenth and New York, Nineteenth and H).[11] After the First World War, most new office building construction occurred along Fourteenth and Fifteenth Streets and to the west, consolidating some of the territory staked out in previous years.

Still, the landscape remained a patchwork, with numerous large commercial edifices standing in small groups or in isolation. No one street or sequence of key intersections formed a distinct heart of the office precinct. Instead, centrality appears to have been viewed in somewhat vaguer terms that reflected the dispersed layout of the city as a whole. Sites were at least potentially desirable if they lay close to one of the several nodes established by federal offices and also were convenient to some of the numerous middle-class residential areas that framed the core to the north and east. A map featured in the promotional

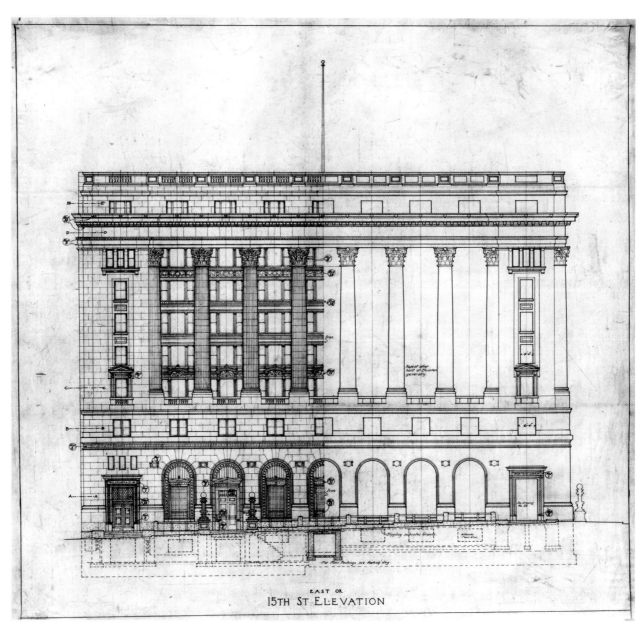

EAST OR
15TH ST. ELEVATION

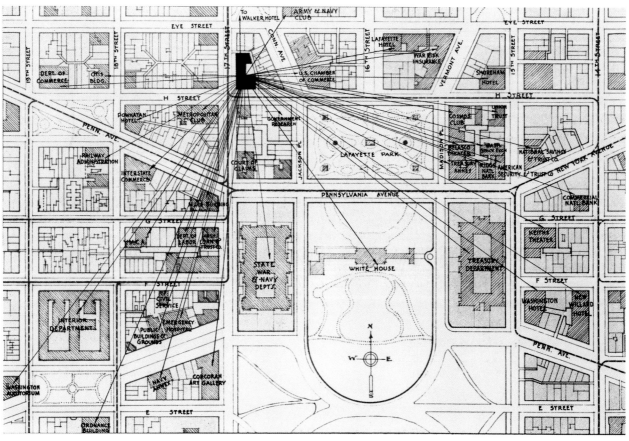

brochure of Waddy Wood's 1923–1924 Transportation Building at Seventeenth and H Streets suggests how the loose grouping of new office facilities around Lafayette Square, each within a few blocks of the White House and what had become a primary commuter route (Connecticut Avenue), was presented as a locational asset (FIG. 4.16).[12]

Much the same scattering occurred with banks. In 1890 most financial institutions were clustered either along the Seventh Street corridor or near the intersection of Fifteenth Street and New York and Pennsylvania avenues. A quarter century later, more than a half-dozen major new banking facilities had been erected in the latter area, rendering it in the minds of many people as the city's financial and office core. Yet almost as many competing institutions had built new headquarters as far afield as Tenth and G, Ninth and K, and Seventh and E Streets.[13]

The trend continued after World War I when Washington Loan and Trust commissioned Arthur Heaton to design a nine-story addition to its offices at Ninth and F Streets (1926–1927), making the facility one of the largest in Washington. Three years earlier, Heaton had prepared plans for the company's West End branch at Seventeenth and G Streets (FIG. 4.17), which was as grand as many banks' main buildings.[14]

The siting of major department stores was similarly diffused. Five of these establishments—Kann's, Lansburgh's, Hecht's, King's Palace, and Goldenberg's—could be found along the seven-block stretch of Seventh Street between Pennsylvania Avenue and Mount Vernon Square. All five companies undertook ambitious expansion campaigns during the 1910s and 1920s, thus ensuring the street's continued role as a primary magnet of retail activity.[15] However,

the first local emporium to construct a large, elaborate building designed for the specific purpose of housing a wide array of departments was the Palais Royal (1892–1893) at Eleventh and G Streets, apart from the retail core but closer to the prosperous districts where its target audience resided. The company that became Washington's biggest department store, Woodward & Lothrop, had occupied a site on F Street one block to the south since 1887 but oriented its huge addition of 1902–1903 to the Palais Royal.[16] Arguably the most prestigious department store in the city, Julius Garfinckel & Company, had, by the 1910s, acquired and added to its own quarters several blocks to the west at Thirteenth and F Streets. An even larger building, erected across the street in 1914, was initially planned as a department store. Two years earlier, a proposal had been made for yet another such facility at Twenty-first and I Streets, which would have been far removed from any shopping area of consequence.[17] The furthest west a large emporium was actually realized before the branch store development that began in the 1940s was Fourteenth and F Streets, where an elegant new Garfinckel's opened in 1930 (PLATE 4.2) (ADE-UNIT 751, no. 1).[18]

Nevertheless, these anchors of trade extended over an area of more than sixteen linear blocks in a T configuration. That pattern was quite different from what could be found even in much larger cities such as Chicago, where major department stores lay within seven blocks of one another on State Street, or Philadelphia, where the arrangement extended over six blocks on Market Street. As early as 1906, an observer remarked that it was increasingly difficult to determine where the center of Washington's business district lay.[19] The matter could only have seemed more perplexing two decades later.

Small Buildings in the Urban Core

It was small buildings, however, that first defined the city's urban core. Until the last quarter of the nineteenth century, buildings of relatively modest dimensions—twenty to fifty feet wide and two to four stories tall—made up most of those in downtown Washington and in most other cities as well. Although the size of major facilities for trade, finance, and services increased significantly after that, many small buildings continued to be erected within a few blocks of them. Outside the choicest locations, the cost of land, coupled with the generally small-scale and independent ownership of most businesses and the abundance of people eager to invest substantial, but not enormous, amounts of capital into commercial real estate contributed to this persistence of a traditional pattern. Small commercial buildings continued to be an especially prominent part of new work in downtown Washington through the first half of the twentieth century because the core was so diffused.

The Mulletts, Heaton, and, to a lesser degree, Waggaman and Ray all contributed to the continued development of small commercial buildings downtown during the 1910s and 1920s. The Mulletts' work fits well within the mainstream of early twentieth-century commercial design, both in Washington and nationwide. Ultimately derived from classical sources and often from the compositional conventions of French academic practice, the exteriors reflect the high median standard attained during that period (FIG. 4.18). Nothing about these buildings was exceptional; yet, they bear evidence of the care that was invested in both the design and construction of even the most routine facilities in the city center.

Heaton's work downtown similarly adheres to period conventions, but it tends to embody an even greater concern for the development of the design. The meticulousness of these schemes stands quite apart from personal style. The architect seems consciously to have avoided the pursuit of overt trademarks, instead lavishing time on refinement of mass, proportion, and detail. Heaton drew from a wide range of historical sources, and although he remained a staunch traditionalist in outlook, he also accepted some modernist tendencies, as was the case with the dignified Art Deco building on Fourteenth Street that he designed for Shannon & Luchs in 1927.[20]

The fact that the market for modest-sized buildings remained strong downtown, even during such

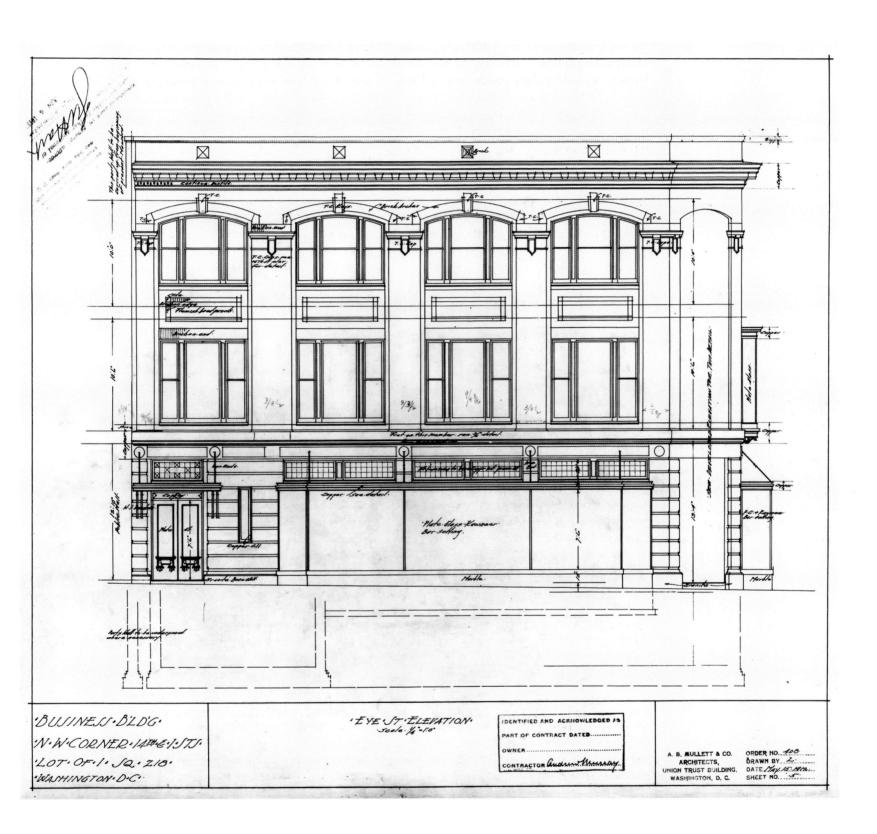

·BUSINESS·BLD'G·
·N·W·CORNER·14TH**E·I·STS·**
·LOT·OF·I·SQ·218·
·WASHINGTON·D·C·

·EYE·ST·ELEVATION·
Scale 1/4"=1'0"

| IDENTIFIED AND ACKNOWLEDGED AS |
| PART OF CONTRACT DATED............ |
| OWNER................................ |
| CONTRACTOR Andrew Murray |

A. B. MULLETT & CO.
ARCHITECTS,
UNION TRUST BUILDING,
WASHINGTON, D.C.

ORDER NO. 100
DRAWN BY L
DATE May 15 1912
SHEET NO. 5

intense periods of development as the second half of the 1920s, helped explain why many property owners were willing to spend substantial sums on appearances. Heaton's work shows that small projects could justify exteriors that were just as elaborate as the showiest large office and retail blocks nearby. Yet most of these small buildings were speculative enterprises. Seldom was the owner also an occupant, although a number of plans did entail interiors tailored to the needs of a specific tenant. In most cases, however, the interior layout was kept general enough to accommodate the great spectrum of businesses that were harbored in the urban core.

In contrast to the scattered pattern of development for major commercial facilities, a clear path was established during the early twentieth century for expansion of small downtown businesses. Connecticut Avenue between Lafayette Square and Florida Avenue formed the spine of this new precinct, with extensions to either side along H, I, and K Streets. Since the 1870s, this area had been the preferred residential quarter of the city's elite, but by the eve of World War I, many residences were either being demolished for, or converted to, commercial uses.[21] Some developers harbored visions of the entire area being transformed into a dense new business corridor, which is reflected in Heaton's studies for the twelve-story Embassy Building (1932) at Connecticut Avenue and N Street (PLATE 4.3). North of I and west of Fifteenth Streets, however, such large-scale work remained the exception until after World War II. The overwhelming majority of new construction before then followed existing residential property lines and seldom exceeded the height of the preceding residence by more than one story.

Goods and services purveyed along the Connecticut Avenue corridor catered primarily to the elite and prosperous middle class who now lived in a steadily expanding ring of neighborhoods to the north and west. The blocks around Fifteenth and K Streets became a new locus for real estate firms, which were, of course, the principal shaping forces of those new residential enclaves. A number of real estate offices also located along Connecticut Av-

enue, but the street became primarily known as the city's most fashionable shopping district. Few of the stores were oriented to basic goods and services that could be found in neighborhood business centers. Most units housed specialty shops for clothing and accessories, furniture, china and glassware, antiques, imported goods, or expensive new kinds of appliances. Personal services included tailors, dressmakers, beauticians, and music and dance instructors. There were some household services (decorators, caterers, upholsterers) and a large number of professional services (doctors, dentists, lawyers, architects, and photographers).

The transformation of Connecticut Avenue into a commercial destination, tangential to, but also removed from, the traditional core, had parallels in other American cities: Newberry and Boyleston Streets in Boston's Back Bay, Walnut Street in the Rittenhouse Square area of Philadelphia, and Madison Avenue on New York's Upper East Side. The main difference was that Washington was a much smaller city; Boston had nearly twice and Philadelphia more than four times the population in 1930. Numerically, the nation's capital stood more on a par with cities such as Cincinnati, Minneapolis, Newark, and New Orleans, none of which could boast of similar quarters.[22] The great concentration of wealth in Washington rendered Connecticut Avenue as an elegant commercial corridor much like Massachusetts Avenue was rendered a splendid residential corridor. Lining both streets was unusually impressive architecture that rivaled any designed for the elite in the largest of cities. Connecticut Avenue also differed from counterparts elsewhere in the United States because of its great width and the absence of tall buildings along most of its course. Visually, the assemblage imparted some of the qualities associated with nineteenth-century Parisian boulevards and was relatively atypical among American shopping streets.

Both the structure and function of earlier residential development affected Connecticut Avenue's character as a new commercial district. In general, new buildings possessed an intricate scale and details derived from historical domestic sources. Few ex-

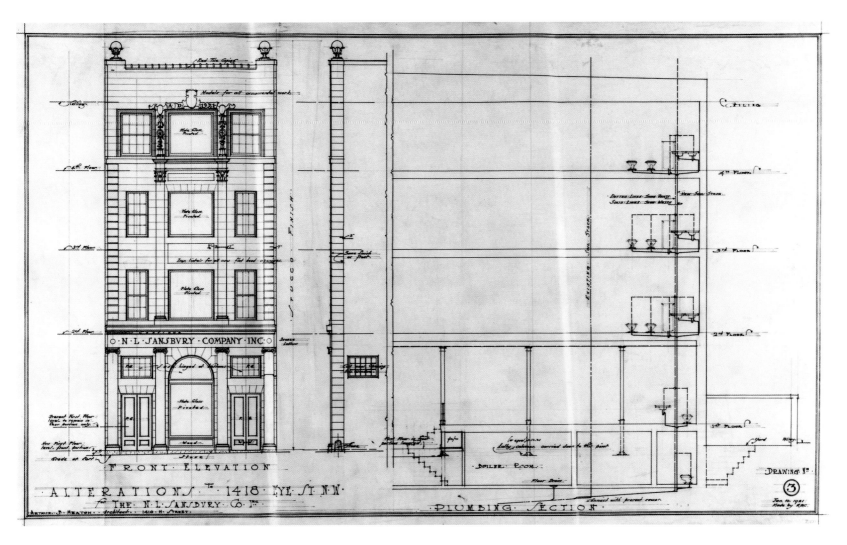

FRONT ELEVATION

ALTERATIONS to 1418 EYE ST. N.W.
for THE N. L. SANSBURY CO. INC.
ARTHUR B. HEATON Architect. 1410 H. STREET.

PLUMBING SECTION

DRAWING N°
③

amples could be confused with houses; yet, the general effect was far more suggestive of an idealized preindustrial city—genteel and urbane—than of the modern metropolis. A number of architects contributed to the distinctive qualities of the district. Heaton helped set the tone among real estate offices with his building for N. L. Sansbury Company of 1921 (FIG. 4.19).[23] But no architectural office came close to matching the involvement of Waggaman and Ray. The firm became the predominant architectural force in the area, not only by setting a high standard of design at the outset of the district's transformation but by the sheer number of buildings it created in the precinct. Waggaman's work began as early as

1913; after World War I, Ray prepared plans for more than two dozen new and remodeled buildings along Connecticut Avenue and worked on almost as many nearby.

Ray developed a readily identifiable style for his commercial buildings that lent much to the Connecticut Avenue corridor's distinction. His imprint was based in large part on consistency in compositional pattern, using a treatment that was at once additive and unifying, one that owed a debt to both English and French traditions but was essentially new to the period. Irrespective of whether the building had a narrow or wide frontage, a strong differentiation existed between its upper and lower zones. For

FIG. 4.19. Arthur B. Heaton, architect. E. Burton Corning, delineator. Alterations to an office building for N. L. Sansbury Co., Inc., 1418 I Street, N.W., Washington, D.C. Front elevation, plumbing section. Ink, wash, and graphite on linen. 1921. Building no longer standing. ADE-UNIT 912, no. 15, E size. LC-USZ62-116915.

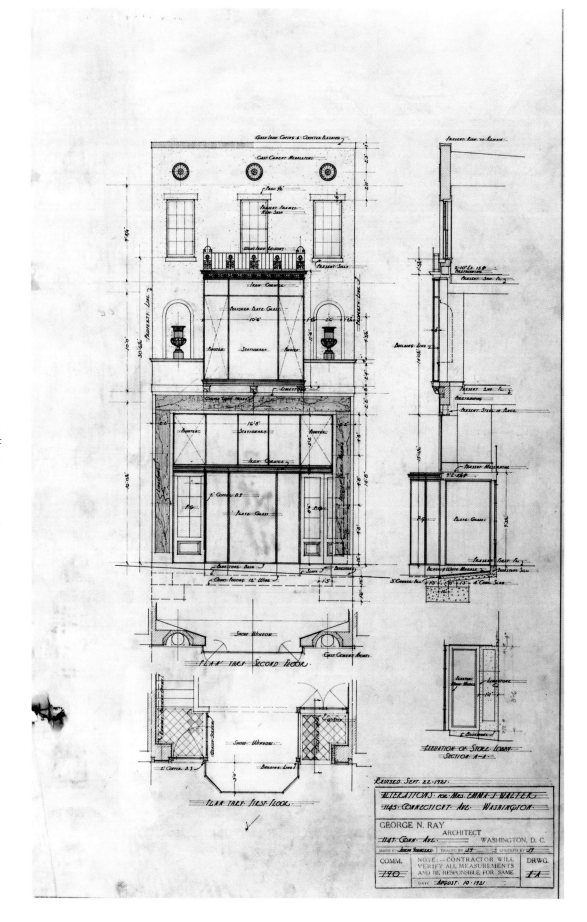

Fig. 4.20. George N. Ray, architect. Joseph Younger, delineator. Alterations to a store building for Emma J. Walter, 1145 Connecticut Avenue, N.W., Washington, D.C. Plans, elevation, section, and detail. Ink, graphite, and colored ink on linen. ADE-UNIT 246, no. 10, C size. LC-USZ62-133453.

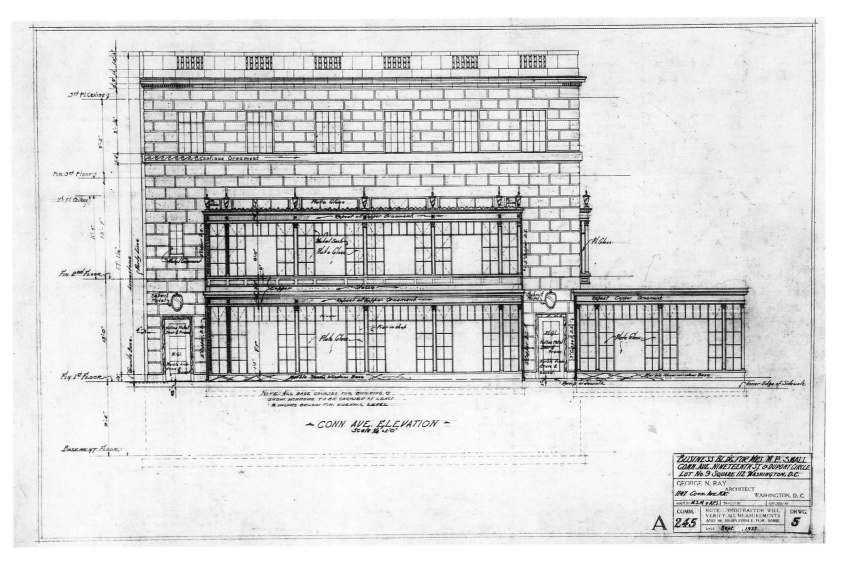

the lower zone, the emphasis was generally on a large-scale void (show windows, doors, etc.), while the upper zone's arrangement emphasized mass, with elements more residential in scale and in character. At the same time, unity was achieved by a pervasive sense of restraint, intricacy in detail, and harmonious use of materials.

Ray proved adept at varying this repertoire in a seemingly limitless number of ways. The palette was further enriched by a wide spectrum of historical allusions, drawing from grand urban dwellings in Italy, France, and England, which spanned from the late fifteenth to the early nineteenth centuries and

were interpreted in a suave, often lively, manner (FIGS. 4.20, 4.21, 4.22). Much of the distinction of this work lies with the fact that its effect suggests neither overly decorated neighborhood stores nor scaled-down versions of the large commercial blocks in the city center. Even when the dimensions involved were considerable, as with the headquarters of the B. F. Saul Company real estate firm, the character is much the same as with the small shops (ADE-UNIT 272, no. 14). In contrast, Heaton's twin quarters for Shannon & Luchs and the Wardman Construction Company (1925–1927) employs a composition identical to that of many tall buildings of the period (FIG. 4.23).[24]

FIG. 4.21. George N. Ray, architect. Store building ("business building") including a flower shop, for Mrs. M[iriam] E. Small, Connecticut Avenue and 19th Streets, N.W., Washington, D.C. Graphite on linen. 1923. ADE-UNIT 265, no. 13, E size. LC-USZ62-133462.

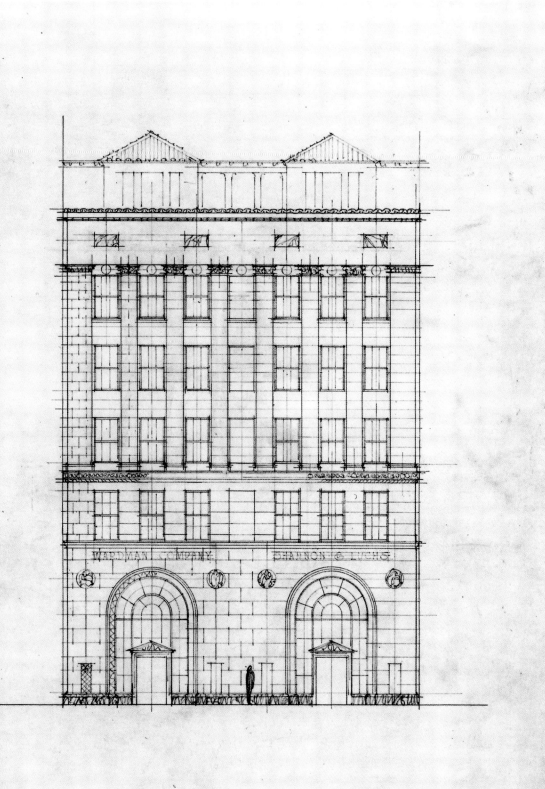

FIG. 4.22 (*opposite*). Waggaman & Ray, architects. "B. F. Saul Company," 15th Street, N.W., Washington, D.C. Perspective and sketch details. Graphite and colored pencil on tracing paper. 1923. ADE-UNIT 272, no. 23, C size. LC-USZ62-116918.

FIG. 4.23. Arthur B. Heaton, architect. Office buildings for Wardman Co. and Shannon & Luchs, 1435 and 1437 K Street, N.W., Washington, D.C. Elevation. Graphite on tracing paper. 1927. Building demolished mid-twentieth century. ADE-UNIT 911, no. 9, C size. LC-USZ62-133456.

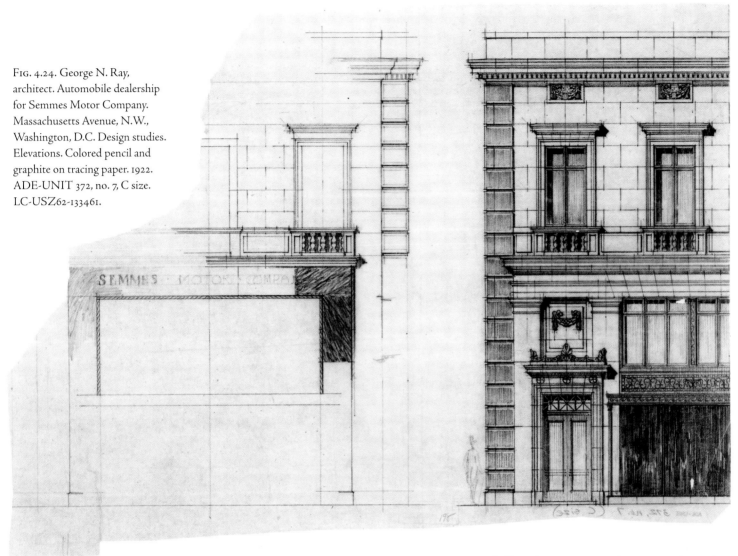

FIG. 4.24. George N. Ray, architect. Automobile dealership for Semmes Motor Company. Massachusetts Avenue, N.W., Washington, D.C. Design studies. Elevations. Colored pencil and graphite on tracing paper. 1922. ADE-UNIT 372, no. 7, C size. LC-USZ62-133461.

FIG. 4.25 (*opposite*). George N. Ray, architect. Store ("Business Building") for Mr. William E. Furey (originally for Trenholm Abrams), 1529 14th Street, N.W., Washington, D.C. Elevations. Graphite on linen. ADE-UNIT 120, no. 10, E size. LC-USZ62-133473.

Automobile Sales, Service, and Storage Facilities

At an early stage of its transformation, Connecticut Avenue began to host a new form of retail activity: automobile sales. Three dealerships were located there as early as 1910. A decade later, there were twenty-one—nearly one-third of those in the city—eighteen of them clustered in the 1000 to 1200 blocks of the avenue. Most of these buildings were small, their fronts indistinguishable from those of other stores nearby, as can be seen in Heaton's 1913 design for a Hudson dealership (ADE-UNIT 774, no. 1). After World War I, however, larger, more elaborate facilities became increasingly common. The automobile showroom emerged as a pretentious place, embellished to a degree paralleled only by a major bank-

ing hall or a large store specializing in costly goods.[25] George Ray's 1922–1923 design for the Semmes Motor Company, a Dodge dealership, indeed might be confused with a bank in both its appearance and prominent Dupont Circle location (FIG. 4.24).[26]

Connecticut Avenue was a logical setting for automobile showrooms because the elite comprised the main clientele of many dealers. Yet as the mass market for cars grew rapidly during the 1910s and especially the 1920s, less constricted sites became increasingly needed. The rise in demand for automobiles was matched by the demand for on-site service facilities; automobile dealers found sales were bolstered by the prospect of reliable maintenance and repair capacities and by having them conveniently located.[27] Dealerships thus remained close to the city center—where their patrons worked and shopped—but still apart from where land values were at their highest and from the areas where traffic congestion was the most intense. By the mid-1920s, numerous dealerships had constructed new buildings that combined sales and service on sites ringing the urban core. By far the greatest concentration of these lay north of Massachusetts Avenue along Fourteenth Street, then the primary route from many of the city's new middle-class residential districts to downtown. At the decade's end, thirty outlets were situated there (again a third of the metropolitan area's total); with the next highest concentrations on M Street, N.W. (twelve), and H Street, N.E. (nine).

The exterior treatment of large automobile dealerships posed a challenge because these buildings had to function as both ornate showplaces and utilitarian storage and repair plants. George Ray and Heaton, like many of their colleagues across the country, sought to attain a balance in their designs by employing classical compositions and some elaborate details but also elements such as large, steel-frame windows that bespoke the special nature of the facility. Ray's 1928 design for a Nash dealership on Fourteenth Street is among the more decorated of the era locally, yet is still clearly indicative of its genre (FIG. 4.25).

A similar equilibrium was sought for a related new building type, the multideck automobile parking garage. While predominantly utilitarian in purpose, these buildings were given an external sense of decorum commensurate with their great size and prominent sites in the city center. By the mid-1920s, the demand for parking space far exceeded the curbside area in downtown Washington and cities elsewhere coast to coast. Surface car lots could alleviate some pressure, but land values were still too high for such usage near the blocks where the need was greatest. To be an economically viable enterprise in the core area, off-street parking had to be undertaken on a grand scale, housed in buildings that could be as big as a major office block or department store. Heaton's Capital Garage supplied by far the largest example locally, and one of the most ambitious projects of its kind nationwide when it opened in 1926 on New York Avenue, a short distance from the Fifteenth Street

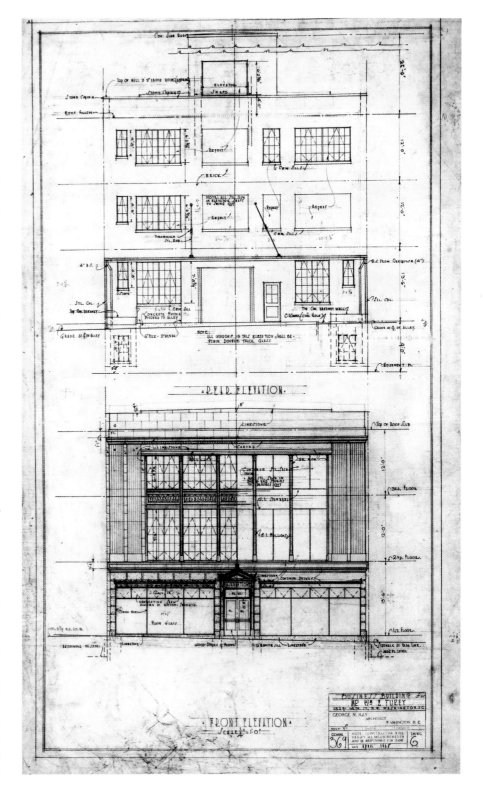

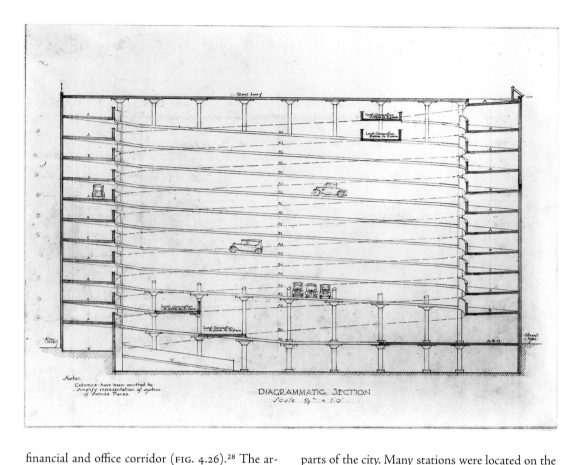

DIAGRAMMATIC SECTION
Scale 1/8" = 1'.0"

FIG. 4.26. Arthur B. Heaton, architect. "Capital Garage" for Capital Garage Co., 1312–1320, New York Avenue, N.W., Washington, D.C. Diagrammatic section. Graphite on tracing paper. Ca. 1926. Building demolished 1974. ADE-UNIT 1008, no. 11, E size. LC-USZ62-121277.

FIG. 4.27 (opposite). George N. Ray, architect. "Gasoline Service Station," for Randall H. Hagner, at Florida Avenue near Connecticut Avenue, N.W., Washington, D.C. Elevations, sections, and detail. Ink, colored ink, and graphite on linen. Unknown if building realized. ADE-UNIT 237, no. 3, D size. LC-USZ62-116869.

financial and office corridor (FIG. 4.26).[28] The architect in 1932 also made studies for at least one other giant facility to have been situated near numerous retail outlets. Heaton's elevation sketches for this latter scheme reveal the attention paid to creating an exterior at once dignified and purposeful (PLATE 4.4). Other drawings also underscore the complex nature of a program that required maximum efficiency in both the movement and storage of unwieldy vehicles (ADE-UNIT 1008, no. 6; LC-USZ62-116907).[29]

During the interwar decades, the other most conspicuous type of facility devised to serve the automobile was the gasoline station. Buildings designed specifically for the sale of petroleum and motor oil were virtually unknown in 1910 but proliferated in the years that followed. By 1930, some 250 of these outlets, a growing number of which also provided related services to the motorist, were operating in the District of Columbia. Examples could be found in virtually all parts of the city. Many stations were located on the periphery of the business district, many others could be found along major arteries where zoning permitted commercial uses, and some were sequestered on residential blocks. The ubiquitousness of these facilities, combined with their inherently utilitarian function, stoked fears of urban blight.[30] Major petroleum companies and independent dealers responded by having new outlets designed that would make respectable neighbors. George Ray's 1920 scheme for a filling station on Florida Avenue, a short distance from Connecticut Avenue, is a good illustration of the tendency at an early stage (FIG. 4.27).[31]

The degree to which some owners pursued making the gasoline station a public ornament is evident in several plans prepared by Arthur Heaton during the early 1930s. Probably no project in Washington and few elsewhere were as elaborate as the studies made for an American Oil Company station at Louisiana and Constitution avenues. Facing the

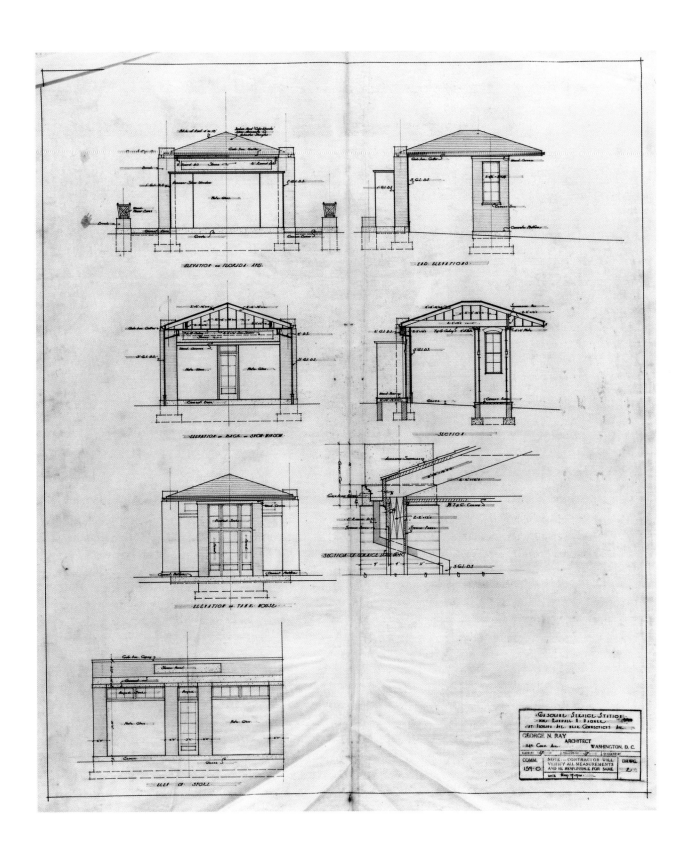

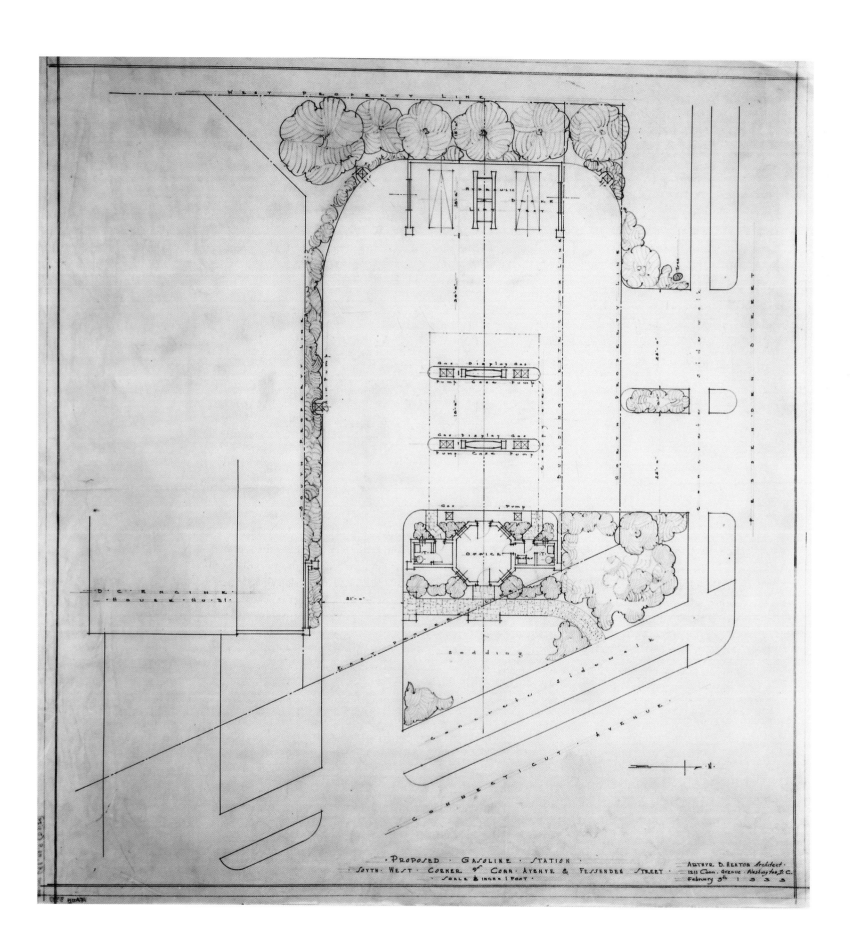

· PROPOSED · GASOLINE · STATION ·
SOUTH WEST CORNER OF CONN. AVENUE & FESSENDEN STREET ·
SCALE ⅛ INCH = 1 FOOT ·

ARTHUR B. HEATON Architect ·
1211 Conn. Avenue Washington D.C.
February 5th 1 9 3 3

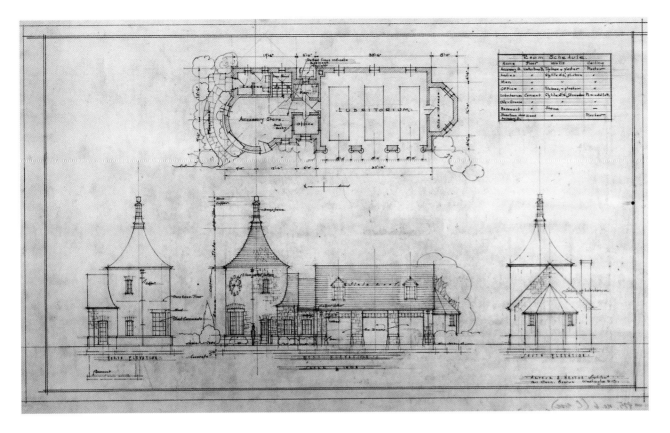

FIG. 4.28. Arthur B. Heaton, architect. American Oil Company (AMOCO) automobile service station, Massachusetts and Wisconsin Avenues, N.W., Washington, D.C. Plan and elevations. Graphite on tracing paper. 1934. Project. ADE-UNIT 975, no. 6, C size. LC-USZ62-116854.

Capitol grounds, the design at this stage suggested a memorial or a small museum more than its actual purpose (PLATE 4.5).[32] Studies in 1934 of an unbuilt station at Massachusetts and Wisconsin avenues allude to the vernacular-inspired houses found in the best residential tracts to which those arteries led (ADE-UNIT 1511, ADE-UNIT 975; FIG. 4.28). Another scheme prepared the previous year was located amid the sylvan neighborhoods along upper Connecticut Avenue and was ingeniously laid out to minimize the visual affect of its considerable extent. Here the service area was surrounded by landscaping and lay to the rear of an office kiosk inspired by the cupola of the reconstructed Governor's Palace at Williamsburg (FIG. 4.29).

Retail Facilities in Outlying Areas

The gasoline station was only one indicator of how routine automobile use fundamentally affected siting and configuring commercial development during the interwar decades. In 1910 few concentrated business districts lay outside downtown Washington. The

oldest such district was, of course, along M Street and Wisconsin Avenue in Georgetown. Others of vintage lay along Pennsylvania Avenue and Eighth Street, S.E., on Capitol Hill, and along Fourth-and-a-half and Seventh Streets, servicing the southwest quadrant. Around the turn of the twentieth century, business nodes began to develop along H Street east of Fourth Street, N.E., serving the new residential sections in that quadrant and at Eighteenth Street and Columbia Road, Fourteenth and U Streets, and Fourteenth Street and Park Road, near affluent neighborhoods of the northwest quadrant.[33] In their arrangement, appearance, and function, these quarters were of a traditional kind, resembling the centers of sizable towns. Like towns, they provided basic goods and services to the people living around them; the choices available, in quantitative terms and often in qualitative ones as well, were more limited than those downtown.

During the 1920s, the role of some outlying business centers in large American cities began to shift, with the development of a much greater range of facilities. For a growing number of goods and services,

FIG. 4.29 (opposite). Arthur B. Heaton, architect. "Sun Oil Co. Gas Station" for Hanse Hamilton, Connecticut Avenue and Fessenden Street, N.W., Washington, D.C. Site plan. Graphite and colored pencil on trace. 1933. Project. ADE-UNIT 658, no. 5, D size. LC-USZ62-133463.

FIG. 4.30. George N. Ray,
architect. Riggs National Bank
Building. 14th Street and
Park Road, N.W., Washington,
D.C. Design study. Perspective.
Photographic print. 1922.
ADE-UNIT 161, no. 34 (Photo).
LC-USZ62-114097.

these districts became ever more competitive with the urban core, in effect functioning as downtowns in miniature. The primary instance of this phenomenon in Washington was the business center at Fourteenth Street and Park Road. The change began as early as 1909, with the conversion of a trolley barn into the immense Arcade Market. With some forty concessions, the enterprise offered the greatest variety of food products found outside the city center. Above rose a huge auditorium for sporting events ("the Madison Square Garden of Washington") and other entertainment facilities. By 1916 nearly one hundred businesses could be found on blocks nearby. That number increased by more than 50 percent during the

next fourteen years, but the most significant change entailed the addition of large chain stores, more specialty shops, and other ventures that would attract patrons from a considerable distance. In 1924, the Tivoli Theater opened as the largest movie house (two thousand five hundred seats) outside downtown and one of the most palatial in the city.[34] Concurrently, work was under way across the street on a branch of the Riggs National Bank and an attached office building for the Charles H. Tompkins Construction Company, both designed by George Ray (FIG. 4.30).[35] With nearly twenty stores and two floors of office space as well as the banking hall, the building was similarly the most ambitious of its kind outside

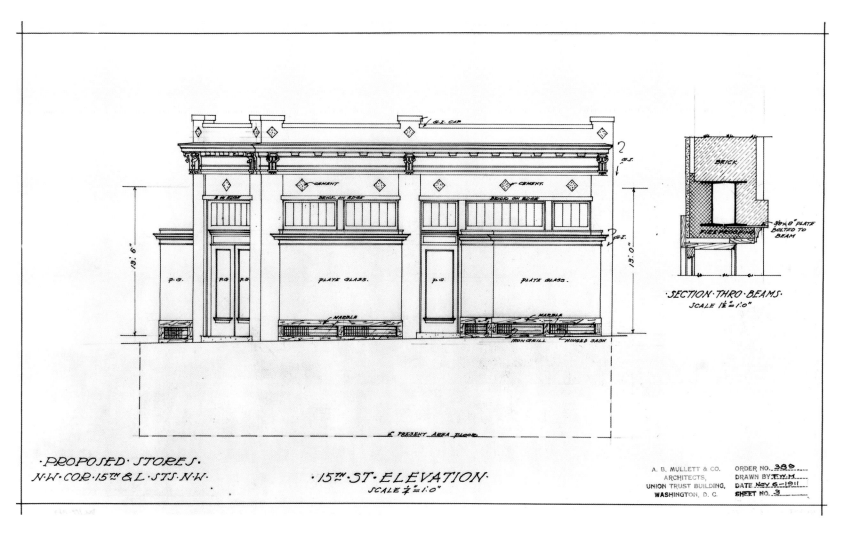

·PROPOSED·STORES·
N·W·COR·15TH·&·L·STS·N·W·

·15TH·ST·ELEVATION·
SCALE ⅛"=1'·0"

·SECTION·THRO·BEAMS·
SCALE 1½"=1'·0"

A. B. MULLETT & CO.
ARCHITECTS,
UNION TRUST BUILDING,
WASHINGTON, D. C.

ORDER NO. 388
DRAWN BY T.W.M
DATE Nov 6-1911
SHEET NO. 3

the city center. In both image and scale, its grand exterior elevations were of a kind previously unknown in outlying areas and aptly symbolized the rise of this new district as a prominent business center.

At the time of its completion in 1922, the Riggs-Tompkins complex presented a strong contrast to the norm for commercial development in outlying areas. Whether located in business nodes or in scattered sites serving just the immediate environs, most buildings represented a modest investment. The taxpayer block, so-called because it could defray landholding costs until the market for a more ambitious undertaking arose, became one of the most ubiquitous types in outlying areas of Washington af-

ter 1900. In general, of no more than a single story and containing from two to eight store units, examples were said to number in the hundreds by the early 1910s.[36] The Mullett office's 1911 scheme for a two-unit edifice at Fifteenth and L Streets, then still a residential area, is a good representative of the type, its exterior comprising mostly openings punctuated by a few, stock decorative details (FIG. 4.31). Advocates of the City Beautiful Movement tended to hold the taxpayer block in disdain, branding it a generator of blight on new neighborhoods and on established ones as well. Early on, some efforts were made to have taxpayers that were more respectful of their environs, with decorous building fronts, such

FIG. 4.31. A. B. Mullett & Co., architects. "Proposed Stores," 15th and L Streets, N.W., Washington, D.C. Elevation and section. Ink and colored ink on tracing paper. 1911. Unknown if building realized. ADE-UNIT 16, no. 3, C size. LC-USZ62-114100.

FIG. 4.32. Arthur B. Heaton, architect. J. A. Parks, delineator. Chevy Chase Savings Bank, Connecticut Avenue and Morrison Street, N.W., Washington, D.C. Perspective. Photostat. 1926. ADE-Unit 653, no. 51, A size. LC-USZ62-133450.

as that designed in 1920 by George Ray for Florida Avenue (ADE-UNIT 236, no. 1).

By the mid-1920s, upgrading the design of commercial establishments in outlying areas became a distinct priority in a number of cities.[37] The change was spurred perhaps more by increasing competition than a concern for visual harmony. Not only was the market rapidly swelling, which induced more and more businesses to locate in such areas, but routine automobile use meant that consumers were no longer tied to stores in their own immediate neighborhood. One could now drive with considerable ease to adjacent areas if the businesses there were preferred. In an effort to secure the local trade and sometimes to attract customers from other precincts, companies could make considerable investments in their buildings, which was the case with the 1926 Chevy

Chase Savings Bank, designed by Heaton and located on Connecticut Avenue near the District line (FIG. 4.32). Even small enterprises might assume a degree of embellishment unthinkable a generation previous. Heaton's circa 1936 studies for the Blue Bell Restaurant, a fast-food outlet at D Street and Pennsylvania Avenue, N.W., indicate the attention that could be lavished on creating a favorable impression (PLATE 4.6).

Heaton also developed many innovative solutions in response to other changes rendered by widespread automobile use. As early as 1926, he drew preliminary plans for a multiuse complex in Bethesda, a bedroom community just beyond the District in Montgomery County, Maryland (FIGS. 4.33, 4.34). While approaching the size of the Riggs-Tompkins buildings at Fourteenth and Park, this facility would have

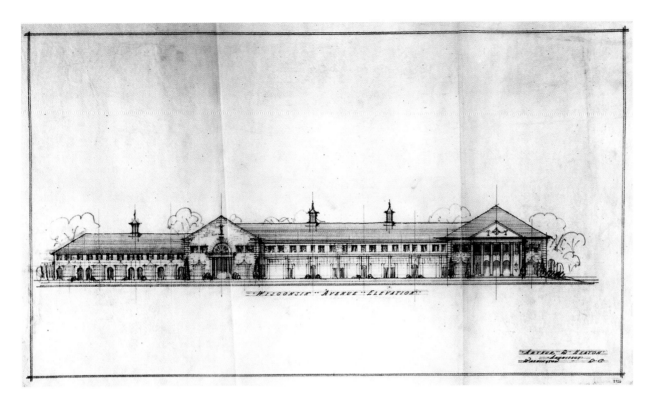

FIG. 4.33. Arthur B. Heaton, architect. Commercial building ("Sacks Theater Group") for George P. Sacks, Wisconsin Avenue and Leland Street, Bethesda, Maryland. Graphite on tracing paper. 1927. Project. ADE-UNIT 1026, no. 11, D size. LC-USZ62-133470.

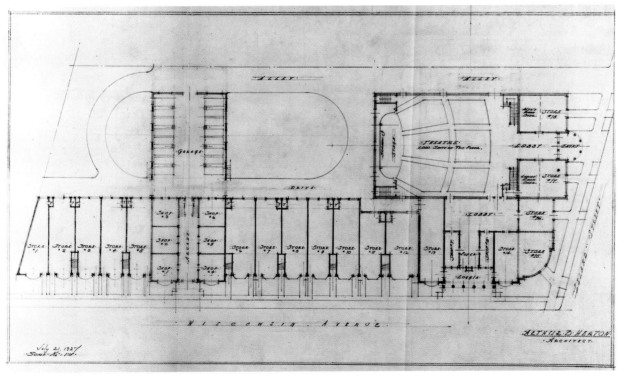

FIG. 4.34. Arthur B. Heaton, architect. Commercial building ("Sacks Theater Group") for George P. Sacks, Wisconsin Avenue and Leland Street, Bethesda, Maryland. Site and ground-floor plan. Graphite on tracing paper. 1927. Project ADE-UNIT 1026, no. 9, D size. LC-USZ62-116872.

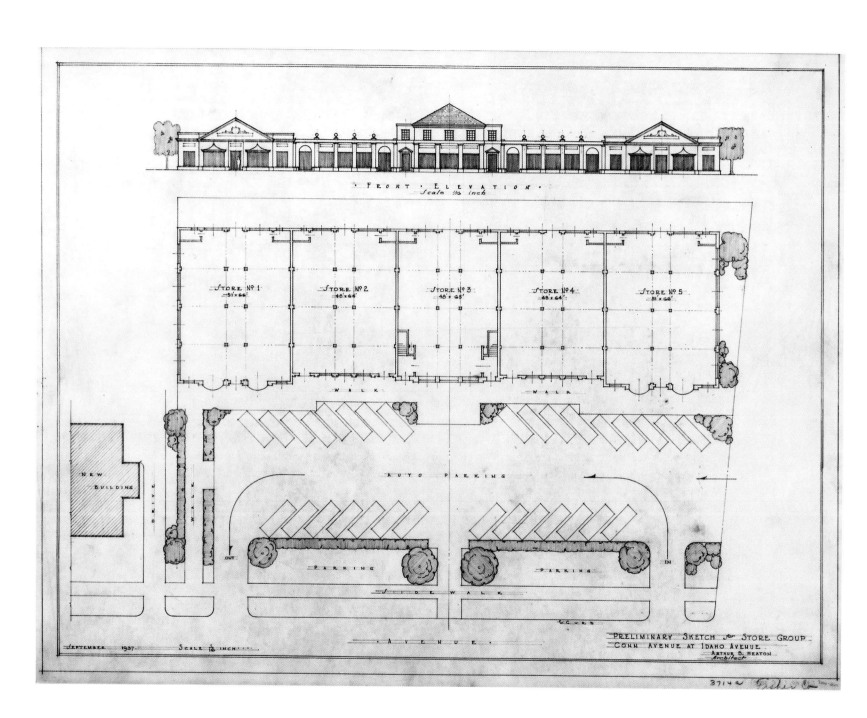

· FRONT · ELEVATION ·
Scale ¼ inch

STORE Nº 1
51'×66'

STORE Nº 2
48'×64'

STORE Nº 3
48'×65'

STORE Nº 4
48'×64'

STORE Nº 5
51'×66'

WALK

WALK

NEW
BUILDING

DRIVE

WALK

AUTO PARKING

OUT

PARKING

PARKING

IN

SIDEWALK

CURB

AVENUE

SEPTEMBER 1937   SCALE ½ INCH

PRELIMINARY SKETCH for STORE GROUP
CONN AVENUE AT IDAHO AVENUE
ARTHUR B. HEATON
Architect

stood well removed from any concentrated business development. The closest commercial facilities consisted of only a few modest buildings nearby on Wisconsin Avenue. With twenty-four stores and a one thousand–seat movie theater, Heaton's building would have become an important destination in itself, possessing sufficient critical mass to attract patronage from a number of the residential subdivisions for the well-to-do and middle class that lay all around. The fact that it was not in an area already built up, yet could be conveniently reached by arteries extending in several directions, would have been considered an advantage among motorists who wished to avoid congestion while shopping. The scheme further departed from conventional practices of previous decades in its use of imagery derived from domestic sources. Despite its size, the project was clearly intended to be compatible with the new neighborhoods of single-family houses that dominated the environs, carrying no vestiges of the urban character that typified large commercial enterprises of the period.

Four years later, Heaton realized what would become a major contribution to retail development in outlying areas with his design for the Park and Shop (ADE-UNIT 896, no. 1).[38] Located in the Cleveland Park neighborhood along what had become a primary automobile commuter route into the city, the complex was the first of its kind in the nation to synthesize the concept of the neighborhood shopping center (a facility purveying a balanced mix of basic goods and services and managed as an integrated business development) with the drive-in concept (a building and site arrangement organized around off-street parking space for customers). Heaton also proved adept at simplifying and abstracting traditional imagery so that the complex, wrapped around a large forecourt, could cast a memorable impression for the motorist at a fleeting glance. After the worst years of the Depression, the Park and Shop became a paradigm for shopping center development both locally and in many other parts of the country as well.[39]

During the next decade, Heaton made studies for a number of other pacesetting drive-in facilities, none of which advanced beyond the preliminary stage. Among them was a shopping center for Charles Glover, which probably would have been located on part of his extensive holdings near Glover Archbold Park (PLATE 4.7). The complex was as large as any of its type in the United States before World War II and suggests it was intended as the principal retail outlet serving the many blocks of row houses and garden apartments that had developed north of Georgetown over the previous decade. Both the configuration and imagery also bespeak a village center, updated for the automobile age, more than a facility oriented to the fast-moving traffic of the boulevard.

In a 1937 scheme for a shopping complex located north of Cleveland Park, Heaton experimented in yet a different vein (FIG. 4.35). Given its elaborate facade, the small number of stores, and the unusually sizable dimensions of each unit, this project may well have been conceived as a fashion center, a place oriented to the sale of stylish clothing, accessories, and other specialty goods. If such was the case, the concept was an unorthodox one at that time. In Washington and most other cities, few outlets existed beyond the urban core where one could purchase the high-end wares purveyed by leading retailers. The move to create branch locations for downtown emporia had gained some momentum by the late 1920s in the largest metropolitan areas such as New York and Philadelphia; yet, even these branches were seldom grouped in a coordinated development. The pattern had scarcely changed a decade later, as indicated by the creation of several branch facilities, each as an independent project, near the site of Heaton's scheme.[40] Only in the 1950s, with the advent of the regional shopping center as a driving force in commercial development, did major retailers begin regularly to join forces in a project.

In the meantime, department stores became the leading agents in the expansion of goods available outside the city center. The first local example was the branch of Garfinckel's, which opened in 1942 on Massachusetts Avenue, a few blocks from the District line (FIG. 4.36).[41] The site was owned by the W. C. & A. N. Miller Company, which had developed nearby Spring Valley as one of the region's most prestigious residential enclaves and now sought to create shopping facilities of a commensurate kind that would draw

FIG. 4.35. Arthur P. Heaton, architect. "Store Group." Shopping center and parking lot for Thos. J. Fisher & Co., Connecticut Avenue at Idaho Avenue, N.W., Washington, D.C. 1937. Site and floor plans; front elevation. Project. ADE-UNIT 693, no. 1, C size. LC-USZ62-133446.

FIG. 4.36. W. C. and A. N. Miller, developers and designers. Department store ("Spring Valley Store") for Julius Garfinckel & Co., Massachusetts Avenue and Fordham Road, N.W., Washington, D.C. Perspective rendering. Photographic print. 1942. Building altered. ADE-UNIT 2419, no. 1 (Photo). LC-USZ62-116827.

customers from many parts of the metropolitan area's affluent northwest sector. With nothing save a few neighborhood-oriented shopping facilities nearby and a large off-street parking area to one side, lacking the crowds and congested streets endemic to downtown, the location seemed more rural than urban.

Postwar Development

After World War II, commercial development began to diffuse at a very rapid rate. Before that time, most facilities in outlying areas still were limited in the array of goods and services they purveyed. With a downtown that remained the overwhelmingly dominant force in business activities of most kinds, Washington ranked among the most centralized U.S. cities in 1940. A decade later, the situation was changing dramatically. Most new residential development now occurred outside the District. By 1950, 46 percent of people residing in the metropolitan area lived in Maryland or Virginia jurisdictions; in 1960, that portion had grown to 62 percent. Between 1939 and 1954, the percentage of the metropolitan area's retail activity in the District dropped from more than

eighty-three to fifty-nine, declining further to forty-four by 1963.[42]

The growth of outlying commercial districts during the postwar years was not only marked by a great increase in the number of stores but also in their size and variety. Designs by the firm of E. Burton Corning and Raymond G. Moore, by Luther Ray, and by Donald Drayer afford a valuable sampling of the broad scope of commercial development that occurred between the mid-1940s and mid-1960s. Both Corning and Moore had worked for Heaton and seemed to have inherited his interest in responding to the demands of the decentralizing metropolis. After the war, their practice became one of the most prolific in the local commercial sphere. As much as any other firm, Corning and Moore helped to define the nature of the new retail development. Luther Ray's practice was smaller and more limited in scope. From the late 1930s to the 1960s, much of his work entailed the application of metal veneers on both remodeled and new commercial buildings.

Ray's business, the Structural Porcelain Enamel Company, served as the local outlet for two manufacturers of porcelain enamel steel panels in the

FIG. 4.37. Donald Hudson Drayer, architect. "Store Building, Appliances by Sheff," Washington Boulevard and North Highland Street, Clarendon, Virginia. Perspective rendering. Charcoal on tracing paper. 1945. ADE-UNIT 1607, no. 1, B size. LC-USZ62-113982.

Midwest and was one of many outside the architectural profession in the United States to give character to the commercial landscape. However, Drayer was an architect with a general practice; commercial buildings formed a relatively minor part of his output. Many of the schemes he developed in this vein were not executed, and almost all of them, like Ray's, were of a modest sort. The surviving documents from both these offices provide a now rare view of a genre that was once ubiquitous, which received almost no publicity when it was new, and often no longer exists, at least in recognizable form.

Although little significant retail growth occurred after World War II in established business districts of Washington, modernization of the existing fabric was extensive. The longstanding practice of store remodeling gained fresh impetus during the Depression in a drive to compete for scarce dollars. A second objective, which dominated the 1940s, was to stem the erosion of trade to new commercial developments. Many of Luther Ray's commissions were generated by this phenomenon and were located not in the city center but in neighborhood precincts, perhaps no more than two decades old, which were likewise feel-

ing the effects of a shifting population (PLATE 4.8).

Some of the most intense competition for trade during the immediate postwar years came from large, new retail centers that could satisfy many shoppers' needs much of the time. Locally, the principal upstarts in this realm were Silver Spring in Montgomery County, Maryland, and Clarendon in Arlington County, Virginia. Both were basically traditional in structure: unplanned, accretive, and oriented to a major artery and one or more intersecting streets.[43] By the early 1950s, both also included a substantial amount of office space and a galaxy of retail enterprises. However, Silver Spring and Clarendon differed from predecessors of the 1920s, such as that at Fourteenth and Park, in that they had large department and variety stores (Hecht's, Sears, Penney's, Murphy's) and, at the same time, were less densely developed. Ever growing, though never sufficient, amounts of peripheral land were devoted to car lots, and many buildings rose no higher than a single story (ADE-UNIT 2145). Often land prices were low enough to allow a medium-sized store, such as the appliance sales facility Drayer designed for Clarendon, to spread on one level over a considerable amount of ground space (FIG. 4.37).[44]

WASHINGTON & LEE SHOPPING CENTER
ARLINGTON, VIRGINIA
E BURTON CORNING & RAYMOND G. MOORE
ARCHITECTS
© CORNING & MOORE, ARCHITECTS

FIG. 4.38. E. Burton Corning & Raymond G. Moore, architects. "Washington & Lee Shopping Center," Arlington, Virginia. Bird's-eye perspective rendering. Building demolished. Photostat. Ca. 1946. ADE-UNIT 2150, no. 1 (A size). LC-USZ62-116831.

Concurrently, the neighborhood shopping center became a ubiquitous fixture in new outlying areas.[45] Although shopping centers were still oriented to a geographically narrow trade, they now tended to include larger stores, such as the supermarket, and often more store units as well. Both the increase in size and a persistent uncertainty among some merchants about having their stores separated from the street by a forecourt led to deviations from the Park and Shop model. Off-street parking was now considered an essential feature for any planned retail complex; however, the location of optimal parking spaces was subject to widespread debate. Corning and Moore's Washington & Lee Shopping Center (1945), just off U.S. Route 50 in Arlington, is a good example of the experiments that were attempted (FIG. 4.38). Here a side street separated the building from the car lot so that motorists could pass at least a few shop fronts before parking.

Sketches prepared by Drayer in 1947 for another shopping center in Arlington County indicate the variety of layouts that might be studied at the beginning of the design process (FIGS. 4.39, 4.40). Site configuration was not only a crucial matter to resolve in itself but affected the size of the building and the number of cars that could be accommodated. A sec-

ond plan for the same property, designed ten years later, reflects the general resurgence of the forecourt configuration as the dominant design and also a marked proportional increase in the amount of space devoted to cars (FIG. 4.41). During the immediate postwar years a lot capacity of one hundred automobiles may have seemed large for a complex of ten or twelve stores, but by the mid-1950s, developers had learned from experience such estimates fell way below peak shopping-period demands. Drayer's new layout includes room for more than three times the number of automobiles provided in the earlier designs; yet, it still falls below what had by then become the standard: ten car spaces for every one thousand square feet of gross building area.[46]

Some experimentation also occurred in tenant structure. A major objective of any shopping center's program was to have a balanced mix of stores, with the presence of each reinforcing those of the others. The mix was hierarchical; one or two anchor tenants provided much of the customer draw for the rest. In the neighborhood shopping center, the anchors were usually a market and sometimes a large drug store. Variety stores or junior department stores served the same purpose in the bigger "community" shopping centers that began to be built in the 1940s. A major department

CAPITAL DRAWINGS

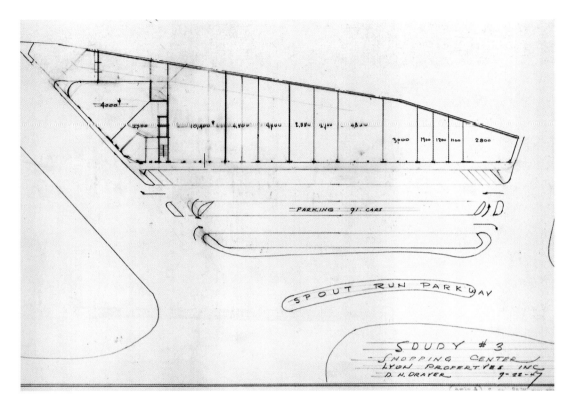

FIG. 4.39. Donald Hudson Drayer, architect. "Study #3, Shopping Center," Lee Highway and Spout Run Parkway, Arlington County, Virginia. Site and floor plans. Project. Graphite on tracing paper. 1947. ADE-UNIT 1598, no. 2, A size. LC-USZ62-114067.

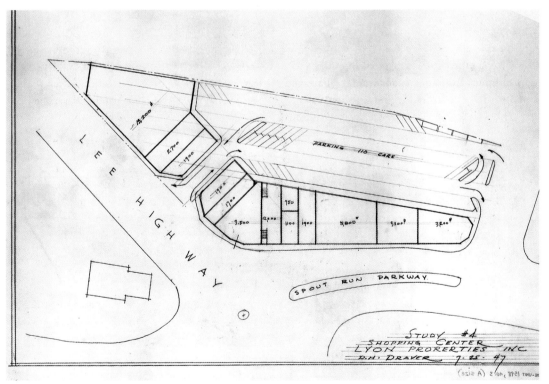

FIG. 4.40. Donald Hudson Drayer, architect. "Study # 4, Shopping Center," Lee Highway and Spout Run Parkway, Arlington County, Virginia. Site and floor plans. Graphite on tracing paper. 1947. Project. ADE-UNIT 1598, no. 3, A size. LC-USZ62-114068.

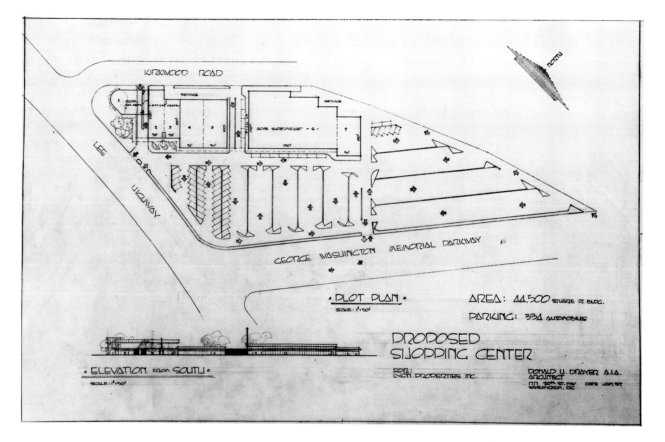

FIG. 4.41. Donald Hudson Drayer, architect. "Proposed Shopping Center for Lyon Properties, Inc.," Lee Highway and George Washington Memorial Parkway (i.e., Spout Run Parkway), Arlington, Virginia. Plot and floor plan; elevation from the south. Graphite on tracing paper. 1957. Project. ADE-UNIT 1597, no. 1, D size. LC-USZ62-133479.

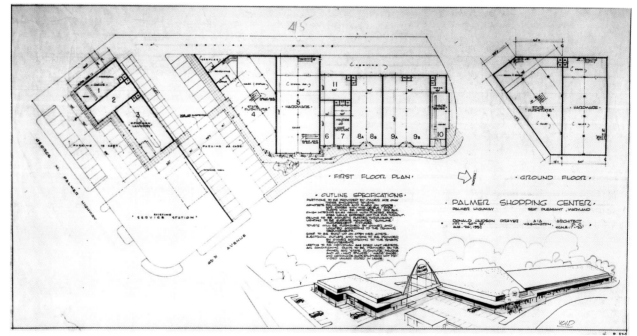

FIG. 4.42. Donald Hudson Drayer, architect. "Palmer Shopping Center," Palmer Highway and 65th Avenue, Seat Pleasant, Maryland. Bird's-eye perspective, floor plans, and outline specifications. Graphite and colored pencil on tracing paper. 1957. Project. ADE-UNIT 1646, no. 4, E size. LC-USZ62-133483.

store branch provided the essential focus for the huge regional centers.[47] At the same time, some developers pursued a less conventional mold, creating, for example, a complex where numerous small shops, rather than a few large stores, were the primary attraction. Another approach is evident in Drayer's 1957 scheme for the Palmer Shopping Center in Prince George's County, Maryland, where major furniture and hardware outlets were primary tenants, while the remainder provided standard basic goods and services for a complex of this size (FIG. 4.42).

The design of larger shopping centers was even more varied since few appropriate models existed for integrated retail development on that scale.[48] Even as Silver Spring and Clarendon were emerging as major commercial nodes for the metropolitan area, some developers pursued alternative strategies further afield that would prove more convenient to motorists, more efficient as business operations, and more coherent and unified trading centers. Among the schemes proposed for the Washington area, few got beyond the preliminary stage before the mid-1950s.[49] Nevertheless, these early large-scale designs document the struggle to conceive a large commercial district as a single entity, while not resorting to conventional arrangements by then considered obsolete. Corning and Moore's 1947 project for the community shopping center at Annandale in Fairfax County, Virginia, is both a good example of this nascent phase and of the pace of postwar growth into what had previously been a rural area eight miles west of Washington (FIG. 4.43).[50]

FIG. 4.43. E. Burton Corning & Raymond G. Moore, architects. "Annandale Business Center for Robertson Development Co.," Annandale, Fairfax County, Virginia. Bird's-eye and ground-level perspective renderings. Photographic print. Ca. 1947. Project. ADE-UNIT 2159, no. 1 (Photo). LC-USZ62-113950.

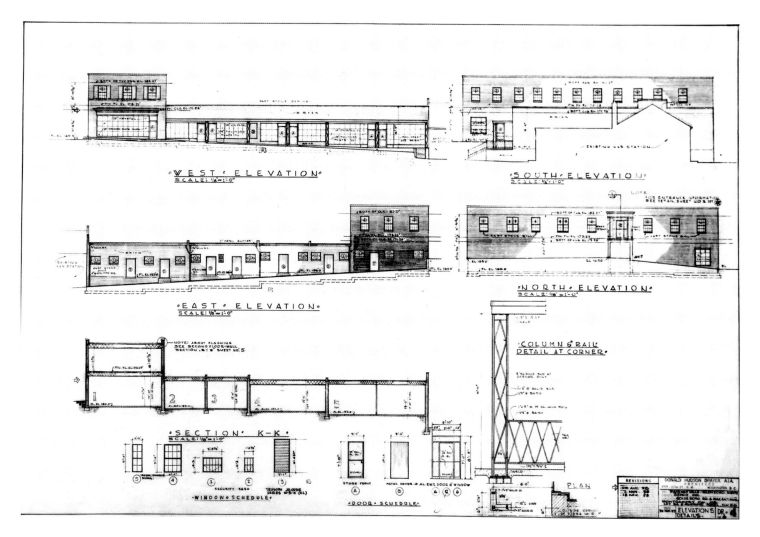

FIG. 4.44. Donald Hudson Drayer, architect. Fairway Hills–Glen Echo Shops for Benco Inc. MacArthur Boulevard and Goldsboro Road, Glen Echo, Montgomery County, Maryland. Elevations, section, and details. Graphite on paper. 1958. Building altered 1990–91. ADE-UNIT 1180, no. 4, D size. LC-USZ62-133475.

Despite the creation of ever-larger planned retail developments, many projects undertaken during the postwar years were far more modest in scope. Some, such as the five-unit complex Drayer designed in 1957–1958 for the Glen Echo section of Montgomery County, were isolated from established retail activity and fulfilled part of the shopping center's functions even if they were too small to be so classified (FIG. 4.44). In many other cases, the project entailed a single building, such as a bank, with perhaps one or two tangent stores, to use the lot more fully, as a component of an accretive and uncoordinated arterial development (FIG. 4.45). Both the scale of and the fast-moving traffic along major commercial strips being

developed during the 1950s made off-street parking virtually essential for each establishment, however modest the operation. The drive-in concept was increasingly used under these circumstances, particularly when the building itself occupied only a small portion of the property. Drayer's additions to the Blue Ribbon Laundry in Arlington well illustrate the tendency to create a minimal shelter and a freestanding object that would stand out among the cars around it and catch the eye of the passing motorist (FIG. 4.46). Even small enterprises, such as the Little Tavern restaurants, which traditionally were sited on vestigial intown lots and oriented entirely to a pedestrian trade, began to include off-street parking spaces with units

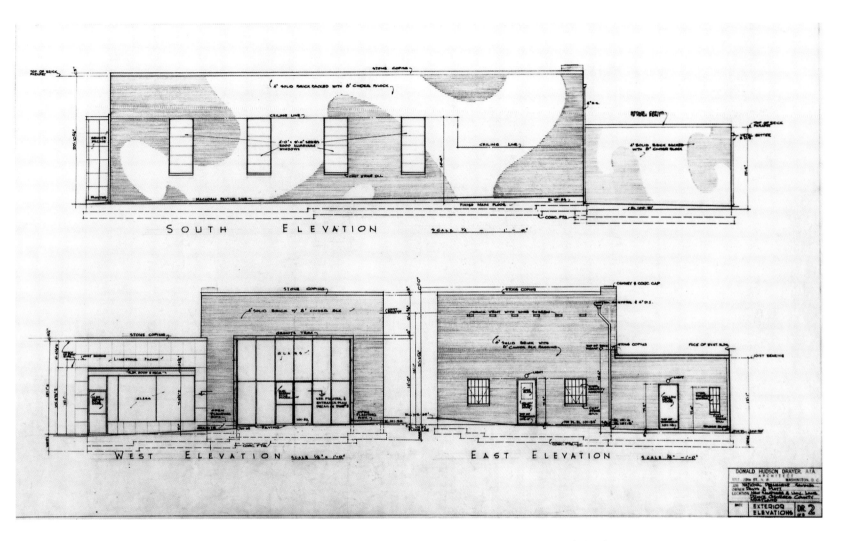

SOUTH ELEVATION

WEST ELEVATION

EAST ELEVATION

located in new outlying areas (ADE-UNIT 1270).

By the 1960s, the shifts in population and retail activity to places well removed from the city center were generating a significant demand for office building construction on the urban fringe. Office facilities in earlier outlying business centers such as Silver Spring were at first primarily oriented to professional services, such as medicine, that had long been tied to shopping areas downtown. This relationship continued with new development in subsequent years, as can be seen in a 1971 study by Drayer for an office-tower addition to a regional shopping mall in Laurel, Maryland.

As early as the 1920s, the idea of isolating a large office building from any form of concentrated business development had been inaugurated elsewhere in the United States by insurance companies for use as their main or regional offices. However, erecting such a complex as a speculative venture was new to the mid-twentieth century and did not become a standard practice locally until the late 1960s. Drayer's 1970 proposal for such a venture embodies the salient characteristics of the type: separation from existing thoroughfares; enormous amounts of space devoted to parking, most of it underground; mid-rise buildings set amid landscaped surroundings; expansive paved areas employed to unify the ensemble; and the absence of other functions, save perhaps a restaurant or newsstand for employees (FIG. 4.47;

FIG. 4.45. Donald Hudson Drayer, architect. Bank building ("National Permanent Savings") for Davis & Platt and Gude & Abrahams, New Hampshire Avenue and University Lane (now Boulevard), Langley Park, Prince George's County, Maryland. Elevations. Graphite on tracing paper. 1959. ADE-UNIT 1391, no. 3, E size. LC-USZ62-133482.

FIG. 4.46. Donald Hudson Drayer, architect. Addition to a cleaning establishment ("Blue Ribbon Laundry Cleaning") for Lyon Incorporated, Lee Highway and Irving Street, Lyon Village, Arlington, Virginia. Building no longer standing. Plot and floor plans, elevations, section, and details. Graphite on tracing paper. 1954. ADE-UNIT 1635, no. 1, E size. LC-USZ62-1126873.

FIG. 4.47 (*opposite*). Donald Hudson Drayer, architect. "Proposed Development of Van Dorn Property for the Commonwealth Management Corporation," Oakwood Road and Van Dorn Street South, Alexandria, Virginia. Elevations. Graphite on tracing paper. 1970. Project. ADE-UNIT 1372, no. 5, E size. LC-USZ62-133466.

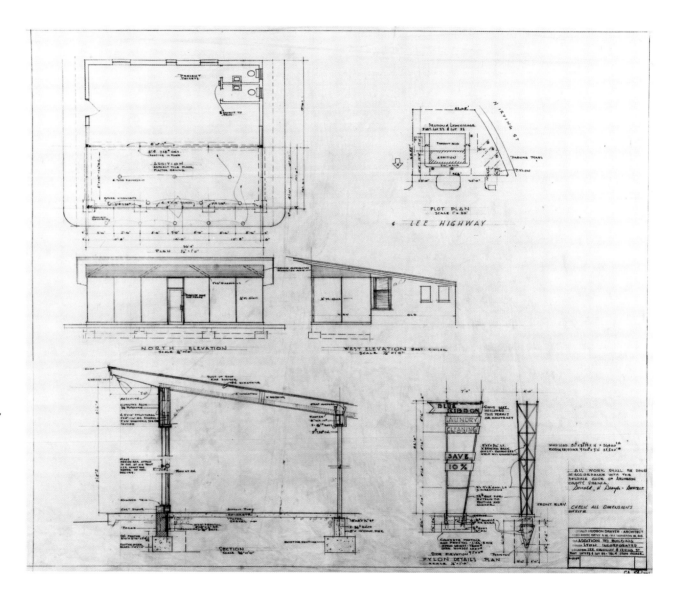

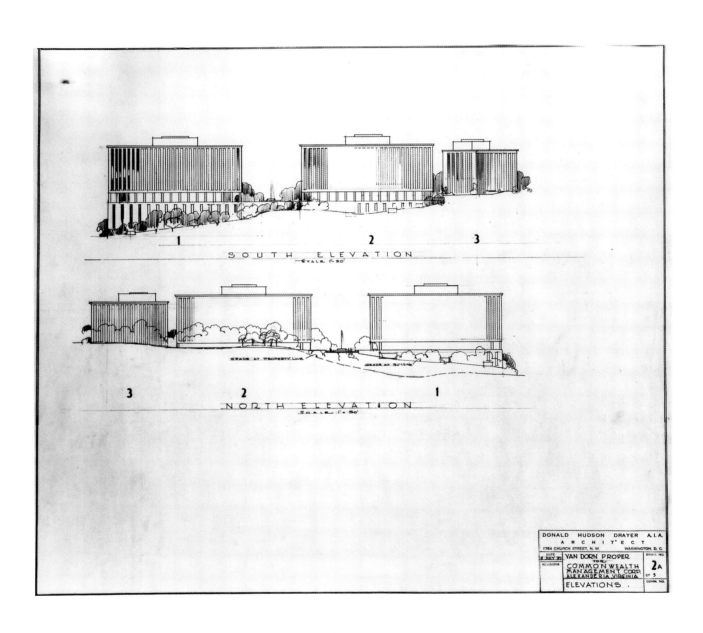

1   2   3

SOUTH ELEVATION
Scale 1"=50'

3   2   1

GRADE AT PROPERTY LINE   GRADE AT BUILDING

NORTH ELEVATION
Scale 1"=50'

DONALD HUDSON DRAYER A.I.A.	
ARCHITECT	
1784 CHURCH STREET, N. W. WASHINGTON, D. C.	

DATE 8 JULY 70	VAN DORN PROPER	DRWG. NO.
REVISIONS	TO COMMONWEALTH MANAGEMENT CORP. ALEXANDERIA VIRGINIA	**2**A OF 3
	ELEVATIONS .	COMM. NO.

FIG. 4.48. Donald Hudson Drayer, architect. Office building for 910 20th Street Partnership, 910 20th Street, N.W., Washington, D.C. Perspective rendering. Graphite on tracing paper. ADE-UNIT 1374, no. 1, E size. LC-USZ62-133478.

ADE-UNIT 1372). The buildings themselves express efficiency and order, at least in the abstract, but are purposely rendered as anonymous containers of minimally defined space. Precisely the same latter characteristics marked office-building development then occurring at a fast pace in downtown Washington (FIG. 4.48).

Drayer's work is a reflection of the mainstream locally and nationally. The approach and the attitudes toward the environment were quite different from those that had given shape to the tall office building and the metropolis at the turn of the twentieth century. Since Drayer's time, his genre of work has fallen from favor; it has indeed fallen as much as the Victorian legacy among champions of the City Beautiful. We may or may not view this material from a different perspective a generation hence. The record preserved here in these collections should prove to be of no small value in understanding the metropolis of the mid-twentieth century.

CHAPTER FIVE

TWENTIETH-CENTURY HOUSING

———

Single-Family Residences, Apartment Buildings, and Planned Communities

GWENDOLYN WRIGHT

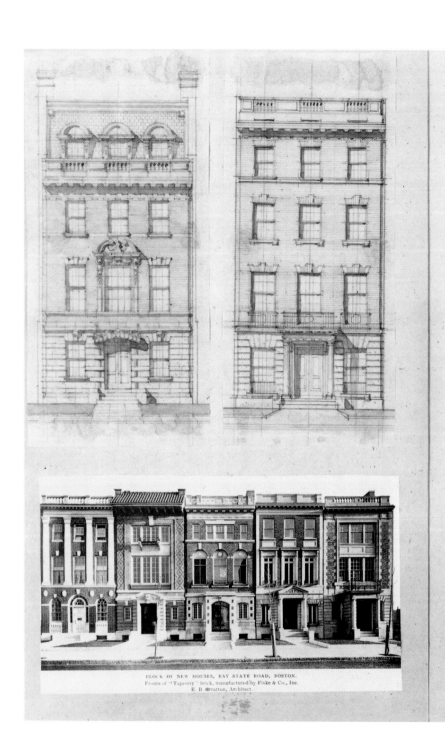

BLOCK OF NEW HOUSES, BAY STATE ROAD, BOSTON.
Fronts of "Tapestry" brick, manufactured by Fiske & Co., Inc.
E. B. Stratton, Architect.

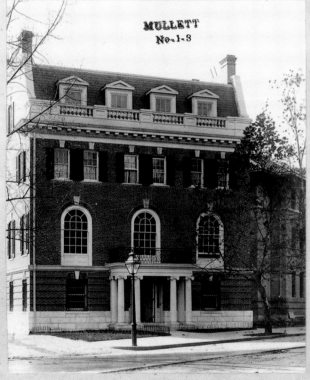

MULLETT
No. 1-3

THE WASHINGTONIANA PROJECT surprises us with several variations on the more familiar repertoire of isolated single-family houses and apartment houses that prevail throughout the Washington, D.C., metropolitan area. "Housing," the generic term for such alternatives, suggests both a distinctive scale of production and several rather disparate clients. On the one hand, the word is used for medium-density enclaves with subsidized rents, commissioned by nonprofit philanthropies, institutions, or government agencies. "Housing" also applies to planned suburbs or townhouse groups built by profit-motivated developers and intended for middle-class families. Examples in this collection include both low- or moderate-cost public projects sponsored by the federal government and private developments aimed toward a speculative market.[1]

Researchers will find well-intended efforts to achieve efficiency and economy. The range in scale is considerable, from immense complexes for several thousand single-room occupancy units to two or three detached single-family dwellings built alongside each other. Little real innovation distinguishes most of these architectural designs. However, if one looks for normative patterns rather than exceptional reforms, this part of the collection takes on considerable interest. Many dwellings usually categorized as separate commissions for "houses," even here, were in fact conceived and built as "housing."

The work comes from several Washington-area firms, most notably, and in chronological order, those of Waddy Butler Wood, Waggaman & Ray, Arthur B. Heaton, Donald Hudson Drayer, and Chloethiel Woodard Smith. Most often a government agency or a private developer provided the impetus; yet, these architects all showed a commendable desire to go beyond professional rhetoric about social responsibility and the need for large-scale planning, whether in the suburb or in the inner city. By no means avant-garde, they did not seek to impose new forms or living arrangements; the iconic American house and yard remained the norm in most cases. These offices represent solid, but never daring, examples of professional concern about the nation's "housing problem" over a half-century's time, including conscious efforts not to stigmatize housing as "projects."[2]

By far the most significant aspect of this documentation is the light it casts on the design process. Focusing on one type and scale of production highlights more general trends, both in the architectural profession and in the field of residential development. Such standard patterns are, of course, far more pervasive than the exceptional work of master architects or other path-breaking reforms that are usually the focus of architectural history. For example, these offices emphasized teamwork and the diligent reworking of a problem, rather than the unique parti. One seldom discerns a polemical voice or the hand of an individual architect, even a principal, inscribing a personal vision. Here, instead, architects are subsumed within an organization that replicated certain basic design and sociological concepts, then explored various possible modifications, and finally—though not too long afterward—provided working drawings and construction supervision. Much of this repetitious work is today being taken over by computer-aided design.

Despite the process of their offices, none of these architects espoused anonymity. They actively promoted themselves, their clients, and their work. Techniques for publicity received increasing attention during the twentieth century. A. B. Mullett & Company put together small volumes of interchangeable prints and photographs (FIG. 5.1; LOT 13041) in the 1910s, promising potential buyers the possibility of customized row house façades at an economical price. A decade later one clearly discerns the growing importance of marketing. Architects produced sales brochures that celebrated high-end townhouses (FIG. 5.2; LOT 13036). Various signage possibilities trumpeted the name of the architect, the developer (FIG. 5.3; ADE-UNIT 104), or the governmental agency.

Not incidentally, the progression of firms reveals a dramatic shift in the architect's professional training, from the continued reliance on an office apprentice system (often accompanied by a year or more of European travel and study) at the time of World War I to the post–World War II dominance of university-based architecture schools.[3] This transformation visibly affected the preferred styles and representational techniques found here. For example, the favored draw-

FIG. 5.1. A. B. Mullett & Co., architect. City houses between party walls. Elevations and views. Graphite on tracing paper, photomechanical prints, photographic print. Ca. 1900–1920. LOT 13041, no. 4, A size. LC-USZ62-133297.

RESIDENCE FOR GEORGE HOWARD, ESQ., WASHINGTON, D. C.

RESIDENCE OF GEO. W. WICKERSHAM, ESQ.,
WASHINGTON, D. C.

RESIDENCE OF ALLERTON CUSHMAN, ESQ.
WASHINGTON, D. C.

J. H. de Sibour, *Architect*

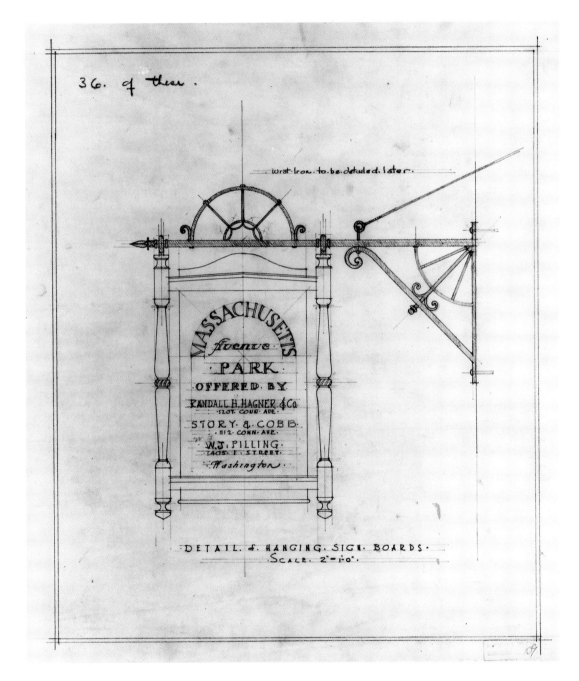

36. of these.

wrot Iron. to. be. detailed. later.

MASSACHUSETTS
Avenue
PARK
OFFERED BY
RANDALL H. HAGNER & Co.
·1207· CONN· AVE·
STORY· & · COBB ·
· 1112· CONN· AVE·
W.J· PILLING ·
·1405· T · STREET·
· Washington ·

· DETAIL· of· HANGING· SIGN· BOARDS ·
·SCALE· 2"= 1'·0"·

FIG. 5.2 (*opposite*). Jules Henri de Sibour, architect. *Architectural Catalog / J. H. de Sibour, Architect* (Washington, D.C., 1923), 32. LC-USZ62-110781.

FIG. 5.3. Clarke Waggaman, architect. "Detail of Hanging Sign Boards. Massachusetts Avenue Park," Washington, D.C. Elevation. Graphite on tracing paper. 1907–1919. ADE-UNIT 104, no. 3, C size. LC-USZ62-114112.

ings for office study and client presentations shifted from softly colored perspectives to bolder axonometric projections in vivid hues or crisp black and white.

Professional training also changed the procedures for architectural design and the kinds of problems that architects or clients believed they could address through good design. These shifts too are well documented. A Beaux-Arts emphasis on the plan as generator dominates the earlier housing studies, with their marked axial symmetry. Wood, Waggaman & Ray, and Heaton sought to provide a sense of civic monumentality in the overall plan, while still paying homage to familiar domesticity in the details of porches or rooflines. In marked contrast, a preponderance of charts, bubble diagrams, and statistics embellishes the housing proposals of the 1960s. Chloethiel Woodard Smith showed a particular interest in construction technology, financing methods, and social scientific theories.[4] She eagerly explored new techniques that might buttress her firm's professional status and help it address complex social and economic problems.

In both eras, while drawings represented a particular set of professional concerns and techniques, the actual buildings did little to explore new ground. The sheets of multiple studies for various projects suggest a formulaic approach to the problems of multiple-unit housing. Time always seemed of the essence. Marginal notes alluded to the client's need for new schemes and ideas "in double-quick time." Accordingly, the architects focused on fast-track approaches to design and construction, which precluded the possibility of venturing too far afield from conventional plans, construction technology, or sociological profiles. They limited their evaluation to problems of time, dimensions, and efficient planning. Typically, with each succeeding scheme the architects would further reduce the square footage devoted to private space. When the project involved large numbers of units, the succeeding designs could therefore add on a few more. To compensate for the anonymity, designers then highlighted the formal harmony of the façades and site plan.

The sequence of steps remained much the same no matter what the scale or type of housing, whether the

clients were to be single workers or upper-middle-class families. In each case, this organization of architectural work provided visual order and a modicum of individuality for the residents, with real economies of scale and production for the builder. Stylistic references varied somewhat, although a respect for the city's historic precedents remained strong. The largest and most imposing housing schemes included in the Washingtoniana Project are among the earliest and the most recent examples. Specific details of the drawings suggest important continuities as well as distinct differences in approach. For example, the use of classical proportions and historic details continued well into the late twentieth century, exemplified by Donald Drayer's infusions of revival styles into his ranch house (FIG. 5.4) and townhouse designs (FIG. 5.5).

The collection begins in 1918, after the United States had entered World War I, when Congress authorized housing for munitions and clerical workers who had joined the war effort.[5] Prominent among these were three gargantuan groups of dormitories in the capital. Each group would become home to several thousand residents—an unprecedented number to house in one centralized enclave (FIG. 5.6). All three commissions were given to the office of Waddy B. Wood (ADE-UNITS 1145, 1170, 1172–1176).

Intended as temporary residential quarters during a national emergency, this architecture required maximum expediency. As the nation's first example of public subsidies for housing, the buildings also took on exceptional ideological weight. Wood responded well to both imperatives. The drawings show his careful balance of mammoth scale with sensitive infill, efficiency with familiarity. He rigorously explored various arrangements and orientations for the blocks and the *Existenzminimum* dimensions of dormitory rooms, and then applied the same care to demure Colonial Revival elevations for every scheme.

Union Plaza Dormitories (also known at various times as the Washington Dormitories, Washington Residence Hall, and the Government Hotels; ADE-UNIT 1172) typify Wood's design approach and preferences. Eighteen dormitories eventually occupied fifteen acres (four city blocks) between Union Station and the Senate Office Building (FIG. 5.7). The

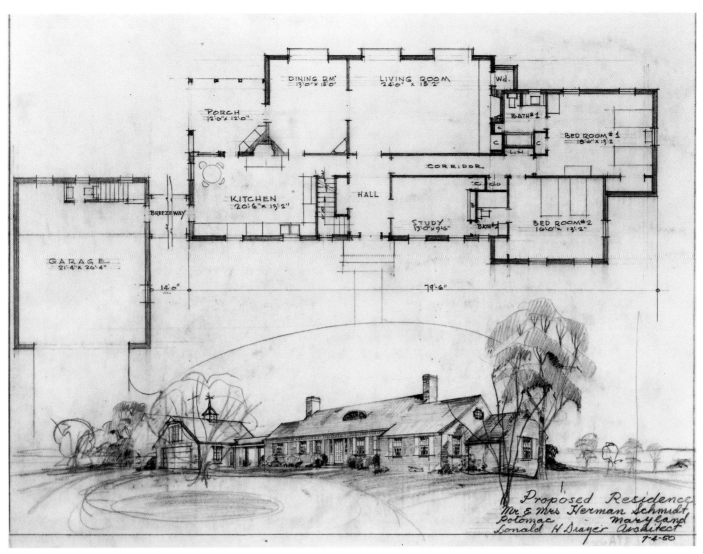

DINING RM.
13'-0" x 15'-0"

LIVING ROOM
24'-0" x 15'-2"

Wd.

BATH #1

BED ROOM #1
18'-0" x 13'-2"

PORCH
12'-0" x 12'-0"

c

c

Lin.

CORRIDOR

c cdo

KITCHEN
20'-6" x 13'-2"

HALL

b

BED ROOM #2
16'-0" x 13'-2"

BREEZEWAY

STUDY
13'-0" x 9'-6"

BATH #2

GARAGE
21'-4" x 26'-4"

14'-0"

79'-6"

Proposed Residence
Mr & Mrs Herman Schmidt
Potomac   Maryland
Donald H Drayer   Architect
7-4-50

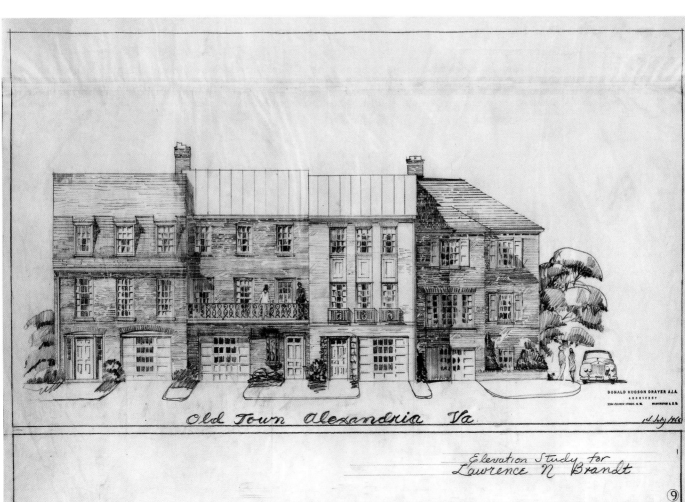

Old Town Alexandria Va

DONALD HUDSON DRAYER A.I.A.
ARCHITECT
2304 CHURCH STREET, N.W.   WASHINGTON 6, D.C.

1st July 1960

Elevation Study for
Lawrence N Brandt

⑨

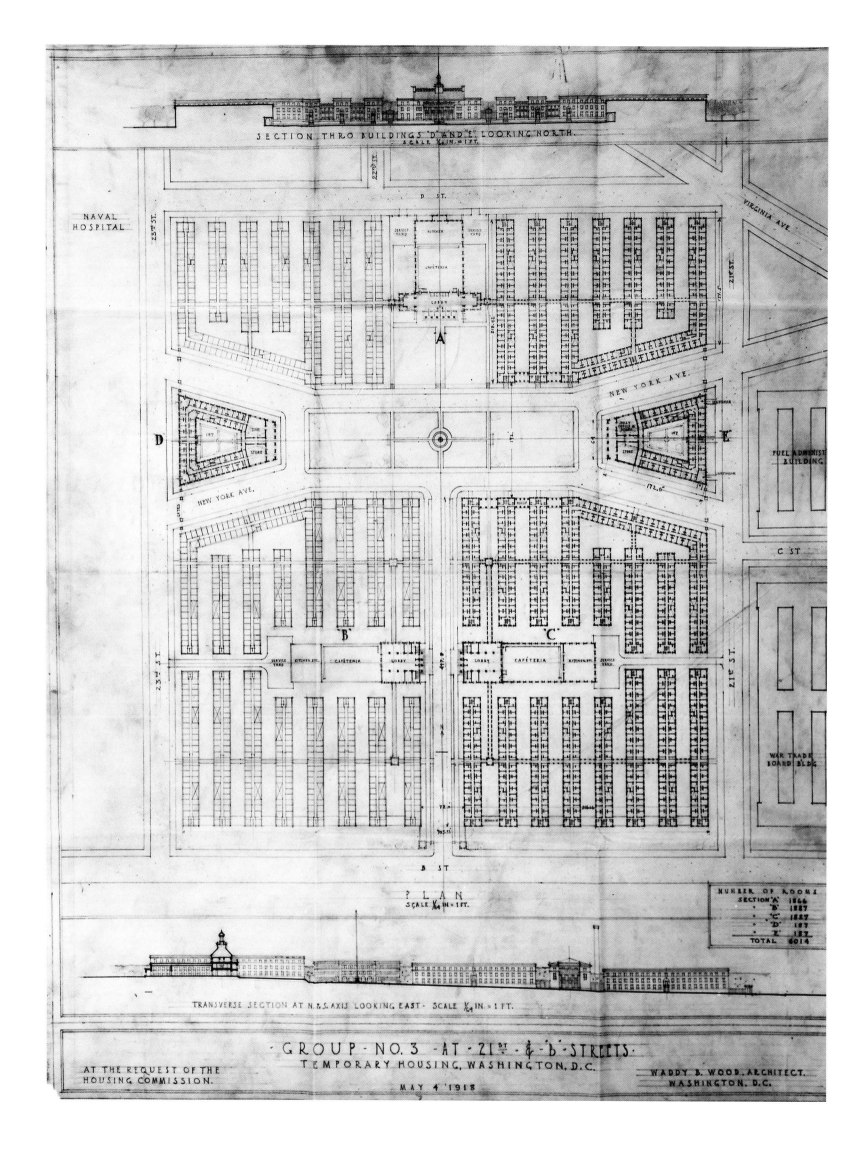

SECTION THRO BUILDINGS "D" AND "E" LOOKING NORTH.
SCALE 1/64 IN.= 1 FT.

NAVAL
HOSPITAL

D ST.

VIRGINIA AVE.

SERVICE YARD   KITCHEN   SERVICE YARD

CAFETERIA

LOBBY

A

NEW YORK AVE.

D   187   STORE

STORE

187   E

FUEL ADMINIST
BUILDING

NEW YORK AVE.

C ST

B   SERVICE YARD   KITCHEN ETC.   CAFETERIA   LOBBY   LOBBY   CAFETERIA   KITCHEN ETC.   SERVICE YARD   C

WAR TRADE
BOARD BLDG

B ST

PLAN
SCALE 1/64 IN.= 1 FT.

NUMBER OF ROOMS	
SECTION "A"	1866
"B"	1887
"C"	1887
"D"	187
"E"	187
TOTAL	6014

TRANSVERSE SECTION AT N. & S. AXIS LOOKING EAST - SCALE 1/64 IN.= 1 FT.

GROUP · NO. 3 · AT · 21ST · & · B · STREETS
TEMPORARY HOUSING, WASHINGTON, D.C.

AT THE REQUEST OF THE
HOUSING COMMISSION.

MAY 4 '1918

WADDY B. WOOD. ARCHITECT.
WASHINGTON, D.C.

architect considered rows of *Zeilenbau* barracks and perimeter blocks linked by porticoes as well as U- and H-shaped slab blocks.[6] In each case, however, the buildings were rotated to align with existing streets, not prevailing sunlight. On-site sketches then explored potential views from various directions.

Wood quickly decided on two clusters: one a grand radial plan focusing on Union Station; the other a collection of U-shaped units linked by Georgian Revival porticoes (FIG. 5.8). This allowed the dormitories to harmonize with the quite different streets and structures of their vicinities. He also chose to focus attention on a monumental common building and dining hall that purposefully overshadowed the residential structures.

Construction commenced while the architects were still elaborating details for the façades and interior spaces. Each specification evokes a tension between the desire for gracious surroundings and the need for efficiency. Remarkably, the first stage of work was completed in only a few months, just at the time of the armistice; construction of the other buildings continued, though with less urgency, over two more years. The dormitories were eventually razed in 1930, to be replaced by a park and a Senate parking garage.

Chloethiel Woodard Smith chose a strikingly different approach for her architectural embellishments. The Washingtoniana Project includes more than five hundred drawings from her office, most notably plans for housing in the Southwest Urban Renewal Area done primarily in the 1950s and 1960s. Smith invariably sought to provide a modern focus on clean lines and rhythmic patterns. Yet this predilection did not signal hostility to history. Indeed, Harbour Square (1968) (ADE-UNIT 1877) incorporated a row of eighteenth-century houses, using these to enclose a quadrangle and smooth the transition into the new development.

Smith's drawings also highlight the greater complexity of architectural offices after World War II, as

FIG. 5.6 (*opposite*). Waddy B. Wood, architect. Temporary war housing, "Group No. 3 at 21st & B Streets," N.W., Washington, D.C., for U.S. Housing Corporation ("Housing Commission"). Site and floor plans, elevations. Graphite and ink on tracing paper. 1918. ADE-UNIT 1176, no. 1, D size. LC-USZ62-133474.

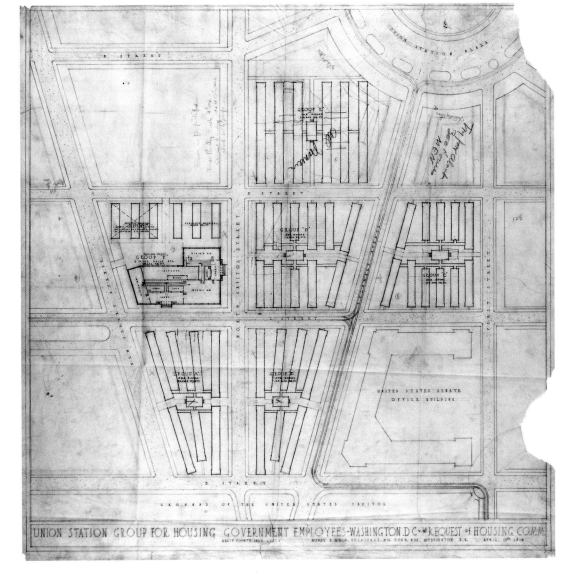

FIG. 5.7. Waddy B. Wood, architect. Temporary war housing, "Union Station Group for Housing Government Employees, Washington, D.C., at request of the Housing Comm." (U.S. Housing Corporation), North Capitol and C Streets. Site and floor plans. Graphite and colored pencil on tracing paper. 1918. ADE-UNIT 1172, no. 2, E size. LC-USZ62-116874.

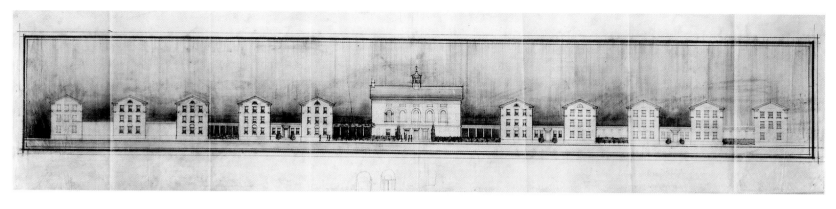

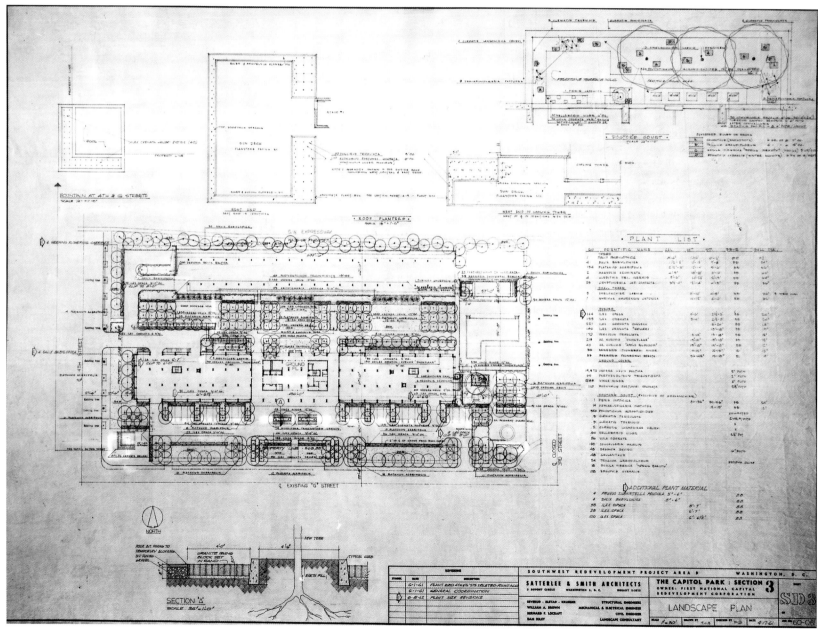

FOUNTAIN AT 4TH & G STREETS

ROOF PLANTERS

PLANT LIST

NORTH

SECTION 'A'

REVISIONS

SATTERLEE & SMITH ARCHITECTS
3 DUPONT CIRCLE   WASHINGTON 6, D.C.

SEVERUD - ELSTAD - KRUEGER   STRUCTURAL ENGINEERS
WILLIAM A. BROWN   MECHANICAL & ELECTRICAL ENGINEER
BERNARD F. LOCRAFT   CIVIL ENGINEER
DAN KILEY   LANDSCAPE CONSULTANT

SOUTHWEST REDEVELOPMENT PROJECT AREA B   WASHINGTON, D.C.

THE CAPITOL PARK : SECTION 3
OWNER: FIRST NATIONAL CAPITAL
REDEVELOPMENT CORPORATION

LANDSCAPE PLAN

SD3

well as the momentous responsibilities ascribed to architects who designed housing. Early in 1952, Smith and Louis Justement helped define a new master plan for Southwest Washington, calling for the demolition of nearly all existing structures and approximately five thousand new dwelling units. A major part of Smith's master plan involved an area called Capitol Park, consisting of five high-rises and four hundred condominium townhouses (ADE-UNITS 1882–1885, 1889). The repeated pattern of balconies defines the tall buildings as modern screens, maximizing light but shutting off access. The apartment towers mark the boundaries of the redevelopment project, and the street plan virtually prohibits through traffic.

One can again note, however, the firm's efforts to emphasize continuities with the existing and pre-existing city, using both historical and urbanistic techniques. Smith maintained the familiar pattern of retail streets, unlike the succeeding scheme by I. M. Pei that called for a large shopping mall. In addition, the lush landscaping (by Dan Kiley) (FIG. 5.9) and public amenities around the periphery (FIG. 5.10) purposefully linked this community to other new developments in the area. Overall, this array of her

drawings for public and private housing exhibits a consistent pattern of genuine social concerns and related modernist design preoccupations. Each example focused early on the street, fitting the new development into the existing fabric, then adding innovations or adaptations—in particular, accommodating larger numbers of cars—that would modernize the particular site.

With this priority in mind, multiple studies explored the formal rhythm and economy of various site plans. Within basic order and regularity, some investigations then sought to maximize a sense of visual particularity and physical comfort for the individual units. Informal marginal notes, followed later by elaborate charts and diagrams, show how the designers evaluated these options and took account of the many factors, intricate and open-ended, that affect housing design.

If Smith's work emphasized site planning and urban design, this too links her with the other architects being considered here. Many design teams provided carefully differentiated outdoor places for children's play, social life, gardens, and pedestrian traffic. Reworking a plan often generated a more compelling or economical pattern of buildings, but the architects usu-

FIG. 5.8 (*opposite, top*). Waddy B. Wood, architect. Temporary war housing, "Union Station Group for Housing Government Employees, Washington, D.C., at request of the Housing Comm." (U.S. Housing Corporation), North Capitol and C Streets. Elevation. Graphite on tracing paper. 1918. ADE-UNIT 1172, no. 6, F size. LC-USZ62-133293.

FIG. 5.9 (*opposite, bottom*). Satterlee & Smith, architects. Dan Kiley, landscape architect. Landscape plan, the Capitol Park: Section 3, Southwest Redevelopment Project for the First National Capital Redevelopment Corporation, Delaware Avenue and G Street, S.W., Washington, D.C. Site and planting plan. Ink and graphite on brown line print. 1961. ADE-UNIT 1885, no. 79, E size. LC-USZ62-133292.

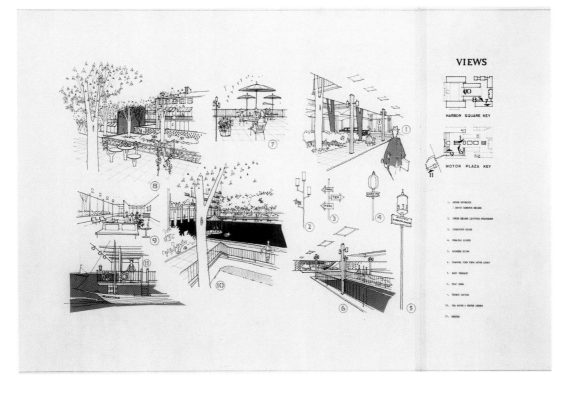

FIG. 5.10. Chloethiel Woodward Smith & Associated Architects. Landscaping, terrace and balcony elements, street furniture, signage and lighting, "Harbour Square" housing development for Harbour Square, Inc., 4th and N Streets, S.W., Washington, D.C. Key plans, perspectives, and details. Ink, graphite, and adhesive shading film on tracing paper. Ca. 1962–1969. ADE-UNIT 1877, no. 2, E size. LC-USZ62-114185.

FIG. 5.11. Associated Architects & Engineers. G. V. Stone & D. H. Drayer, architects. "Arlington Towers Apartments," F.H.A. Rental Housing Project, Arlington [Rosslyn], Virginia. Bird's-eye perspective rendering. Charcoal and graphite on tracing paper. 1954. ADE-UNIT 1618, no. 1, E size. LC-USZ62-114199.

FIG. 5.12 (*opposite, left*). Waddy B. Wood, architect. "All States Hotel for Women," 514 19th Street, N.W., Washington, D.C. Typical floor plan. Colored pencil on blueprint. 1927. ADE-UNIT 1130, no. 3, A size. LC-USZ62-113959.

FIG. 5.13 (*opposite, right*). Waggaman & Ray, architects. Seven-family building, type C, war "housing for Navy Yard Employees," for U.S. Department of Labor, Bureau of Industrial Housing and Transportation, U.S. Housing Corporation, at an eight-block site bordered by 17th Street, 18th Street, East Capitol Street, and Massachusetts Avenue, S.E., Washington, D.C. Elevation. Blueprint. 1918. ADE-UNIT 137, no. 38, E size. LC-USZ62-133289.

ally checked these formal resolutions against their finely honed understanding of the site as a complex stage set for day-to-day events and experiences. Landscaping too emerges as a consistent strength of these various housing projects, and professional landscape architects often joined the design teams (PLATES 5.1, 5.2; ADE-UNITS 1508, 1650).

Especially marked, whatever the stylistic preference or client group, was a focus on the services, amenities, and attention to the larger city scale that designers would later call "urban design." This took many forms. Arthur Heaton used recreational space as a link to the existing neighborhood. Both Heaton and George N. Ray often integrated small shops and convenience stores into groups of apartments or row houses. Every architect underscored formal and functional connections to the city of Washington. From Wood to Smith, designers accepted the block and setback pattern of adjacent buildings. They adapted to the rhythm of existing streets, rather than seeking to isolate their housing from its surroundings. Equally constant was the focus on transportation services. From the 1920s on, both public and private developments devoted considerable attention to garages and open-air parking spaces that would accommodate the private car. Streets functioned as an internal arterial network and as conduits to the larger city (FIG. 5.11, PLATE 5.3).

In all these ways, Washington's housing echoed the dominant themes of twentieth-century suburban expansion: outdoor recreation, contact with nature, friendly homogeneity, familial privacy, and reliance on the automobile. Centralized or communal facilities sometimes provided an important exception to the preoccupation with privacy that characterized the suburban myth. After all, the pooling of services and sharing of activities remains an inherent value in housing. For subdivisions and townhouses of the 1960s, Drayer and Smith routinely supplied elaborate recreational areas to be used by all residents (ADE-UNIT 1625, 1877).

Even earlier Waddy B. Wood had incorporated similar facilities in his World War I dormitories (ADE-UNIT 1145, 1170, 1172–1176). These included elaborate schemes for outdoor tennis courts, swimming pools, and gardens, as well as collective laundries,

infirmaries, and dining halls inside the dorms. In the commodious kitchens, serving meals for up to two thousand residents, one sees Wood's use of a Taylorist approach to spatial organization: specific work tables and storage areas were allocated to diverse foods and food preparation. One should remember, of course, that these dormitories were intended as temporary structures, rather than alternative models for normal residential life. Yet Wood's explorations did affect his 1927 All States Hotel for Women in Northwest Washington (FIG. 5.12; ADE-UNIT 1130), which also featured many centralized services and amenities behind a façade of staid conventionality.

The most important projects in the collection pertain to the federal government's efforts to address housing problems.[7] Washington remained conservative in its taste, never a site for radical experimentation in architecture, whether under public or private auspices. Perhaps design control played too large a role in the nation's capital, especially after the McMillan Commission and the 1930 Shipstead-Luce Act, which required the Federal Arts Commission to approve any new or altered private building that faced a government edifice.

The most thorough documentation concerns the provision of residences for the influx of some forty thousand new Washington residents during World War I, most of whom joined the war agencies or worked in munitions factories. As we have seen, Waddy Wood undertook dormitories for clerical employees on three different sites. To accommodate shipbuilders, Clarke Waggaman and George N. Ray designed groups of small houses for two, three, or seven families, as part of a more general reorganization of the outdated Navy Yard (FIG. 5.13) (ADE-UNIT 137). Once again, none were completely finished by the time of the armistice in November 1918.

Another chapter in the city's history concerns the Alley Dwelling Authority of the New Deal, created in 1934. This office sought to resolve the problem of crowded, unhealthy alley slums that housed thousands of black families. Had the act been passed when drafted in 1930, private builders might have cooperated in putting up inexpensive housing for the displaced persons. Instead, constrained by a recent

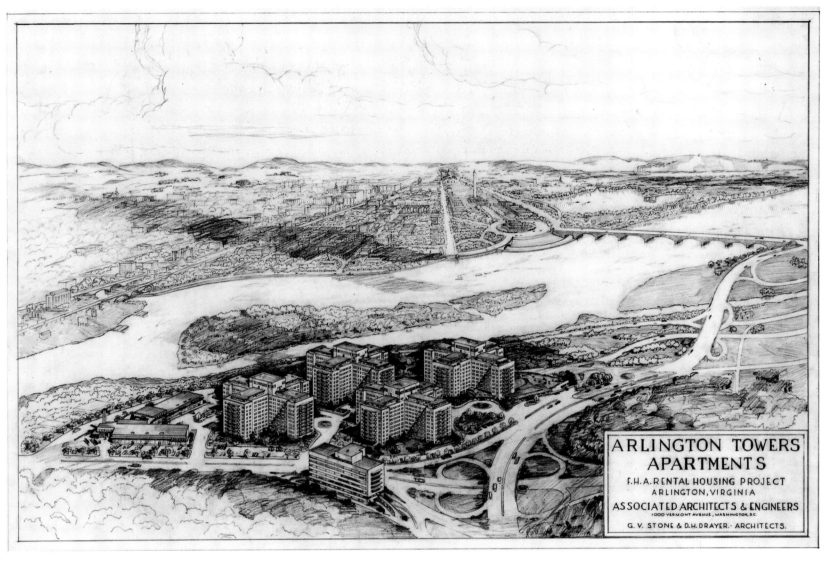

ARLINGTON TOWERS
APARTMENTS

F.H.A. RENTAL HOUSING PROJECT
ARLINGTON, VIRGINIA

ASSOCIATED ARCHITECTS & ENGINEERS
1000 VERMONT AVENUE, WASHINGTON, D.C.

G.V. STONE & D.H. DRAYER · ARCHITECTS.

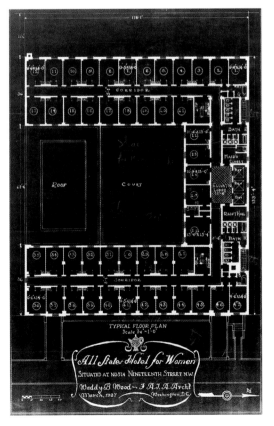

TYPICAL FLOOR PLAN
Scale ¼"=1'-0"

All States Hotel for Women

SITUATED AT NO.814 NINETEENTH STREET N.W.

Waddy B. Wood ~ F.A.I.A. Archt

March, 1927   Washington, D.C.

REAR ELEVATIONS · SEVEN-FAMILY BUILDINGS · TYPE C · FACING SOUTH

END ELEVATIONS · SEVEN-FAMILY BUILDINGS · TYPE C · THE OTHER END · SAME · EXCEPT REVERSED

FRONT ELEVATIONS · THREE-FAMILY BUILDINGS · TYPE A ·

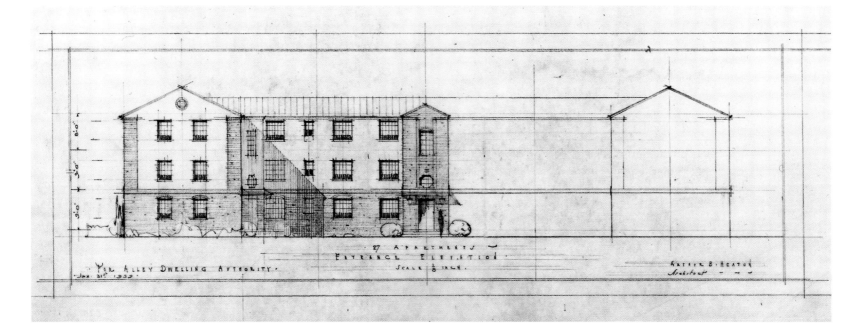

27 APARTMENTS
ENTRANCE ELEVATION
SCALE ½ INCH

FOR ALLEY DWELLING AUTHORITY
Jan 21st 1935

ARTHUR B HEATON
Architect

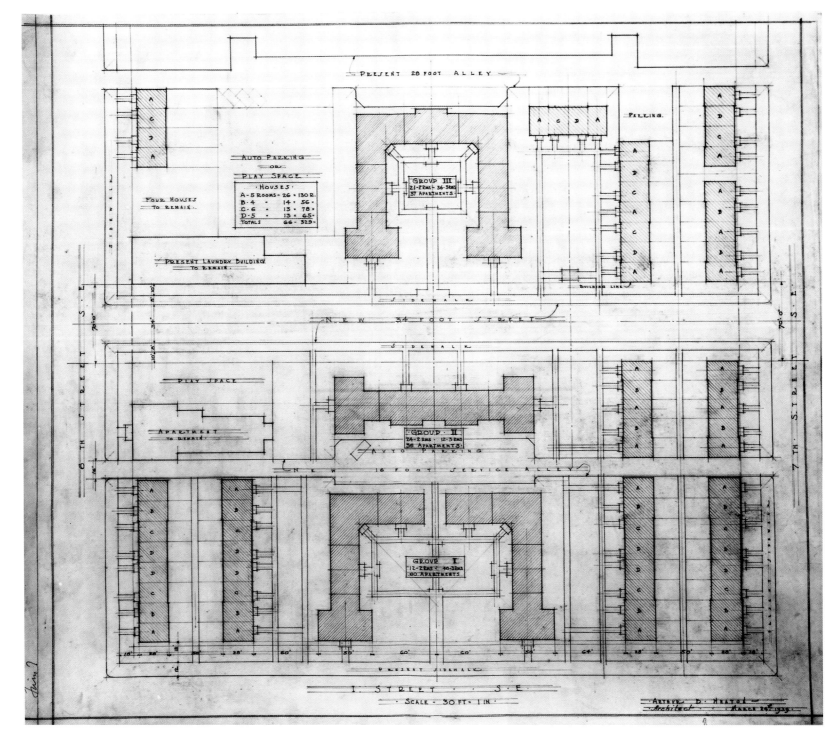

PRESENT 28 FOOT ALLEY

PARKING

AUTO PARKING
OR
PLAY SPACE

HOUSES
A - 5 ROOMS - 26 - 130 R.
B - 4   "   - 14 - 56
C - 6   "   - 13 - 78
D - 5   "   - 13 - 65
TOTALS   66 - 329

FOUR HOUSES
TO REMAIN

PRESENT LAUNDRY BUILDING
TO REMAIN

GROUP III
21 - 2 RMS. 36 - 3 RMS
57 APARTMENTS

BUILDING LINE

SIDEWALK

6TH STREET S.E.

NEW   34   FOOT   STREET

SIDEWALK

PLAY SPACE

APARTMENT
TO REMAIN

GROUP II
24 - 2 RMS. 12 - 3 RMS
36 APARTMENTS

AUTO PARKING

7TH STREET S.E.

NEW   16   FOOT   SERVICE   ALLEY

GROUP I
12 - 2 RMS. 40 - 3 RMS
80 APARTMENTS

PRESENT SIDEWALK

I STREET S.E.
SCALE 30 FT. 1 IN

ARTHUR B HEATON
Architect   MARCH 20th 1935

upsurge in private construction in other nearby areas, the government agency found its role mostly limited to documentation and planning studies. Extensive photographic reports emphasized the dangerous or idle population who resided in the alleys, even more than the rundown structures. Design proposals focused on traffic and parking facilities, sometimes to the exclusion of any recommendations for housing.[8]

When improvements did take place, they usually involved the restoration of alley houses along with the gentrification of the neighborhoods. In fact, over the protests of the director, John Ihlder, the agency sometimes cleared an area and sold the land to private developers, instead of using it for new low-rental developments. In 1938–1939, when the Alley Dwelling Authority proposed to raze several blocks of slum housing near Navy Place, Arthur Heaton was asked to redesign the area, adding new row houses and low-rise apartments (FIGS. 5.14, 5.15) (ADE-UNIT 959, no. 5). Although Ihlder hoped to house low-income families, Heaton realized that well-designed philanthropic housing could be converted into middle-class private developments and left an ambiguous sense of the future residents.

The individual units received relatively little attention, though Heaton, like Wood, favored Georgian Revival brick façades with historical ornament: tiny slate porches, octagonal windows, newel posts for the interior stairways. The architect focused primarily on the street plan, exploring various ways to fit the new development into the existing fabric, then adding modifications—in particular, courtyards and play spaces for the residents, as well as large amounts of parking for their cars. Multiple studies explored the formal rhythm and economy of various site plans, each group encompassing between thirty-eight and sixty buildings. Informal marginal notes show how the architects evaluated different options. Yet the open-ended nature of the commission proved somewhat frustrating, and the site never developed Heaton's characteristic sense of ordered variety.

Most of Heaton's work pertained to the Washington suburbs. Here, too, one finds abundant material in the collections describing both routine office practice and occasional forays into uncharted design territory. Although the vast majority of his commissions dealt with private single-family dwellings, a surprising number document the creation of small speculative groups ranging from two to thirty houses. Again, the continuities and distinctions between these two closely related types of work are of particular interest.

As early as 1919, Heaton designed a group of nine houses (ADE-UNIT 552) for the development firm of Shannon & Luchs, who would remain a steadfast client. This early incarnation treated the arrangement quite formally, using a classical rhythm that placed the largest houses at the two ends and in the center (ADE-UNIT 552, no. 1). Two basic variations in floor plan and façade gave the semblance of distinctiveness to each dwelling. A few years later, in 1923, Heaton undertook five houses in the northwest area of Washington (ADE-UNIT 768). Here the site plan (FIG. 5.16), developed with landscape architect John H. Small, groups the units in a broad U-pattern to create a more informal feeling. Drawings show new economies of construction, such as reversing window or porch details on adjacent dwellings.

A preliminary study for stores, apartments, and row houses bordering Rock Creek Park (ADE-UNIT 712), built for Capital Transit in 1935, followed much the same procedure. After his office had explored five site plans, Heaton chose a scheme with a spacious central court that linked off-street parking to a covered arcade of shops. This mixed-use project thereby initiated an early innovation in commercial site planning.

Heaton's office also designed more than five hundred houses in Burleith (ADE-UNIT 925–931, 960). Among his most interesting designs are those for the subdivision of Wrenwood (ADE-UNIT 978), another Shannon & Luchs project, built in 1931. The architect could again concentrate on street configurations and their relationship to the block plans. In particular, he made innovative use of Radburn-like cul-de-sacs to foster a sense of close-knit isolation among neighbors and the earlier precedent of alleyways to emphasize a connection with traditional street layouts in the Washington area. Houses were

FIG. 5.14. Arthur B. Heaton, architect. "Entrance elevation, 27 Apartments," Navy Place Housing Project "for Alley Dwelling Authority," United States Housing Authority, 6th and 7th Streets between H and I Streets, S.E. (square 878), Washington, D.C. Half-elevation. Graphite and colored pencil on tracing paper. 1939. ADE-UNIT 959, no. 16, C size. LC-USZ62-133449.

FIG. 5.15. Arthur B. Heaton, architect. Navy Place Housing Project "for Alley Dwelling Authority," United States Housing Authority, 6th and 7th Streets between H and I Streets, S.E. (square 878), Washington, D.C. Site plan. Graphite on tracing paper. 1939. ADE-UNIT 959, no. 40, E size. LC-USZ62-133481.

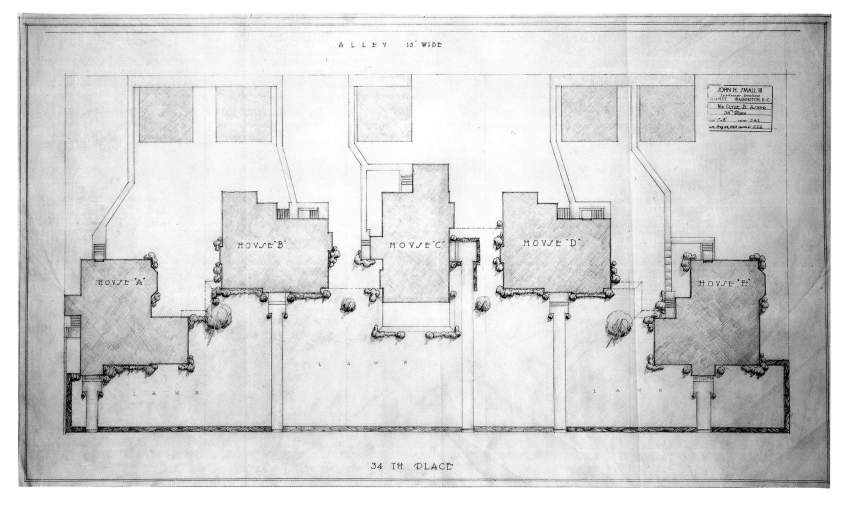

ALLEY 15' WIDE

HOUSE "A"   HOUSE "B"   HOUSE "C"   HOUSE "D"   HOUSE "E"

L A W N

34 TH PLACE

FIG. 5.16. Arthur B. Heaton, architect. John H. Small III, landscape architect. "Group of houses" for Clyde B. Asher, 2705–2713 34th Place, N.W., Washington, D.C. Site plan. Graphite and colored pencil on tracing paper. 1923. ADE-UNIT 768, no. 5, C size. LC-USZ62-133288.

designed in groups of four to seven, with one larger house in each cluster. Contrasts among the dwellings were achieved by alternating brick and wood, roof heights and pitches, and other façade treatments, often using stock parts, accentuating the apparent uniqueness of each dwelling. These same variations would then be repeated throughout the subdivision. Heaton's office provided a preliminary model (FIG. 5.17) and site plan (FIG. 5.19) that showed twenty-eight houses, indicating such modifications.

Elevations drawn in colored pencil evoked the distinctive suburban charm the developers sought to promote for Wrenwood (ADE-UNIT 978; FIG. 5.19; PLATE 5.4). Heaton's office also prepared the marketing brochure for this subdivision in which distinct segments were directed toward women and

men, extolling the aspects of house design, neighborhood, and financial investment they might find especially attractive.

A major New Deal enterprise involved the Greenbelt towns, represented here by Arthur Heaton's Union Built Homes (1938) at Greenbelt, Maryland (ADE-UNIT 979). Although the lyrical color sketches (FIG. 5.20; PLATE 5.5) and the site plans evoke the utopian ideals of the program and its emphasis on collective identity, Union Built Homes is not fundamentally different from other work in Heaton's office. Both the design process and the basic typology closely resembled his more conventional suburban housing, reminding us of the architectural and social diversity in the Greenbelt towns.

Only a few contemporary drawings document de-

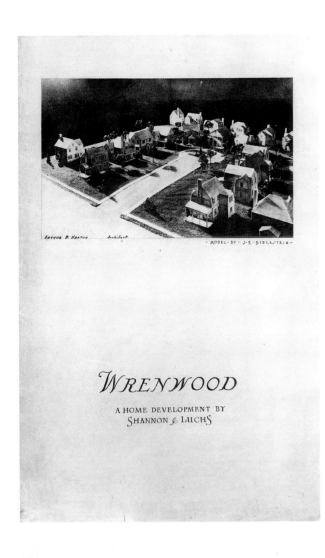

WRENWOOD

A HOME DEVELOPMENT BY
SHANNON & LUCHS

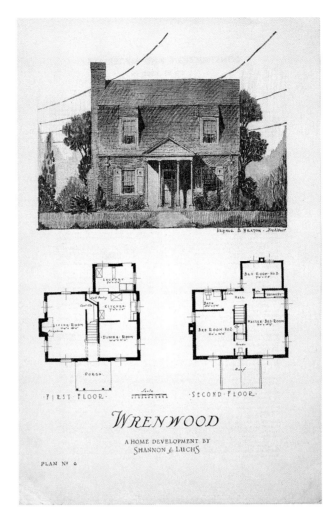

WRENWOOD

A HOME DEVELOPMENT BY
SHANNON & LUCHS

PLAN Nº 6

FIG. 5.17 (*top left*). Arthur B. Heaton, architect. J. E. Biberstein, model. Cover, promotional brochure for "Wrenwood, A Home Development by Shannon & Luchs," Quesada Street, Rittenhouse Street, Broad Branch Road, and 6000–6010 34th Place, N.W. (lots 31–39, square 2010), Washington, D.C. 1930–1931. ADE-UNIT 978, no. 34, C size. LC-USZ62-133457.

FIG. 5.18 (*top right*). Arthur B. Heaton, architect. House plan no. 6, promotional brochure for "Wrenwood, A Home Development by Shannon & Luchs," Quesada Street, Rittenhouse Street, Broad Branch Road, and 6000–6010 34th Place, N.W. (lots 31–39, square 2010), Washington, D.C. 1930–1931. ADE-UNIT 978, no. 51, C size. LC-USZ62-133444.

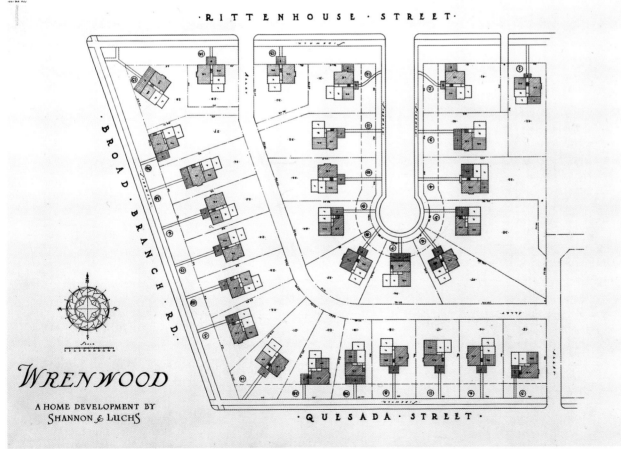

WRENWOOD

A HOME DEVELOPMENT BY
SHANNON & LUCHS

FIG. 5.19. Arthur B. Heaton, architect. Site plan, promotional brochure for "Wrenwood, a Home Development by Shannon & Luchs," Quesada Street, Rittenhouse Street, Broad Branch Road, and 6000–6010 34th Place, N.W. (lots 31–39, square 2010), Washington, D.C. Elevation and floor plans. Colored pencil on photomechanical print. 1930–1931. ADE-UNIT 978, no. 39, C size. LC-USZC4-11485.

·UNION·HOMES· AT·
·GREENBELT· MD ·
· ARTHUR B. HEATON ·
Architect.   Washington.D.C.

FIG. 5.20. Arthur B. Heaton, architect. "Union Homes at Greenbelt," Maryland, "Greenbelt Project—Union Green" for Union Homes, Inc. Perspective. Graphite and colored pencil on tracing paper. 1938. ADE-UNIT 979, no. 14, A size. LC-USZ62-114012.

FIG. 5.21 (*opposite*). Heaton & Chatelain, architects. Berrall & Locraft, site engineers. H. F. Hoppe, mechanical engineer. Rose Greely, landscape architect. Site improvement plan and details, "Lanham Act War Housing Project No. VA-44231" for National Housing Agency, bordered by 18th Street, 23rd Street, Eads Street, and Fern Street, Arlington, Virginia. Blueprint. 1942. ADE-UNIT 580, no. 3, E size. LC-USZ62-133290.

fense housing projects built under the U.S. Housing Authority (USHA) during World War II.[9] Three of these—at Falls Church (ADE-UNIT 581), in Arlington County (ADE-UNIT 580), and in Hillwood Square, each built in 1942—also came from Heaton's office. Despite the characteristic attention to site planning (FIG. 5.21), this architecture seems rather sparse and routine. It is a pity that George Howe's West Potomac dorms or Grainger & Johanson's Westpark in Bremerton are not included. Here and elsewhere, architects of World War II housing frequently experimented with demountable or prefabricated construction and daringly modern design, as in Frank Lloyd Wright's unbuilt Cloverleaf project (ADE-UNIT 2449) for Pittsfield, Massachusetts, and Aluminum City Terrace in New Kensington, Pennsylvania, by Walter Gropius and Marcel Breuer, both of 1942—the latter recorded extensively by the Historic American Buildings Survey in 1994 (FIGS. 5.22, 5.23; HABS PA-302). The Washingtoniana drawings cannot match the Li-

brary of Congress's extensive photographic record, especially rich for the New Deal and World War II, available in the FSA/OWI (Farm Security Administration/Office of War Information) collections, also in the Prints and Photographs Division (FIGS. 5.24, 5.25).

Equally important, though often obscured under the privatized rubric of single-family homes, were private developers' schemes for suburban tracts.[10] Donald Hudson Drayer's work explores the concept of "cluster housing," popular in the 1960s and 1970s, which grouped dwellings close together to maximize open space, economize on utilities, and protect the environment.[11] Despite enthusiastic rhetoric about a revolutionary new approach, we can see that this phenomenon had cautiously and unobtrusively taken shape much earlier in the century.

Suburban expansion first began to attract white middle-class and upper-middle-class families to Chevy Chase, Arlington, and Bethesda during the 1920s.[12] The exodus was fueled by the standardiza-

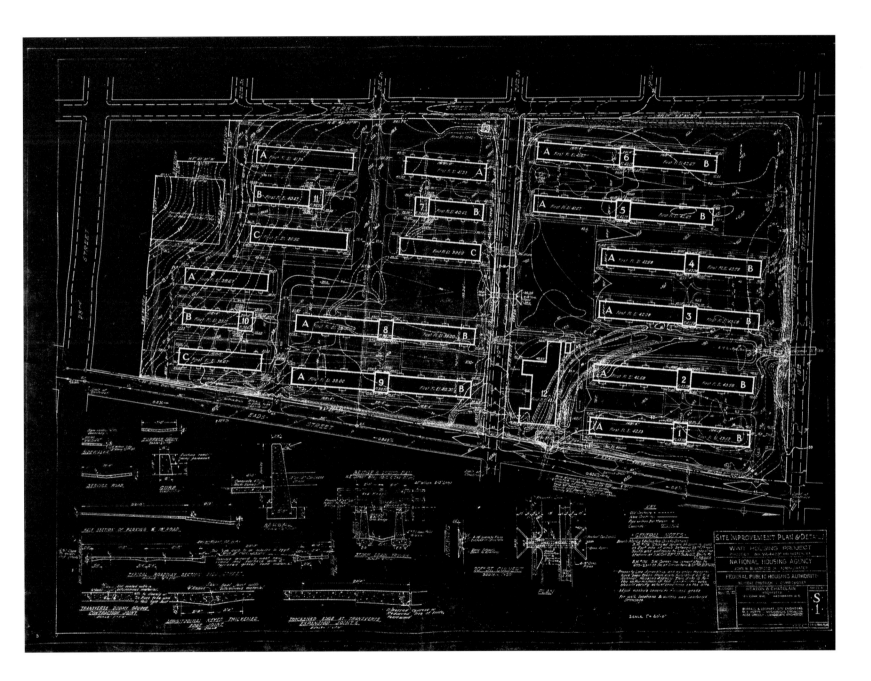

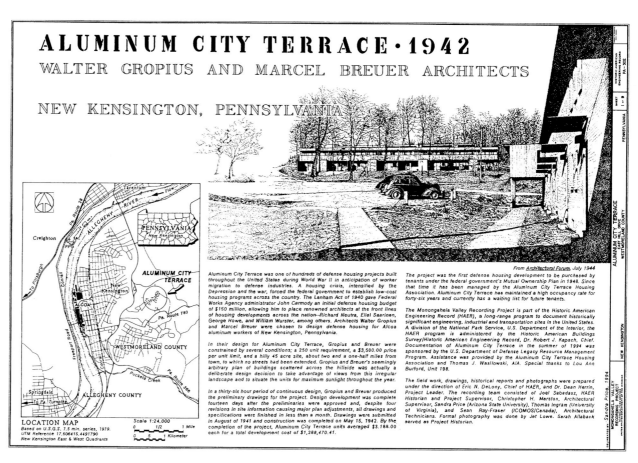

FIG. 5.22. Historic American Engineering Record. Sandra Price, delineator. Walter Gropius and Marcel Breuer, architects. Aluminum City Terrace [Defense Housing Project], East Hill Drive, New Kensington, Westmoreland County, Pennsylvania. Measured drawing; location map based on U.S.G.S. series and perspective rendering based on illustration in *Architectural Forum*, July 1944. Ink on polyester film, 1994. Digital file of HAER PA-302, sheet 1 of 9.

FIG. 5.23. Historic American Engineering Record. Sean Ray Fraser, delineator. Walter Gropius and Marcel Breuer, architects. Assembly and services, typical three-bedroom unit, Aluminum City Terrace [Defense Housing Project], East Hill Drive, New Kensington, Westmoreland County, Pennsylvania. Measured drawing; isometric section. Ink on polyester film. 1994. Digital file of HAER PA-302, sheet 7 of 9.

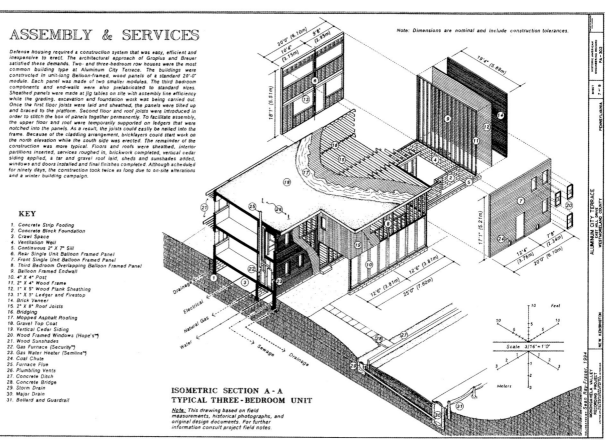

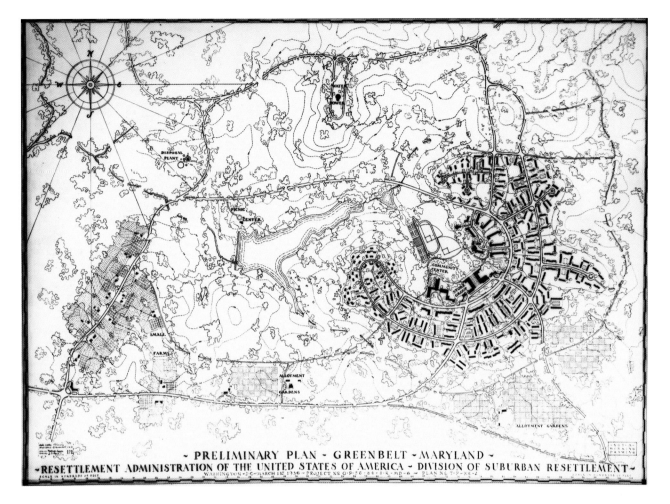

FIG. 5.24. Preliminary Plan, model community, Greenbelt, Maryland, Project No. O.P.156-84-8.R-MD-6 for the Resettlement Administration of the United States of America, Division of Suburban Resettlement. Site plan. Photographic print. LOT 1360, F size. LC-USF341-548-ZB.

FIG. 5.25. Duplex house, model community, Greenbelt, Maryland, Project No. O.P.156-84-8.R-MD-6 for the Resettlement Administration of the United States of America, Division of Suburban Resettlement. Perspective rendering. Photographic print. LOT 1360, F size. LC-USF344-927-ZB.

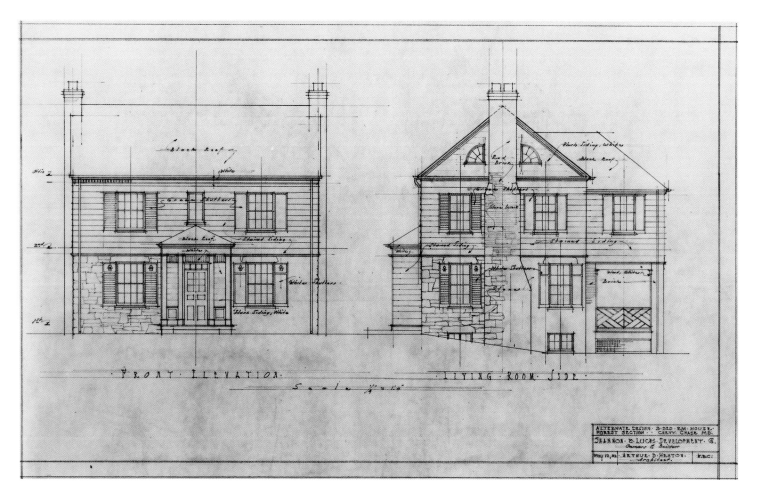

· F R O N T · E L E V A T I O N ·

· L I V I N G · R O O M · S I D E ·

S c a l e   ¼" = 1'-0"

FIG. 5.26. Arthur B. Heaton, architect. Front and living room side, alternate design for a three-bedroom house, housing development ("Forest Section") for Shannon & Luchs Development Co., owners and builders, Leland Street, Ridgewood Avenue, and Oak Lane, Chevy Chase, Maryland. Elevations. Graphite on tracing paper. 1932. ADE-UNIT 775, no. 2, C size. LC-USZ62-133709.

tion of building materials and methods, longer-term mortgages, federal highway legislation, the growth of government employment, and the economies of scale in speculative developments. Whereas small building and loan associations had generated the capital for most residential properties in the nineteenth century, the larger national banks began to fund major local developers during the decade of the 1920s. Although these developers continued to market the image of individualized, custom-built "manors," they hired architects to build aggregations of dwellings. Even in exclusive neighborhoods architects often produced plans for two, three, four, and often nine or more adjacent houses. Heaton's work of the 1920s and 1930s is especially well documented, with more than ten dwellings on two blocks of Leland Street in

Chevy Chase (FIG. 5.26), all built speculatively for the Washington developer Shannon & Luchs (ADE-UNIT 775–777, 779, 781–782, 784–787).

Indeed, the extensive Heaton holdings, which include designs for apartment buildings and single-family residences, government housing, and dormitories, exemplify the value of the materials made available for study by the Washingtoniana Project. Comprising more than nine thousand drawings in more than 693 units, Heaton's work represents the most voluminous archive of any Washington architect in the library's collections. In its variety and its consistency, this rich compendium dramatizes an important aspect of architectural scholarship. Here one can see both the actual process of design in a successful office and the real mechanisms of residential development in this city.

CHAPTER SIX

THE VIETNAM VETERANS MEMORIAL

——

Grateful Memory, Lost Bravado

PAMELA SCOTT

In March 1979, twenty-nine-year-old Vietnam veteran Jan C. Scruggs began the effort to erect in Washington, D.C., a national memorial to commemorate veterans of the bitterly divisive and controversial sixteen-year U.S. military struggle in Southeast Asia. On July 1, 1980, President Jimmy Carter signed legislation authorizing a privately sponsored memorial on the Mall. Maya Lin's winning design, a V-shaped, polished black granite wall inscribed with the names of all the dead and missing, was dedicated on Veterans Day, November 11, 1982 (FIG. 6.1). Two years later—after much criticism of Lin's somber design—the government placed a figurative sculpture group by Frederick E. Hart and a flag in a grove of trees at the southwest entrance to the memorial grounds. No other national monument in Washington rose as rapidly, no earlier competition for an executed monument generated as much public interest and comment, and none achieved such immediate popular and critical success.[1]

As a professional adviser hired by the Vietnam Veterans Memorial Fund (VVMF), Washington architect Paul Spreiregen helped formulate the competition program, select the eight-person jury, and oversee the competition process from advertising for competitors to returning designs (ADE-UNIT 2246). Announcements of the competition went to art and architecture schools and to architecture and landscape architecture firms. Advertisements appeared in professional art and architecture journals, and directors of the fund issued a widely circulated press release.

On November 24, 1980, the VVMF published a twelve-page registration booklet that included a copy of the law authorizing the memorial, four aerial and two ground-level photographs of the Mall site, the competition rules, and registration forms. The booklet also outlined the "purpose and philosophy" of the memorial and suggested readings on both the history

FIG. 6.1. Maya Lin, architect. Interface Architects, Paul Stevenson Oles, delineator. Study looking toward the Lincoln Memorial with snow, Vietnam Veterans Memorial, Constitution Gardens, Constitution Avenue and Henry Bacon Drive, N.W., Washington, D.C. Perspective. Black wax-based pencil on watercolor paper. 1981. DLC/PP-1999.015.119, A size. LC-USZ62-133443.

of the war and its effect on its veterans. The memorial sought "to recognize and honor those who served and died;" its philosophy was to "make no political statement regarding the war or its conduct . . . [but to] begin a healing process, a reconciliation." The memorial was intended to be a "symbol of national unity . . . a focal point for remembering the war's dead, the veterans, and the lessons learned through a tragic experience." The memorial's sponsors wished that "through the memorial both supporters and opponents of the war may find a common ground for recognizing the sacrifice, heroism, and loyalty which were also a part of the Vietnam experience."[2]

The two-acre site in Constitution Gardens (established in 1976) "was chosen for its prominence and for its proximity to the Lincoln Memorial, itself a symbol of reconciliation after the Civil War." The competition was open to all American designers—artists, sculptors, architects, and landscape architects—who were eighteen years old at the time of registration, December 29, 1980. The sole physical criterion was that the memorial design "provide for the inscription of the names of all 57,661 Americans who died in Vietnam, as well as the names of the approximately 2,500 who remain unaccounted for." These numbers later changed as updated lists were provided by the Department of Defense and as veterans died from wounds received in Vietnam. (Names have been and will continue to be added to the memorial owing to the latter circumstance.) In this initial registration booklet, abstract issues, both philosophical and visual, which required the judgment of the competing designers, were addressed by the sponsors. "The memorial should be reflective and contemplative in character. It should be harmonious with its site and with its surroundings, particularly the national monuments in and near the area." Individuals and design teams were invited to register for a fee of $20.

A double-sided map of Washington's central core with the site clearly outlined on two maps of different scales, and a well-illustrated, eighteen-page design program were sent to more than five thousand registrants. The booklet gave detailed information on the Constitution Gardens site, its relationship to all nearby natural and built features, including topography, subsoil conditions, trees and vegetation, ground cover, lighting, and accessibility by pedestrians and motorists. Photographs into and from the site under differing seasonal conditions were supplemented by a text that stressed the importance of designing in harmony with the existing conditions, noting that while the immediate area would have the "advantage of a sense of enclosure, and hence repose, it is not isolated visually . . . It is a place in itself, but not a place apart."

"A profile of the dead and unaccounted for" preceded fourteen design requirements. Thus entrants were provided with the average age of the dead (23.3 years), their sex, race, marital status, branch of service, and the country in which they died. However, the fifth point in the design requirements noted that the full names only of those sacrificed would be presented with "no information as to rank, dates, places, or service branch." Among the fourteen design requirements, eight were directly concerned with the physical characteristics of the site. Three stipulated that the memorial design should be "contemplative and reflective in character" and should not "challenge or detract from the views of the existing memorials visible from the site," but be "harmonious . . . an integral part of Constitution Gardens," and should be planned for small-scale "gatherings for commemorative ceremonies or reflection." Materials should be "enduring in time." The estimated construction budget was $3 million; the VVMF eventually raised $10 million. The sponsors reiterated that the proposed memorial was to honor "the service and memory of the war's dead, its missing, and its veterans, not the war itself," and thus the designs should in no way make a political statement.

In an introduction to the presentation requirements, "substantive ideas" rather than "elaborately rendered illustrations" were stressed as the goal of the sponsors. Designs were to be submitted on one, or two, rigid 30 × 40–inch panels hung vertically, with illustrations in any medium allowed, although mechanical and press-on lettering were not permissible. No three-dimensional models could be used, only photographs of them. Color was to be employed only "insofar as necessary to explain the design."

Three illustrations were required on one board: a site plan oriented with north upward, an elevation, and a cross section. All had to be on the scale of one inch to thirty feet. Additional optional illustrations could include eye-level views, explanatory drawings indicating interrelationships between the Vietnam Veterans Memorial, the Lincoln Memorial, and the Washington Monument, and some indication of "how the required names will be displayed." Materials should be noted, as well as any proposed special features, such as inscriptions, "aspects of diurnal, nocturnal, or seasonal variation" or the use of "sound, wind, or sun angle." A brief explanatory text was optional. Simplicity of presentation was urged.

All competing entries were to be judged anonymously so no names or other identifying marks on the panels were allowed. Questions, to be submitted in writing no later than January 30, 1981, would be compiled with answers sent to all entrants, and the submissions deadline was set at midnight on March 31, 1981. Names of the eight jury members, consisting of two architects, Pietro Belluschi and Harry Weese; two landscape architects, Garrett Eckbo and Hideo Sasaki; three sculptors, Richard H. Hunt, Constantino Nivola, and James Rosati; and an author, Grady Clay (who had written a best-selling book on Vietnam), were listed in the registration booklet and not repeated in the design program.

On February 10, 1981, a list of 230 "Questions and Answers" grouped under seven headings—rules, information, design, names, illustrations, communications and shipping, and afterthoughts—were sent to the competitors. New information included the significant dates of American involvement in Vietnam, the number of dead organized by year and by home state, commonwealth, and U.S. possession, the legal height limitation of buildings on the site (385 feet above sea level), statistical data on nearby buildings and natural features, and species of trees in the locale. Of the fifty-one questions grouped under design, many were concerned with clarifying the VVMF's position on respecting the surrounding area. Repeatedly entrants were admonished to not overwhelm the site: "our intention is that the memorial be carefully integrated into the existing Constitution Gardens; that

it be an intrinsic part of it, sensitively wedded to it."

The Vietnam Veterans Memorial was the first national competition to adhere to guidelines and ethical standards for architectural competitions developed by the American Institute of Architects in 1980. The registration booklet explicitly stated that the VVMF, jury, and professional adviser were bound by the competition rules and program. Completed registration forms are part of the VVMF archive in the Prints and Photographs Division. These registration forms required name, profession or occupation, date of birth, address, telephone numbers, and the signed pledge that entrants had read and agreed to abide by the competition rules. Rule 9.3, "Ownership and Use of Designs," stipulated that if the VVMF used a "feature from a design other than the first prize winning design" it would be done "only with the agreement of the author of the feature and the author of the first-prize design." In the registration packet, entrants were told that all designs would be the property of the VVMF and disposed of; in a letter dated April 13, 1981, entrants were advised that designs would be returned for a $10 packing and shipping fee.

In the records of the VVMF, the official number of entries varies slightly from 1,418 to 1,421—the largest number in a design competition ever held in America or Europe. Numbered slides (processed in April 1981) of 1,418 entries correspond with a computerized list of names and addresses entitled "Memorial Contest Entrants," organized in entry number sequence and dated April 14, 1981. Most entrants were young; many of them were students. Few architects or sculptors with national reputations entered the competition. Jean Paul Carlhian, Richard Lippold, William Turnbull Jr., and Anne Tyng submitted designs, as did many young members of major firms, but entries by numerous principals of the important firms are conspicuously absent.

The judges did their work between April 29 and May 1, 1981, at Hangar No. 3 at Andrews Air Force Base. Yale University architecture student Maya Lin's design was the unanimous choice of the jury for the first prize of $20,000. The second prize of $10,000 was awarded to a team headed by architect Marvin Krosin-

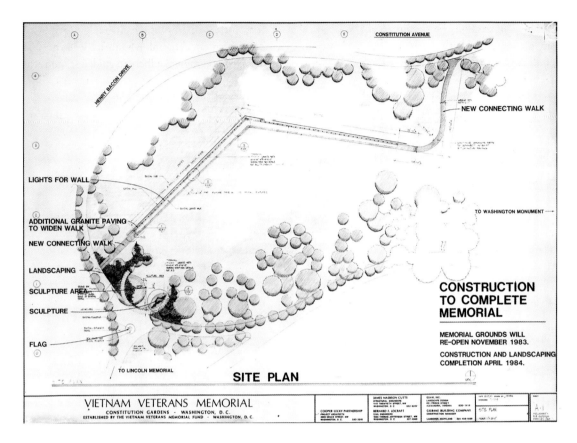

FIG. 6.2. Maya Lin, architect. Cooper-Lecky Partnership, project architects. Preliminary site plan (for bidding purposes only), construction to complete memorial, Vietnam Veterans Memorial, Constitution Gardens, Constitution Avenue and Henry Bacon Drive, N.W., Washington, D.C. A-1. Colored pencil on diazoprint mounted on foam core. 1983. ADE-UNIT 2337, no. 2, E size. LC-USZ62-114202.

sky of Island Park, New York. The third-prize ($5,000) winners were a team headed by Alexandria, Virginia, landscape architect Joseph E. Brown. Honorable mentions each received $1,000. In addition, forty-four designs were judged as "meritorious" and included in an exhibition with the winning design held in the winter of 1981–1982. Among this total of sixty-two honored designers or design teams, three submissions, in addition to Lin's, were headed by women, although women were members of many teams. On May 28, 1981, Doubek and Spreiregen sent all entrants a letter listing of prizewinners and honorable mentions and enclosed a *Washington Post* article by Wolf von Eckardt praising Lin's design, the jury report, and a copy of Lin's explanatory statement that had been an integral part of her design. For two days, May 28–29, 1981, all the competition entries were on public view at Hangar #3.

Lin's original boards (ADE-Unit 2228; PLATE 6.1) and those of a number of other prizewinning designs

are preserved in the Prints and Photographs Division. They, and the nearly complete set of slides recording the competitors' designs, constitute a unique resource for the study of many aspects of late twentieth-century American design. They represent primarily a young generation bombarded by numerous aesthetic and philosophical theories ranging from abstraction to superrealism, from postmodernism to mystical religions. The VVMF collection offers scholars an unparalleled study collection of professional and amateur designs at a moment in the twentieth century when an unusually broad spectrum of traditional attitudes as well as innovative ideas were both current and acceptable.

Because designs were received from all fifty states and U.S. possessions, they represent a cross section of regional and national trends in architectural and design education, which can be studied here in detail. In both the competition entries and the design and construction documents (PLATE 6.2; FIG. 6.2), a

FIG. 6.3. Maya Lin, architect. Cooper-Lecky Partnership, project architects. Model, Vietnam Veterans Memorial, Constitution Gardens, Constitution Avenue and Henry Bacon Drive, N.W., Washington, D.C., 1981. Lot 13034, no. 79, H size. LC-USZ62-133459.

wide range of presentation methods, primarily architectural drawings from drafted to freehand, but also architectural models (FIG. 6.3) and sculptural maquettes (see FIG. 6.4), are available for examination. The collection offers an excellent opportunity to study the work of design teams, an important part of contemporary architectural education. Because the visual and factual data provided entrants were both extensive and directed toward specific philosophical and design goals, future studies of the collection might focus on literal interpretations of the stated program versus ideological design statements. Iconographers will find in the memorial entries rich materials to document and study the reemergence of symbolism in the postmodern era. Women partici-

pated in the Vietnam Veterans Memorial competition in significant numbers; future study of their entries vis-à-vis those of their male colleagues might focus on gender issues relating to aesthetics.

Particularly interesting will be future comparisons of the jury's choices with the entire collection of entries because large numbers of the designs fell into a limited number of typologies (PLATES 6.3, 6.4). Designs predicated on circles dominated because of the geometry of the site, a large horseshoe-shaped meadow nearly enclosed by trees. Walls and pylons often suggested themselves as the armature on which to display the names. The entries offer a particularly rich collection with which to explore the interaction of historicism with modernism in all areas of design. A large number of Washington-area designers entered the competition; six were among the sixty-two top designs.

Although few submissions included representational sculpture, both the second- and third-prize designs (team submissions) featured prominent figural groups. Frederick E. Hart and the team he belonged to won third place with an idea that provided the impetus for his design of three soldiers—one an African American—supporting each other in the travails of war. The Park Service dedicated this bronze group, with flagstaff and surrounding landscaping, in November 1984. Hart had entered two figural groups in the competition entry of 1981, a single running figure facing two figures supporting one another, placed at each end of a concave, semicircular wall.[3]

Because many women in military service did not feel that those who had served in Vietnam were adequately commemorated in the memorial's walls, the Vietnam Women's Memorial Fund was founded in 1984. Glenna Goodacre's realistic sculptural group of three women in nurses's uniforms aiding fallen soldiers was dedicated on Veterans Day, November 11, 1993. Located in a grove along the pathway leading to Hart's sculpture from Constitution Gardens, Goodacre's figures are separated from Lin's wall by a line of trees and a meadow. While Lin's wall can be seen from both Hart's and Goodacre's works, they can only be glimpsed when trees are bare of leaves. This isolation of each of the artworks was intentional because each was conceived separately by their creators and each has a distinct history in the overall effort to commemorate both the living and the dead whose lives were changed by the Vietnam War.[4]

The records generated by the Vietnam Veterans Memorial Fund (approximately forty-three thousand items), a nonprofit organization incorporated on April 27, 1979, are located primarily in the Library of Congress. The Manuscript Division has 130 boxes of records organized into six series: the office files (including blueprints and construction plans); files of Robert W. Doubek, co-founder and executive director of the fund (includes blueprints and construction drawings); files relating to the National Salute to Vietnam Veterans that took place between November 10 and 14, 1982; fund-raising files; miscellaneous documents including posters; and card files of addresses of donors and veterans. The Motion Picture, Broadcasting, and Recorded Sound Division preserves audio- and videotapes of various ceremonies and press conferences connected with the memorial.

Related records of federal agencies involved in the location, design selection process, and implementation of the monument include documents compiled by the Commission of Fine Arts, which reviewed Lin's design for acceptance and held public meetings where praise and criticism of it were voiced. The National Capital Planning Commission (NCPC) also held public hearings as part of their approval process; minutes of these meetings are among the Manuscript Division's holdings, but additional records are maintained by NCPC. The National Park Service, which maintains the memorial, has a large collection of construction and postconstruction photographs and slides, as well as the commissioned model. Objects of a permanent nature left at the memorial are housed in the National Archives. The Vietnam Generation Project at the National Museum of American History, Smithsonian Institution, collects documents relating to the memorial.

A clipping file on the Vietnam Veterans Memorial, primarily from the *Washington Post*, continues to be compiled by the Washingtoniana Division of the Martin Luther King Library. The American Institute of Architects held an exhibition of the winning and meritorious designs at the Octagon from November 11, 1981, to January 3, 1982, for which they have some visual and textural records, but many are duplicated in the Library of Congress's holdings.

The extensive literature on the Vietnam Veterans Memorial has concentrated on two major issues, the history and significance of the postcompetition controversy and interpretations of Lin's design. Her design has been explained within political, aesthetic, moral, and psychological contexts. Much of the initial criticism of Lin's design focused on it as an anti–Vietnam War comment; the abstraction of her design has been viewed as elitist in opposition to Hart's realism, seen as representing populist taste; and, many commentators have noted its sacred ambiance and emotionally powerful effect.[5]

Fig. 6.4. Frederick E. Hart, sculptor. Study of a maquette for the "Three Fighting Men," proposed Addition to Vietnam Veterans Memorial, Constitution Gardens, Constitution Avenue and Henry Bacon Drive, N.W., Washington, D.C. Gouache on photoprint. 1982. ADE-UNIT 2259 (Photo size). LC-USZ62-114093.

COLOR PLATES

PLATE 1.1. William Thornton,
architect. Proposed West Front,
U.S. Capitol, Washington, D.C.
Elevation. Graphite, ink, and water-
color on paper. Ca. 1795–1797.
ADE-UNIT 2470, no. 5, C size.
LC-USZ62-4712.

PLATE 1.2. Stephen Hallet, architect. Conference Room, scheme
"E," U.S. Capitol, Washington,
D.C. Section and partial elevation.
Ink, wash, and watercolor on
paper. 1793. ADE-UNIT 2461,
no. 9, D size. LC-USZC4-1094.

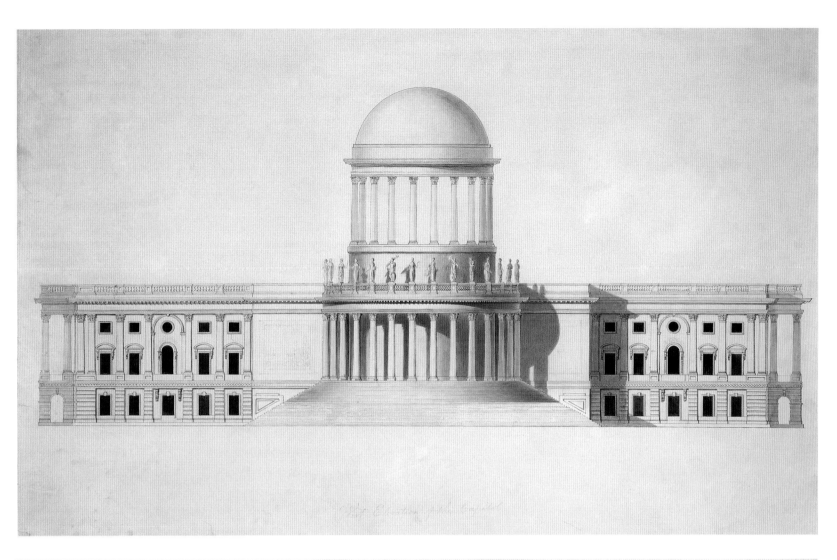

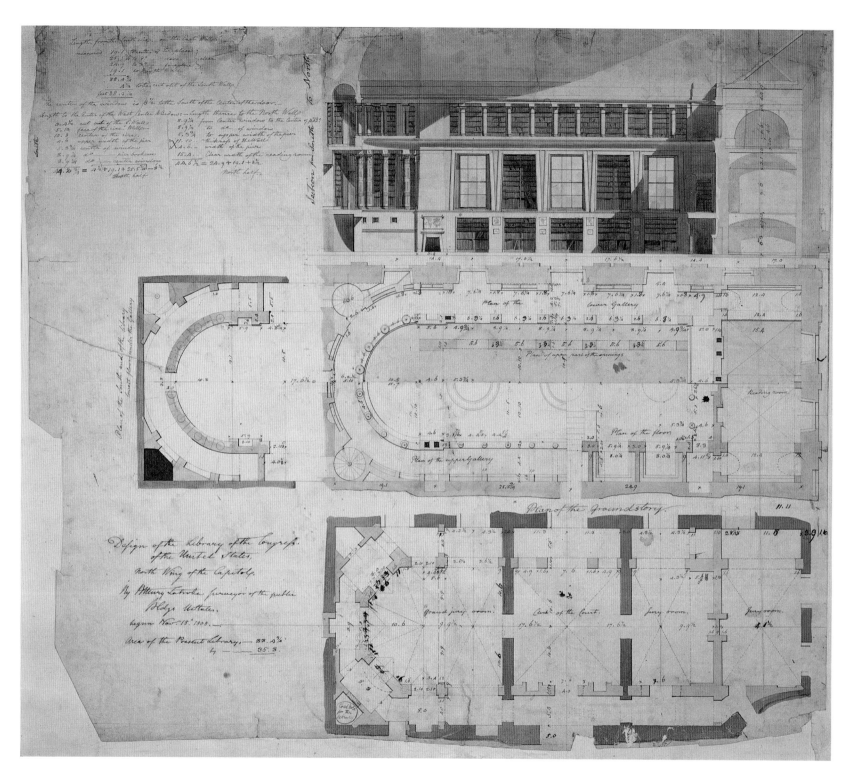

PLATE 1.3. B. Henry Latrobe,
architect. "Design of the Library of
the Congress of the United States,
North Wing," United States
Capitol, Washington, D.C. Plans
and section from south to north.
Watercolor, wash, graphite, and ink
on paper. 1808. ADE-UNIT 2462,
no. 33, D size. LC-USZC4-226.

PLATE I.4. B. Henry Latrobe, architect. South (principal) front, proposed design for a House for John Tayloe, Washington, D.C. Elevations. Graphite, ink, and watercolor on paper. 1796–1799. ADE-UNIT 2886, no. 20, C size. LC-USZC4-35.

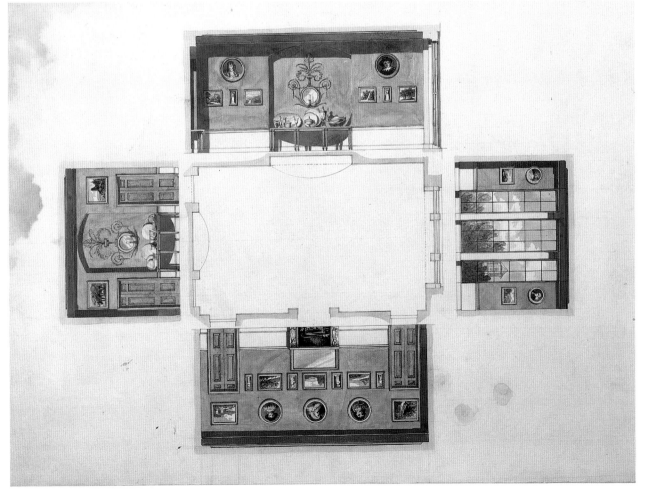

PLATE I.5. B. Henry Latrobe, architect. Dining room, proposed design for a house for John Tayloe. Washington, D.C. Plan and elevations. Graphite, ink, and watercolor on paper. 1796–1799. ADE-UNIT 2886, no. 23, C size. LC-USZC4-3730.

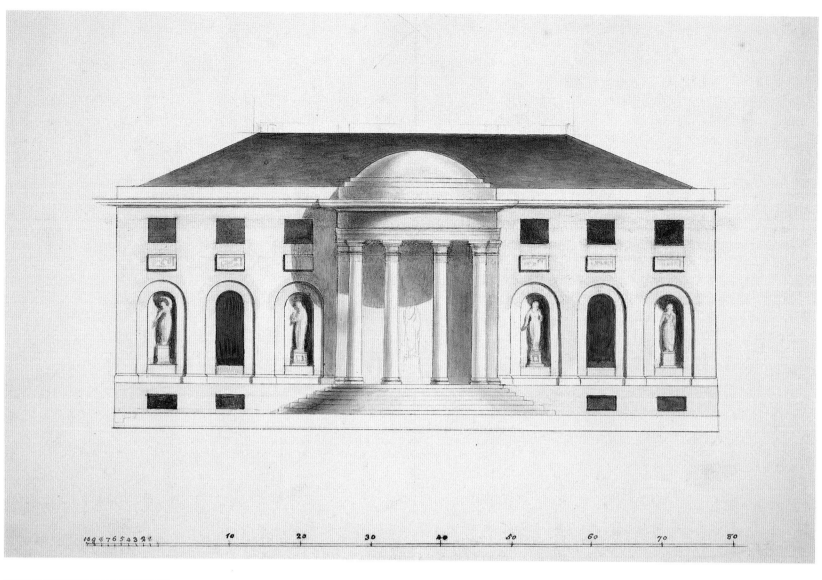

PLATE 1.6 (*opposite, top*).
William Thornton, architect.
Preliminary design, house for
Robert Peter. *Tudor Place*,
1644 31st Street, N.W., Washington, D.C. Elevation. Ink, watercolor, and graphite on paper.
1808–1811. ADE-UNIT 2588,
no. 4, A size. LC-USZC4-233.

PLATE 1.7 (*opposite, bottom*).
B[enjamin]. F. Smith Jr., designer
and lithographer. F. Michelin
(New York), printer. "Washington,
D. C., with projected improve-
ments. Respectfully dedicated to
the President and Citizens of the
United States by the publishers,
Smith & Jenkins, N.Y." Bird's-eye
perspective view. Color lithograph
by B. F. Smith. Printed in tints
by F. Michelin, New York.
Ca. 1852. PGA-SMITH, B. F.,
F size-Washington Monument.
LC-USZC4-579.

PLATE 1.8. Adolph E. Melander,
architect. "Library of Congress Art
Gallery." Competition for the
Library of Congress, Washington,
D.C. Interior perspective. Ink,
colored ink, and gouache on paper.
1873. ADE-UNIT 2436, no.6,
D size. LC-USZC4-3729.

PLATE 1.9. Paul W. Bartlett,
sculptor. Glenn Brown,
architect. The Alfred Noble
Memorial Fountain, E Street
and New York Avenue, N.W.,
Washington, D.C. Elevation
and partial plan. Photographic
print/watercolor on paper. 1920.
ADE-UNIT 2188, no. 33
(Photo size). LC-USZC4-3715.

PLATE 1.10. Frank Lloyd Wright, architect. Gordon Strong Automobile Objective, Sugar Loaf Mountain, Montgomery County, Maryland. Perspective. Graphite and colored pencil on Japanese paper. 1925. Gift of Donald D. Walker, copyright Frank Lloyd Wright Foundation, reproduced by permission. ADE-UNIT 2605, no. 1, D size. LC-USZC4-2195.

PLATE 1.11. George N. Ray, architect. House for George H. Kennedy, Worcester, Massachusetts. Elevation and details. Graphite and colored pencil on trace. 1927. ADE-UNIT 401, no. 19, C size. LC-USZC4-3703.

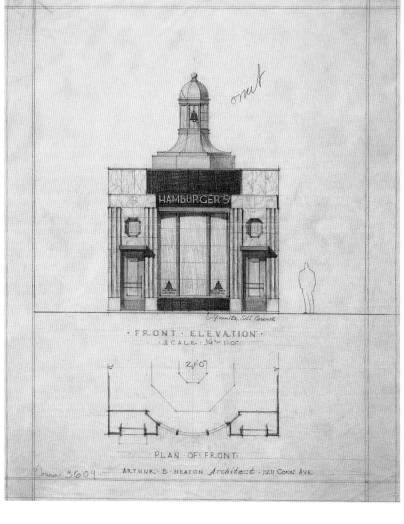

PLATE 1.12. Arthur B. Heaton, architect. "Blue Bell System Hamburger" restaurant, 1011 D Street at Pennsylvania Avenue, N.W., Washington, D.C. Front elevation and plan. Graphite and colored pencil on trace. 1936–1937. ADE-UNIT 721, no. 5, A size. LC-USZC4-3709.

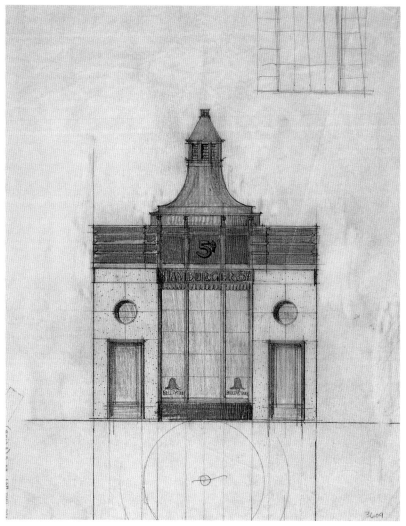

PLATE 1.13. Arthur B. Heaton, architect. "Blue Bell System Hamburger" restaurant, 1011 D Street at Pennsylvania Avenue, N.W., Washington, D.C. Front elevation and plan. Graphite and colored pencil on trace. 1936–1937. ADE-UNIT 721, no. 12, C size. LC-USZC4-3704.

Flood Light
Reflector

PLATE 1.14. Arthur B. Heaton, architect. "Blue Bell System Hamburger" restaurant, 1011 D Street at Pennsylvania Avenue, N.W., Washington, D.C. Front elevation and plan. Graphite and colored pencil on trace. 1936–1937. ADE-UNIT 721, no. 4, A size. LC-USZC4-19.

¼" Scale

PLATE 1.15. Arthur B. Heaton, architect. "Blue Bell System Hamburger" restaurant, 1402 Park Road, N.W., Washington, D.C. Front elevation and plan. Graphite and colored pencil on trace. 1936–1937. ADE-UNIT 721, no. 8, A size. LC-USZC4-11990.

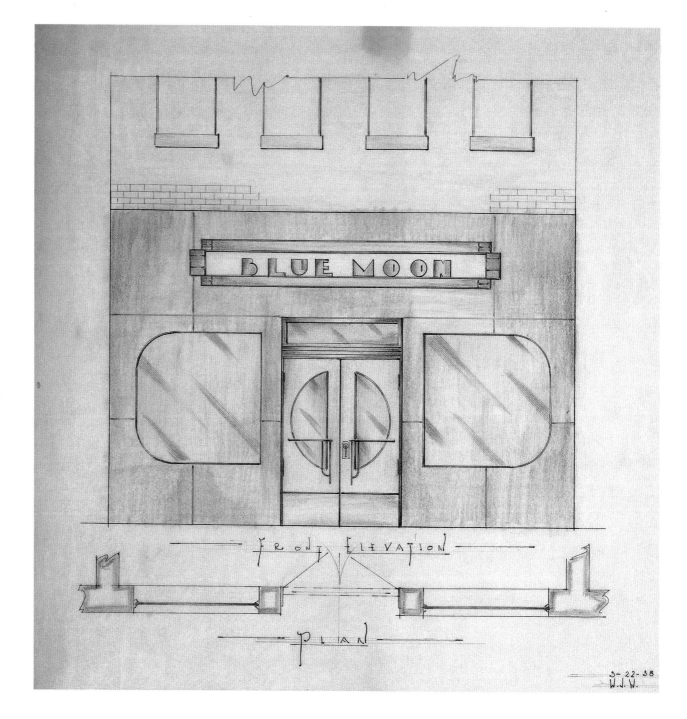

PLATE 1.16. Luther R. Ray, architect, W.J.W, draftsman. "Blue Moon," Washington, D.C. (?). Elevation and plan of front. Graphite and colored pencil on trace. 1938. ADE-UNIT 2753, no. 1, B size. LC-USZC4-3737.

PLATE 1.17. Winold Reiss, designer. "Sketch for Madrillon Restaurant," Washington, D.C. Interior perspective and details. Graphite and tempera on paper. Ca. 1930–1940. ADE-UNIT 2765, no. 1, B size. LC-USZC4-3717.

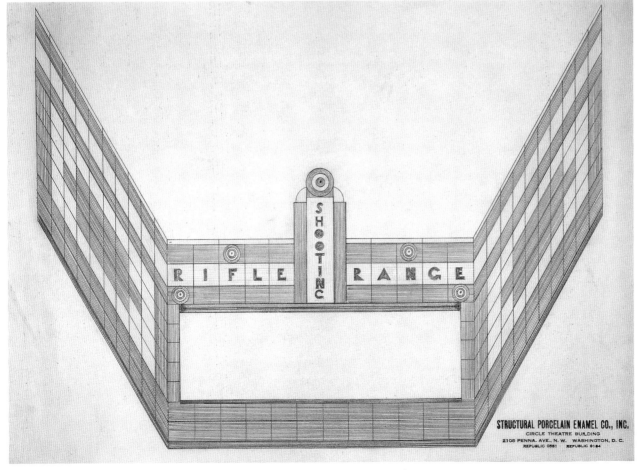

PLATE 1.18. Luther R. Ray, architect. Structural Porcelain Enamel Co., Inc. "Rifle Shooting Range." Perspective. Graphite and colored pencil on trace. After 1937. ADE-UNIT 2706, no. 1, B size. LC-USZC4-3738.

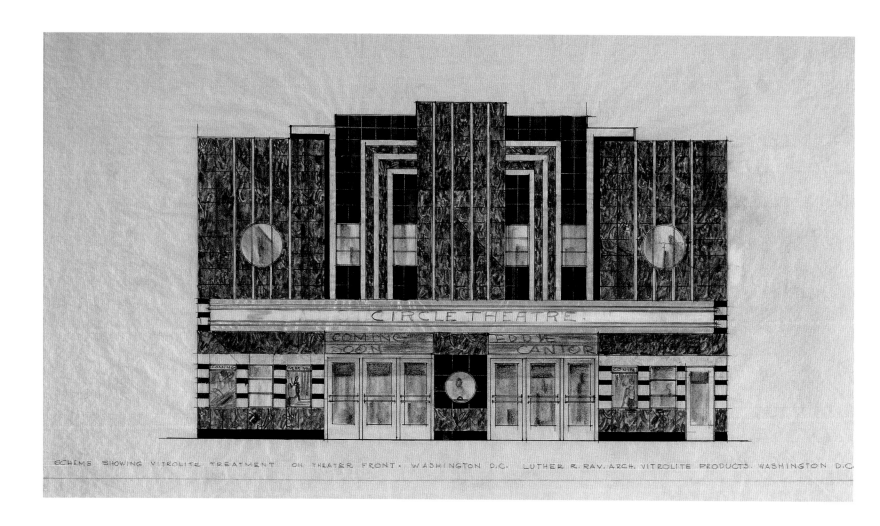

PLATE 1.19. Luther R. Ray,
architect. "Scheme showing
Vitrolite Treatment on Theater
Front," "Circle Theatre,"
2105 Pennsylvania Avenue,
N.W., Washington, D.C. Front
elevation. Graphite, ink, and
colored pencil on trace. 1932–1933.
ADE-UNIT 2750, no. 1, B size.
LC-USZC4-3702.

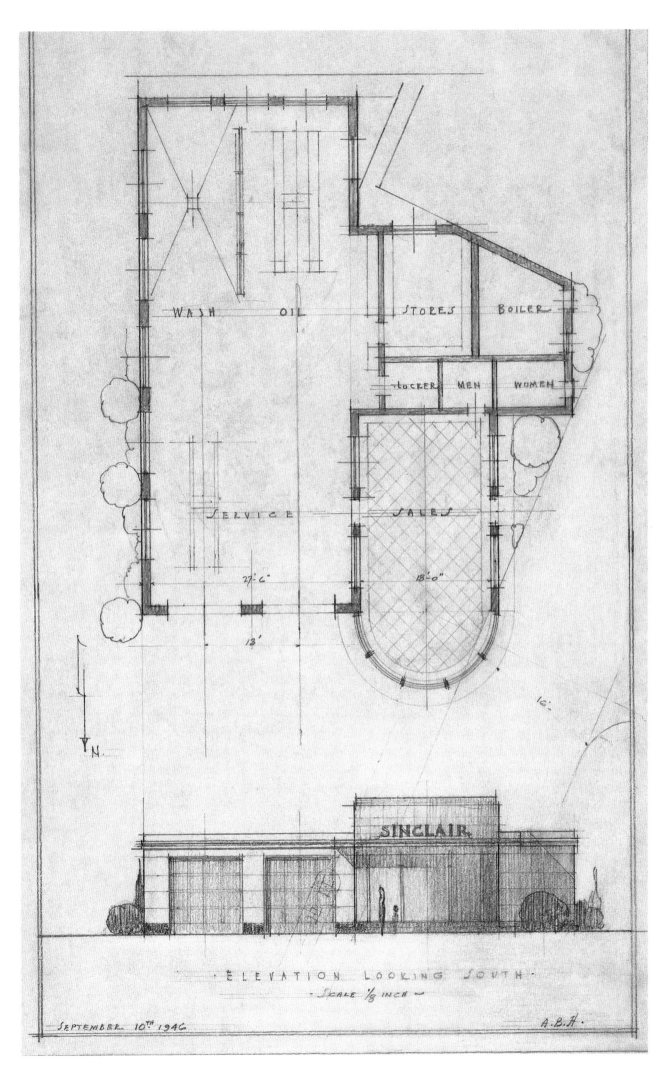

WASH   OIL   STORES   BOILER

LOCKER MEN WOMEN

SERVICE   SALES

27'-6"   18'-0"

13'

16'

N

SINCLAIR

·ELEVATION LOOKING SOUTH·

·SCALE ⅛ INCH~

SEPTEMBER 10ᵀᴴ 1946   A.B.H.

PLATE 1.20. Arthur B. Heaton
for Berla & Abel, architects.
One of two studies for a "Sinclair"
automobile service station.
Plan and elevation. Graphite
and colored pencil. 1946.
ADE-UNIT 952, no. 1, B size.

PLATE 1.21. Kevin Roche John Dinkeloo and Associates, architects. Office of Charles and Ray Eames, consultants for program and exhibit design. Proposed National Aquarium, Ohio and Buckeye Drives, S.W., Washington, D.C. Perspective. Mixed media on transparency, film overlays. 1966–1971. The Work of Charles and Ray Eames, bequest of Ray Eames. ADE-UNIT 2810, no. 441, A size. LC-USZC4-11484.

PLATE 1.22 (*opposite*, *top*). Anonymous. Entry, Vietnam Veterans Memorial Design Competition, Constitution Gardens, Constitution Avenue and Henry Bacon Drive, N.W., Washington, D.C. Perspectives. Tempera on paper mounted on board. 1981. ADE-UNIT 2242, no. 1, E size. LC-USZC4-3767.

PLATE 1.23 (*opposite*, *bottom*). Doug Michels, architect. "Dolphin America" Hotel. Massachusetts Avenue and I Street, N.W., Washington, D.C. Section. Graphite, ink, and colored pencil on trace. 1989. ADE-UNIT 1983, no. 11, C size. LC-USZC4-3700.

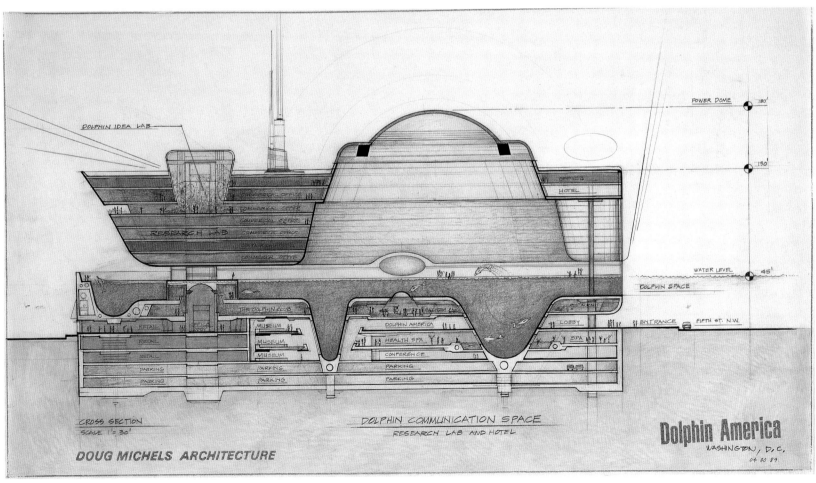

CROSS SECTION
SCALE 1"=30'

DOUG MICHELS ARCHITECTURE

DOLPHIN COMMUNICATION SPACE
RESEARCH LAB AND HOTEL

Dolphin America
WASHINGTON, D.C.
04 30 89

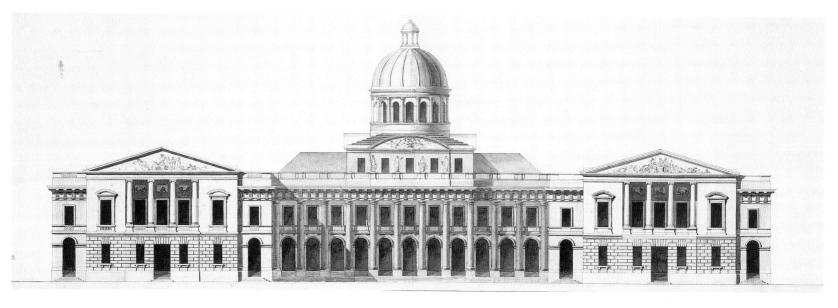

PLATE 2.1 (*opposite, top*). Stephen Hallet, architect. Principal front, scheme "B," U.S. Capitol, Washington, D.C. "B2" or "the Fancy Piece." Elevation. Ink, wash, and watercolor on paper. 1791. ADE-UNIT 2458, no. 2, E size. LC-USZC4-1454.

PLATE 2.2 (*opposite, center*). Stephen Hallet, architect. "Principal front," scheme "C," U.S. Capitol, Washington, D.C. "C3." Elevation. Ink, wash, and watercolor on paper. 1792. ADE-UNIT 2459, no. 3, E size. LC-USZC4-221.

PLATE 2.3 (*opposite, bottom*). Stephen Hallet, architect. "Principal front," scheme "D," U.S. Capitol, Washington, D.C. "D2." Elevation. Ink, wash, and watercolor on paper. 1793. ADE-UNIT 2460, no. 2, E size. LC-USZC4-7191.

PLATE 2.4 (*above*). William Thornton, architect. East front, U.S. Capitol, Washington, D.C. Elevation. Ink, graphite, and watercolor on paper. Ca. 1795–1797. ADE-UNIT 2470, no.4, C size. LC-USZC4-1097.

PLATE 2.5 (*opposite, top*). Stephen
Hallet, architect. West front,
scheme "E," U.S. Capitol, Washington, D.C. Elevation. Ink,
wash, and watercolor on paper.
March, 1793. ADE-UNIT 2461,
no. 7, E size. LC-USZC4-1088.

PLATE 2.6 (*opposite, bottom*).
B. Henry Latrobe, architect.
"West elevation," U.S. Capitol,
Washington, D.C. Ink
and watercolor on paper. 1811.
ADE-UNIT 2462, no. 4,
D size. LC-USZC4-276.

PLATE 2.7. B. Henry Latrobe,
architect. "South elevation," U. S.
Capitol, Washington, D.C. Ink,
wash, and watercolor on paper.
1810–1811. ADE-UNIT 2462,
no. 5, D size. LC-USZC4-197.

PLATE 2.8. George Munger,
artist. View of the ruins
of the United States Capitol,
Washington, D.C. Watercolor on
paper. 1814. DLC/PP-2001:064.
LC-USZC4-11489.

PLATE 2.9. Charles Bulfinch, architect. "Section of Rotunda," U. S. Capitol, Washington, D.C. Ink, wash, and graphite on paper. Ca. 1821–1822. ADE-UNIT 2474, no. 7, B size. LC-USZC4-352.

PLATE 2.12. Constantino Brumidi, artist. Sketch for a decorative frieze, after Jean Le Pautre. Elevation. Ink, graphite, and watercolor on paper. n.d. Lot 13061 (H). LC-USZC4-3797.

PLATE 2.10 (*opposite, top*). William Thornton, B. Henry Latrobe, and Charles Bulfinch, architects. Alexander Jackson Davis, delineator. East front, U.S. Capitol, Washington, D.C. Measured drawing, elevation. Ink, wash, and watercolor on paper. 1834. ADE-UNIT 2464, no. 6, C size. LC-USZC4-1278.

PLATE 2.11 (*opposite, bottom*). John Rubens Smith, artist. West front, U.S. Capitol, Washington, D.C. Ink and watercolor on paper. 1828. DLC/PP-1996:032.6. LC-USZC4-3671.

PLATE 3.1. B. Henry Latrobe, architect. "Looking glass frame for President's House," Washington, D.C. Elevation. Ink, watercolor, wash on paper. 1809. ADE-UNIT 2462, no. 1, A size. LC-USZC4-47.

PLATE 3.2. B. Henry Latrobe, architect. "View of the East Front of the President's House, with the Addition of the North & South Porticos," Washington, D.C. Elevation. Ink, watercolor, wash on paper. 1807–1817. ADE-UNIT 2464, no. 4, B size. LC-USZC4-1495.

PLATE 3.3. B. Henry Latrobe, architect. "Elevation of the South Front of the President's House, copied from the design as proposed to be altered in 1807," Washington, D.C. Elevation. Ink, watercolor, wash on paper. 1817. ADE-UNIT 2464, no. 3, B size. LC-USZC4-249.

PLATE 4.1 (*right*). Waddy B. Wood, architect. Presentation drawing, office building, 15th and G Streets, N.W., Washington, D.C. Perspective rendering. Graphite, watercolor, and ink on paper. Ca. 1925–1930. Project. ADE-Unit 1683, no. 1, C size. LC-USZC4-3728.

PLATE 4.2 (*opposite, top*). Starrett & Van Vleck, architects; F. L. Cruess (?), delineator. "Julius Garfinckel & Co.," 14th and F Streets, N.W., Washington, D.C. Perspective. Colored pencil, watercolor, and gouache on photoprint mounted on board. 1929. ADE-UNIT 2420, no. 1, C size (Photo). LC-USZC4-3725.

PLATE 4.3 (*opposite, bottom*). Arthur B. Heaton, architect. Embassy Building, Connecticut Avenue and N Street, N.W., Washington, D.C. South Elevation. Colored pencil on photostat. 1932. Project. ADE-UNIT 646, no. 10, A size. LC-USZC4-3754.

STARRETT & VAN VLECK Architects
NEW YORK.

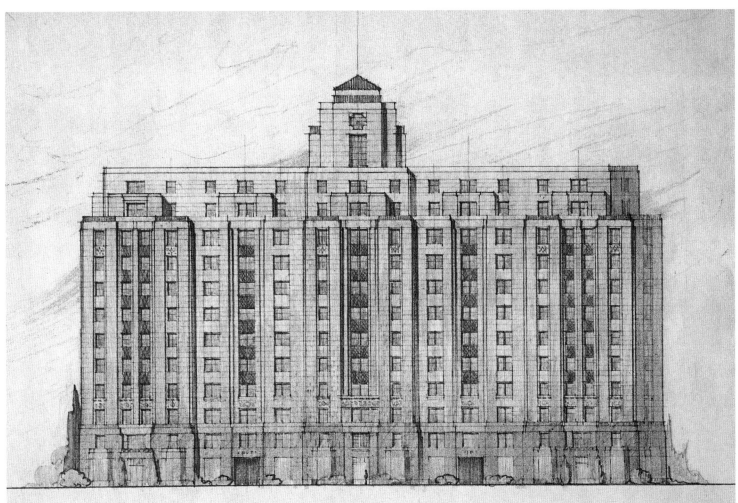

· S O U T H · E L E V A T I O N ·
· Scale 1/16 inch ·

ARTHUR B. HEATON Architect
WASHINGTON · D · C ·

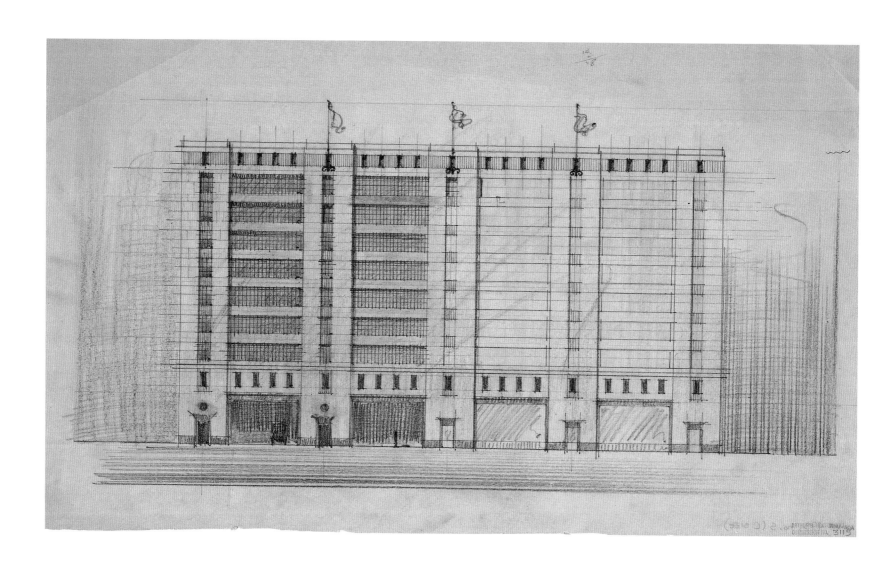

PLATE 4.4. Arthur B. Heaton,
architect. Parking garage with
stores for McLachlen. 10th and
G Streets, N.W., Washington,
D.C. Design study. Elevation.
Graphite and colored pencil on
tracing paper. Ca. 1926. Project.
ADE-UNIT 475, no. 5, C size.
LC-USZC4-3780.

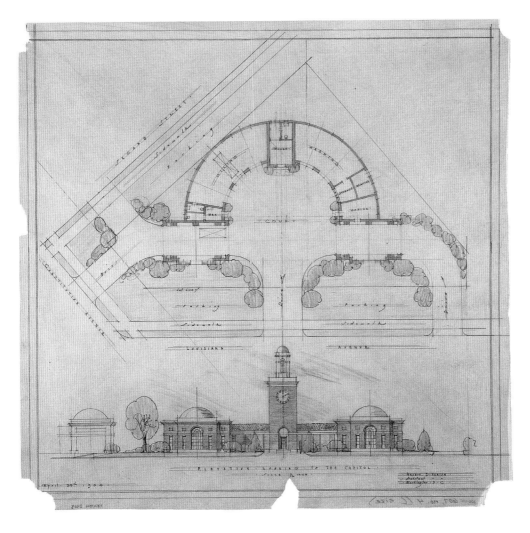

PLATE 4.5. Arthur B. Heaton, architect. American Oil Company (AMOCO) gasoline and oil service station for Bliss Properties. 2nd Street, Constitution and Louisiana Avenues, N.W., Washington, D.C. Site plan and elevation "looking to the Capitol." Graphite and colored pencil on tracing paper. 1934. Building demolished. ADE-UNIT 607, no. 4, C size. LC-USZC4-3731.

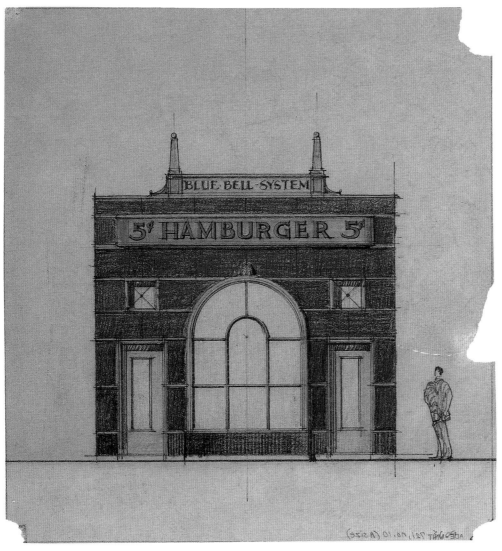

PLATE 4.6. Arthur B. Heaton, architect. "Blue Bell System Hamburger Restaurant," 1011 D Street at Pennsylvania Avenue, N.W., Washington, D.C. Front elevation. Graphite and colored pencil on trace. 1936–1937. Building demolished. ADE-UNIT 721, no. 10, A size. LC-USZC4-3708.

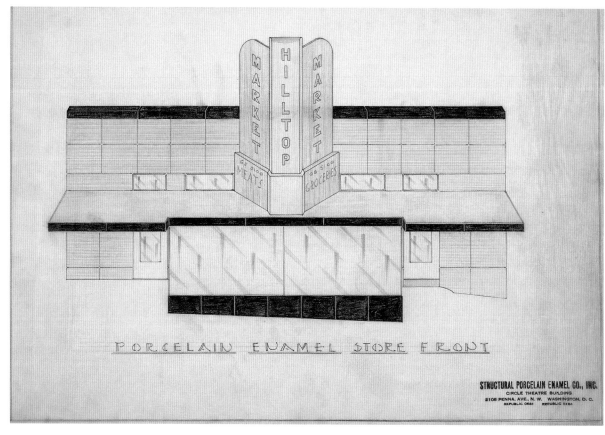

Plate 4.7 (*above*). Arthur B. Heaton, architect. Himmelieber, delineator. Shopping center for Charles C. Glover Jr., P Street, N.W., Washington, D.C. Bird's-eye perspective. Colored pencil on photostat. 1935. Project. ADE-UNIT 712, no. 8, C size. LC-USZC4-11480.

Plate 4.8. Structural Porcelain Enamel Co. Alterations ("porcelain enamel storefront") for Hilltop Market, 5706 Georgia Avenue, N.W., Washington, D.C. Perspective rendering. Graphite and colored pencil on trace. Ca. 1938. ADE-UNIT 2701, no. 1, B size. LC-USZC4-11481.

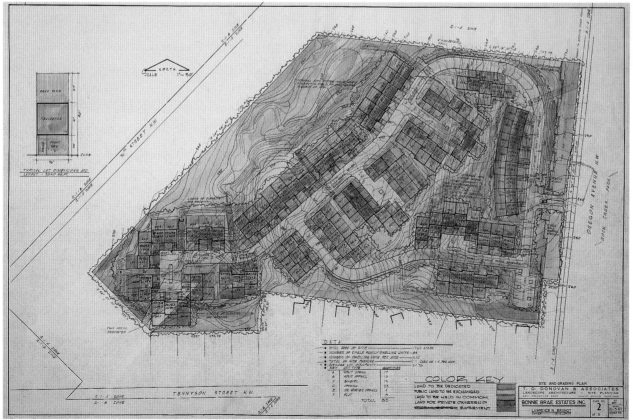

PLATE 5.1 (*above*). Donald Hudson Drayer, architect. "The Promenade" Apartment House for Landow & Company, 4710 Bethesda Avenue, Bethesda, Maryland. Bird's-eye perspective rendering. Photographic print. 1971–1973. ADE-UNIT 1508, no. 2 (Photo). LC-USZC4–3712.

PLATE 5.2. Donald Hudson Drayer, architect. T. D. Donovan & Associates, landscape architects. "Bonnie Brae Estates" housing development for Lawrence N. Brandt, Great Universal Development Co., Inc., Oregon Avenue, Unicorn Lane, and 31st Street, N.W., Washington, D.C. Site and grading plan. Fluid marker and watercolor on diazoprint. 1967. ADE-UNIT 1650, no. 8, E size. LC-USZC4-11479.

The Admiral

APARTMENTS
ADMIRAL BARNEY CIRCLE
WASHINGTON   D.C.

★ ★ ★ ★

DONALD H. DRAYER   ARCHITECT.
1413 H. ST. N.W.   WASHINGTON, D.C.

PLATE 5.3. Donald Hudson
Drayer, architect. "The Admiral
Apartments," Admiral Barney
Circle, Washington, D.C. Bird's-eye
perspective rendering. Colored
pencil on photostat. Ca. 1941–1948.
ADE-UNIT 1280, no. 1, B size.
LC-USZC4-3716.

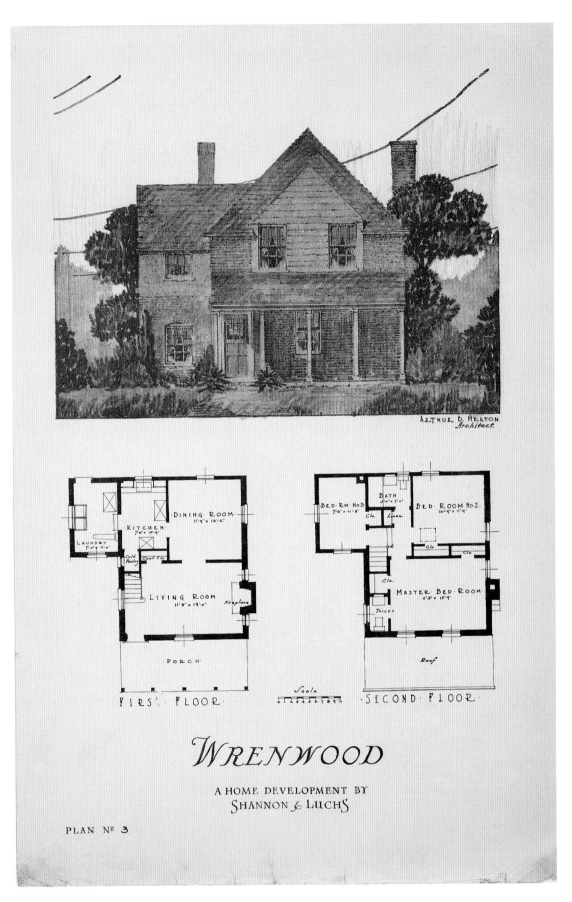

WRENWOOD

A HOME DEVELOPMENT BY
SHANNON & LUCHS

PLAN № 3

PLATE 5.4. Arthur B. Heaton, architect. Plan No. 3, promotional brochure for "Wrenwood, A Home Development by Shannon & Luchs," Quesada Street, Rittenhouse Street, Broad Branch Road, and 6000–6010 34th Place, N.W. (lots 31–39, square 2010), Washington, D.C. Elevation and floor plans. Colored pencil on photomechanical print. 1930–1931. ADE-UNIT 978, no. 37, C size. LC-USZC4-11482.

PLATE 5.5. Arthur B. Heaton, architect. Preliminary study, housing development, "Greenbelt Project—Union Green," for Union Homes, Inc., Greenbelt, Maryland. Elevation. Graphite and colored pencil on tracing paper. 1938. ADE-UNIT 979, no. 4/5/6 /10, C size; 8/9, E size). LC-USZC4-3783.

IN MEMORIAM

TROJAN LETTER TYPE: 3/4"

"Walking through this park-like area, the memorial appears as a rift in the earth — a long, polished black stone wall, emerging from and receding into the earth. Approaching the memorial, the ground slopes gently downward, and the low walls emerging on either side, growing out of the earth, extend and converge at a point below and ahead. Walking into the grassy site contained by the walls of this memorial we can barely make out the carved names upon the memorial's walls. These names, seemingly infinite in number, convey the sense of overwhelming numbers, while unifying these individuals into a whole. For this memorial is meant not to be a monument to the individual, but rather as a memorial to the men and women who died during this war, as a whole.

The memorial is composed not as an unchanging monument, but as a moving composition, to be understood as we move into and out of it; the passage itself is gradual, the descent to the origin slow, but it is at the origin that the meaning of this memorial is to be fully understood. At the intersection of these walls, on the right side, at this wall's top is carved the date of the first death. It is followed by the names of those who have died in the war, in chronological order. These names continue on this wall, appearing to recede into the earth at the wall's end. The names resume on the left wall, as the wall emerges from the earth, continuing back to the origin, where the date of that death is carved, at the bottom of this wall. Thus the war's beginning and end meet; the war is 'complete', coming full circle, yet broken by the earth that bounds the angle's open side, and contained within the earth itself. As we turn to leave, we see these walls stretching into the distance, directing us to the Washington Monument, to the left, and the Lincoln Memorial, to the right, thus bringing the Vietnam Memorial into historical context. We, the living, are brought to a concrete realization of these deaths.

Brought to a sharp awareness of such a loss, it is up to each individual to resolve or come to terms with this loss. For death is in the end a personal and private matter, and the area contained within this memorial is a quiet place meant for personal reflection and private reckoning. The black granite walls, each 200 feet long, and 10 feet below ground at their lowest point (gradually ascending towards ground level) effectively act as a sound barrier, yet are of such a height and length so as not to appear threatening or enclosing. The actual area is wide and shallow, allowing for a sense of privacy, and the sunlight from the memorial's southern exposure along with the grassy park surrounding and within its walls contribute to the serenity of the area. Thus this memorial is for those who have died, and for us to remember them.

The memorial's origin is located approximately at the center of this site; its legs each extending 200 feet towards the Washington Monument and the Lincoln Memorial. The walls, contained on one side by the earth, begin at ground level at their point of origin, gradually lessening in height, until they finally recede totally into the earth at their ends. The walls are to be made of a hard, polished black granite, with the names to be carved in a simple Trojan letter, 3/4 inch high, allowing for nine inches in length for each name. The memorial's construction involves recontouring the area within the walls' boundaries so as to provide an easily accessible stable growth, but as much of the site as possible should be left untouched (including trees). The area should be made into a park for all the public to enjoy."

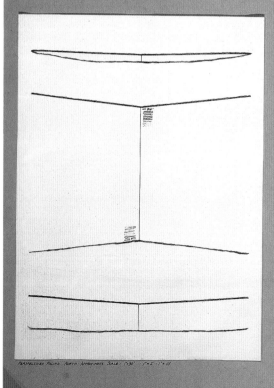

PERSPECTIVES FACING NORTH APPROXIMATE SCALE 1:30   1"=2'—1"=10'

PLATE 6.1 (*opposite*). Maya Lin, architect. No. 1026, panel 1, winning entry, Vietnam Veterans Memorial Design Competition, Constitution Gardens, Constitution Avenue and Henry Bacon Drive, N.W., Washington, D.C. Plans, perspective, and elevations. Ink and mixed media on paper mounted on board. 1981. ADE-UNIT 2228, no. 1, E size. LC-USZC4-1353.

PLATE 6.2. Maya Lin, architect; Interface Architects, Paul Stevenson Oles, delineator. Study below grade, Vietnam Veterans Memorial, Constitution Gardens, Constitution Avenue and Henry Bacon Drive, N.W., Washington, D.C. Perspective. Black wax-based pencil and colored pencil on watercolor paper. 1981. DLC/PP-1999.015.119, A size. LC-USZC4-11477.

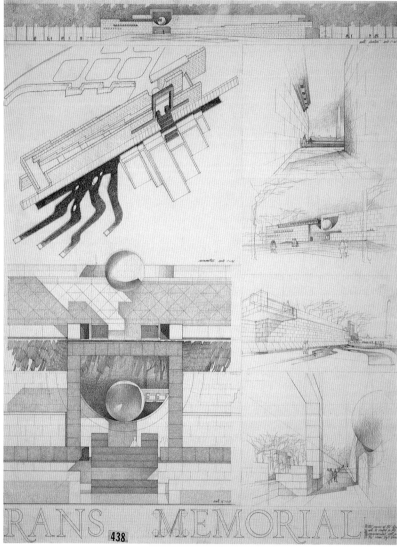

PLATE 6.3. Henry F. Arnold, architect. No. 235, entry. Vietnam Veterans Memorial Design Competition, Constitution Gardens, Constitution Avenue and Henry Bacon Drive, N.W., Washington, D.C. Plans, perspectives, and details. Graphite, colored pencil, fluid marker on illustration board. 1981. ADE-UNIT 2434, no. 5, E size. LC-USZC4-3773.

PLATE 6.4. Richard Samuel Shank, architect. No. 138, entry, Vietnam Veterans Memorial Design Competition, Constitution Gardens, Constitution Avenue and Henry Bacon Drive, N.W., Washington, D.C. Elevations, perspectives, and details. Graphite and colored pencil on paper mounted on masonite. 1981. ADE-UNIT 2430, no. 1, E size. LC-USZC4-3786.

ACKNOWLEDGMENTS

This publication and the work that it represents in the conservation, housing, and processing of more than forty thousand architecture, design, and engineering drawings and related documents are the result of the Washingtoniana II Project (1986–present), funded entirely through the generosity of a series of grants from the Morris and Gwendolyn Cafritz Foundation. Its predecessor, the Washingtoniana I Project (1983–1989), was also supported through series of grants from the Cafritz Foundation and similarly made available more than seven hundred fifty thousand photographic images relating the Washington, D.C., metropolitan area, and culminated in the publication of Kathleen Collins's *Washingtoniana: Photographs: Collections in the Prints and Photographs Division of the Library of Congress* (Washington, D.C.: Library of Congress, 1989).

Many individuals contributed to the Washingtoniana II Project, and we take this opportunity to thank them. The idea and original grant requests for the project were conceived and administered by myself and Renata V. Shaw and Elisabeth Betz Parker, both former assistant chiefs in the Prints and Photographs Division at the Library of Congress. Stephen E. Ostrow, Linda Ayres, Ellen Hahn, and Jeremy Adamson, all chiefs of the Prints and Photographs Division, continued to administer and support the project to its completion and were aided in this task by Doris Lee, Robert Lisbeth, James Carroll, and other members of the division's administrative staff. Head curators Bernard Reilly and Harry Katz also helped to guide the work of the project, as did various heads and team leaders in the division's Technical Services section, including Helena Zinkham, Brett Carnell, and Sarah Rouse, as did Mary Ison in its Reference Section. Peter Waters and Doris Hamburg in the library's Conservation Office guided the conservation survey and treatment, which was carried out by conservators Michele Hamill and Anne Fuhrman. Initial cataloging information was gathered by Anne Mitchell and Karen Chittenden, who later worked to complete more than 2,900 new LOT and UNIT records, following processing meetings that included myself and staff members from the division's Curatorial (Cristina Carbone, Maricia Battle), Reference (Marilyn Ibach, Samuel V. Daniel), and Technical Services (Elisabeth Parker, Helena Zinkham, Karen Chittenden, Anne Mitchell, Brett Carnell, Grey Marcangelo, Richard Herbert) sections.

The publication reflects the dedication of many people. I had the privilege to select the various authors and to suggest their topics, and to work with them to choose their illustrations. Leslie Freudenheim, Diane Tepfer, and Pamela Scott all provided valuable editorial assistance during the course of the project; Pamela most extensively helped to edit all of the essays and to draft the great majority of the biographical entries. Samuel V. Daniel, Maricia Battle, and I drafted the captions for most of the illustrations. After an initial system was set up to track photographic reproduction orders for the publication, Sarah Hadley, Marica Battle, and I carried this work to completion. Marilyn Ibach drafted the guidelines for users.

The director of the Library of Congress's Publishing Office, W. Ralph Eubanks, and senior editor Evelyn Sinclair provided unfailing support in helping to shape and refine the publication and in negotiating a publishing agreement with the Johns Hopkins University Press, where acquisitions editor Robert J. Brugger and his assistant Melody Herr gave it their patient support, and Andre Barnett skillfully honed its ultimate form.

Our gratitude to the authors who gave so much of their time and talent to make this publication and broader project so successful also is immense. They include William C. Allen, Frances Brousseau, Karen Chittenden, Jeffrey Cohen, Leslie Freudenheim, James M. Goode, Donald Jackson, Michele Hamill, C. M. Harris, Antoinette J. Lee, Hélène Lipstadt, Richard Longstreth, Denys Peter Myers, James F. O'Gorman, William Seale, Thomas Somma, Pamela Scott, Damie Stillman, Diane Tepfer, Barbara Wolanin, Gwendolyn Wright, and Tony P. Wrenn.

Reference assistance was provided to the authors by Mary Ison, Marilyn Ibach, Samuel V. Daniel, Maja Keech, Jan Grenci, Diane Tepfer, and Leslie Freudenheim. Kathy Hoban, Donna Collins, Kit Arrington, Phil Michel, and Barbara Hoyniak in the Prints and Photographs Division all provided invaluable technical assistance and support. Yvonne Burton helped to get copies of the illustrations and essays to the authors. My colleagues in the Curatorial section were always supportive and patient as the project took me away from our shared obligations. The library's Photoduplication Service provided the photographic prints for the book's illustrations; and Georgia Zola was especially helpful, as were Pam Miller and Denise King. Many other offices and individuals in the Library of Congress contributed to this effort, from Mary Klutz in Financial Services to Larry Stafford in the Development Office.

This book could not have been completed without the support and patience of colleagues, my friends, and my family. In this regard, I in particular must express my heartfelt thanks to Pamela Scott, Evelyn Sinclair, Maricia Battle, R. N. Anderson Jr., and Margaret S. Peatross.

APPENDIX A

Ordering Reproductions and Exploring the Architecture, Design, and Engineering Collections

To Order Photographic Reproductions of Images Illustrated in This Book:

Reproductions may be ordered from the Library of Congress, Photoduplication Service, once the call number and any existing reproduction numbers for an individual item have been determined.

Individual items are identified by CALL NUMBER and REPRODUCTION NUMBER, both of which are found in the illustration captions. An example of a caption showing the call number and reproduction number is

ADE-UNIT 2810, no. 30, C size [call number]. Kevin Roche, John Dinkeloo & Associates [creator]. National Aquarium, Ohio and Buckeye Drives, S.W., Washington, D.C. Perspective and plan [title]. Graphite [medium]. 1966–1971 [date(s)]. LC-USZ62-114111 [reproduction number; describes a black-and-white film negative].

The reproduction number may be used to order the exact type of illustration shown; for example, if the illustration is in black and white, the reproduction number will be for a black-and-white illustration. If the illustration is color, the reproduction number given will be for a color illustration. If a black-and-white reproduction of a color illustration is desired, or vice versa, cite the call number and send a copy of the caption when ordering.

Photographic copies (8" × 10" and larger black-and-white prints, and 2" × 2" and 4" × 5" color transparencies) of the architectural drawings are available. The quality of the copy will vary depending on the quality of the original.

Photoreproductions can be ordered by mail, e-mail, or fax from the Library of Congress, Photoduplication Service, Washington, D.C., 20540-4570, telephone number 202-707-5640; fax number 202-707-1771; e-mail to photoduplication@loc.gov. More information is available at:

www.loc.gov/preserv/pds/order.html

To Consult Materials Mentioned but Not Illustrated in This Book:

Throughout *Capital Drawings* the reader will find many references to ADE-UNITs and LOTs. ADE-UNITs are groups of drawings in the Architecture, Design, and Engineering Collection related to a specific project; they include items that are served to readers as individual pieces. LOTS are groups of items also related to a specific project that have been cataloged as a group and which are served as a group.

A full listing of all ADE-UNITs and some related LOTs is available online at:

www.loc.gov/rr/print/catalog.html

Readers may do an "all collections" search by first clicking on "Search the Catalog" to reach the "Search ALL RECORDS in this catalog" page and typing in keywords [example: for Waggaman & Ray commission no. 203, enter "Waggaman and 203"; for Charles Bulfinch's stove notebook, type in "Bulfinch stove"]. For specific ADE-UNITs or LOTs mentioned in the body of *Capital Drawings*, readers may select "Search in number field" in the pull-down list to perform a number search. An example of a number search would be "ADE-UNIT 1827," which would detail holdings related to the reconstruction of the capitol building in Williamsburg.

The results of these searches usually will be of group records, either ADE-UNITs or LOTs. Occasionally, individual architectural drawings with full descriptions will be found.

The group records and individual items in each ADE-UNIT are listed in an unpublished finding aid in the Prints and Photographs Division Reading Room. The finding aid includes both the group description found online, plus the individual items found within that UNIT, which generally are not listed online.

Examples of the types of information found in the unpublished finding aid are given below:

An example of a group record (found in the finding aid and online) is

Title: Architectural drawings for an *official residence* ("*Executive Mansion*") for Mary Newton Foote Henderson, 16th Street NW, Washington, D.C.

Call Number: ADE-UNIT 2802

Summary: Presentation drawings showing executive mansion as perspective projections; renderings.

Medium: 3 items: ink and photographic print; in folder(s) 117 × 192 cm or smaller.

Date: 1898.

Creator: Pelz, Paul J., 1841–1918, architect.

Related name(s): Henderson, Mary F. (Mary Foote), 1842–1931, client.

Note(s): UNIT title devised.

Address and client's name from information in P&P Curatorial Files.

Source: Transfer, Architect of the Capitol; 1991; (DLC/PP-1991:268).

Card no.: 95861049 /PP

Individual items within the group record shown above of ADE-UNIT 2802 (found in full only in the unpublished finding aid) are

Call number:	ADE-UNIT 2802, no. 1, F size
Notable subject(s):	Perspective rendering
Media/support:	Ink on paper
Note(s):	
Reproduction number(s):	LC-USZ62-105251

Call number:	ADE-UNIT 2802, no. 2, F size
Notable subject(s):	Perspective rendering
Media/support:	Ink on paper
Note(s):	
Reproduction number(s):	LC-USZ62-105250

Call number:	ADE-UNIT 2802, no. 3 (Photo)
Notable subject(s):	Perspective rendering
Media/support:	Photographic print on emulsion paper
Accession no.:	DLC/PP-1991:268
Note(s):	
Reproduction number(s):	
Specifications:	none
Misc. supplementary materials:	none
Associated photographs:	none

Access to Individual Drawings Not Mentioned in This Book

Because all individual drawings are not listed in *Capital Drawings* or online, researchers who may want to explore the collections further may do so by either visiting the Prints and Photographs Division Reading Room, or by consulting with the reference staff by telephone.

Visiting the Prints and Photographs Reading Room. ADE-UNITs may be served by appointment in the Prints and Photographs Reading Room. It usually takes two visits to view ADE-UNITs, one for selecting individual drawings, and another appointment for viewing them. This is because many of the drawings require preparation to be served. On occasion individual drawings are ready for immediate service.

Consulting staff by telephone. Researchers may telephone the Prints & Photographs Division Reading Room at 202-707-6394 for further information. Depending on the amount of material involved, the staff can advise on how to proceed.

Types of Reproductions Offered

Please note that individual ADE drawings cannot be photocopied (Xeroxed) or copied full size as diazoprints. Photographic copies (8" × 10" and larger black-and-white prints, and 2" × 2" and 4" × 5" color transparencies) of the architectural drawings are available, as are copy film negatives. The quality of the copy will vary depending on the quality of the original. Xeroxes cannot be provided from the original items. *Full-size diazo process copies are not available from the original drawings.* In most cases where no negative exists, a $20 surcharge for the handling of fragile items will be added to the cost of photoduplication.

Photoreproductions can be ordered by mail or fax from the Library of Congress, Photoduplication Service, Washington, D.C., 20540-4570, telephone number 202-707-5640; fax number 202-707-1771. When placing an order for an item, it is necessary to cite the full call number. Please see the following example:

ADE-UNIT 1650, no. 1, E size, for a street grading plan for "Bonnie Brae Estates" plus any reproduction number(s) cited

APPENDIX B

Architects, Designers, and Engineers: A Listing of Online Resources

A. B. Mullett & Co. (firm active 1889–ca. 1942)
James F. Denson (active Washington ca. 1886–1890)
Alfred Bult Mullett (1834–1890). *See* main entry for Alfred Bult Mullett
Frederick William Mullett (ca. 1869–1924)
Thomas Augustine Mullett (1868–1935)
Howard G. Abel (b. 1939)
Joseph Henry Abel. *See* Berla & Abel
Richard Aber (b. 1948)
Percy Crowley Adams (1869–1953). *See* Averill & Adams
Jim Allegro (?)
Allied Architects (firm active ca. 1925–1935)
Allied Bridge Designers (active ca. 1925–1935)
David Olney Almy (b. 1938). *See* Sullivan & Almy, Inc. (firm active 1957–1970)
Alexander Pearson Almond (1904–?). *See* DeWitt, Poor, Swanke, Shelton, and Almond (associated 1965–1979)
A. M. Schneider & Co. (firm active ca. 1905–ca. 1923)
Anderson, George M. (1869–1916). *See* Elzner & Anderson (firm)
Anthony Ames (b. 1944)
Architect of the White House (title used 1940s)
Architectural Service Corporation (firm active 1916–1922)
Marion Henry Argyll (1900–1984)
John Ariss (ca. 1725–1799)
Henry F. Arnold (?)
W. S. Arrasmith (1898–1966). *See* Wischmeyer, Arrasmith & Elswick (firm active 1928–1941)
Arthur Cotton Moore Associates (firm active 1965–present)
Arthur Cotton Moore (b. 1935)
Art Metal Construction Company (firm active 1898–1968)
Snowdon Ashford (1868–1927)
Associated Architects & Engineers (firm active 1940s and 1950s)
Associated Engineers (firm active 1920s to present)
Robert Bruce Atkinson (1884–1952)

Atkinson & White (firm active 1919–ca. 1923)
Robert Bruce Atkinson (1884–1952). *See* main entry for Robert Bruce Atkinson (1884–1952)
Jarrett Carlisle White (1894–1947). *See* main entry for Jarrett Carlisle White (1894–1947)
Charles B. Atwood (d. 1895). *See* D. H. Burnham & Company
Averill & Adams (firm active 1909–1915)
Frank L. Averill (?)
Percy Crowley Adams (1869–1953)

Francis H. Bacon (1856–1940)
Clifton John Balch (b. 1954)
John Lakin Baldridge (1892–1967)
Harry Barrett (1902–1978)
John A. Barrows (1906–1931). *See also* Waterman & Barrows (firm active ca. 1928–1931)
Frederic Auguste Bartholdi (1834–1904)
Paul Wayland Bartlett (1865–1925)
Barton, Price & Wilson (firm active 1920s)
William O. Barton
Morris Price
Elsie Cobb Wilson
Emerlich H. Bauer (?)
Beale & Meigs, Engineers (firm active 1910–1920)
Carroll Beale (?)
Orton L. Meigs (?)
Leon Beaver (active ca. 1868–1888)
LeRoy C. Becker (?)
Piromis Hulsey Bell (1858–1956)
Lawrence Stevens Bellman (1876–1951). *See* Mills, Rhines, Bellman & Nordhoff (firm active 1912–1944)
Jules Jacques Benois Benedict (1879–1948)
Cletus William Bergen (1895–1966)
Bergstrom and Witmer
George Edwin Bergstrom (1876–1955)
David J. Witmer (1888–1973)
Berla & Abel (firm active 1941–1972)
Julian Emerson Berla (1902–1976)
Joseph Henry Abel (1905–1985)
Frederick A. Berlin (?)
Walter F. Beyer (?)
Federic H. Bicknell (?)
George Blagden (ca. 1769–1826)
Arthur L. Blakeslee (1880–1982)
J. A. Blanton (?)

Eleanor Boaz (?)
William C. Bond (?)
Booton and Boynton (?)
Borhek. *See* Brown-Borhek Co.
William Lawrence Bottomley (1883–1951)
Harold Lester Boutin (1910–ca. 1992). *See* Johnson & Boutin (firm active 1948–1968)
Forrest Dodge Bowie (1914–1979)
Boynton. *See* Booton and Boynton (?)
Alfred Laurens Brennan (1853–1921)
George Bridport (d. 1819)
George Sheperd Brock Jr. (1901–1973)
Charles Summers Bromwell (1869–1915)
William Brotherhead (active 1849–ca. 1894)
Bedford Brown IV (1880–1952). *See* Glenn Brown & Bedford Brown IV (firm active 1907–1921)
Glenn Brown (1854–1932). *See* Glenn Brown & Bedford Brown IV (firm active 1907–1921); Glenn Brown and James Rush Marshall (firm active ca. 1919)
William Hoskins Brown (1910–1976)
Brown-Borhek Co. (firm active 1820–?)
Bruce Price and de Sibour (firm active ca. 1902–1909)
Bruce Price (1843–1903)
Jules Henri de Sibour (1872–1938). *See also* main entry for Jules Henri de Sibour (1872–1938)
Joseph Goldsborough Bruff (1804–1889)
Constantino Brumidi (1805–1880)
Bryant and Bryant (firm active 1969–present)
Charles Irving Bryant (b. ca. 1930)
Robert E. Bryant (ca. 1932–1995)
Samuel Buck (?). *See* T. T. Waterman and Samuel Buck (active 1947)
Charles Bulfinch (1763–1844)
Gordon Bunshaft (1909–1990)
John Henry Burgee (b. 1933). *See* Johnson/Burgee (firm active 1968–1982)
D. H. Burnham. *See* D. H. Burnham & Company
Edward Everett Burr (1895–1986)
Harold Bush-Brown (1888–1983)
Henry Kirke Bush-Brown (1857–1935)
Charles Butler (ca. 1871–1953). *See* R. D. Kohn and Charles Butler, Associated Architects (firm active ca. 1911–ca. 1953)

Frances F. Campani (?)

Campbell Green Cunzolo (firm active 1960–present)

  James Stephen Campbell (b. 1922)

  Samuel J. Green (?)

  Napoleon John Cunzolo (b. 1928)

William F. Cann (?)

Thomas Carhart (b. 1944)

Carlhian of Paris, Inc. (firm active 1920s)

Carrère & Hastings (firm active 1885–ca. 1929)

  John Merven Carrère (1858–1911)

  Thomas Hastings (1860–1929)

Carter, Drayer Company (firm active ca. 1934)

  Harry B. Carter (1903–?)

  Donald H. Drayer (1909–1973). *See also* main entry for Donald H. Drayer (1909–1973)

Edward Pearce Casey (1864–1940)

Thomas Lincoln Casey Jr. (1831–1896)

Cement Gun Company (firm active 1922–1960)

Francis Ward Chandler (1844–1926)

Charles Wellford Leavitt & Son (firm active ca. 1900–ca. 1940)

  Charles Wellford Leavitt (1871?–1928)

  Gordon Leavitt (?)

Volney Ogle Chase Jr. (1902–1975)

Leon Chatelain Jr. (1902–1979)

Chatelain, Gauger, and Nolan (firm active 1956–1969)

  Leon Chatelain Jr. (1902–1979). *See also* main entry for Leon Chatelain Jr. (1902–1979)

  Earl Victor Gauger (1900–1986)

  James Nolan (?)

Chesapeake Iron Works (firm active ca. 1900–1927)

Appleton Prentiss Clark Jr. (1865–1955)

Edward Clark (1822–1902)

Warren & Clark (firm active ca. 1913–1925)

  Warren (?)

  Samuel Adams Clark (?)

Clarke, Rapuano & Holleran (firm active 1944–?)

  Gilmore David Clarke (1892–1982)

  Michael Rapuano (1904–1975)

  Leslie G. Holleran (?)

Cluss & Schulze (firm active 1877–1889)

  Adolph Cluss (1825–1905)

  Paul Schulze (1828–1897)

Albert Winslow Cobb (1858–1941)

Henry Ives Cobb (1859–1931)

Theodore Irving Coe (1872–1960)

Collins, Kronstadt, and Associates (firm active 1956–?)

  Collins, Richard Edward (1910–ca. 1981)

  Arnold M. Kronstadt (?)

The Commission of Fine Arts

Cooper, Lightbown & Son (firm active ca. 1930–ca. 1950)

James E. Cooper (1877–1930). *See* Simmons & Cooper (firm active ca. 1913–ca. 1917)

Copeland, Novak & Israel (firm active ca. 1960–ca. 1980)

  Peter Copeland (?–1975)

  Adolph Novak (b. 1912)

  Lawrence J. Israel (b. 1918)

Corning & Moore (firm active ca. 1942–ca. 1957); Corning, Moore, and Fischer (firm active ca. 1957–1969)

  Edward Burton Corning (1889–1957)

  Raymond Gilbert Moore (1889–1963)

R. Ernest Covert (1905–1988)

Allyn Cox (1896–1982)

Cram and Ferguson (firm active 1915–ca. 1938)

  Ralph Adams Cram (1863–1942). *See also* main entry for Thomas Tileston Waterman (1900–1951)

  Frank Ferguson (1861–1926)

Norris Ingersoll Crandell (1891–?)

Thomas Crawford (1813–1857)

Paul Philippe Cret (1876–1945). *See* Kelsey & Cret (firm active 1907–ca. 1910)

Robert Cronbach (b. 1908)

Daniel A. Crone (1880–ca. 1939)

Jules T. Crow (?)

Harry Francis Cunningham (1888–1959)

Napoleon John Cunzolo. *See* Campbell Green Cunzolo

Curtis & Davis (firm active 1936–?)

Cutler & Woodbridge (firm active 1920–1921)

  Howard Wright Cutler (1883–1948)

  Carlin H. Woodbridge (active in Washington 1920–1921)

D. Green Associates (firm active 1962–present)

D. H. Burnham & Co. (firm active 1894–1912)

  Daniel Hudson Burnham (1846–1912)

  Ernest Robert Graham (1868–1936)

  E. C. Shanklin [Shankland?] (?)

  Charles B. Atwood (d. 1895)

David J. Howell and Son, Civil Engineers (firm active 1920s)

Henry D. Dagit & Sons (firm active 1888–present)

Davis, Wick & Rosengarten (firm active 1970s)

Alexander Jackson Davis (1803–1890). *See also* Town & Davis (firm active 1829–1835; 1842–1843)

Lawrence N. Davis (?). *See* Hunting Davis Company (firm active 1910–?)

Stuart O. Dawson (b. 1935). *See* Sasaki, Dawson, DeMay Associates, Inc. (firm active 1963–1975)

Edward Clarence Dean (1879–1950)

Hal M. Dean (b. 1935)

Ruth Dean (1889–1932)

Jacques Marcel DeBrer (b. 1935)

Frederic C. DeKrafft (fl. 1817–32)

Richard Delafield (1798–1873)

DeLong & DeLong Associates (firm active 1940s)

  Ellwood F. DeLong (1879–1967)

  Victor W. DeLong (?)

Kenneth DeMay (b. 1932). *See* Sasaki, Dawson, DeMay Associates, Inc. (firm active 1963–1975)

William I. Deming (1871–1939). *See* Wood, Donn & Deming (firm active 1902–1912)

James F. Denson. *See* A. B. Mullett & Co.

Jules Henri de Sibour (1872–1938). *See also* Bruce Price & de Sibour (firm active ca. 1902–1909)

Jules Henri Gabriel de Sibour. *See* Jules Henri de Sibour (1872–1938)

Leon Emile Dessez (1858–1918)

DeWitt, Poor & Shelton (associated 1958 to 1964). *See* Alfred Easton Poor (1899–1988) and DeWitt, Poor, Swanke, Shelton, and Almond (associated 1965–1979)

  Roscoe DeWitt (1894–1975)

  Alfred Easton Poor (1899–1988). *See* main entry for Alfred Easton Poor (1899–1988)

  Albert Homer Swanke (1909–1996)

  Jesse Markham Shelton (1895–1976)

  Alexander Pearson Almond (1904–?)

  A. J. Tatum (b. 1921)

George Dickie (b. 1938)

John Gerald Dinkeloo (1918–1981). *See* Kevin Roche John Dinkeloo and Associates (firm active 1966–1980)

District of Columbia, Office of the Municipal
    Architect
District of Columbia Office of the Surveyor.
    See Office of the Surveyor of the District
    of Columbia
District of Columbia Redevelopment Land
    Agency
Mark Andrew Dodds (b. 1956)
Edward Wilton Donn Jr. (1868–1953). *See also*
    Wood, Donn & Deming (firm active
    1902–1912)
John Mahon Donn (ca. 1872–1931)
William Douden (1869–1946)
Doxiadis Associates (firm active 1951–ca. 1975)
Vladimir Joseph Dragan (b. 1953)
Donald Hudson Drayer (1909–1973). *See also*
    Carter, Drayer Co. (firm active ca. 1934)
Maria Ramona Drayer (b. 1920)
Duane & Lawrence (firm active 1955–?)
Anthony F. Dumas (active ca. 1916–1937)
Walter Kremer Durham (1896–1978)
David VanDuzer (b. 1947). *See* Rounds
    VanDuzer Associates (firm active
    1977–present)

Charles Eames (1907–1978). *See* Office of
    Charles and Ray Eames (firm active
    1941–1984)
Ray Eames (1913–1988). *See* Office of Charles
    and Ray Eames (firm active 1941–1984)
E. C. (Edward Curtis) Earl
EDAW, Inc. (firm active 1964–present)
Edw. F. Caldwell & Co.
Edward J. Murray Inc.
Harry L. Edwards (1902–1958)
Edwin Weihe/Katherine Gibbs (firm active
    1946–1948)
    Edwin Armstrong Weihe (1907–1994)
    Katherine Gibbs (b. 1907)
Eero Saarinen and Associates (firm active
    1950–1961). *See also* Kevin Roche John
    Dinkeloo and Associates (firm active
    1966–1980)
    Eero Saarinen (1910–1961)
Eggers & Higgins (firm active 1937–1970).
    See also John Russell Pope (1874–1937)
    Otto Reinhold Eggers (1882–1964)
    Daniel Paul Higgins (1886–1953)
Eidlitz & Ross Incorporated (firm active
    ca. 1942)

Frank Eliscu (b. 1912)
Francis Lawrence Ellingwood (1856–ca. 1929)
William Parker Elliot (1807–1854)
Benjamin Paul Elliott (b. 1920)
Fred H. Elswick (1907–1959). *See* Wischmeyer,
    Arrasmith & Elswick (firm active
    1928–1941)
Elzner & Anderson (firm)
    Alfred O. Elzner (1845–1933)
    Anderson, George M. (1869–1916)
Emily Malino Associates
Albert P. Erb (1893–1972)
Robert James Erikson (b. 1945)
Alexander Rice Esty (1826–1881)
Etudes et créations d'ambiances
J. Owen Evans (active 1930s)
Tox Bronté Evermann (1879?–1941)
Ewin Engineering Corporation (firm active
    1950s)

Daniel Cox Fahey Jr. (?)
Faulkner, Fryer & Vanderpool
    Avery Coonley Faulkner (b. 1929)
    Frederick Lear Fryer (1918–1983)
    Wynant Davis Vanderpool Jr. (1914–1986)
Faulkner, Kingsbury & Stenhouse
    Herbert Winthrop Waldron Faulkner
        (1898–1979)
    Slocum Kingsbury (1893–1987)
    John Warren Stenhouse (1904–1984)
Federal Seaboard Terra Cotta Corporation
    (New York, N.Y.) (firm active 1930s)
Samuel A. Fite (active ca. 1867–ca. 1886)
Ernest Flagg (1857–1947)
Formica Insulation Co.
William Forsyth (active ca. 1888–1900)
Frank R. White & Co., Architects
    Frank Russell White (1889–1961)
Kenneth Franzheim (1890–1959)
Fred S. Gichner Ironworks (Washington, D.C.)
    (firm active ca. 1898–present)
Frost and Granger, Architects (firm active
    1898–1910)
Frederick Lear Fryer (1918–1983). *See* Faulkner,
    Fryer & Vanderpool
T. J. D. (Thomas James Duncan) Fuller
    (1870–1946)
Robert Fulton (1765–1815)

Edgar William Garbisch (1899–1979)
Joseph C. Gardner (?)
Charles Jefferson Garner (1879–1968)
Earl Victor Gauger (1900–1986). *See* Chatelain,
    Gauger and Nolan (firm active 1956–1969)
Joseph William Geddes (1890–1969)
Geiffert, Alfred Jr. (1890–1957)
Geno (?)
George Stone Associates
Arthur C. Giacalone (1913–1989)
Katherine Gibbs (b. 1907). *See* Edwin Weihe/
    Katherine Gibbs (firm active 1946–1948)
Elsa Gidoni (1901–1978). *See also* Kahn & Jacobs
    (firm active 1940–1966)
Cass Gilbert (1859–1934)
Gill, Maurice Bernard (1893–1982)
Romaldo Giurgola (b. 1920). *See* Mitchell/
    Giurgola with Frank Schlesinger Associates
    (firm active since 1958)
Glenn Brown & Bedford Brown IV (firm active
    1907–1921)
    Glenn Brown (1854–1932)
    Bedford Brown IV (1880–1952)
Glenn Brown and James Rush Marshall
    (firm active ca. 1919)
Glenn Brown (1854–1932. *See* main entry
    for Glenn Brown & Bedford Brown IV
    (firm active 1907–1921)
    James Rush Marshall (1851–1927)
Albert Goenner (1860–1918). *See* Schulze and
    Goenner (firm active 1892–1894)
Goldwin Starrett & Van Vleck. *See* Starrett &
    Van Vleck (firm active 1904–1930s)
Gortner Associates
Ernest Robert Graham (1868–1936). *See* D. H.
    Burnham & Co. (firm active 1894–1912)
Michael Graves (b. 1934)
William Bruce Gray (active ca. 1876–1901)
Rose Ishbel Greely (1887–1969)
Bernard Richardson Green (1843–1914)
Samuel J. Green (?). *See* Campbell, Green,
    Cunzolo (firm active 1960–present)
Allan Greenberg (b. 1938)
Gregg & Leisenring (firm active 1910–ca. 1928)
    Charles Gregg (1872–1950)
    Luther Morris Leisenring (1895–1965). *See also*
        main entry for Luther Morris Leisenring
        (1895–1965)
Victor Gruen (1903–1980). *See* Victor Gruen
    Associates (firm active 1951–1967)

Hahn Engineering Co.

Earl S. Haislip (1896–1981)

R. E. Hall & Company. *See* R. E. Hall & Company, Inc. (active ca. 1926–ca. 1928)

Stephen (Étienne Sulpice) Hallet (1755–1825)

William Deane Ham (?)

Walker Kirtland Hancock (b. 1901)

Harbeson, Hough, Livingston & Larson, Architects (firm active 1945–present)
   John Frederick Harbeson (1888–1986)
   William Jarrett Hallowell Hough (1888–1969)
   William Henry Livingston (1898–1965)
   Roy F. Larson (1893–1973)

H. J. (Henry Janeway) Hardenbergh (1847–1918)

Clarence Lowell Harding (1872–?)

Hardy Holzman Pfeiffer Associates (firm active 1967–present)
   Hugh Hardy (b. 1932)
   Malcolm Holzman (b. 1940)
   Norman Pfeiffer (b. 1940)

Harley, Ellington & Day (firm active 1942–1960)

A. C. (Artemas Canfield) Harmon (1873–ca. 1943)

John Haro (b. 1928)

J. H. (James Henry) Harper (?)

Albert Lewis Harris, 1868–1933

W. H. (William Howieson) Harrold (1887–1956)

Harry Wardman/Eugene Waggaman, Architects (firm active 1920–1924)
   Harry Wardman (1872–1938)
   Eugene Waggaman (?)

Frederick E. Hart (1943–1999)

Harvey L. Page & Company (firm active 1885–1897)
   Harvey L. Page (1889–1934)

Thomas Hastings (1860–1929). *See* Carrère & Hastings (firm active 1885–ca. 1929)

Wm. M. (William Max) Haussmann (1906–1988)

Arthur B. (Arthur Berthrong) Heaton (1875–1951)

Andrew Hopewell Hepburn (1880–1967). *See* Perry, Shaw & Hepburn (firm active 1923–1951)

Christian S. (Christian Stanger) Heritage Jr. (1907–1939)

Ricardo C. Herring (b. 1947)

Herring-Hall-Marvin Safe Co.

Daniel Paul Higgins (1886–1953). *See* Eggers & Higgins (firm active 1937–1970)

James G. (James Green) Hill (1841–1913)

Historic American Buildings Survey (active 1933–present)

Hitchings & Co.

James Hoban (ca. 1762–1831)

G. H. Hoffmann (?)

Henry Hofmeister (ca. 1891–1962). *See* Reinhard & Hofmeister (firm active 1928–1956)

Holden, McLaughlin & Associates (firm active 1930–1953)
   Arthur Cort Holden (1890–1993)
   Robert William McLaughlin (1900–1989)

Leslie G. Holleran (?). *See* Clarke, Rapuano & Holleran (firm active 1947–?)

Malcolm Holzman (b. 1940). *See also* Hardy Holzman Pfeiffer Associates (firm active 1967–present)

Daniel M. C. Hopping (1905–1990)

Hornblower & Marshall, Architects (firm active 1883–1927)
   Joseph Coerten Hornblower (1848–1908)
   James Rush Marshall (1851–1927)

Hot Shoppes Inc. (company established 1927)

William Jarrett Hallowell Hough (1888–1969). *See* Harbeson, Hough, Livingston & Larson (firm active 1945–present)

Vinnie Ream Hoxie (1847–1914)

Hugh Hardy & Associates (1962–1967). *See* Hardy Holzman Pfeiffer Associates (firm active 1967–present)

Hunting Davis Company (firm active 1910–?)
   Eugene N. Hunting (?)
   Lawrence N. Davis (?)

Addison Hutton (1834–1916)

ISD, Incorporated

The Iron-Craftsmen (firm active 1920–1965)

Lawrence J. Israel (b. 1918). *See* Copeland, Novak & Israel (firm active ca. 1960–ca. 1980)

Albert Ely Ives (1898–1966)

J. H. Burton & Co. (firm active 1910s)

J. L. Smithmeyer & Co. (firm active 1875–1888). *See also* Smithmeyer & Pelz (firm active 1873–1888)
   John L. Smithmeyer (1832–1908)
   Paul Johannes Pelz (1841–1918)

Zuleima Bruff Jackson (1843–1915)

Jacobs Poor & Eggers. *See* Alfred Easton Poor (1899–1988)
   Robert Allan Jacobs (1905–1993). *See* Kahn & Jacobs (firm active 1940–1966)

Hugh Newell Jacobsen (b. 1929)

Chih-chen Jen (b. 1929)

Denzil Jenkins (1927–1992)

Johannes & Murray (firm active 1945–?)
   Dana Berry Johannes Jr. (1910–1972)
   Loren L. Murray (1909–1987)

Johnson & Boutin (firm active 1948–1968)
   Donald Steele Johnson (1905–1974)
   Harold Lester Boutin (1910–ca. 1992)

Johnson & Burgee (firm active 1968–1982)
   Philip Cortelyou Johnson (b. 1906)
   John Henry Burgee (b. 1933)

Alonzo B. Jones (ca. 1847–1907)

Philip M. (Philip Morrison) Jullien (1875–1963)

Louis Henri E. Justement (1891–1968)

Albert Kahn (1869–1942)

Kahn & Jacobs (firm active 1940–1966). *See also*
   Elsa Gidoni (1901–1978)
   Ely Jacques Kahn (1884–1972)
   Robert Allan Jacobs (1905–1993)

Walter Thompson Karcher (1881–1953). *See* Walter T. Karcher & Livingston Smith (firm active 1910–1953)

John W. Kearney (b. 1873)

Albert Kelsey (1870–1950)

Kelsey & Cret (firm active 1907–ca. 1910)
   Albert Washburn Kelsey (1870–1950). *See also* main entry for Albert Washburn Kelsey (1870–1950)
   Paul Philippe Cret (1876–1945. *See also* main entry for Paul Philippe Cret (1876–1945)

Kevin Roche, John Dinkeloo and Associates (firm active 1966–1980). *See also* Eero Saarinen & Associates (firm active 1950–1961)
   Kevin Roche (b. 1922)
   John Gerald Dinkeloo (1918–1981)

Keyes, Smith, Satterlee & Lethbridge (firm active 1951–1956)
   Arthur Hawkins Keyes Jr. (b. 1917)
   Francis D. Lethbridge (b. 1920)
   Chloethiel Woodard Smith (1910–1992). *See also* main entry for Chloethiel Woodard Smith (1910–1992); Smith & Satterlee
   Nicholas Satterlee (1915–1974)

Slocum Kingsbury (1893–1987). *See* Faulkner, Kingsbury & Stenhouse

John S. Kistler II (?)

Charles Z. (Charles Zeller) Klauder (1872–1938)

Kenneth Joseph Klima (b. 1945)

Russell O. (Russell Ormond) Kluge (1894–1967)

R. D. Kohn & Charles Butler, Associated Architects (firm active ca. 1911–ca. 1953)
  Robert D. Kohn (ca. 1870–1953)
  Charles Butler (ca. 1871–1953)

Vlastimil Koubek (b. 1927)

Arnold M. Kronstadt (?). *See* Collins, Kronstadt, and Assoc. (firm active 1956–?)

T. F. (Theodore Frederick) Laist (1868–1939)

The Lamson Company (firm active 1939–?)

J. G. Langdon (?)

Roy F. Larson (1893–1973). *See* Harbeson, Hough, Livingston & Larson (firm active 1945–present)

B. Henry Latrobe (1764–1820)
  Hazlehurst Boneval Latrobe (1803–1891)

P. J. (Peter J.) Lauritzen (?)

Henry H. Law (active 1880s and 1890s)

Belle D. Lawrason (?)

H. A. Lee (?)

W. Duncan Lee (1884–1952)

Luther Morris Leisenring (1875–1965). *See also* Gregg & Leisenring (firm active 1910–ca. 1928)

Stanley W. Leonard (?)

M. G. (Matthew Giles) Lepley (1886–1953)

Lethbridge, Francis D. (b. 1920). *See* Keyes, Smith, Satterlee & Lethbridge

Harold Randolph Lewis (b. 1941)

Stanley T. Lewis (b. 1927)

Maya Ying Lin (b. 1959)

E. G. (Edmund George) Lind (1829–1909)

L. G. (Lawrence G.) Linnard (1901–1983)

William Henry Livingston (1898–1965). *See* Harbeson, Hough, Livingston & Larson (firm active 1963–present)

Joseph A. Lockie (1881–1949). *See* Porter and Lockie (firm active 1922–?)

Lockman Associates/Architects PC (firm active 1961–present)

Alan J. Lockman (b. 1932)

Raymond Loewy (1893–1986)

Sir Edwin Landseer Lutyens (1869–1944)

David Lynn (1873–1961)

G. E. (Gordon Earl) MacNeil (ca. 1883–1945)

Loren Madsen (b. 1943)

Toshiyuki (James) Maeda (b. 1919)

Harold Van Buren Magonigle (1867–1935)

Marcellus Wright & Son (firm active 1938–present)

Marquis & Stoller (firm active 1955–1975)
  Robert Marquis (b. 1927)
  Claude Stoller (b. 1921)

Marsh & Peter (firm active 1898–1926)
  William Johnston Marsh (1863–1926)
  Walter Gibson Peter, Sr. (1868–1945). *See also* main entry for Walter Gibson Peter Sr. (1868–1945)

James Rush Marshall (1851–1927). *See* Hornblower & Marshall, Architects (firm active 1883–1927)

Thomas Worth Marshall (1872–1952)

Maurice S. May (1891–1968)

P. A. McHugh (?)

McKim, Mead & White (firm active 1879–1960s)
  Charles Follen McKim (1847–1909)
  William Rutherford Mead (1846–1928)
  Stanford White (1853–1906)

Martin Hawley McLanahan (1865–1929). *See* Price and McLanahan (firm active 1903–1916)

Robert William McLaughlin (1900–1989). *See* Holden, McLaughlin & Associates (firm active 1930–1953)

Francis K. McNerhany (?)

Marcia Mead (1879–1967). *See* Schenck & Mead (firm active ca. 1914–ca. 1922)

William Rutherford Mead (1846–1928). *See* McKim, Mead & White (firm active 1879–1960s)

Montgomery C. (Montgomery Cunningham) Meigs (1816–1892)

Adolph E. (Adolph Emil) Melander (1845–1933)

John Ogdon Merrill (1896–1975). *See* Skidmore, Owings & Merrill (firm active 1936–present)

W. E. (William Emery) Merrill (1837–1891)

M. (Mihran) Mesrobian (1889–1975)

Doug Michels (b. 1943)

Thomas Yancey Milburn (1890–1977)

Miles Pneumatic Tube Company

Allison W. Miller (1891–?). *See* W. C. & A. N. Miller, Realtors and Builders (firm active 1912–present)

Hal Arluck Miller (1903–1953)

William Cammack Miller (1886–?). *See* W. C. & A. N. Miller, Realtors and Builders (firm active 1912–present)

David C. Milling (?). *See* Osler/Milling Architects (firm active 1981–present)

Alan B. (Alan Balch) Mills (ca. 1887–1963)

George Stafford Mills (1866–1939). *See* Mills, Rhines, Bellman & Nordhoff (firm active 1912–1944)

Robert Mills (1781–1855)

Mills, Rhines, Bellman & Nordhoff (firm active 1912–1944)
  George Stafford Mills (1866–1939)
  George Volney Rhines (1875–1938)
  Lawrence Stevens Bellman (1876–1951)
  Charles M. Nordhoff (1877–1950)

Mims, Speake & Co. (firm active 1939–?)
  James Raymond Mims (1886–1965)
  Cecil Speake (?)

Minoru Yamasaki and Associates (firm active 1949–ca. 1986)
  Minoru Yamasaki (1912–1986)

Mitchell/Giurgola Architects with Frank Schlesinger (firm active since 1958)
  Ehrman Burkman Mitchell Jr. (b. 1924)
  Romaldo Giurgola (b. 1920)
  Frank Schlesinger (b. 1925)

Moline Furniture Works (firm active 1898–1955)

Arthur Cotton Moore (b. 1935). *See* Arthur Cotton Moore/Associates (firm active 1965–present)

M. F. (Maurice F.) Moore (?)

Raymond Gilbert Moore (1889–1963). *See* Corning & Moore (firm active ca. 1942–ca. 1957); Corning, Moore, and Fischer (firm active ca. 1957–1969)

Joseph G. (Joseph Gerard) Morgan (1903–1956)

E. P. Morrill (?)

Rudolph B. Moscau (?)

A. B. (Alfred Bult) Mullett (1834–1890)

Barbara Lee Mullins (b. 1938)

Loren L. Murray (1909–1987). *See* Johannes & Murray (firm active 1945–?)

Naramore, Bain, Brady & Johanson (firm active ca. 1942–?)

National Small House Competition (active 1920s)

Edwin Fairfax Naulty (b. 1869)

Edwin A. (Edwin Amil) Newman

Charles Henry Niehaus (1855–1935)

James Nolan (?). *See* Chatelain, Gauger, and Nolan (firm active 1956–1969)

John Nolan (?). *See* Nugent & O'Connor (firm active mid-1940s)

W. Clark Noble (1858–1838)

Charles M. Nordhoff (1877–1950). *See* Mills, Rhines, Bellman & Nordhoff (firm active 1912–1944)

L. (Lemuel) Norris (1848–1930)

James H. Northcott (?)

Adolph Novak (b. 1912). *See* Copeland, Novak & Israel (firm active ca. 1960–ca. 1980)

Samuel G. Nugent (1901–1966). *See* Osmundson & Staley (firm active 1944–1965)

E. Jerome O'Connor. *See* Edward Aloysius Jerome O'Connor (1891–1977) and Osmundson & Staley (firm active 1944–1965)

Edward Aloysius Jerome O'Connor (1891–1977)

Office of Alfred Easton Poor 1952–1971. *See* Alfred Easton Poor (1899–1988)

Office of Building, Library of Congress

Office of Charles and Ray Eames (firm active 1946–1984)
    Charles Eames (1907–1978)
    Ray Eames (1913–1988)

Office of Chief Engineer, M, W & S

Office of John Russell Pope. *See* John Russell Pope (1874–1937) and Eggers & Higgins (firm active 1937–1970)

Office of the Quartermaster Corps, Construction Division

Office of Supervising Architect

Office of the Superintendent, State, War, and Navy Building

Office of the Surveyor of the District of Columbia

Timothy W. (Timothy Wayne) O'Keefe (b. 1946)

Paul Stevenson Oles (b. 1936)

Michele Rose Ortega (b. 1960)

Osler/Milling Architects (firm active 1957–present)
    David William Osler (b. 1921)
    David C. Milling (?)

Osmundson & Staley (firm active 1944–1965)
    Theodore Osmundson Jr. (b. 1921)
    John Hedges Staley Jr. (b. ca. 1918–?)
    Samuel G. Nugent (1901–1966)
    E. Jerome O'Connor (1891–1977). *See also* main entry for Edward Aloysius Jerome O'Connor (1891–1977)

F. D. (Frederick Dale) Owen (active 1882–1909)

Nathaniel Alexander Owings (1903–1984). *See* Skidmore, Owings & Merrill (firm active 1936–present)

Panama Canal Company, Department of Operation and Maintenance

Joseph A. (Joseph Algernon) Parks (1890–1977)

Partridge, Bogan & O'Connor (firm active 1950s)
    C. Warren Bogan
    Seymour T. Partridge
    E. Jerome O'Connor (1981–1977)

Ralph D. Patterson (?)

Horace Whittier Peaslee (1884–1959)

Cesar Pelli (b. 1926)

Paul J. (Paul Johannes) Pelz (1841–1918). *See* J. L. Smithmeyer & Co. (firm active 1873–1888) and Smithmeyer & Pelz (firm active 1873–1888)

Vincent Perez (?)

George B. Perkins (active 1840s)

Perry, Shaw & Hepburn (firm active 1923–1951). *See* main entry for Thomas Tileston Waterman (1900–1951)
    William Graves Perry (1883–1975)
    Thomas Mott Shaw (1878–1965)
    Andrew Hopewell Hepburn (1880–1967)

Walter Gibson Peter Sr. (1868–1945). *See also* Marsh & Peter (firm active 1898–1926)

Norman Pfeiffer (b. 1940). *See* Hardy Holzman Pfeiffer Associates (firm active 1967–present)

Eugene H. Phifer (1899–1989)

Pierson & Wilson (firm active 1920s and 1930s)
    Frank G. Pierson (1870–?)
    A. Hamilton Wilson (1892–1956)

Edward Morris Pitt (1905–1969)

Thos. M. (Thomas M.) Plowman (active ca. 1868–1879)

O. M. (Orlando Metcalfe) Poe (1832–1895)

Alfred Easton Poor (1899–1988). *See also* Rodgers & Poor (firm active 1927–1932) and DeWitt, Poor, Swanke, Shelton, and Almond (associated 1965–1979)

Poor and Swanke & Partners (associated 1972–). *See* Alfred Easton Poor (1899–1988)

Poor, Swanke, Hayden and Connell (associated 1978–1979). *See* Alfred Easton Poor (1899–1988)

John Russell Pope (1874–1937). *See also* Eggers & Higgins (firm active 1937–1970)

Porter and Lockie (firm active 1922–?)
    Irwin Stevens Porter (1888–1956)
    Joseph A. Lockie (1881–1949)

James Christopher Postell (b. 1958)

William Appleton Potter (1842–1909)

William Gibbons Preston (1842–1910)

Henry Brooks Price (1873–1936)

Bruce Price. *See* Bruce Price and de Sibour (firm active ca. 1902–1909)

Morris Price. *See* Barton, Price & Wilson (firm active 1920s)

Price and McLanahan (firm active 1903–1916)
    William Lightfoot Price (1861–1916)
    Martin Hawley McLanahan (1865–1929)

Laurens N. Prior (?)

Frank B. (Frank Baker) Proctor (1893–1956)

Taxiarchis Protopapas (1896–1959)

Frederic Bennett Pyle (1867–1934)

Quartermaster Corps, Construction Division. *See* Office of the Quartermaster Corps, Construction Division

August C. Radziszewski (?)

Michael Rapuano (1904–1975). *See* Clarke, Rapuano & Holleran (firm active 1947–?)

Ratcliffe (?)

George N. (George Nicholas) Ray (1887–1959). *See also* Waggaman & Ray (firm active 1917–1919)

Luther Reason Ray (1892–1978)

R. D. Kohn and Charles Butler, Associated Architects (firm active ca. 1911–ca. 1953)
    Robert D. Kohn (ca. 1870–1953)
    Charles Butler (ca. 1871–1953)

R. E. Hall & Co., Inc. (firm active ca. 1926–ca. 1928)

Margaret W. Read (?)

Reinhard & Hofmeister (firm active 1928–1956)
    L. Andrew Reinhard (ca. 1892–1964)
    Henry Hofmeister (ca. 1891–1962)
Winold Reiss (1886–1953)
James Renwick Jr. (1818–1895)
George Volney Rhines (1875–1938). *See* Mills,
    Rhines, Bellman & Nordhoff (firm active
    1912–1944)
Isidor Richmond (1893–1988). *See* Waterman,
    Richmond and Walsh (firm active 1920s)
William Henry Rinehart (1825–1874)
Ring Engineering Co. (?)
T. Kent Roberts (active ca. 1909–ca. 1916)
Edward F. Robinson (?)
Kevin Roche (b. 1922). *See* Kevin Roche
    John Dinkeloo and Associates (firm active
    since 1966)
Rodgers & Poor (firm active 1927–1932)
    Robert Perry Rodgers (1895–1934)
    Alfred Easton Poor (1899–1988). *See also* main
        entry for Alfred Easton Poor (1899–1988)
Albert Randolph Ross (1869–1948)
Rounds VanDuzer Associates (firm active
    1977–present)
    Anthony Rounds (b. 1943)
    David VanDuzer (b. 1947)
George Cooper Rudolph (b. 1912)

Eero Saarinen (1910–1961). *See* Eero Saarinen
    and Associates (firm active 1950–1961)
George Thomas Santmyers (1889–1960)
Alfred D. Sardella (b. 1912)
Sasaki, Dawson, DeMay Associates (firm active
    1963–1975)
    Hideo Sasaki (b. 1919)
    Stuart O. Dawson (b. 1935)
    Kenneth DeMay (b. 1932)
Nicholas Satterlee (1915–1974). *See* Keyes,
    Smith, Satterlee & Lethbridge (firm active
    1951–1956); Satterlee & Smith (firm active
    1957–1964)
Satterlee & Smith (firm active 1957–1964)
    Nicholas Satterlee (1915–1974)
    Chloethiel Woodard
Schenck & Mead (firm active ca. 1914–ca. 1922)
    Anna Pendleton Schenck (1874–1915)
    Marcia Mead (1879–1967)
Frank Schlesinger (b. 1925). *See* Mitchell/
    Giurgola with Frank Schlesinger (firm
    active since 1958)

John L. Schmidtmeier. *See* John L. Smithmeyer
    (1832–1908)
Anthony F. A. Schmitt (active 1900–1935)
Albert M. Schneider. *See* A. M. Schneider & Co.
    (firm active ca. 1905–ca. 1923)
T. F. (Thomas Franklin) Schneider (1858–1938)
Schulze & Goenner (firm active 1892–1894)
    Paul Schulze (ca. 1827–1897). *See* main entry
        for Cluss & Schulze (firm active,
        1877–1889)
    Albert Goenner (1860–1918)
Paul Schulze or Schultze (1827/28–1897). *See*
    Cluss & Schulze (firm active, 1877–1889)
    and Schulze & Goenner (firm active
    1892–1894)
Schumann & Lautrup (firm active 1873)
    Franz (Francis by 1873) Schumann
        (ca. 1843–1911)
    Paul C. Lautrup (?)
Senate Park Commission (1901–1902)
Richard Samuel Shank (b. 1944)
E. C. Shanklin [Shankland?] (?). *See* D. H.
    Burnham & Co. (firm active 1894–1912)
R. E. Shaw (?)
Thomas Mott Shaw (1878–1965). *See* Perry,
    Shaw & Hepburn (firm active 1923–1951)
Jesse Markham Shelton (1895–1976). *See*
    DeWitt, Poor, Swanke, Shelton, and
    Almond (associated 1965–1979)
Arthur A. (Arthur Asahel) Shurtleff
    (1870–1957)
Jules Henri de Sibour (1872–1938). *See also*
    Bruce Price & de Sibour (firm active
    ca. 1902–1909)
Sibour. *See* Jules Henri de Sibour (1872–1938)
R. H. E. Siebert (?)
Howard Sill (1865–1927)
Lawrence Fletcher Simmons (1895–1969)
Simmons & Cooper (firm active ca. 1913–
    ca. 1917)
    Francis A. Simmons (?)
    James E. Cooper (1877–1930)
Henry Simpson (?)
Skidmore, Owings & Merrill (firm active
    1936–present)
    Louis Skidmore (1897–1962)
    Nathaniel Alexander Owings (1903–1984)
    John Ogdon Merrill (1896–1975)
Samuel Sloan (1815–1884)
John H. Small III (1889–ca. 1967)

Chloethiel Woodard Smith (1910–1992). *See
    also* Keyes, Smith, Satterlee & Lethbridge
    (firm active 1951–1956), Satterlee & Smith
    (firm active 1957–1964)
Delos H. (Delos Hamilton) Smith (1884–1963)
Livingston Smith (1879–1961). *See* Walter T.
    Karcher and Livingston Smith (firm active
    1910–1953)
John L. Smithmeyer (1832–1908). *See* J. L.
    Smithmeyer & Co. (firm active 1876–1888?)
    and Smithmeyer & Pelz (firm active
    1873–1888?)
    John L. Smithmeyer (1832–1908)
    Paul Johannes Pelz (1841–1918)
John Edgar Sohl (1877–?)
Arnold Southwell (b. 1903–?)
Cecil Speake (?). *See* Mims, Speake & Co.
    (firm active ca. 1914–?)
Spencer, White & Prentis Incorporated
Richard Phené Spiers (1838–1916)
Paul David Spreiregen (b. 1931)
Stacor Visionaire Corp. (business active 1963–?)
John Hedges Staley Jr. (b. ca. 1918–?).
    See Osmundson & Staley (firm active
    1944–1965)
Standard Oil Company of New Jersey
Stanley Matthews (firm active 1925–1926)
N. G. (Norris Garshon) Starkweather
    (1818–1885)
Starrett & Van Vleck (firm active 1904–1930s)
    Goldwyn (or Goldwin) Starrett (1876–1918)
    Joseph Van Vleck (1876–1948)
Robert Stead (1856–1943)
John Warren Stenhouse (1904–1984).
    See Faulkner, Kingsbury & Stenhouse
Robert A. M. Stern (b. 1939)
Stern & Tomlinson (firm active ca. 1918–ca. 1927)
Sternfeld, Harry (1888–1976)
J. George Stewart (1890–1970)
Claude Stoller (b. 1921). *See* Marquis & Stoller
    (firm active 1955–1975)
Stone, George V. (1905–1958)
Structural Porcelain Enamel Co. (firm active
    1937–?)
F. or T. R. Stuart (active 1850s)
Abby P. Suckle (b. 1952)
Francis Paul Sullivan (1885–1958)
Sullivan & Almy Inc. (firm active 1957–1970)
    John Henry Sullivan Jr. (b. 1925)
    David Olney Almy (b. 1938)

Thoralf M. Sundt (d. 1969)
Albert Homer Swanke (1909–1996).
    See DeWitt, Poor, Swanke, Shelton, and
    Almond (associated 1965–1979)

Tadjer-Cohen Assoc. Inc. (firm active
    1962–present)
A. J. Tatum (born 1921). See DeWitt, Poor,
    Swanke, Shelton, and Almond (associated
    1965–1979)
W. W. (William Waverly) Taylor (1896–1986)
T. D. Donovan & Associates (firm active
    1959–present)
Adolph Frederick Thelander (1899–1976)
Theodore G. Thomas (b. 1896)
Thomas Meehan & Sons
Anna Maria Brodeau Thornton (1774–1865)
William Thornton (1759–1828)
Tilghman Moyer Company
Timber Engineering Company (company active
    1933–?)
Toledo Porcelain Enamel Products Company
    (firm active 1928–1952)
George Oakley Totten (1866–1939)
Town & Davis (firm active 1829–1835;
    1842–1843)
    Ithiel Town (1784–1844)
    Alexander Jackson Davis (1803–1890). See also
        main entry for Alexander Jackson Davis
        (1803–1890)
T. T. Waterman and Delos H. Smith (firm active
    ca. 1945)
    Thomas Tileston Waterman (1900–1951).
        See also main entry for Thomas Tileston
        Waterman (1900–1951)
    Delos Hamilton Smith (1884–1963). See also
        main entry for Delos Hamilton Smith
        (1884–1963)
T. T. Waterman and Samuel Buck (active 1947)
    Thomas Tileston Waterman (1900–1951).
        See also main entry for Thomas Tileston
        Waterman (1900–1951)
    Samuel Buck (?)
Tuskegee Normal and Industrial Institute

United States Army. Quartermaster Corps.
    See Office of the Quartermaster Corps,
    Construction Division
United States. Bureau of Agricultural
    Engineering

United States. Department of the Treasury.
    Office of Supervising Architect. See Office
    of Supervising Architect
United States. Public Buildings Service (agency
    active 1949–present)
United States. Public Works Administration
    (active 1933–1935)
United States. Senate Park Commission.
    See Senate Park Commission (1901–1902)
United States Superintendent of State, War,
    and Navy Building. See Office of the
    Superintendent, State, War, and Navy
    Building

Wynant Davis Vanderpool Jr. (1914–1986).
    See Faulkner, Fryer & Vanderpool
Joseph Van Vleck (1876–1948). See Starrett &
    Van Vleck (firm active 1904–1930s)
Henry Vaughan (1845–1817)
Victor Gruen Associates (firm active 1951–1967)
    Victor Gruen (1903–1980)
David Volkert & Associates (firm active
    1957–present)

W. C. & A. N. Miller, Realtors and Builders
    (firm active 1912–present)
    William Cammack Miller (1886–?)
    Allison W. Miller (1891–?)
Waggaman & Ray (firm active 1917–1919)
    Clarke Waggaman (1877–1919)
    George Nicholas Ray (1887–1959). See also
        main entry for George Nicholas Ray
        (1887–1959)
Eugene Waggaman (?). See Harry Wardman/
    Eugene Waggaman, Architects (firm active
    1920–1924)
Harold Eugene Wagoner (1905–1986)
Robert C. (Robert Craighead) Walker
    (1894–1966)
Walker Bin Co. (firm active ca. 1915–1928)
Walker & Gillette and Alfred Easton Poor
    (1946–1947). See Alfred Easton Poor
    (1899–1988)
Walker & Poor (associated 1947–1952).
    See Alfred Easton Poor (1899–1988)
Charles James Walsh (1893–?). See Thomas T.
    Waterman and Charles J. Walsh
    (associated, 1927) and Waterman,
    Richmond and Walsh (firm active 1920s)
Thomas Ustick Walter (1804–1887)

Walter T. Karcher and Livingston Smith (firm
    active 1910–1953)
    Walter Thompson Karcher (1881–1953)
    Livingston Smith (1879–1961)
Harry Wardman (1872–1938). See Harry
    Wardman-Eugene Waggaman, Architects
    (firm active 1920–1924)
Warren & Clark (firm active ca. 1913–1925)
    Warren (?)
    Samuel Adams Clark (?)
Harvey Hodgson Warwick Sr. (1893–1972)
Washington Housing Associates (active mid-
    1930s)
Thomas Tileston Waterman (1900–1951). See
    also Thomas T. Waterman and Charles J.
    Walsh (associated, 1927); Waterman &
    Barrows (firm active ca. 1928–1931);
    Waterman, Richmond, and Walsh (firm
    active 1920s)
Waterman & Barrows (firm active ca. 1928–1931)
    Thomas Tileston Waterman (1900–1951).
        See main entry for Thomas Tileston
        Waterman (1900–1951)
    John A. Barrows (1906–1931). See also main
        entry for John A. Barrows (1906–1931)
Thomas T. Waterman and Charles J. Walsh
    (associated, 1927)
    Thomas Tileston Waterman (1900–1951).
        See also main entry for Thomas Tileston
        Waterman (1900–1951)
    Charles James Walsh (1893–?)
Waterman, Richmond and Walsh (firm active
    1920s)
    Thomas Tileston Waterman (1900–1951)
    Isidor Richmond (1893–1988)
    Charles James Walsh (b. 1893). See also
        Waterman & Walsh
Gerald R.W. Watland (ca. 1905–1974)
Ronald G. Watson (b. 1941)
David G. Watt (?)
Edwin Armstrong Weihe (1907–1994).
    See Edwin Weihe/Katherine Gibbs
    (firm active 1946–1948)
Julius Wenig (1872–1940)
Claughton West (1885–1978)
Vivian Westerman (?)
John Joseph Whelan (1902–1961)
E. B. (Edward Brickell) White (1806–1882)
Gilbert White (?)
Jarrett Carlisle White (1894–1947)

Lucius Read White Jr. (1887–1970)

Stanford White (1853–1906). *See* McKim, Mead & White (firm active 1879–1960s)

Francis Marion Wigmore (b. 1890)

James Rowland Willett (1831–1907)

M. J. (Morley Jeffers) Williams (1886–1977)

A. Hamilton Wilson (1892–1956). *See* Pierson & Wilson (firm active 1920s and 1930s)

Elsie Cobb Wilson. *See* Barton, Price & Wilson (firm active 1920s)

Joseph Miller Wilson (1838–1902)

Mark Leonard Wilson (?)

Wischmeyer, Arrasmith & Elswick (firm active 1928–1941)
    Kenneth Edward Wischmeyer (1908–1996)
    W. S. Arrasmith (1898–1966)
    Fred H. Elswick (1907–1959)

David J. Witmer (1888–1973). *See* Bergstrom and Witmer

Otto C. (Otto Charles) Wolf (1856–1916)

Wolverine Porcelain Enameling Co. (firm active ca. 1924–?)

Ralph S. Wood (?)

Waddy B. (Waddy Butler) Wood (1869–1944). *See also* Wood, Donn & Deming (firm active 1902–1912)

Wood, Donn & Deming (firm active 1902–1912)
    Waddy Butler Wood (1869–1944). *See* main entry for Waddy Butler Wood (1869–1944)
    Edward Wilton Donn Jr. (1868?–1953). *See also* main entry for Edward Wilton Donn Jr. (1868?–1953)
    William I. Deming (1871–1939)

Carlin H. Woodbridge (active in Washington 1920–1921). *See* Cutler & Woodbridge (firm active 1920–1921)

Richard Christopher Woods (b. 1950)

Frank Lloyd Wright (1867–1959)

N. C. (Nathan Corwith) Wyeth (1870–1963)

Minoru Yamasaki (1912–1986). *See* Minoru Yamasaki and Associates (firm active 1949–ca. 1986)

Ammi B. (Ammi Burnham) Young (1799–1874)

Joseph Arthur Younger (1892–1932)

Charles H. Zeller (?)

NOTES

Chapter One. Washington, D.C.

1. For one of the most extensive and valuable compilations of unrealized designs, spanning two centuries of American history, see Alison Sky and Michelle Stone, *Unbuilt America: Forgotten Architecture in the United States from Thomas Jefferson to the Space Age* (1976; repr., New York: Abbeville Press, 1983), with an introduction by George R. Collins, which came to the author's attention after the completion of this chapter. The study illustrates designs discussed herein for the U.S. Capitol by Stephen Hallet and William Thornton; various designs by B. Henry Latrobe, but with a mistaken identification of Latrobe's proposal for a monument to George Washington as that for his Richmond, Virginia, theater memorial; designs for the Washington Monument by Robert Mills and Peter Force and proposals for its completion by others; a number of Franklin Webster Smith's schemes for the "aggrandisement" of the city of Washington; and J. J. B. Benedict's designs for a summer "capitol" in Colorado.

2. The selections, in general, are arranged chronologically throughout the chapter, although sometimes by building type or common characteristics. They include examples that in some instances have been treated in greater depth or from a different point of view in the subsequent chapters. They are intended to illustrate the collections' depth and breadth, not only relating to the expected governmental architecture (official, national, federal) but also to the less known, appreciated, and studied commercial and domestic architecture of Washington, D.C., and the politically, socially, and economically ambitious, grandiose, sometimes ill-considered, often or potentially (still) influential schemes of a wide range of architects, engineers, designers, speculators, entrepreneurs, reformers, interlopers, and visionaries. They also are intended to prompt researchers to consult the biographical entries prepared as part of this project and the additional essays available online. These sources, which are listed in Appendix B, are available under "Biographical Information: Architects, Designers, and Engineers," and "Capital Drawings" in the online P&P Site Index at www.loc.gov/rr/print/, as are the more complete records for the documents, UNITs, and LOTs cited, under "Prints & Photographs Online Catalog (PPOC)" at the same Web address.

3. Letter from L'Enfant to Washington, New York, Sept. 11, 1789, as quoted in H. Paul Caemmerer, *The Life of Pierre Charles L'Enfant* (New York: Da Capo Press, 1950), 172–79, quoted in John W. Reps, *Washington on View, The Nation's Capital Since 1790* (Chapel Hill: University of North Carolina Press, 1991), 2, and n. 9.

4. John W. Reps, *Monumental Washington, the Planning and Development of the Capital Center* (Princeton: Princeton University Press, 1967), 9.

5. Lisa A. Torrance, "Owings, Nathaniel Alexander," *American National Biography Online*, www.anb.org/articles/index.html (accessed July 2001). For discussion of the development and illustrations of the plans and models of the SOM plan for Pennsylvania Avenue, the Mall, and the National Square, see Nathaniel Owings, *The Spaces In Between; An Architect's Journey* (Boston: Houghton Mifflin, 1973), 229–45; Reps, *Washington on View*, 179–91. For the reasons for the demise of the National Square proposal, see Sue A. Kohler, *The Commission of Fine Arts: A Brief History, 1910–1990* (Washington, D.C.: Government Printing Office for the Commission of Fine Arts, 1990), 105–6.

6. Reps, *Washington on View*, 34.

7. Pamela Scott, *Temple of Liberty, Building the Capitol for a New Nation* (New York: Oxford University Press, 1995), 39, 49–50. The author also points out that Charles Bulfinch's short-lived Capitol dome was a popular place for viewing the city and its surrounds, quoting Robert Mills's *Guide to the Capitol and National Executive Offices*: "Those fond of picturesque and panoramic scenery will be fully repaid for ascending to the giddy summit of the great dome. Those more timid will be satisfied to view the landscape from the general level of the roof; . . . from the galleried apex of the dome, you can take a bird's eye view embracing the whole horizon. In whatever direction here the vision is cast, there is something interesting to be seen. On one hand a rising city, with its numerous avenues, branching off in all directions, like radii from a centre, its splendid public buildings, and hum of active life; on the other hand, the noble Potomac . . ."; and p. 53: "Thornton's drawing of the revised west front shows fourteen traditional allegorical figures standing atop the balustrade of the conference room colonnade. Each is in classical garb; those who can be identified by the various implements include Mars carrying a shield, Justice with scales, Abundance with a cornucopia, Hope with an anchor, and History with a mirror." See also Scott's "Stephen Hallet's Designs for the United States Capitol," *Winterthur Portfolio* 27 (1992): 145–70, 155: "Hallet also planned the dome to serve as a belvedere, accessed by a monumental circular staircase, from which to view the city. Belvederes for viewing landscapes and vistas were part of a newly perceived relationship between humans and their environment, formulated by the eighteenth-century picturesque aesthetic"; and her "Stephen (Étienne Sulpice) Hallet," are available under "Biographical Information: Architects, Designers, and Engineers" in the online P&P Site Index at www.loc.gov/rr/print/.

8. "B. Henry Latrobe," available under "Biographical Information: Architects, Designers, and Engineers" in the online P&P Site Index at www.loc.gov/rr/print/.

9. George Washington had discussed his idea for a national university with Latrobe as early as 1796, had set aside land for the purpose, and willed his shares in the Potomac Canal Company for its support, but Congress had delayed the matter until his bequest was worthless and the political climate did not support it, as discussed in Reps, *Monumental Washington*, 36–7, who also quotes Constance Green on the subject. The scheme is also illustrated and discussed in Pamela Scott and Antoinette Lee, *The Buildings of the District of Columbia*, The Buildings of the United States (New York: Oxford University Press, 1993), 65–66; and most extensively in Jeffrey A. Cohen and Charles E. Brownell, *The Architectural Drawings of Benjamin Henry Latrobe*, The Papers of Benjamin Henry Latrobe, ed. Edward C. Carter II. Ser. 2, pt. 2 (New Haven, Conn.: Yale University Press, 1994), 2:671–76.

10. The cataloger's transcription of Latrobe's accompanying explanation of the vignette in the title page reads: "During my residence in Virginia from 1795 to 1799, the applications to me for designs were very numerous, and my fancy was kept employed in building castles in the air, the plans of which are contained in this Volume. The only two buildings which were executed from the drawings were CAPTN Pennocks house at Norfolk, and Colonel Harvies at Richmond (p. 1 & ——). The former stands on terra firma in the background to the left, the latter on the hill in the middle ground. The Wings of Col. Harvie's were never built, & are thus following the other buildings into the sky.

Higher up among the clouds, are the buildings which may easily be known by looking over the following drawings. To the right hovers the figure of the Architects imagination, such as she is. With the Model of the Bank of Pennsylvania in her hand, she is leaving the Rocks of Richmond & taking her flight to Philadelphia. The idea of the Figure is imitated from a figure by Flaxman, the celebrated Sculptor."

11. Cohen and Brownell, *Architectural Drawings,* ser. 2, pt. 1, 2:169–176; William Beiswanger to C. Ford Peatross, August 23, 2001: "[Bed] alcoves are listed in Jefferson's Bill of scantling," dated November 1796 (Nichols no. 147B, p.1). The list identifies the framing members needed for floors, partitions, etc. Alcoves are described on another sheet from Jefferson's building notebook (Nichols no. 145, p. 14): "Alcoves. 7 feet being the soffites of the door, those of the alcoves for the beds should be the same, and their architraves the same with those of the doors, as to both breadth & height. Leiper's alcove was 6 f. 9 I. Long & 4.f. Wide." Jefferson's note is not dated but very likely it is from 1796 or soon thereafter.

12. Cohen and Brownell, *Architectural Drawings,* pt. 1, 2:291–303.

13. Ibid., 2:114–125; they discuss and illustrate Latrobe's Tayloe project as a whole and drawing by drawing; Orlando Ridout V, *Building the Octagon* (Washington, D.C.: American Architectural Foundation, 1989), 1–3, 15–49, 61–69, provides a chapter concerning Latrobe's proposal in addition to Tayloe family history and a thorough exposition of Thornton's subsequent work for them; C. M. Harris, ed., and Daniel Preston, asst. ed., *Papers of William Thornton, 1781–1802,* vol. 1 (Charlottesville: University Press of Virginia, 1995), xxxii, 574–94; Thornton's architectural projects up to 1802 are discussed.

14. Acquired as the headquarters of the American Institute of Architects in 1902, the Octagon today serves as a museum and the headquarters of the American Architectural Foundation.

15. Discovered in the National Archives by researchers working for the Dunlap Society in the 1970s, the original drawings of 1912 may have been done for Pope by Rockwell Kent. Now in NARA Record Group 121, they are illustrated in Bates Lowry, *Building a National Image: Architectural Drawings for the American Democracy* (Washington, D.C.: National Building Museum, 1985), plates 104–6.

16. The majority of Boullée's drawings for his various proposals for triumphal, memorial, or funerary monuments are in the Bibliothèque Nationale in Paris, although the drawing for a truncated pyramid most similar to Force's can be found in a Florentine archive. They are discussed and handsomely illustrated in Jean-Marie Prouse de Montclos, *Étienne-Louis Boullée, Architect* (Paris: Flammarion, 1994), 142–43, 150–65, 182–83, 187, 196. In Pamela Scott, "Robert Mills and American Monuments," in *Robert Mills, Architect* (Washington, D.C.: American Institute of Architects Press, 1989), 158, the author explains Mills's undated description of his proposal for a "National Monument to Washington," for which no drawing apparently exists, in the form of a rusticated, stepped pyramid, 1,000 feet square and 680 feet high, surmounted by a 100-foot statue of Washington and with 350-foot obelisks at each corner. "Inclined planes" would have allowed pedestrians and carriages to make their way up the sides to the summit. The form and character of such monuments is further discussed in Jean Starobinski, *The Invention of Liberty, 1700–1789* (New York: Rizzoli, 1987), 205: "The constructions, and even more the plans, of Boullée, Ledoux, or Poyet, are striking for their monumental proportions, their vigor, their impressive use of simple mass. They manifested a new eloquence (which was probably to some extent indebted to the majesty of Rome, to Seneca, and the Sant'Angelo tower). As opposed to the eloquence of the Baroque, the effect sought after was not movement and profusion, but an elemental force whose energy would appear controlled and static. We are in the presence of a sense of purpose which has voluntarily renounced its normal external characteristics and turned itself purely into *mass.* The aesthetic of the grand décor has been replaced by an aesthetic of restrained sublimity. In this way man's Promethean willpower could counterbalance nature's "titanic" strength. In searching for what Quatremere de Quincy called a 'standard of imitation' in nature, man invented a *style of strength* to stand in contrast to the strength of nature. Nature was infinite, but there was, according to Burke, an artificial infinite which consisted of "a uniform succession of great parts." Moreover, this willpower was not simply concentrated in an impressive simplicity of form; it was perceptible in the tendency to show clearly the purpose of particular

buildings, by symbolizing their *finality.* This constituted what Georges Cattaui has called "architectural symbolics"—the most perfect example being Boullée's plan for the Cenotaph for Newton. If in this instance one can speak of expressive finality, other works can be said to show a functional finality (using the term *functional* in its most modern sense): libraries, hospitals, prisons, tenements were so conceived that their structure had the double attribute of indicating and complying strictly with their function."

17. See "Robert Mills," available under "Biographical Information: Architects, Designers, and Engineers" in the online P&P Site Index at www.loc.gov/rr/print/.

18. A second copy of this print has been identified in the I. N. Phelps Stokes Collection at the New York Public Library. Benjamin Franklin Smith and his three brothers produced more than twenty views of American cities between 1848 and 1855. They sold their business during the financial panic of 1857 and headed west, working as bankers and merchants. Benjamin founded the Bank of Omaha and later retired to an estate called Warrenton Park on Penobscot Bay in his native Maine. See Harry T. Peters, *America on Stone: The Other Printmakers to the American People* (New York: Arno Press, 1976, 1931); *The Old Print Shop Portfolio* 8, 5 (January 1954): 98–102; and I. N. Phelps Stokes and Daniel C. Haskell, *American Historical Prints, Early Views of American Cities, etc., from the Phelps Stokes and other Collections* (New York: New York Public Library, 1932), 179–80.

19. Pamela Scott, "Robert Mills and American Monuments," in *The Mall in Washington, 1791–1991: Studies in the History of Art* 30, Center for Advanced Study in the Visual Arts, Symposium Papers 15, ed. Richard Longstreth (Washington, D.C.: National Gallery of Art, 1991), 166; Changes in Mills's design were represented in Smith's lithograph, which followed suggestions for possible modifications requested by the board of the Washington National Monument Society and provided in an 1848 report by Mills and James Renwick. For Latrobe's corn order, see Cohen and Brownell, *Architectural Drawings,* vol. 2, pt. 1, 270; vol. 2, pt. 2, 11, 365, 393, 583–4, 586, 604.

20. See Therese O'Malley, "'A Public Museum of Trees': Mid-Nineteenth Century Plans for the Mall," in *The Mall in Washington, 1791–1991: Studies*

in the History of Art 30, Center for Advanced Study in the Visual Arts, Symposium Papers 15, ed. Richard Longstreth (Washington, D.C.: National Gallery of Art, 1991), 63–76.

21. See "Vinnie Ream Hoxie" by Diane Tepfer available under "Biographical Information: Architects, Designers, and Engineers" in the online P&P Site Index at www.loc.gov/rr/print/.

22. As completed, following the suggestions of George Perkins Marsh and under the supervision of Lieutenant Colonel Thomas Lincoln Casey of the Army Corps of Engineers, Mills's design for the Washington Monument was "corrected" to conform more accurately to the proportions of a true Egyptian obelisk. For Casey's 1884 drawing for his modified *Project for a Marble Pyramidion*, including plans, sections, elevations, and details, see ADE-UNIT 2518, no. 2 (Photo).

23. See "Joseph Goldsborough Bruff" available under "Biographical Information: Architects, Designers, and Engineers" in the online P&P Site Index at www.loc.gov/rr/print/.

24. The architectural development of the Library of Congress is discussed by Frances Brousseau in her illustrated essay available under "Capital Drawings" in the online P&P Site Index at www.loc.gov/rr/print/, beginning with its home in the Capitol, but giving particular attention to the complicated history of the Thomas Jefferson building in the late nineteenth century.

25. See "Alexander Rice Esty" by Frances Brousseau, available under "Biographical Information: Architects, Designers, and Engineers" in the online P&P Site Index at www.loc.gov/rr/print/.

26. See "Smithmeyer & Pelz (firm active 1873–1888): John L. Smithmeyer (1832–1908), Paul Johannes Pelz (1841–1918)" by Frances Brousseau and Pamela Scott, available under "Biographical Information: Architects, Designers, and Engineers" in the online P&P Site Index at www.loc.gov/rr/print/.

27. Donald Beekman Myer, *Bridges and the City of Washington* (Washington, D.C.: Commission of Fine Arts: 1974), 17–18 and cover.

28. James M. Goode, "Henderson's Castle," in *Capital Losses: A Cultural History of Washington's Destroyed Buildings* (Washington, D.C.: Smithsonian Institution Press, 1979), 106–8. The archival materials and photographs assembled for this section of his book can be found in Prints and Photographs Division LOT 11800-D5. John Russell Pope's designs for the Lincoln Memorial on the Meridian Hill site are illustrated in Lowry, *Building a National Image*, plate 100, and the Historic American Buildings Survey (HABS) documentation for Meridian Hill Park (HABS DC-532), which includes twenty-five measured drawings, fifty-six photographs, and sixty-nine data pages. Mrs. Henderson's role in the development of the Meridian Hill area, works proposed and executed there by John Russell Pope, and the park itself are discussed and illustrated in *Washington Renaissance, Architecture and Landscape of Meridian Hill* (Washington, D.C.: Meridian House International, 1989).

29. Franklin Webster Smith, *A Design and Prospectus for a National Gallery of History and Art at Washington* (Washington, D.C.: Gibson Bros., 1891); *National Galleries of History and Art* (Washington, D.C.: Government Printing Office, 1900); [*Propositions and suggestions for aggrandizement of Washington, From the Halls of the Ancients . . .*] (Washington, 1903); *Washington Magazine. In Advocacy of a National Society for the Aggrandizement of Washington* (Washington, 1904); Goode, "Halls of the Ancients," in *Capital Losses*, 106–8; Curtis Dahl, "Mr. Smith's American Acropolis," *American Heritage* (June 1956): 39–43, 104–5; Reps, *Monumental Washington*, 70–72.

30. Franklin W. Smith, Architect, C. Wilkinson, del., Prints and Photographs Division LOT 11800-J5, LC-G7-1681.

31. See "Paul Wayland Bartlett," available under "Biographical Information: Architects, Designers, and Engineers" in the online P&P Site Index at www.loc.gov/rr/print/.

32. See "Jules Jacques Benois Benedict" by Pamela Scott, available under "Biographical Information: Architects, Designers, and Engineers" in the online P&P Site Index at www.loc.gov/rr/print/; Thomas J. Noel and Barbara S. Norgren, *Denver, The City Beautiful and Its Architects, 1893–1941* (Denver: Historic Denver, 1987), 188–89; "Benedict, Jules Jacques Benois" available under Colorado Architects Biographical Sketch, www.coloradohistory-oahp.org/guides/architects/benedict.pdf (accessed February 2004).

33. Terence Riley, ed., with Peter Reed, *Frank Lloyd Wright, Architect* (New York: Museum of Modern Art, 1994), figs. 89, 98, 125, 151.

34. See David G. De Long, "Designs for an American Landscape, 1922–1932," in *Frank Lloyd Wright: Designs for an American Landscape, 1922–32*, ed. David G. De Long (New York: Harry N. Abrams, in association with the Canadian Centre for Architecture, the Library of Congress, and the Frank Lloyd Wright Foundation, 1996), 80–100, fig. 116. This is a catalog of an exhibition cosponsored by the Canadian Centre for Architecture and the Library of Congress. Frank Lloyd Wright wrote in a letter to Gordon Strong (December 1924), quoted by De Long: "You wanted something *rational* but *unforgettable* and reasonably *economical*. Well, this would be the talk of the world—as is the Leaning Tower of Pisa, the Hanging Gardens of Babylon, King Solomon's Temple, King Tutankamen's Tomb, etc. etc. And it is all delightfully simple and sensible. It is fearfully difficult to draw on account of the curving ramps and eats up office time like a devouring dragon. . . . With all its simplicity it is a difficult thing to draw—more so than to build eventually" (85). The online version of the exhibition will continue to be available at www.loc.gov/exhibits/flw/flw.html.

35. See "Joseph William Geddes" by Diane Tepfer and Pamela Scott, available under "Biographical Information: Architects, Designers, and Engineers" in the online P&P Site Index at www.loc.gov/rr/print/.

36. Records concerning the commission's deliberations on this topic are available in its offices in Washington, D.C.

37. In 2001 the Prints and Photographs Division acquired several hundred additional design and construction drawings, as well as photographs, promotional materials, letters, and financial records from the papers of Cass Gilbert and Cass Gilbert Jr. relating to the Woolworth Building, Oberlin College, the Scott Fountain, the Detroit Public Library, the Louisiana Purchase Exposition, and other built works and projects (PR 13 CN 2001:084).

38. See "Cass Gilbert (1859–1934)" by Diane Tepfer available under "Biographical Information: Architects, Designers, and Engineers" in the online P&P Site Index at www.loc.gov/rr/print/.

39. Allied Architects included, in addition to those already mentioned (with the exception of Gilbert LaCoste): P. C. Adams, Robert F. Beresford, Fred H. Brooke, Ward Brown, A. P. Clark, William Deming, J. H. deSibour, E. W. Donn Jr., William Douden, W. H. Irwin Fleming, B. C. Flourney, Charles Gregg, Arthur B. Heaton, A. L. Kundzin,

L. M. Leisenring, O. Harvey Miller, Victor Mindeleff, Thomas A. Mullett, Fred V. Murphy, Fred B. Pyle, George H. [*sic*] Ray, Fred J. Ritter, Delos H. Smith, Alex. H. Sonneman, Francis P. Sullivan, Maj. George O. Totten, L. P. Wheat Jr., and Lt. Col. George C. Will. See "Allied Architects (firm active ca. 1925–1935)" by Diane Tepfer, available under "Biographical Information: Architects, Designers, and Engineers" in the online P&P Site Index at www.loc.gov/rr/print/.

40. Joel Garreau, *Edge City: Life on the New Frontier* (New York: Doubleday, 1991). The author provides his definition and description of the characteristics of an "edge city" (4–15), quoting from *The Machine in the Garden* by and an interview with the noted cultural historian, Leo Marx, concerning its origins in and kinships with America's other new frontiers (12–13) and writes (14): "Edge City may be the result of Americans striving once again for a new, restorative synthesis. Perhaps Edge City represents Americans taking the functions of the city (the machine) and bringing them out to the physical edge of the landscape (the frontier). There, we try once again to merge the two into a newfound union of nature and art (the garden), albeit one in which the treeline is punctuated incongruously by office towers." The ruling "machine" in the twentieth century also has been interpreted to be the automobile and that is how it is used in this chapter.

41. See "Arthur Berthrong Heaton" by Diane Tepfer, available under "Biographical Information: Architects, Designers, and Engineers" in the online P&P Site Index at www.loc.gov/rr/print/.

42. Richard Longstreth was the first scholar to recognize the importance of Heaton's Park & Shop Store on upper Connecticut Avenue as a paradigm for the early shopping center, and expands his assessment of Heaton's contributions further in chapter 4, as does Gwendolyn Wright in chapter 5. James Goode and Pamela Scott discuss Heaton's designs for hotels and domestic architecture in their illustrated essays devoted to those subjects available under "Capital Drawings" through the online "P&P Site Index," www.loc.gov/rr/print/.

43. See "Washington, Hallowed Ground," in *Edge City*, 343–77.

44. See chapter 4, "Building for Business: A Century of Commercial Architecture in the Washington Metropolitan Area," by Richard Longstreth, which illustrates proposals by Donald Hudson

Drayer in the 1940s and 1950s for the commercial development of the same area at the junction of Lee Highway (figs. 7.49, 7.50).

45. See "Waggaman and Ray (firm active 1917–1919)," "Clarke Waggaman," and "George Nicholas Ray" by Diane Tepfer and Pamela Scott, available under "Biographical Information: Architects, Designers, and Engineers" in the online P&P Site Index at www.loc.gov/rr/print/.

46. See "Luther Reason Ray" by Diane Tepfer, available under "Biographical Information: Architects, Designers, and Engineers" in the online P&P Site Index at www.loc.gov/rr/print/. More modest, shingled versions, the "Mitchell" and the "Willard" models described as an "English type bungalow" and an "English Cottage," appear on the cover and inside the catalog of what was then the world's largest dealer of building materials. *1929 Honor Bilt Modern Homes* (Chicago: Sears, Roebuck, 1929), 39, 72.

47. Important studies that have contributed to the recognition, appreciation, and understanding of the qualities and significance of America's commercial vernacular buildings are Robert Venturi, Denise Scott Brown, and Steven Izenour, *Learning from Las Vegas* (Cambridge, Mass.: MIT Press, 1977); Paul Hirshorn and Steven Izenour, *White Towers* (Cambridge, Mass.: MIT Press, 1979); Chester H. Liebs, *Main Street to Miracle Mile* (Boston: Little, Brown, 1985): Philip Langdon, *Orange Roofs, Golden Arches: The Architecture of American Chain Restaurants* (New York: Alfred A. Knopf, 1986); and Alan Hess, *Googie, Fifties Coffee Shop Architecture* (San Francisco: Chronicle Books, 1985).

48. See "Fritz Winold Reiss" by C. Ford Peatross available under "Biographical Information: Architects, Designers, and Engineers" in the online P&P Site Index at www.loc.gov/rr/print/; Peatross, "Winold Reiss: A Pioneer of Modern Design," *Queen City Heritage* 51 (Summer/Fall 1993): 38–57.

49. At the time of his gift, Roy S. Thurman allowed the Library of Congress to copy his prospectus and publicity materials for the Crystal Heights project, also called "Crystal City" on the leather binder that held them. They are available as "miscellaneous supplementary materials" associated with ADE-UNIT 2451. Included are copies of a description of Wright as the "world's greatest living architect"; a description and topographical plat of the site; a detailed economic analysis of the nature, size,

and buying power of the resident and tourist populations of the metropolitan area and their growth over time; an analysis of the features of the projected development; and contemporary local newspaper articles and publicity photographs (including images of Wright, Thurman, and the drawings).

50. See Michael Sorkin, "Hollin Hills: Happy Experiment in Modernity"; John A. Burns, "The Postwar Housing Phenomenon"; Gregory K. Hunt, "The Architecture of Hollin Hills"; Dennis Carmichael, "The Landscape of Democracy"; and Joseph Rosa and Catherine Hunt, "The Modern Interior and the Hollin Hills House" in *Hollin Hills: Community of Vision* (Alexandria, Va.: Civic Association of Hollin Hills, 2000), 34–39, 40–45, 46–69, 70–77; bibliography, 178–180.

51. See also Hélène Lipstadt's essay "'Needful Buildings: Federal and National Architecture in the Collections of the Prints and Photographs Division" available under "Capital Drawings" in the online P&P Site Index at www.loc.gov/rr/print/. In the late 1930s and early 1940s, in a period of rising modernism and reaction against the Beaux-Arts tradition in architecture, the designs for both the National Gallery of Art and the Jefferson Memorial were the subject of critical condemnation, which more recently has been subject to revision. Paul Goldberger, "Awakening to the Power and Passion of a Museum," *New York Times*, June 30, 1991; "John Russell Pope and the Building of the National Gallery of Art" (exhibition brochure, Washington: National Gallery of Art, 1991); Stephen McLeod Bedford, *John Russell Pope, Architect of Empire* (New York: Rizzoli, 1998), 198, 222, 200; Joseph Hudnut, "The Last of the Romans," *Magazine of Art* 34 (April 1941): 169–73.

52. In 1963 the editors of *Architectural Forum* (then including Douglas Haskell, Donald Canty, and Peter Blake) produced an issue devoted to Washington, D.C., and wrote the following with the above project in mind: ". . . the record of J. George Stewart, who has held the title of Architect of the Capitol since 1954, is remarkable. Stewart's door is not only closed, it is hermetically sealed against the prying press and public. He is Washington's acknowledged master of the *fait accompli* . . . Stewart, of course, is no architect at all. Prior to his appointment, he was a builder, a surveyor, and one-term Congressman from Delaware, chief clerk to the Senate District Committee, and an engineering

consultant. He is, however, an accomplished politician who knows precisely how the bread gets buttered on Capitol Hill. Stewart's chief monuments are the pompous new Senate and House office buildings and the 'improved' East Front of the Capitol, remodeled over the collective dead body of the American architectural profession . . . It is worth keeping in mind, therefore, that Stewart is determined to remodel the West Front of the Capitol as well. At budget hearings for fiscal 1963, in fact, he suggested that the West Front be extended as soon as possible. He estimated the cost of the work at $18.2 million." *Architectural Forum* 118 (January 1963): 52.

53. "Ein Elysium bei Washington (Stafford Harbor, VA); Paul Rudolph, architect," *Deutsche Bauzeitung* 102 (April 1968): [229]–268; "A New Town that Conserves the Landscape," *Architectural Record* 141, no. 4 (April 1967): [151]–158. In an issue devoted to innovative and modular housing schemes, Stafford Harbor is included with Rudolph's residential skyscraper with manufactured units and Safdi's Habitat '67: "Proposed Trailer Tower, Architect: Paul Rudolph"; "Habitat '67, Montreal, Architect: Moishe Safdie with David, Barott and Boulva"; "Stafford Harbor, Virginia, Architect: Paul Rudolph," *Perspecta: The Yale Architectural Journal* 11 (1967): 191, 206–8, 178–218. In the 1960s, Rudolph also produced a number of projects for Washington's renewal areas and an article discussing civic design, Washington's monuments and buildings, and the principles of L'Enfant's plan deserving further attention: "Two projects for Northwest 1 urban renewal area, Washington, D.C.; Paul Rudolph, archt.," *Architectural Record* 143, no. 7 (June 1968): [147]–166; "A View of Washington as a Capitol—Or What is Civic Design?" *Architectural Forum* 118 (January 1963): 64–70. For the organization of structures along ridges and with roadways in Wright's Doheny Ranch Development in Beverly Hills, California, in the early 1920s, see De Long, *Designs*, 16–31, and for discussion and images of his Marin County Civic Center, see Neil Levine, *The Architecture of Frank Lloyd Wright* (Princeton, N.J.: Princeton University Press, 1996), 404–17.

54. Chloethiel Woodard Smith, "The New Town: Concept and Experience," *Building Research* 3, no. 1 (January–February 1966): 10–12.

55. See "Kevin Roche John Dinkeloo and Associates (firm active 1966–1981); Kevin Roche (b. 1922);

John Gerald Dinkeloo (1918–1981)," by Pamela Scott, available under "Biographical Information: Architects, Designers, and Engineers" in the online P&P Site Index at www.loc.gov/rr/print/; "National Aquarium in Washington," *Domus* 452 (May 1968): 8–12; and "Aquarium," *Architectural Design* 39 (February 1969): 91–94.

56. "Aquarium: National Fisheries Center and Aquarium," *Architectural Design* 2 (Feb. 1969): 91–94; Yukio Futagawa, ed. and photographer, *Kevin Roche John Dinkeloo and Associates, 1962–1975*, preface by J. Irwin Miller, introduction by Henry-Russell Hitchcock (New York: Architectural Book Pub. Co., 1977), 160–63; Kevin Roche with Francesco Dal Co, ed., *Kevin Roche* (New York: Rizzoli, 1985), 140–41; John Neuhart, Marilyn Neuhart, and Ray Eames, *Eames Design: the Work of the Office of Charles and Ray Eames* (New York: Abrams, 1989), 315–17. The exhibitions, as developed by the Eames Office, were to have seven major themes: (1) systematic and evolutionary biology, (2) biogeography, (3) biological disciplines, (4) aquatic environments, (5) levels of complexity in natural biological associations, (6) research techniques and equipment, and (7) "Man's responsibility for maintenance of the ecosystem," in U.S. Department of the Interior, *National Fisheries Center and Aquarium* (Washington, D.C.: U.S. Department of the Interior, 1969), 8.

57. Paul Rudolph, "A View of Washington as a Capital," 68–69.

58. Gregory K. Hunt, "From Generic Issues to Speculative Visions: Urban Design Charrettes in Washington, D.C., The Portal and King Street Metro Sites," in *Capital Visions: Reflections on a Decade of Urban Design Charrettes and a Look Ahead*, Iris Miller and Ronald Grim, eds. (Washington: Library of Congress Geography and Map Division, 1995), 11–14.

59. See "Doug Michels" by Diane Tepfer and James Goode, available under "Biographical Information: Architects, Designers, and Engineers" in the online P&P Site Index at www.loc.gov/rr/print/ and Ant Farm, *Automerica: A Trip Down U.S. Highways from World War II to the Future* (New York: E. P. Dutton, 1976); Wendy Hamilton, "In Search of Dolphin Links," *Canberra Times*, April 5, 1978; Ann Holmes, "Ambassadors to the Sea: A Dolphin Embassy," *Houston Chronicle*, March 25, 1979; Jennifer Harper, "Far-Out Idea: Think Tank

in Space," *Insight* (September 1, 1986): 64–65; Robert Engelman, "Dolphins and Humans Will Check into New Hotel," *Richmond Times-Dispatch*, June 25, 1989; Julia Mashburn and Joe Mashburn, "Doug Michels and a Visionary Texas Frontier," *Texas Architect* (July/August 1989): 30–35; Susan Tamulevich, "Flipper Does D.C.?," *Washington Post Magazine*, April 23, 1989, 15; and Doug Michels Architecture, "Dolphin America, The Future Is Coming to Power City," press release, 1989.

60. Thomas Jefferson to James Madison, September 20, 1785, Thomas Jefferson Papers, Library of Congress. Julian P. Boyd, ed., *The Papers of Thomas Jefferson* (Princeton, N.J.: Princeton University Press, 1950), 8:535.

Chapter *Two. The United States Capitol*

1. Library of Congress, L'Enfant Papers, printed in Elizabeth S. Kite, *L'Enfant and Washington, 1791–1792* (Baltimore: Johns Hopkins Press, 1929), 34.

2. *U.S. v. Martin F. Morris, et al.*, Records of the Supreme Court of the District of Columbia, 7 (1898): 2155–59, published in Saul K. Padover, ed., *Thomas Jefferson and the National Capital* (Washington: U.S. Government Printing Office, 1946), 30–36.

3. Jefferson to L'Enfant, early March 1791, in A. A. Lipscomb and A. E. Bergh, eds., *The Writings of Thomas Jefferson* (Washington, D.C.: Issued under the auspices of the Thomas Jefferson Memorial Association, 1903), 8:140; published in Kite, 35. In addition to these published compilations and Padover, ed., for Jefferson's writings, see also Julian P. Boyd et al., eds., *The Papers of Thomas Jefferson* (Princeton, N.J.: Princeton University Press, 1950–).

4. Letter of April 10, 1791, in Lipscomb and Bergh, eds., 8:163; published in Padover, ed., 59. The drawing based on the Pantheon is Massachusetts Historical Society, N388. This was discussed in some detail by Charles E. Brownell, "Jefferson, The U.S. Capitol, and Civic Architecture for a New American Nation" (Creating the Federal Image: Art for a New Nation, American Art Symposium, University of Delaware, April 5, 1991).

5. Letter of July 12, 1812, Library of Congress, Latrobe Papers, printed in Padover, ed., 471.

6. In July 1791, one of the original commissioners for the District of Columbia, David Stuart, wrote Governor Randolph of Virginia that "Ms l'Enfant is about drawing a model for the house of

legislature. I have mentioned to him the one sent in by Mr. Jefferson, which he desires to see. If there is no impropriety I would beg you to send it to him by stage" (Calendar of Virginia State Papers, quoted by Fiske Kimball, *Thomas Jefferson, Architect* [Boston: Printed for private distribution at the Riverside Press, Cambridge, 1916], 520; and Alexandra Cushing Howard, "Stephen Hallet and William Thornton at the U.S. Capitol: A Re-evaluation of Their Role in the Original Design of the Federal Capitol, 1791–1797" [master's thesis, University of Virginia, 1974], 116).

7. Library of Congress, Jefferson Papers, in Padover, ed., 111.

8. Letter from Washington to Jefferson, February 22, 1792, in John C. Fitzpatrick, ed., *The Writings of George Washington* (Washington, D.C.: U.S. Government Printing Office, 1931–44), 31: 483, and in Padover, ed., 93.

9. Library of Congress, L'Enfant Papers, published in Kite, 99. This argument and that which follows have also been presented by Bates Lowry, *Building a National Image: Architectural Drawings for the American Democracy, 1789–1912* (Washington, D.C.: National Building Museum, 1985), 16–17, 21; as well as Pamela Scott, "Stephen Hallet's Designs for the United States Capitol," *Winterthur Portfolio* 27 (1992): 145.

10. Drawings at the Maryland Historical Society, Baltimore, 76.88, include those of Andrew Mayfield Carshore (.22, .23, .27, and .28), James Diamond (.49–.53), Dobie (.39–.41), Abraham Faw (.7), Philip Hart (.12–.18), Robert Goin Lanphier (.19–.21), McIntire (.44–.48), Jacob Small (.4–.5, .29–.35), Charles Wintersmith (.42–.43), and an unidentified design (.11). Other drawings possibly connected with the competition include four by John Trumbull (New-York Historical Society, Trumbull Album, 60–62b). Designs were also submitted by Leonard Harbaugh, Samuel Blodgett, and George Turner, but these apparently have not survived, although see the next paragraph. For Blodgett and Harbaugh, see letter from commissioners to Blodgett, August 29, 1792 (House of Representatives, *Documentary History of the Construction and Development of the United States Capitol Buildings and Grounds*, 58th Cong., 2d sess., HR 646 [Washington, D.C.: U.S. Government Printing Office, 1904], 19). Most of the others are illustrated, at least in part, and discussed in Jeanne F.

Butler, "Competition 1792: Designing a Nation's Capitol," *Capitol Studies* 4, no. 1 (1976). See also Fiske Kimball and Wells Bennett, "The Competition of the Federal Buildings, 1792–93," *Journal of the American Institute of Architects* 7 (1919): 8–12, 98–102, 202–10, 355–61, 521–28; and 8 (1919): 117–21.

11. Letter from Washington to the commissioners, July 23, 1792, Library of Congress, Letterbook 11, p. 228; printed in *Records of the Columbia Historical Society* 17 (1914): 57–58. In his view, its principal flaw, shared by all the others, was "the want of an Executive apartment." The other factor that Washington wanted was the extension of the "Pilastrade . . . around the semi-circular projection at the end." Even better would be the surrounding of Turner's plan "with Columns and a colonade like that which was presented to you by Monsr. Hallet."

12. See "William Thornton" by Charles M. Harris, available under "Biographical Information: Architects, Designers, and Engineers" in the online "P&P Site Index" at www.loc.gov/rr/print/.

13. This source was first noted by Pamela Scott in 1991 and was subsequently published in her "Stephen Hallet's Designs."

14. See letter from Hallet to Jefferson, September 21, 1792, Library of Congress, Jefferson Papers. For Hallet's role at the Capitol, see also Pamela Scott's essay on Hallet, available under "Biographical Information: Architects, Designers, and Engineers" in the online "P&P Site Index"; Scott, "Stephen Hallet's Designs"; and Wells Bennett, "Stephen Hallet and His Designs for the National Capitol, 1791–1794," *Journal of the American Institute of Architects* 4 (July–October 1916): 290–95, 324–30, 376–83, 411–18.

15. Library of Congress, Jefferson Papers.

16. Thornton to Commissioners, December 12, 1792, Library of Congress, Thornton Papers, box 18, p. 3. See also, his letters of November 9, Library of Congress, Thornton Papers, box 18, p. 73; and July 12, Glenn Brown, *History of the United States Capitol* (Washington, D.C.: U.S. Government Printing Office, 1900–1903), 1:7. For Thornton's role in the story of the Capitol, see also C. M. Harris's essay on Thornton online; Harris, ed., and Daniel Preston, asst. ed., *The Papers of William Thornton* (Charlottesville: University Press of Virginia, 1995–); and Fiske Kimball and Wells Bennett, "William Thornton and the Design of the United States Capitol," *Art Studies* 1 (1923): 76–92.

17. Letter to Daniel Carroll, in Lipscomb and Bergh, eds., *Writings of Jefferson*, 9: 8; published also in Padover, ed., 171, and *Documentary History*, 23.

18. The French text is published in Bennett, "Stephen Hallet," 418.

19. National Archives, RG 42, Letters Sent by the Commissioners, 1:177. Jefferson's transmission of Hallet's description to Washington is in National Archives, Records of Dept. of State, Misc. Letters, March–April 1793; the English translation also sent is printed in Padover, ed., 180–81.

20. Commissioners to Washington, June 23, 1793, *Documentary History*, 26.

21. Dorothy Twohig, ed., *The Journal of the Proceedings of the President, 1793–1797* (Charlottesville: University Press of Virginia, 1981), 189 (June 24, 1793). In addition to this work and Fitzpatrick, ed., see "The Writings of George Washington Relating to the National Capital," *Records of the Columbia Historical Society* 17 (1914): 3–232.

22. Jefferson to Washington, July 17, 1793 (National Archives, Records of the Department of State, Miscellaneous Letters, July–August 1793), in *Documentary History*, 26–27, and Padover, ed., 184–86.

23. See, e.g., letter from Thornton to Samuel Blodgett, February 21, 1800, Letterbook, Thornton Papers, Library of Congress, printed in *Papers of William Thornton, vol. 1, 1871–1802*, ed. C. M. Harris, Daniel Preston, asst. ed. (Charlottesville: University Press of Virginia, 1995–), 537.

24. Hadfield's intention is noted in a letter from Thornton to Washington, November 2, 1795, Library of Congress, Thornton Papers, 2:207. The drawings at the Maryland Historical Society (76.88.1–.2), grouped with the competition drawings, have also been attributed to Hallet and even to Thornton, though they do not resemble his work at all. For the guilloche belt course, see Pamela Scott and Antoinette J. Lee, *Buildings of the District of Columbia* (New York: Oxford University Press, 1993), 116.

25. For Latrobe's role at the Capitol, see also "B. Henry Latrobe," by Jeffrey A. Cohen, available under "Biographical Information: Architects, Designers, and Engineers" through the online P&P Site Index; Cohen and Charles E. Brownell, eds., *The Architectural Drawings of Benjamin Henry Latrobe* (New Haven, Conn.: Yale University Press, 1994); John C. Van Horne and Lee H. Formwalt, eds., Darwin H. Stapleton, assoc. ed., and Jeffrey A. Cohen and

Tina H. Sheller, asst. eds., *The Correspondence and Miscellaneous Papers of Benjamin Henry Latrobe* (New Haven, Conn.: Yale University Press, 1984–88); Paul F. Norton, "Latrobe, Jefferson, and the National Capitol" (Ph.D. diss., Princeton University, 1952; publ., New York, 1977); Virginia Daiker, "The Capitol of Jefferson and Latrobe," *Library of Congress Quarterly*, Spring 1975, 25–32; Brownell, "Latrobe, His Craftsmen, and the Corinthian Order of the Hall of Representatives," *The Craftsman in Early America*, A Winterthur Book, ed. Ian M. G. Quimby (New York: Norton, 1984), 247–72; and Cohen, "Forms into Architecture: Reform Ideals and the Gauntlets of the Real in Latrobe's Surveyorships at the U. S. Capitol, 1803–1817," *The United States Capitol: Designing and Decorating a National Icon*, ed. Donald R. Kennon (Athens: Ohio University Press, 2000), 23–55.

26. A very similar drawing to Latrobe's inscribed on the back by the sculptor Giovanni Andrei is in the collection of the Architect of the Capitol (003150.1685), and a letter from Latrobe to Jefferson of July 12–18, 1815, with another drawing of the House (Library of Congress, Jefferson Papers), elaborates in detail on the damage. There were parts that were not significantly damaged (e.g., the corncob capitals of the ground-floor vestibule of the north wing), as established by the following comment by Latrobe in a letter to Jefferson of November 5, 1816 (Library of Congress, Jefferson Papers): "The Columns & Capitals as executed, and standing in the Vestibule of the North wing of the Capitol on the ground floor, were not much injured by the British, so little indeed, that, as I wish some part of the building to remain as they left it— I do not propose to repair them, unless the president shall order it to be done."

27. The statement about two architects, with both Bulfinch and McComb mentioned, is from a letter to Bulfinch from Harrison Gray Otis, December 2, 1817, where Otis is quoting President Monroe, published in Ellen S. Bulfinch, ed., *The Life and Letters of Charles Bulfinch* (Boston: Houghton Mifflin, 1896), 206. Three days later, December 5, 1817, in a letter to McComb, James Renwick asked whether he "would accept the appointment at Washington made vacant by the resignation of Mr. Latrobe" (New-York Historical Society, Miscellaneous MSS McComb). For Bulfinch's role at the Capitol, see also James F. O'Gorman's essay avail-

able under "Biographical Information: Architects, Designers, and Engineers" in the online P&P site Index; Pamela Scott, "Charles Bulfinch: Well-Connected, Refined Gentleman Architect," *The United States Capitol: Designing and Decorating a National Icon*, ed. Kennon, 56–84; and Harold Kirker, *The Architecture of Charles Bulfinch* (Cambridge, Mass.: Harvard University Press, 1969).

28. Nos. 003150.1670, .1671, and .1679–.1683.

29. Message to Congress, December 2, 1852.

30. *Documentary History*, 341–49; and August Schoenborn, "Sketch of My Education and Connection with the Extension of the United States Capitol, Washington, D.C." (Washington, D.C., 1895), and Schoenborn, "Contribution to the History of the Building of the Capitol Extension . . . by an Eye-witness" (Washington, D.C., 1898), both in Turpin C. Bannister, "The Genealogy of the Dome of the United States Capitol," *Journal of the Society of Architectural Historians* 7, nos. 1–2 (January–June 1948): 17–31. See also Susan Brizzolara Wojik, "Thomas U. Walter and Iron in the United States Capitol: An Alliance of Architecture, Engineering, and Industry" (Ph.D. diss., University of Delaware, 1998).

31. *Documentary History*, 859, 1025–27; Schoenborn, "Sketch of My Education," 7, in Bannister, 19; Wojik, "Thomas U. Walter and Iron in the United States Capitol"; and James Moore Goode, "Architecture, Politics, and Conflict: Thomas Ustick Walter and the Enlargement of the United States Capitol, 1850–1865" (Ph.D. diss., George Washington University, 1995). For Walter's role at the Capitol, see also "Thomas Ustick Walter" by William C. Allen, available under "Biographical Information: Architects, Designers, and Engineers" at the online "P&P Site Index"; Allen, *The Dome of the United States Capitol: An Architectural History* (Washington, D.C.: U.S. Government Printing Office, 1992); Goode, "Thomas U. Walter and the Search for Propriety," *The United States Capitol: Designing and Decorating a National Icon*, ed. Kennon, pp. 85–109; and Homer T. Rosenberger, "Thomas Ustick Walter and the Completion of the United States Capitol," *Records of the Columbia Historical Society* 50 (1948–50): 272–322.

32. Schoenborn, "Contribution to the History of the Building of the Capitol Extension," 2–3, in Bannister, 24; Wojik, "Thomas U. Walter and Iron in the United States Capitol"; and Goode, "Thomas U. Wal-

ter and the Search for Propriety." For Meigs's role at the Capitol, see also Donald C. Jackson's essay on Meigs available under "Biographical Information: Architects, Designers, and Engineers" in the online P&P site Index; Russell F. Weigley, "Captain Meigs and the Artists of the Capitol: Federal Patronage of the Arts in the 1850's," *Records of the Columbia Historical Society* 47 (1969–70): 285–305; Weigley, *Quartermaster General of the Union Army* (New York: Columbia University Press, 1959); David W. Miller, *Second only to Grant* (Shippensburg, Penn.: White Maine, 2000); and William C. Dickinson, Dean A. Herrin, and Donald R. Kennon, eds., *Montgomery C. Meigs and the Building of the Nation's Capitol* (Athens: Ohio University Press, 2001).

33. Schoenborn, "Contribution to the History of the Building of the Capitol Extension," 5–6; published in Bannister, 25.

34. Schoenborn, "Contribution to the History of the Building of the Capitol Extension," 3; published in Bannister, 24. For the Library, see Schoenborn, "Sketch of My Education," 15; published in Bannister, 21. O. Sonnemann, an assistant to Meigs, also submitted designs for the construction of the dome (see Schoenborn, "Sketch of My Education," 15; published in Bannister, 21).

35. Schoenborn, "Contribution to the History of the Building of the Capitol Extension," 3, 13; published in Bannister, 28, 24.

36. For these, see, esp., Robert B. Ennis, "Handlist: Thomas Ustick Walter, Architect: An Exhibition at the Athenaeum of Philadelphia," October 29–December 28, 1979. The Athenaeum's Walter drawings number 503 for about eighty-eight projects, with some for the Capitol; Winterthur's holdings in its Joseph Downs Collection of Manuscripts and Printed Ephemera comprise fourteen items; and the American Architectural Foundation owns a bound volume of drawings for the north wing.

37. Schoenborn, "Sketch of My Education," 20; published in Bannister, 23.

38. For this, see Frances Brousseau, "The Library of Congress, 1873–1897: The Building, Its Architects, and the Politics of Nineteenth-Century Architectural Practice" (Ph.D. diss., University of Delaware, 1998).

39. For these, see drawings in the collection of the Architect of the Capitol; and Alfred Easton Poor, "Report and Recommendations for the Extension of the West Central Front of the United

States Capitol, Washington, D.C., March 1978" (copy, Library of Congress, Prints and Photographs Division).

40. In addition to this report, cited also in the preceding note, see Mario E. Campioli, "The Proposed Extension of the West Central Front of the Capitol," and Charles C. McLaughlin, "The Capitol in Peril: The West Front Controversy from Walter to Stewart," *Records of the Columbia Historical Society* 47 (1969–1970): 212–36 and 237–65, respectively.

41. In addition to the works cited in the preceding notes, I am also indebted to the following: the Digges-L'Enfant-Morgan, Jefferson, Latrobe, Thornton, and Washington Papers in the Manuscript Division of the Library of Congress; the Proceedings and Letterbooks of the District of Columbia Commissioners and of the Office Concerned with Public Buildings in Record Group 42 at the National Archives, a guide to which is provided by Mary-Jane M. Dowd, ed., *Records of the Office of Public Buildings and Public Parks of the National Capital* (Washington, D.C.: National Archives and Records Administration, 1992); U.S. Department of the Interior, *Annual Reports*, 1851–61 and 1862–68; U.S. Department of War, *Annual Reports*, 1855–61; John R. Kerwood, ed., *The United States Capitol: An Annotated Bibliography* (Norman: University of Oklahoma Press, 1973); William C. Allen, *The United States Capitol: A Brief Architectural History* (Washington: U.S. Government Printing Office, 1990); Ihna T. Frary, *They Built the Capitol* (Richmond, Va.: Garrett & Massie, 1940); Wilhelmus B. Bryan, *A History of the National Capital* (New York: Macmillan, 1914–16); Charles E. Fairman, *Art and Artists of the Capitol of the United States of America* (Washington, D.C.: U.S. Government Printing Office, 1927); and Egon Verheyen, "John Trumbull and the U.S. Capitol," *John Trumbull*, ed. Helen A. Cooper (New Haven, Conn.: Yale University Art Gallery, 1982), 260–75.

Since this essay was written in the early 1990s, a number of significant works have appeared, and it has been possible to incorporate information and ideas from them into later revisions. These include Pamela Scott, *Temple of Liberty: Building the Capitol for a New Nation*, exhibition catalog, Library of Congress, February 24–June 24, 1995 (New York: Oxford University Press, 1995); *Papers of William Thornton, Vol. 1: 1781–1802*, ed. C. M. Harris, David Preston, asst. ed. (Charlottesville: University Press of Virginia, 1995–); William C. Allen, *History of the United States Capitol: A Chronicle of Design, Construction and Politics* (Washington, D.C.: U.S. Government Printing Office, 2001); and three volumes of collected essays derived from papers given at symposia sponsored by the U.S. Capitol Historical Society, the first two edited by Donald R. Kennon. The first of these is *A Republic for the Ages* (Charlottesville: Published for the U.S. Capitol Historical Society by the University Press of Virginia, 1999), which includes the following relevant essays: Charles E. Brownell, "Thomas Jefferson's Architectural Models and the United States Capitol," 316–401; James Stevens Curl, "The Capitol in Washington, D.C., and its Freemasonic Connections," 214–67; Pamela Scott, "Power, Civic Virtue, Wisdom, Liberty, and the Constitution: Early American Symbols and the United States Capitol," 402–47; and Damie Stillman, "From the Ancient Roman Republic to the New American One: Architecture for a New Nation," 271–315. The second is *The United States Capitol: Designing and Decorating a National Icon* (Athens: Published for the U.S. Capitol Historical Society by Ohio University Press, 2000), which includes essays cited in preceding notes by Cohen, Goode, and Scott and the following additional essays: William C. Allen, "'Seats of Broils, Confusion, and Squandered Thousands': Building the Capitol, 1790–1802," 3–22; William B. Bushong, "Right Hand Men: The Development of the Office of the Architect of the Capitol, 1865–1954," 110–33; and Richard Guy Wilson, "The Historicization of the U.S. Capitol and the Office of the Architect, 1954–1996," 134–68, as well as three articles on Brumidi by Barbara A. Wolanin, Catherine S. Myers, and David Sellin. The third, edited by Dickinson, Herrin, Kennon, is *Montgomery C. Meigs and the Building of the Nation's Capitol.*

Chapter *Three. The White House*

1. *National Intelligencer*, December 9, 1831; November 9, 1833.

2. For Bingham's official papers and some of his historical work, see Records Commissioner of Public Buildings, Record Group 42, National Archives, Washington, D.C.

3. Tracings of the Leinster House remodeling were sent to Bingham but do not survive in the archives. For letters on the subject, see Bingham to the Hon. Joshua Wilbur, Washington, D.C., January 20, 1900, and May 4, 1900, commissioners' letters, National Archives.

4. For the most readily available sketch of the various redecorations from the Kennedy period to the present, consult the *Guides* published by the White House Historical Association. See also James A. Abbott and Elaine M. Rice, *Designing Camelot: The Kennedy White House Restoration* (New York: Van Nostrand Reinhold, 1998).

5. See John Guidas, *The White House: Resources for Research at the Library of Congress* (Washington, D.C.: Library of Congress, 1992).

6. See Record Group 42, National Archives and also the special file on the Truman Renovation, National Archives. Lorenzo Winslow Diary, Office of the Curator, White House.

7. The view of the south front is in the Library of Congress; the dining room photograph is in the James K. Polk Memorial Museum, Columbia, Tennessee.

8. Collection in the International Museum of Photography, George Eastman House, Rochester, New York.

9. Prints and Photographs Division, Library of Congress.

10. See Michael Fazio and Patrick Snadon, "Benjamin Latrobe and Thomas Jefferson Redesign the White House," *White House History*, no. 8 (Fall 2000): 37–53.

11. See Charles M. Harris, "The Politics of Public Buildings: William Thornton and President's Square," *White House History*, no. 3 (Spring 1998): 46–59; and "William Thornton" (1759–1828), by Harris, available in the online P&P Site Index at www.loc.gov/rr/print/.

12. Stephen V. Van Rensselaer to Joseph Elgar, Washington [January 1829]; Hoban to Samuel Lane, Washington, December 12, 1818; and Hoban memorandum, commissioners letters sent and received, Record Group 42, National Archives.

Chapter *Four. Building for Business*

1. For purposes of this essay, I have limited the range of types to those whose dominant function is to house retail, financial, or service businesses, either singly or in combination. The list thus includes office buildings, banks, department stores, shopping centers, specialty stores, and automobile

sales, service, and storage facilities. I have also included a few other commercial types such as restaurants and motels to which the consumer public has traditionally had access. I have not included warehouses or industrial facilities because of the space constraints for this project. The collection has a large amount of such material, which warrants careful examination.

2. Among the firms are Carrère & Hastings, John Eberson, Cass Gilbert, Henry Hardenburgh, Johnson/Burgee, Kohn Pederson Fox, Thomas Lamb, William Lescaze, I. M. Pei & Partners, Bruce Price, Starrett & van Vleck, Warren & Wetmore, and York & Sawyer from New York; D. H. Burnham & Company, Henry Ives Cobb, Holabird & Root, and Jarvis Hunt from Chicago; and Vincent Kling, Mitchell/Giurgola, and James Windrim from Philadelphia. Washington-based architects traditionally have received scant national attention for work in the commercial sphere. Only in recent years has the situation begun to change, particularly with the work of Hartman/Cox and Keyes Condon Florance (now KCF/SHG).

3. At least until recently, the few exceptions are not located in the urban core but rather in outlying business districts. Among the most important examples is the Park and Shop, discussed in the text below. Another work of major significance is the Hecht Company Silver Spring store (1945–1947), among the first of the very large branch department stores constructed outside the Los Angeles area and one which demonstrated that such a facility need not be oriented to an upper-end market nor be elaborate in its design to be highly profitable.

One downtown facility that did attract national attention for its novel plan was the ten-story Cafritz Building (1948–1950; demolished), which included a multideck, 450-car parking garage as its core. The concept, however, does not appear to have been followed elsewhere to any marked degree. See *Architectural Forum* 89 (October 1948): 13; "Integrated Parking for Office Building in Washington, D.C.," *Architectural Record* 106 (December 1949): 12; and Conrad P. Harness, "Cafritz Plans 'Park-at-Your-Desk' Building," *Washington Post* [hereafter *WP*], 29 August 1948, R1.

4. Among other things, such a range of documentation can be very useful in reconstructing the way in which an architect approached the process of design. Studies of that process that fo-

cus on practitioners in the United States are few. For a noteworthy exception, see James F. O'Gorman, "The Making of a 'Richardson Building,' 1874–1886," in *H. H. Richardson and His Office: Selected Drawings* (Cambridge, Mass.: Harvard College Library, 1974), 16–27.

5. For a general background, see Warren James Belasco, *Americans on the Road: From Autocamp to Motel, 1910–1945* (Cambridge, Mass.: MIT Press, 1979); Chester H. Liebs, *Main Street to Miracle Mile: American Roadside Architecture* (Boston: New York Graphic Society, 1985), 169–191; and John A. Jakle, Keith A. Sculle, and Jefferson S. Rogers, *The Motel in America* (Baltimore: Johns Hopkins University Press, 1996).

6. For this essay, I have drawn on material collected in the course of several other projects, including those cited in nn. 36, 39, 43, and 48 below. To supplement these sources, I have gathered some contemporary accounts from local newspapers and a few other period publications. The ideas presented in the paragraphs that follow are not intended as definitive analysis of the subject. Likewise the sources cited in the notes are but a few of those pertinent to a detailed study.

7. For further discussion, see Richard Longstreth, "The Unusual Transformation of Downtown Washington in the Early Twentieth Century," *Washington History* 13 (Fall–Winter 2001–2002): 50–71. Useful background on the development of downtown Washington is contained in Walter F. McArdle, "The Development of the Business Sector in Washington, D.C., 1800–1973," *Records of the Columbia Historical Society* 73–74 (1973–1974), 556–94; and Alison K. Hoagland, "7th Street Downtown, An Evolving Commercial Neighborhood," in *Washington at Home: An Illustrated History*, ed. Kathryn Schneider Smith (Northridge, Calif.: Windsor Publications, 1988), 43–53.

8. "Tall" is, of course, a relative term. When the Sun Building was completed in 1887, it had more floors designed for human occupancy than any other edifice in the city and not many fewer than the tallest buildings then in New York and Chicago. By 1900 tall buildings in those and other major cities were routinely planned with fourteen to sixteen stories, and some exceeded twenty. In Washington, D.C., however, the height of buildings was limited to a maximum of one hundred thirty feet, except on the north side of Pennsylvania Avenue, by fed-

eral legislation of 1899 and 1910. Thus eleven stories has been more or less the maximum number present in local commercial construction.

Concerning the Sun Building, see "The New Sun Building," Washington *Evening Star* [hereafter *ES*], 23 April 1887, 2; "Washington," *American Architect and Building News* 25 (19 January 1889): 34; *Illustrated Washington: Our Capital* (New York: American Publishing and Engraving, 1890), 97; Theodore Turak, "A. B. Mullett: Private Practice in Washington, D.C.," in *A. B. Mullett: His Relevance in American Architecture and Historic Preservation*, ed. D. Mullett Smith (Washington, D.C.: Mullett-Smith Press, 1990), 55–72. Concerning the Atlantic Building, see "Building Operations," *ES*, 22 September 1888, 2. Concerning the Washington Loan & Trust Building, see *ES*, 28 June 1890, 15; and Diane Maddex, *Historic Buildings of Washington, D.C.* (Pittsburgh: Ober Park, 1973), 137–38. For contemporary accounts of changes in prime locations for business property, see *ES*, 8 November 1890, 2; and *ES*, 27 December 1890, 15. Here and in many of the citations below, titles of newspaper articles are abbreviations.

9. Concerning the Evening Star Building, see *ES*, 30 June 1900, 18–19; concerning the Colorado Building, see *ES*, 12 May 1902, 12.

10. "Washington City in White," *WP*, 30 December 1906, III-8; Raymond W. Pullman, "Hub of Business," *WP*, 19 August 1906, II-2; "The City Today," *WP*, 7 October 1909, I-2; "Downtown Property Values," *ES*, 22 April 1911, II-2; "Making Way for Bank," *WP*, 6 February 1910, III-4. George H. Gall, *The New Washington* (Washington, D.C.: Washington Chamber of Commerce, 1913), provides a convenient source of illustration of much of this work when it was new.

Concerning the Union Trust Building, see "Metropolitan Bank," *WP*, 29 July 1906, III-9; "Home of Union Trust," *WP*, 23 June 1907, III-3; "Union Trust at Home," *WP*, 8 December 1907, IV-2; *Inland Architect and News Record* 50 (December 1907), plate; "Union Trust Building, Washington, D.C.," *American Architect & Building News* 43 (April 15, 1908), 128–29, plates; "Recent Bank Buildings of the United States," *Architectural Record* 25 (January 1909), 9, 19–21; "Union Trust Co.," *ES*, 28 January 1927, 14; and *History in the Making: A Pictorial Celebration of Our Landmark Headquarters Building* (Washington, D.C.: First American Bank of Washington, 1983).

For discussion of other examples, see "Metropolitan Bank," *WP*, 20 July 1906, III-9; "Westory Building," *WP*, 4 November 1906, III-6; "New Business Edifice," *WP*, 17 March 1907, III-2; "Flat-iron's Rival Here," *WP*, 11 August 1907, III-5; "In New Home Soon," *WP*, 8 September 1907, III-8; "Adorns Money Center," *WP*, 15 September 1907, III-3; "New Bank Home," *WP*, 13 October 1907, III-6; "Business Landmark to Go," *WP*, 27 September 1907, III-2; "Making Way for Bank," *WP*, 6 February 1910, III-4; "To Rush New Building," *WP*, 4 June 1910, 5; "To Have 11 Stories," *WP*, 5 February 1911, I-8; "Riggs Building Plans," *WP*, 5 February 1911, III-2; "Prospectus of the New Woodward," *WP*, 25 February 1911, 2; "Office Building Planned," *WP*, 2 July 1911, III-2; "New Bank Building," *WP*, 11 September 1911, III-3; "Plan Interstate Building," *WP*, 18 February 1912, 14; and "Offices in Demand," *WP*, 12 May 1912, II-4.

11. For examples, see "New Office Building," *ES*, 4 March 1906, I-8; "Bank Ready to Open," *WP*, 1 December 1907, IV-1; *WP*, 27 June 1909, Real Estate Sect., 1; "Office Structure Begun," *WP*, 13 February 1910, Real Estate Sect., 2; "For Business Purpose," *ES*, 4 June 1910, II-2; "Soon to Start Work," *WP*, 3 November 1912, I-19; "Business Section Grows," *ES*, 16 November 1912, II-2; "Ninth Street Growing," *WP*, 24 May 1913, II-2; "Rebuilt for Business," *WP*, 14 September 1913, III-3; *WP*, 8 March 1914, III-3; and *WP*, 19 April 1914, III-3.

12. Concerning the Transportation Building, see "Himes Takes Title," *WP*, 16 March 1924, III-3.

13. Here and elsewhere in this essay, I have relied on city directories to determine the location of businesses. See nn. 10 and 11 above for references to banks constructed as part of multistory office buildings.

14. "Bank Will Erect," *WP*, 25 July 1926, R-1; "Work Begun Today," *ES*, 14 August 1926, 16; "Washington Loan," *WP*, 15 April 1923, III-2; James M. Goode, *Capital Losses: A Cultural History of Washington's Destroyed Buildings*, rev. ed. (1979; repr. Washington, D.C.: Smithsonian Institution Press, 2003), 322.

15. Contemporary accounts of these emporia include a serialized article by Bernard McDonnell, "Romances of Washington Stores," *WP*: 27 September 1925, Amusements/Features Sect., 10; 11 October 1925, 5; 18 October 1925, 7; 25 October 1925, 5; and 8 November 1925, 11. Concerning expansion, see: "Lansburgh & Brother Enlarge," *WP*,

26 May 1912, I-17; "Addition to Hecht Store," *ES*, 30 June 1912, I-16; "Bigger Stores Here," *WP*, 19 October 1913, III-3; "Like a Real Palace," *WP*, 19 July 1914, III-3; "Added to Big Stores," *WP*, 18 October 1914, I-15; "King's Palace Ready," *WP*, 15 November 1914, I-19; "Beautiful Hecht Home," *WP*, 23 March 1924, III-2; "New Million-Dollar Lansburgh," *ES*, 9 March 1925, 22; "Hecht's Will Open," *WP*, 12 November 1925, 24; and Annette C. Ward, "Nine Decades of Lansburgh Growth," *Women's Wear Daily*, 24 July 1950, 42. The most detailed historical account is Theresa Renee Burr, "Building Fashions: Department Store Architecture in Washington, D.C., 1885–1930" (M.A. thesis, George Washington University, 1996).

16. Concerning the Palais Royal, see: "The New Palais Royal," *ES*, 30 September 1893, 10; "Story of a Business Life," *WP*, 1 October 1893, 7; "Crowned by Dome," *ES*, 6 August 1910, II-1; and "Prepare to Start Work," *ES*, 25 February 1911, II-2. Concerning Woodward & Lothrop, see: "Possession Obtained," *ES*, 14 May 1901, 8; *ES*, 16 December 1902, 7; "Woodward & Lothrop's," *WP*, 7 October 1909, II-14; Bernard McDonnell, "Romances of Washington Stores," *WP*, 4 October 1925, Amusements/Features Sect., 11; "Landmark Store Is Razed," *ES*, 28 March 1926, I-14; and Martha C. Guilford, ed., *From Founders to Grandsons: The Story of Woodward & Lothrop* (Washington, D.C.: Rufus H. Darby Printing, 1955), chaps. 3–4.

17. Known as the Homer Building, the project at Thirteenth and F Streets extended a full block, rose five stories, and was designed to support an additional six stories. It may have been initially planned as new quarters for Kann's, which announced over a decade later that it would occupy the premises. See: "Big Store Rushed," *WP*, 22 March 1914, III-3; "Big F Street Store," *ES*, 8 December 1926, 1; "Kann Sons Company," *ES*, 3 January 1927, 13; and "S. Kann & Co. Will Move," *WP*, 3 January 1928, 11.

The store at Twenty-First and I Streets was to have been eight stories, rivaling the large new addition to Woodward & Lothrop; see "Historic Houses Sold," *WP*, 10 March 1912, III-4.

18. "Garfinckel Buys," *ES*, 28 July 1926, 1; "Garfinckel to Erect," *WP*, 20 May 1928, M-1, 3; "Garfinckel Plans," *ES*, 6 April 1929, 13; *WP*, 7 April 1929, R-1; "New Garfinckel Building," *ES*, October 1930, B-1; "Garfinckel Store," *WP*, 5 October 1930, M-16.

19. Pullman, "Hub of Business District."

20. "Realtors Will Improve," *WP*, 10 July 1927, R 4; "New Structure Framed," *WP*, 15 April 1928, R-4.

21. For contemporary accounts of Connecticut Avenue's transformation, see: "Growth of Business," *ES*, 22 January 1910, II-2; "Business Spreading Out," *ES*, 29 October 1910, II-2; "Will Be Office Building," *WP*, 4 December 1910, III-2; "Business Moving Northward," *ES*, 20 January 1912, II-2; "Growth Continues," *ES*, 29 June 1912, II-3; *WP*, 14 September 1919, III-1; "Conn. Ave. Trade Unites," *WP*, 2 January 1921, III-1; *WP*, "Business Crowding," *WP*, 2 September 1923, III-2; and "Famous Connecticut Avenue," *WP*, 27 February 1926, Home & Garden Sect., 15.

22. In 1930 Washington's population was 486,869. Boston's was 781,188; Philadelphia's 1,951,961; New York's 6,930,446. Washington indeed had substantially fewer people than its neighbor Baltimore (808,874) and other major industrial centers such as Pittsburgh (669,817), St. Louis (821,960), Cleveland (900,429), or even Buffalo (573,076) and Milwaukee (578,249).

23. "Larger Offices," *WP*, 1 May 1921, III-1.

24. "B. F. Saul Company," *WP*, 7 December 1924, III-2; "Two Office Buildings," *WP*, 20 December 1925, III-3; "Shannon & Luchs," *WP*, 6 March 1927, R-6.

25. For background on the type, see Liebs, *Main Street*, 75–86; and Robert Bruegmann, *The Architects and the City: Holabird & Roche of Chicago, 1880–1918* (Chicago: University of Chicago Press, 1997), chap. 18. Many of the Connecticut Avenue showrooms were featured in *WP*; see 21 March 1912, I-16; 17 August 1913, I-11; 30 January 1921, III-3; 8 October 1922, VI-12; 5 November 1922, VI-1; 11 May 1924, V-7; 14 September 1924, IV-5; 7 December 1924, V-7; 30 August 1925, V-4; and 8 November 1925, Automobile Sect., 5.

26. "Future Home," *WP*, 30 April 1922, V-1; *WP*, 1 April 1923, V-6; *WP*, 30 December 1923, V-7; *Architectural Forum* 41 (September 1924): 154. A branch of the Riggs Bank was located next door (ADE-UNIT 379). Built at roughly the same time and also designed by Ray, it was clearly conceived as part of the ensemble. See "Riggs Bank Ends," *WP*, 30 September 1923, III-7; "Riggs Bank Grows, *WP*, 30 June 1933, 13, 14; and "Riggs Complete," *ES*, 31 December 1933, II-8.

27. "Service Stations Becoming Problems," *WP*, 10 August 1924, IV-5. See also "Service Stations

Should Be Landmarks," *WP*, 12 June 1921, I-21. The trend toward consolidation of facilities was a reversal of what occurred some ten years earlier when dealers found it desirable to separate salesrooms from service garages; see "Now Using Showrooms," *WP*, 19 June 1910, III-2.

Coverage in *WP* of large facilities erected during the era after World War I was extensive; see "Buick Co. Buys," 18 April 1920, III-4; "Trew Motor Co.," 9 May 1920, IV-7, 11; "Occupies New Building," 30 May 1920, IV-6; 20 March 1921, III-2; 30 July 1922, V-7; 10 September 1922, VI-1; 22 October 1921, III-1; 28 January 1923, V-6; 4 November 1923, V-9; "3-Story Auto Building," 20 January 1924, III-3; 20 September 1925, V-2; 21 March 1926, IV-3; 9 May 1926, A-7; and 16 May 1926, A-6.

28. "Downtown Garage Planned," *WP*, 13 December 1925, III-5; "The Capital Garage, Washington, D.C.," *American Architect* 131 (June 5, 1927): 761–763; Goode, *Capital Losses*, 458–459.

29. For other local examples of the period, see *WP*, 28 May 1922, III-1; "Garage at 1707 L St.," *WP*, 25 March 1923, III-1; *WP*, 30 September 1923, V-11; "Wardman to Erect Garage," *WP*, 20 January 1924, III-1; and *Architectural Record* 69 (April 1931): 309–10. For a sampling of period accounts of the type, see Harold F. Blanchard, "Ramp Construction Which Saves Space," *Motor Age* 37 (March 11, 1920): 18; Blanchard, "Ramp Design in Public Garages," *Architectural Forum* 35 (November 1921): 169–75; Hugh E. Young, "Day and Night Storage and Parking of Motor Vehicles" (Proceedings of the Fifteenth National Conference of City Planning, Baltimore, 1923), 176–218; Tom Wilder, "City Parking: How Much Will They Pay?" *Motor Age* 50 (September 9, 1926): 16–17; C. Stanley Taylor, "Structural Fire Prevention for Large Garages," *Architectural Forum* 46 (April 1927): 341–44; Hawley S. Simpson, "Downtown Storage Garages," *Annals of the American Academy of Political and Social Science* 133 (September 1927): 82–89; "Technical News and Research: Garages," *Architectural Record* 65 (February 1929), 177–96; and Fred W. Moe, "Downtown Parking Garages," *Building Owner and Manager* 10 (September 1930): 5–7.

30. For general background, see Liebs, *Main Street*, 98–102; John A. Jakle and Keith A. Sculle, *The Gas Station in America* (Baltimore: Johns Hopkins University Press, 1994); and Daniel M. Bluestone, "Roadside Blight and the Reform of Commercial Architecture," in *Roadside America: The Automobile in Design and Culture*, ed. Jan Jennings (Ames: Iowa State University Press, 1990), 170–84.

31. A good comparative sense of examples can be gleaned from coverage in *WP*; see, for example, "Open Largest Gas Station," 9 April 1922, IV-1; 29 October 1922, VI-16; 30 December 1923, V-6; 30 March 1924, V-9; "Columbia Oil Company," 22 June 1924, III-2; 20 June 1924, V-6; 6 July 1924, III-5; 5 April 1925, V-6; 1 November 1925, Automobile Sect., 4; 28 November 1925, 7; 23 May 1926, A-7; 26 December 1926, S-13; and 5 March 1927, 10.

32. As realized, the building was not nearly as elaborate, yet still possessed an unusual degree of decorum for the type.

33. These districts are described in a *WP* series on the city's neighborhoods; see "Southwest Washington," 21 August 1910, I-8; "Northeast Washington," 28 August 1910, I-8; "All Eyes Again Turned," 4 September 1910, I-12; "Stores of Northwest," 11 September 1910, I-3; "Ideal Location," 18 September 1910, I-11; "Northeast Washington," 25 September 1910, II-2; "Merchants of Southeast," 2 October 1910, II-2; "Southwest Is Roused," 9 October 1910, III-2; "Northwest Gets Busy," 16 October 1910, III-5; "Seeks Better Suburb," 23 October 1910, II-11; "Pride in Northeast," 30 October 1910, II-11; and "Revival in Business," 20 November 1910, IV-2.

34. For period accounts of the district, see *The Story of Mount Pleasant and Milestones of Its Latter Day Development* (Washington, D.C.: W. F. Roberts Co., 1923), a commemorative booklet for the opening of the Riggs Bank Building at Fourteenth Street and Park Road; and "Columbia Heights Seen," *WP*, 6 April 1924, II-15. Concerning the Arcade Market, see: *ES*, 22 May 1909, II-2; "Fun Here Tomorrow," *WP*, 13 February 1910, I-16; "Three Thousand Visit," *ES*, 11 December 1910, I-19; and *WP*, 21 November 1926, Pictorial Sect., [7].

Concerning the Tivoli Theater, see: "Crandall to Build," *WP*, 21 August 1921, III-1; "Preliminary Work Begun," *WP*, 10 December 1922, III-1; "Tivoli Theater Dedicated," *WP*, 6 April 1924, II-14, 15, 18.; and Douglas Gomery, "A Movie-Going Capital: Washington, D.C., in the History of Movie Presentation," *Washington History* 9 (Spring–Summer 1997): 7, 9.

For comparison with other movie theaters in outlying areas, see: *WP*, 6 July 1919, III-2; "Belmont Theater," *WP*, 12 June 1921, III-3; "Takoma Park Gets," *WP*, 15 October 1922, III-1; "Careful Planning," *WP*, 7 January 1923, III-1; and "Work Will Begin," *WP*, 19 July 1925, III-1.

35. "Riggs-Tompkins," *ES*, 6 January 1923, 13; "Riggs New Branch," *WP*, 7 January 1923, I-26; "Riggs Uptown Bank," *WP*, 7 January 1923, Magazine Sect., 21; "Riggs Bank at Mt. Pleasant," *United States Investor* 34 (27 January 1923): 36–39; "A Plan for Branch Banks," *United States Investor* 40 (25 May 1929): 40–42; "Riggs Bank Grows," *WP*, 30 June 1933, 13; "Riggs Completes," *ES*, 31 December 1933, II-8.

36. For contemporary accounts, see: "One-Story Stores," *ES*, 14 January 1911, II-2; "Row of One-Story Stores," *ES*, 22 July 1911, II-2; and "Interesting Development," *ES*, 9 November 1912, II-3. For recent discussion of the type generally, see Liebs, *Main Street*, 10–15; and Richard Longstreth, *City Center to Regional Mall: Architecture, the Automobile, and Retailing in Los Angeles, 1920–1950* (Cambridge, Mass.: MIT Press, 1997), 63–71.

37. For a sampling of contemporary writing on the subject, see "Small Buildings," *Architectural Forum* 42 (February 1925): 97–120; Kenneth Kingsley Stowell, "Small Buildings: Recent Small Shops," *Architectural Forum* 49 (July 1928): 73–88; "Stores May Make or Mar Your Community, Which Shall It Be?" *Building Developer* 4 (March 1929): 45; and M. S. C. Wood, "Shop Fronts Must Advertise," *Building Age* 52 (January 1930): 39–41, 95.

38. Contemporary accounts include "Store Plans Provide," *ES*, 19 April 1930, B-1, 2; "'Park and Shop'," *ES*, 6 December 1930, B-2; "New Stores Opened," *WP*, 7 December 1930, III-2, 3; "Washington Gets New 'Park and Shop' Market," *Chain Store Age*, Grocery Products Sect., 7 (July 1931): 4–5, 32; "Drafting and Design Problems: Neighborhood Shopping Centers," *Architectural Record* 71 (May 1932): 325; Clarence S. Stein and Catherine Bauer, "Store Buildings and Neighborhood Shopping Centers," *Architectural Record* 75 (February 1934): 178; "Terminal Facilities—Motor Transport's Greatest Need," *American City* 49 (February 1934), 70; "Park and Shop," *American City* 52 (October 1937): 71–72; F. Wallace Stoever, "Park-and-Shop Projects for Neighborhood Improvement," *Real Estate Record* 141 (5 February 1938): 30–31; Wilbur H. Simonson, "The Roadside Picture: A Hinderance to Traffic, or an Inspiring Asset to Travel?" *Landscape Architecture* 30 (October 1939): 34. See also n. 39.

39. For further discussion, see Richard Longstreth, "The Neighborhood Shopping Center in Washington, D.C., 1930–1941," *Journal of the Society of Architectural Historians* 51 (March 1992): 5–34; and Longstreth, *The Drive-In, the Supermarket, and the Transformation of Commercial Space in Los Angeles, 1914–1941* (Cambridge, Mass.: MIT Press, 1999), 148–161.

40. *WP*, 23 November 1947, 7R; *WP*, 21 March 1948, 8R; "New Jeleff Store Opens," *Women's Wear Daily*, 29 November 1948, 4; "Simon's Opens Unit," *Women's Wear Daily*, 15 September 1948, 10.

41. *ES*, 20 November 1941, A-10; *Women's Wear Daily*, 26 November 1941, 32; Katherine Smith, "New Garfinckel Store," Washington *Times-Herald*, 14 August 1942, 12; "New Garfinckel's Store," *ES*, 14 August 1942, A-2; "Garfinckel's New Shop," *Women's Wear Daily*, 14 August 1942, 32; "Garfinckel's Gives Preview," *WP*, 14 August 1942; Margaret Nowell, "Opening of Garfinckel," *ES*, 15 August 1942, B-2; Virginia Stephens, "Beautiful Garfinckel Store," *Times-Herald*, 16 August 1942, C-1; "Garfinckel Opens," *Women's Wear Daily*, 11 June 1947, 2.

42. Retail figures are taken from the Census of Business. For tabulations, I have used the Washington Standard Metropolitan Statistical Area (SMSA), which includes Montgomery and Prince George's counties in Maryland and Arlington and Fairfax counties, in addition to the cities of Alexandria and Falls Church in Virginia. For discussion, see Rufus S. Lusk, "Washington Escapes," *ES*, 21 June 1941, B-1, 7; "Washington Trends: 1947," *Washington Board of Trade News* 1 (May 1947), supplement, n.p.; "Population Growth Supports Committee Predictions," *Washington Board of Trade News* 3 (November 1949), 8–9; "Shopping Spreads Out: 'Downtown' Is Worried," *U.S. News & World Report*, 7 November 1952, 58, 60, 62–63; "Sales Study, Major Business Project Completed," *Washington Board of Trade News* 7 (November 1952): 5–6; "What's Happening to 'Downtown'?" *Washington Board of Trade News* 7 (December 1952): 5; and "Eight Years of Growth and Change in Greater Washington," *Washington Board of Trade News* 13 (October 1958): 6–7.

43. Concerning Silver Spring, see Richard Longstreth, "Silver Spring: Georgia Avenue, Colesville Road, and the Creation of an Alternative 'Downtown' for Metropolitan Washington," in *Streets: Critical Perspectives on Public Space*, ed. Zeynep Ce-

lik, Diane Favro, Richard Ingersoll (Berkeley: University of California Press, 1994), 247–258; and Longstreth, "The Mixed Blessings of Success: The Hecht Company and Department Store Branch Development after World War II," in *Shaping Communities: Perspectives in Vernacular Architecture*, ed. Carter L. Hudgins and Elizabeth Collins Cromley (Knoxville: University of Tennessee Press, 1997), 6:244–62. Concerning Clarendon, see "Historic Resources in the Clarendon Commercial District," Report of the Historic Affairs and Landmark Review Board to the Arlington County Board, May 1985.

44. *Arlington Daily*, 10 November 1945, 2; *WP*, 27 January 1946, 6R.

45. For general discussion, see Conrad P. Harness, "Builders Get a Whiff," *WP*, 10 November 1946, 1R, 5R; Robert J. Lewis, "D.C. Park-and-Shop," *ES*, 20 September 1947, B-1, B-2; and Robert P. Jordan, "A Growing Greater Washington," *WP*, 24 June 1951, 1R.

46. Both the size of the car lot and its relationship to the stores it served were among the most widely discussed matters in shopping center development of the postwar years. See, for example, Seward H. Mott and Max S. Wehrly, "Shopping Centers: An Analysis," *Urban Land Institute Technical Bulletin* 11 (July 1949): 42; Geoffrey Baker and Bruno Funaro, *Shopping Centers: Design and Operation* (New York: Reinhold, 1951), 31–44; J. Ross McKeever, "Shopping Centers: Planning Principles and Tested Policies," *Urban Land Institute Technical Bulletin*, no. 20 (July 1953): 15–23; and J. Ross McKeever, "Shopping Centers Re-Studied: Emerging Patterns and Practical Experiences," *Urban Land Institute Technical Bulletin*, no. 30, pt. 2 (May 1957): 12–13.

47. Distinctions in size, in scope of services, and in target audience of shopping centers were not formalized until the postwar era, when such variations became commonplace. The precise attributes accorded to each vary somewhat with the account. See, for example, Baker and Funaro, *Shopping Centers*, 10; Gordon H. Stedman, "The Rise of Shopping Centers," *Journal of Retailing* 31 (Spring 1955): 14–15; Jack Hyman, "Shopping Center Here to Stay," *Women's Wear Daily*, 27 December 1955, II-6; and Paul E. Smith, *Shopping Centers: Planning and Management* (New York: National Retail Merchants Association, 1956), 12. For discussion of

trends in the development of major postwar centers, see Longstreth, *City Center to Regional Mall*, chaps. 11 and 12.

48. Integrated shopping centers larger than the neighborhood size (i.e., in general greater than twenty stores) were relatively few before World War II, and all were much more traditional in layout than their successors of the late 1940s and 1950s. For background, see Richard Longstreth, "J. C. Nichols, the Country Club Plaza, and Notions of Modernity," *Harvard Architecture Review* 5 (1986): 120–35; and Longstreth, "The Diffusion of the Community Shopping Center Concept during the Interwar Decades," *Journal of the Society of Architectural Historians* 56 (September 1997), 268–93.

49. All three of the complexes realized were located in Arlington County. The first was Shirlington, begun in 1943; see "Large-Scale Shopping Center Develops," *American City* 61 (December 1946): 69; and Baker and Funaro, *Shopping Centers*, 180–183. The Kann's Virginia and Virginia Square complex near Clarendon center was in fact two projects undertaken as a coordinated development; see McKeever, "Shopping Centers," 51–55. The most ambitious undertaking was Parkington; see Longstreth, "Mixed Blessings," 252–57. For examples not realized, see Conrad P. Harness, "University Lane Area," *WP*, 4 December 1949, 1R; *WP*, 18 December 1949, 6R; and Robert P. Jordan, "Shopping Center," *WP*, 22 April 1951, 1R.

50. "Shop Center Set," *WP*, 10 August 1947, 6R.

Chapter *Five. Twentieth-Century Housing*

1. On this distinction, see Gwendolyn Wright, *Building the Dream: A Social History of Housing in America* (Cambridge, Mass.: MIT Press, 1983); "Housing Tactics," special issue, *Praxis: A Journal of Writing + Building*, no. 3 (Winter 2002); "The Question of Home," special issue, *New Formations: A Journal of Culture/Theory/Politics*, no. 17 (Summer 1992); and "Home, House, Housing," special issue, *Design Book Review* 37/38 (Winter 1996/1997).

2. See Richard Pommer, "The Architecture of Urban Housing in the United States during the Early 1930s," *Journal of the Society of Architectural Historians* 37 (1978): 235–64; and Eric Mumford, "The 'Tower in a Park' in America: Theory and Practice,

1920–1960," *Planning Perspectives* 10 (1995): 17–41.

3. See, for example, Kenneth Frampton with Alessandra Latour, "Notes on American Architectural Education from the End of the Nineteenth Century until the 1970s," *Lotus* 27 (1980): 5–39; Richard Oliver, ed., *The Making of an Architect: Columbia University in the City of New York* (New York: Columbia University Press, 1981); Margaret Henderson Lloyd, ed., *Architectural Education and Boston* (Boston: Boston Architectural Center, 1989); and Gwendolyn Wright and Janet Parks, eds., *The History of History in American Schools of Architecture, 1865–1975* (New York: Princeton Architectural Press, 1990).

4. *Two on Two at the Octagon: Design for the Urban Environment* (Washington, D.C.: American Institute of Architects, 1979).

5. "Housing War Workers in Washington," *American Architect* 114 (December 4, 1918): 661–668; and Edith Elmer Wood, *Recent Trends in American Housing* (New York: Macmillan, 1931).

6. For overviews of European modern housing that provided these models, see Catherine Bauer, *Modern Housing* (Boston: Houghton-Mifflin, 1934); Peter G. Rowe, *Modernity and Housing* (Cambridge, Mass.: MIT Press, 1994); and Roger Sherwood, *Modern Housing Prototypes* (Cambridge, Mass.: MIT Press, 1978).

7. Federal Writers' Project, *Washington, City and Capital* (1942), reissued as *The WPA Guide to Washington, D.C.* (New York: Pantheon, 1983); and John Ihlder, "Public Housing in Washington," *Shelter* 3 (February 1939): 8–11.

8. James Borchert, *Alley Life in Washington: Family, Community, Religion and Folklife in the City, 1950–1970* (Urbana: University of Illinois Press, 1980).

9. See U.S. Housing Authority, *Public Housing Design* (Washington, D.C.: U.S. Government Printing Office, 1946); Catherine Bauer, *War Housing in the United States* (Washington, D.C.: National Housing Agency for the U.N. Conference on International Organization, 1945); Elizabeth Mock, *Built in USA Since 1932* (New York: Museum of Modern Art, 1945); and Donald Albrecht, ed., *World War II and the American Dream: How Wartime Building Changed a Nation* (Washington, D.C., and Cambridge, Mass.: National Building Museum and MIT Press, 1995).

10. For an overview, see Kathryn Schneider Smith, ed., *Washington at Home: An Illustrated History of Neighborhoods in the Nation's Capital* (Northridge, Calif.: Windsor, 1988).

11. See Anne Vernez Moudon, ed., *Master Planned Communities: Shaping the Exurbs in the 1990s* (Seattle: University of Washington Press, 1990); and William Whyte, *Cluster Development* (New York: McGraw-Hill, 1964).

12. On suburban expansion in general, see Peter G. Rowe, *Making a Middle Landscape* (Cambridge, Mass.: MIT Press, 1991); Wright, *Building the Dream*; and Dolores Hayden, *Building Suburbia: Green Fields and Urban Growth, 1820–2000* (New York: Pantheon, 2003).

Chapter Six. The Vietnam Veterans Memorial

1. Robert W. Doubek, "The Story of the Vietnam Veterans Memorial," *Retired Officer*, November 1983, 17–24; and Jan C. Scruggs and Joel L. Swerdlow, *To Heal a Nation* (New York: Harper & Row, 1985).

2. Copies of this registration booklet and all other original documents produced by the Vietnam Veterans Memorial Foundation quoted in this essay are among the foundation's papers in the Manuscript Division of the Library of Congress.

3. Allen Freeman, "An Extra Competition," *American Institute of Architects Journal* 70 (1981): 47–53; and Elizabeth Hess, "A Tale of Two Memorials," *Art in America*, 1983, 121–27.

4. Glenna Goodacre, *Glenna Goodacre: The First 25 Years: A Retrospective Exhibition of Sculpture*, ed. Gary Edson (Lubbock: Museum of Texas Tech University, 1995).

5. William Hubbard, "A Meaning for Monuments," *Public Interest* 74 (1984): 17–30; Nicholas J. Capasso, "Vietnam Veterans Memorial," in *The Critical Edge*, ed. Tod A. Marder (Cambridge: MIT Press, 1985), 189–202; Charles L. Griswold, "The Vietnam Veterans Memorial and the Washington Mall: Philosophical Thoughts on Political Iconography," *Critical Inquiry* 12 (1986): 689–719; Mary McLeod, "The Battle for the Monument: The Vietnam Veterans Memorial," in *The Experimental Tradition*, ed. Hélène Lipstadt (Princeton, N.J.: Architectural League of New York and Princeton Architectural Press, 1989), 115–137; and Jeffrey Karl Ochsner, "A Space of Loss: The Vietnam Veterans Memorial," *Journal of Architectural Education* 50, no. 3 (February 1997): 156–71.

ESSAY ON SOURCES

Hélène Lipstadt was instrumental in the preparation of the following list. For those who wish to pursue the particular topics that are the subjects of the essays that make up this book, the notes will in most cases serve as a guide for further reading. The most extensive, comprehensive and up-to-date bibliography for the historical development of Washington is *A Historical Bibliography of the Built Environment in the Washington, D.C., Metropolitan Area*, compiled by Richard Longstreth, May 2001, and available online at www.loc.gov/rr/print/adecenter/.

The Federal Presence: Architecture, Politics, and Symbols in United States Government Buildings (Cambridge, Mass.: MIT Press, 1978), produced by Lois Craig and the staff of the Federal Architecture Project, remains the only comprehensive historical overview of the building activities of the federal government. It has been supplemented usefully by the ongoing and well-indexed *Records of the Columbia Historical Society*, now *Washington History*; by Bates Lowry's *The Architecture of Washington, D.C.* (2 vols., microfiche; Washington, D.C.: The Dunlap Society, 1976–1979) and his *Building a National Image: Architectural Drawings for the American Democracy, 1789–1912* (Washington, D.C.: National Building Museum, 1985); James M. Goode's *Capital Losses, A Cultural History of Washington's Destroyed Buildings* (Washington, D.C.: Smithsonian Institution Press, 1979) and *The Outdoor Sculpture of Washington, D.C.: A Comprehensive Historical Guide* (Washington, D.C.: Smithsonian Institution Press, 1974); the republication of C. W. Short's 1940 *Survey of the Architecture of Completed Projects of the Public Works Administration* (Microfiche Edition; Alexandria, Va.: Chadwick-Healey, 1986); Sue Kohler's *The Commission of Fine Arts, a Brief History, 1910–1976; with Additions, 1977–1984* (Washington: The Commission of Fine Arts, 1984); *The Mall in Washington, 1791–1991* (Studies in the History of Art, vol. 30; Washington, D.C.: National Gallery of Art, 1991), edited by Richard Longstreth; Pamela Scott and Antoinette Lee's superb *The Buildings of Washington, D.C.* (in the series The Buildings of the United States) (New York: Oxford University Press, 1993), which, in many cases, provides insightful and the first dependable information for many of Washington's buildings; Antoinette Lee's *Supervising Architect's Office, Architects to the Nation: The Rise and Decline of the Supervising Architect's*

Office, Federal Buildings in Context: The Role of Design Review, edited by J. Carter Brown (vol. 50 of Studies in the History of Art) (Washington, D.C.: National Gallery of Art, 1995); Jane Loeffler's *The Architecture of Diplomacy: Building America's Embassies* (New York: Princeton Architectural Press, 1998); Antoinette Lee's *Architects to the Nation: The Rise and Decline of the Supervising Architect's Office* (New York: Oxford University Press, 2000); and, most recently, Willliam Allen's excellent *History of the United States Capitol: A Chronicle of Design, Construction, and Politics* (Washington, D.C.: U.S. Government Printing Office, 2001).

Useful studies predating the *Federal Presence* include Glenn Brown's *History of the United States Capitol*, 2 vols. (Washington, D.C.: U.S. Government Printing Office, 1900–1903); Charles Moore's *Washington, Past and Present* (New York: The Century Co., 1929); H. P. Caemmerer's *Washington, the National Capital* (Washington, D.C.: U.S. Government Printing Office, 1932) and his *A Manual on the Origins and Development of Washington* (Washington, D.C.: U.S. Government Printing Office, 1939); C. W. Short and R. Stanley-Brown's *Public Buildings: A Survey of Architecture of Projects Constructed by Federal and Other Governmental Bodies Between the Years 1933 and 1939* (Washington, D.C.: U.S. Government Printing Office, 1939); Frederick Gutheim's *The Potomac*, rev. ed. (1949; repr., Baltimore: Johns Hopkins University Press, 1986), his *Worthy of the Nation: The History of Planning for the National Capital* (Washington, D.C.: National Capital Planning Commission, 1977), and, with Wilcomb E. Washburn, his *The Federal City: Plans and Realities* (Washington, D.C.: Smithsonian Institution Press with the National Capital Planning Commission, 1976); Constance McLaughlin Green's *Washington, A History of the Capital, 1800–1850* (Princeton, N.J.: Princeton University Press, 1962); John W. Reps's *Monumental Washington: The Planning and Development of the Capital Center* (Princeton, NJ: Princeton University Press, 1967); Daniel D. Reiff's *Washington Architecture 1791–1861: Problems in Development* (Washington, D.C.: U. S. Commission of Fine Arts, 1971); Diane Maddex's *Historic Buildings of Washington, D.C.: A Selection from the Records of the Historic American Buildings Survey* (Pittsburgh: Ober Park Associates, 1973); *A Bibliographic Tour of Washington, D.C.* (Washington, D.C.: Redevelopment Land Agency, 1974), com-

piled by Anne Llewellyn Meglis; *Historic American Buildings Survey, District of Columbia Catalog* (Charlottesville: University Press of Virginia for the Columbia Historical Society, 1976), compiled by Nancy B. Schwartz; and *An Illustrated History, the City of Washington, by the Junior League of Washington* (New York: Alfred A. Knopf, 1977), edited by Thomas Froncek.

Readers are further directed to sources that accompany the more than five hundred new biographical entries and essays written as a part of this project by Pamela Scott, Diane Tepfer, Leslie Freudenheim, and myself, available online through the Prints and Photographs Division (P&P) of the Library of Congress as part of the P&P Site Index at www.loc.gov/rr/print. Among the distinguished contributors and their major subjects are Pamela Scott on "Stephen (Étienne Sulpice) Hallet (1755–1825)," James O'Gorman on "Charles Bulfinch," C. M. Harris on "William Thornton," Jeffrey Cohen on "Benjamin Henry Latrobe," Donald Jackson on "Montgomery Cunningham Meigs," William Allen on "Thomas Ustick Walter," Barbara Wolanin on "Constantino Brumidi," Denys Peter Myer on "Joseph Goldsborough Bruff," Tony Wrenn on "Thomas Tileston Waterman," Antoinette J. Lee on the "Office of the Supervising Architect," and Thomas Somma on "Paul Bartlett."

For information and findings concerning the process of conserving, housing, and cataloging the drawings and related documents in this project, consult Michele E. Hamill's "Washingtoniana II: Conservation of Architectural Drawings at the Library of Congress" in *The Book and Paper Group Annual* (The American Institute for Conservation of Historic and Artistic Works 12 [1993]: 24–31); Karen Chittenden's "Washingtoniana II: Cataloging Architectural, Design, and Engineering Collections in the Prints and Photographs Division of the Library of Congress," *ArtMARC Sourcebook: Cataloging Art, Architecture and Their Visual Images* (Chicago: American Library Association, 1998), 144–53; and Anne Mitchell and Karen Chittenden's "Washingtoniana II Data Dictionary," *ArtMARC Sourcebook: Cataloging Art, Architecture and Their Visual Images* (Chicago: American Library Association, 1998), 223–63. The first two articles also are available on request from the Prints and Photographs Division, Library of Congress, Washington DC 20540-4730.

LIST OF CONTRIBUTORS

RICHARD LONGSTRETH is a professor of American studies and director of the Graduate Program in Historic Preservation at George Washington University. A past president of the Society of Architectural Historians, he has written extensively on nineteenth- and twentieth-century American architecture, landscape, and urbanism. His many publications include *On the Edge of the World: Four Architects in San Francisco at the Turn of the Century* (1983); *The Buildings of Main Street: A Guide to American Commercial Architecture* (1987); *The Mall in Washington, 1791–1991* (1991 and 2002), editor; *City Center to Regional Mall: Architecture, the Automobile, and Retailing in Los Angeles, 1920–1950* (1997); *The Drive-in, the Supermarket, and the Transformation of Commercial Space in Los Angeles, 1914–1941* (1999); and *The Charnley House: Louis Sullivan, Frank Lloyd Wright, and the Making of Chicago's Gold Coast* (2004), editor.

C. FORD PEATROSS is curator of the Architecture, Design, and Engineering Collections in the Prints and Photographs Division of the Library of Congress and has been instrumental in the expansion and dissemination of the Library's collections and in establishing the new Center for Architecture, Design, and Engineering. He helped to conceive the Norton/Library of Congress Visual Sourcebooks in Architecture, Design, and Engineering series and the library's exhibitions on the U.S. Capitol, the work of Charles and Ray Eames, and Frank Lloyd Wright. He has lectured widely on the library's rich collections, is an adjunct professor at Union College, and has been a consultant for the Vitra Design Museum and Universal Studios. His articles and publications include *William Nichols, Architect* (1979) and *Historic America: Buildings, Structures, Sites* (1983).

PAMELA SCOTT is an architectural historian and visiting lecturer for Cornell University in Washington, D.C. Her many books and articles include *The Buildings of the District of Columbia*, with Antoinette J. Lee, and *Temple of Liberty: Building the Capitol for a New Nation*. In addition to frequent lectures, she has curated several architectural exhibitions in the Washington, D.C., area, including the National Building Museum and the Library of Congress.

WILLIAM SEALE, a historian and restorationist based in Washington, D.C., works closely with the White House Historical Association. His expertise has guided restoration projects across the country, including many famous historic houses, several state capitols, governors' mansions, and government buildings. His numerous articles and publications include *The Tasteful Interlude: American Interiors Through the Camera's Eye, 1860–1917* (1975, 1981, 1995); *Temples of Democracy: The State Capitols of the U.S.A.*, with Henry-Russell Hitchcock (1976); *Recreating the Historic House Interior* (1979); *The President's House: A History* (1986); *Virginia's Executive Mansion* (1988); *The White House: History of An American Idea* (1992); *Of Houses and Time: Personal Histories of America's National Trust Properties* (1992); *A Guide to Historic Alexandria* (2000); and *The White House: Actors and Observers* (2002), editor.

DAMIE STILLMAN is professor emeritus of American architecture at the University of Delaware, former editor-in-chief of the Buildings of the United States, and a past president of the Society of Architectural Historians. He has specialized in American architectural history, with special emphasis on the Federal period and neoclassicism here and abroad. His many books and articles include *The Decorative Work of Robert Adam* (1966) and *English Neo-Classical Architecture* (1988).

GWENDOLYN WRIGHT, a professor of architecture and history at Columbia University, is the author of several books and articles on the history of American domestic architecture and was formerly the director of Columbia's Buell Center for the Study of American Architecture. Her many books and articles include *The Politics of Design in French Colonial Urbanism* (1991); *Building the Dream: A Social History of Housing in America* (1981); and *Moralism and the Model Home: Domestic Architecture and Cultural Conflict in Chicago, 1873–1913* (1980).

INDEX

*Page numbers in **bold type** indicate illustrations.*

A&P supermarkets, 43
A.B. Mullett & Co.
  business building, 110, 120, **121**,
    135, 135
  city houses, **152**, 153
Air Force One, design by Loewy
  (1962), 108
Alcoa Research Houses (1950s), 44
Alfred Noble Memorial Fountain,
  29, **188**
Allegro, Jim, 57
Allen, Gerald, 55, 56
Alley Dwelling Authority, 162, 165
Allied Architects (Washington,
  D.C.)
  history of, 37, 233–34n39
  Longworth House Office
    Building, 37
  National Stadium Project, **36**, 37
All States Hotel for Women, 162,
  163
Aluminum City Terrace (New
  Kensington, Pa.), 168, **170**
American Architectural Founda-
  tion, 62, 63, 81, 232n14
American Battle Monuments
  Commission, 34
American Institute of Architects,
  176, 179, 232n14
American Oil Co., service station,
  41, 130, **211**
Anderson, J. Walter, inventor of
  hamburger-on-a-bun, 41
Annandale Business Center, **145**,
  145
Ant Farm (avant-garde architects),
  58
Appliances by Sheff (Clarendon,
  Va.), 141
Arcade Market, 134
Architect of New Buildings (Trea-
  sury and Patent Office), 74
Architect of the Capitol
  collections, 69, 70, 74
  U.S. Capitol extension projects,
    84, 86
  Walter drawings, 81

Architect of the U.S. Capitol
  Extension, 78
architects and architectural firms,
  listing of, 222–30
architectural symbolics, 232n16
Arlington Towers Apartments,
  162, **163**
Arnold, Henry A., Vietnam
  Veterans Memorial design
  competition, **218**
Arzola, Robert R., 107
Athenaeum of Philadelphia, 81
Atlantic Building, 116, 239n8
Avery Coonley House (Riverside,
  Ill.), 30

Ballu and Deperthes, 22
Baltimore Sun Building, 116, **117**,
  239n8
Bartlett, Paul, fountain sculpture
  by, 29, **188**
Belair plantation (Prince Georges
  County, Md.), 12
Belluschi, Pietro, 176
Benedict, Jules Jacques Benois,
  29, 30
Berghof (Adolf Hitler's mountain
  retreat), destroyed, 30
Bergstrom, G. E., 37
Berla & Abel, 195
B. F. Saul Co., 112, 125, **126**, 127
Bingham, Theodore, 89, 102, 238n2
Blagden, George, 98
Blodgett, Samuel, 66, 236n10
Blue Bell System restaurants, 41,
  190, **191**, **211**
Blue Moon (cafe), design by Ray,
  41, **192**
Blue Ribbon Laundry (Arlington,
  Va.), 146, **148**
Bond Building, 116
Boston, Peace Jubilee Naval Tower
  proposal, **32**, 33
Boullé, Étienne-Louis, architec-
  tural designs (1780s), 14,
  232n16
Breuer, Marcel, 168, **170**
Brousseau, Frances, x
Brown, Glenn, memorial fountain
  design proposal, 29, **188**

Brown, Joseph E., 177
Bruff, J. Goldsborough
  California Gold Rush drawings
    by, 18
  Grand National Monumental
    Sphinx, 17–18, **18**
Brumidi, Constantino
  Apotheosis of Washington,
    Capitol dome painting by, 78
  decorative frieze, **205**
Brunelleschi, Filippo, Foundling
  Hospital (Florence), 21
Buehner, Timothy, 89
Bulfinch, Charles
  as Architect of the Capitol,
    60, 73
  President's House, north
    portico, 98, **100**, **101**
  U.S. Capitol: ceiling plans,
    76, **77**; dome study, **76**, **203**,
    231n7; east front, with grand
    staircase, 70, 73, **204**, **205**;
    floor plan, 76, **77**; House
    Chamber, 73; site and land-
    scaping plan, **73**, 73; south
    wing vestibule, 74, **75**; west
    front, Library of Congress,
    73; west front proposal, 86
Burnham, D. H., 84
Butterfield, William, 21

Cadillac Ranch icon (*near* Amar-
  illo, Tex.), 58
Cafritz, Morris and Gwendolyn
  Foundation, iv, vii, x
Cafritz Building, 239n3
California Gold Rush, drawings
  by Bruff, 18
Campbell, Colin, English country
  house at Wanstead, 63
Capital Garage Building, 129–30,
  130
Capitol Building. *See* U.S. Capitol
Carlhian, Jean Paul, 176
Carrère & Hastings (New York),
  30, 83
Carstairs, Thomas, U.S. Capitol,
  conference meeting with
  Jefferson, 66
Carter, Jimmy, 174

Casey, Thomas Lincoln, 14
Cattaui, Georges, 232n16
charette, origin of the term, 55
Charles and Ray Eames (firm),
  53, 196
Charles H. Tompkins Construc-
  tion Co., 134
Chatelain, Leon III, 37
Chevy Chase Savings Bank,
  136, 136
Circle Theatre, 43, **194**
Citizen Kane (film), 30
City Beautiful Movement, 135
City Hall, design proposal
  (Hadfield, 1820), **6**, **7**, 14
Clarendon, commercial develop-
  ment, 141
Clark, Edward, as Architect of the
  Capitol, 81, 83
Clay, Grady, 176
Cleveland Park, shopping center
  development, 139
Clifton (*near* Richmond, Va.), 11
Cobb, Henry Ives, 26
Cohen, Jeffrey, x
College des Quatres Nations
  (Paris), 62
Colorado Building, 116
Columbia University, *Alma Mater*
  sculpture, 34
Columbia University, Avery Archi-
  tectural Archives, 93
commercial architecture, 109–50,
  238–39n1
  automobile dealerships, **128**,
    128–29
  department stores, 119–20,
    240n15
  garages, 129–30, **130**, 210,
    241n29
  motel designs, 113, **114**, **115**
  postwar development, 140–50
  retail/stores development,
    133–40
  service stations, 41, 46, 47, 130,
    131, **132**, **133**, 133, 240–41n27
  tall office buildings, 110, 116, **117**
  "commercial vernacular" buildings,
    41, 234n47
Commission of Fine Arts, 34, 179

Como Orchards Summer Colony (Darby, Mont.), 30
Connecticut Avenue
  automobile dealerships, 128–29
  commercial development, 122–23, **124**, **125**, 125
Constitution Gardens, Vietnam Veterans Memorial site, 175
Corcoran Gallery of Art, 74
Corning and Moore. *See* E. Burton Corning and Raymond G. Moore (firm)
Cram, Ralph Adams, 21
Crawford, Thomas, statue of *Freedom* by, 78, **79**
Crow, Jules T., Executive Mansion at Meridian Hill proposal (1898), **25**, 25
Crystal Heights development proposal, 30, **42**, 43–44, 234n49
Custis, John Parke, 12
Custis, Martha Parke, 12
Custis-Lee Mansion (Va.), 22

Davis, Alexander Jackson
  U.S. Capitol: ceiling and floor plans, drawings by, 74, 76, **77**; east front, watercolor by, 74, **204**, 205
Day the Earth Stood Still, The (film), 44
Design for a National Gallery of History and Art (Smith), 26
Designs of Buildings Erected or Proposed to be Built in Virginia … from 1795 to 1799 (Latrobe), **10**, 11
DeWitt, Poor, and Shelton, 84, 86
District of Columbia. *See* Washington, D.C.
Dobie, Samuel, U.S. Capitol design, 62
Dolphin Embassy, 58
domestic buildings. *See* housing
Doubek, Robert W., 177, 179
Douden, William, Hotel Dewey, 58

Downing, Andrew Jackson
  public grounds design for Washington (1851), 14, **16**, 17
  triumphal arch for President's Park, 14, **16**, 17, 108
Drayer, Donald Hudson, 153
  business buildings, **141**
  housing: Admiral Apartments, **214**; Arlington Towers Apartments, **162**, 162; "Bonnie Brae Estates," **213**; "cluster housing," 168; private residence (Potomac, Md.), 156, **157**; Promenade Apartment House (Bethesda, Md.), **213**; town house development, 156, **157**; war housing, 168, **169**
  "Lady Bird Special Train," 108
  Lyndon Baines Johnson's closet, 108
  motel/hotel designs, 113, **114**, **115**
  office buildings, **147**, 147–50, **148**, **149**, **150**
  shopping centers, 110, 140–47, **143**, **144**, **146**
Dulles International Airport, 53

Eames, Charles, friendship with Saarinen, 53
East Capitol Street, development, 37
E. Burton Corning and Raymond G. Moore (firm), 140, 142
Eckbo, Garrett, 176
Eckhardt, Wolf von, 177
edge city, defined, 234n40
Edge City: Life on the New Frontier (Garreau), 37
Eero Saarinen and Associates, 53
Eggers, Otto R., 48
Eggers & Higgins (firm), National Hall proposal, 47–48, **49**
Egyptian Revival, 8, 17–18
Ellicott, Andrew, plan of Washington (1792), 4
Ellipse (formerly President's Park), 8, **25**, 25, 107

Embassy Building, 122, 208, **209**
Esty, Alexander R., Library of Congress design proposal, **20**, 21, 83
Evening Star Building, 116, 239n9

Farragut, David, 17
Farragut Square, Monument of Farragut, by Hoxie, 17
FDR Memorial Gateway, proposal, 55
Federal District, Congressional approval for, vii
  See also Washington, D.C.
Fenderich, Charles, 14
Fillmore, Millard, 78
Fleck, Glen, national aquarium project, drawings by, 53
Force, Peter, Washington Monument design proposal (1837), 13, 14, **15**
Foundling Hospital (Florence, 1419), 21
Fountain of the Engineers, proposal, 29
Franklin, William B., and U.S. Capitol extension project, 81
Franzen, Ulrich, 55
Freedom, bronze statue of (by Thomas Crawford), 78, **79**
French, Daniel Chester, *Alma Mater*, sculpture by, 34
Frost and Granger (Chicago), 30

garages, 129–30, **130**, 210, 241n29
garden folly, temple-form retreat design, **10**, 11
Garfinckel's (department store), 120
Garreau, Joel, on "Edge City," 37, 234n40
Geddes, Norman Bel, General Motors Democracity at New York World's Fair (1939–40), 50
Geography and Map Division
  Jefferson sketch of White House grounds, 89
  Urban Design Charrettes Collection, 55–57

Georgetown University, Healy Hall, 22
Gilbert, Cass
  U.S. Customs House (New York), 34
  U.S. Supreme Court, 34, **36**, 37, 55
  Woolworth Building (New York), 34
Glover, Charles, shopping center commissioned by, 139, **212**
Goldenberg's (department store), 119
Goodacre, Glenna, Vietnam Memorial sculpture by, 179
Goode, James M., x
Goodhue, Bertram, 26
Goodman, Charles M.
  Hollin Hills development, 44, **46**, 47, 234n50
  Lee family residence (Arlington, Va.), **46**, 47
  modular housing (1939), 44, **45**
  new town developments (*such as* Reston, Va.), 44
  New York World's Fair, U.S. Government Building (1939), 44
  service stations, **46**, 47
  Washington National Airport, 44
Goodman, Dorothy S., 44
Gothic Revival, 21–22
Governor's Palace (Williamsburg, Va.), 133
Graham, Charles, Washington, D.C., bird's-eye perspective, **28**, 29
Grand National Monument Sphinx, Bruff proposal, 17–18, **18**
Grant, Ulysses S., 18
  memorial bridge design, 22, **23**
Greek Revival, 11
Greenbelt (Md.) Project, 166, 168, **215**
Gridley J. F. Bryant (firm), 21
Gropius, Walter, 168, **170**
Guggenheim Museum (New York), 33

Hadfield, George
    City Hall design proposal
        (1820), 6, 7
    U.S. Capitol, as the architect,
        66
Halle au Blé (Paris), 69
Hallet, Stephen
    U.S. Capitol designs, 4, 60–62,
        61, 65, 65–66, 182, 183, 198,
        199, 200, 201; fired as assis-
        tant superintendent, 66;
        modifying Thornton's
        designs, 65–66; Rotunda and
        dome cupola stairway
        proposal (1793), 4, 6, 7
Hall of the Ancients (New York
    Avenue), 26
Harbaugh, Leonard, 236n10
Harbeson, Hough, Livingston &
    Larson, U.S. Capitol, west
    front alterations proposal
    (1963), 48, 49, 86
Harper, J. H., Boston Peace
    Jubilee Naval Tower
    proposal, 32, 33
Harris, Charles M., x, 62, 63, 98
Harrison, Mrs. Benjamin (Caro-
    line), 22, 102, 107
Harrison, Wallace K., 50
Hart, Frederick E., sculpture by,
    174, 179, 180
Harvie House (Richmond, Va.), 11,
    231n10
Hearst, William Randolph, 30
Heaton, Arthur B., 110, 153
    automobile dealerships, 129
    automobile/"drive-in" architec-
        ture, 37–38, 41
    automobile license plate compe-
        tition, 37
    bank buildings, 118, 119, 119, 136,
        136
    Blue Bell System restaurants,
        41, 190, 191, 211
    commercial/business buildings,
        120, 122–23, 127, 137, 208,
        209
    "commercial vernacular" build-
        ings, with new materials, 41,
        234n47

housing developments, 165, 166,
    167, 172, 172; alley house
    development, 164, 165; Union
    Built; Homes—Greenbelt
    Project, 166, 168, 215; Wren-
    wood subdivision, 165, 166,
    167, 215
    Lyon Village Development
        proposal, 37–38, 39
    mixed-use development, 136, 162
    motel designs, 113, 114, 115
    parking garage, 210
    service stations, 41, 47, 130, 132,
        133, 211
    shopping centers, 138, 139, 212
Heaton & Chatelain, 168, 169
Hecht's (department store), 119,
    239n3
Henderson, Mrs. John Brooks
    (Mary), Executive Mansion
    design commissioned by,
    22, 25, 25, 103, 233n28
Henderson's Castle (Meridian
    Hill), destroyed (1949), 25,
    233n28
Hewitt, Jean, 26
Hickel, Walter J., national
    aquarium supporter, 53
Hilltop Market, porcelain enamel
    storefront, 212
Historic American Buildings
    Survey, 89, 108, 168
Hoban, James
    President's House, design
        competition winner, 65, 89
    U.S. Capitol: architect/superin-
        tendent of, 66; conference
        meeting with Jefferson, 66
Hoffman, Josef, 41
Hollin Hills development
    (Fairfax County, Va.), 44, 46,
    47, 234n50
Homer Building, 240n17
Hoppin, F. L. V., Washington,
    D.C., bird's-eye perspective,
    28, 29
Hôtel de Ville (Paris, 1874–92),
    designed by Ballu and
    Deperthes, 22
Hotel Washington, 4

House of Representatives
    Chamber. See U.S. Capitol,
    House Chamber
housing, 151–72
    Alcoa Research Houses (1950s),
        44
    alley house development, 162,
        164, 165
    city houses, 152, 153
    Crystal Heights development
        proposal, 30, 42, 43–44,
        234n49
    Hollin Hills development, 44,
        46, 47, 234n50
    Latrobe unbuilt projects, 7
    Lyon Village development
        (Arlington, Va.), 37–38, 39
    modular, metal housing, 44, 45
    multiunit housing develop-
        ments, 156
    National Homes (Lafayette,
        Ind.), 44
    prefabricated homes, 168, 170
    private residences, 154
    recreational space, 162
    Stafford Harbor proposal,
        48, 50, 51, 52, 235n53
    suburban tracts/"cluster
        housing," 168
    Union Built Homes—Green-
        belt Project, 166, 168, 215
    war housing, temporary, 156,
        158, 159, 159, 166, 168
    Wrenwood subdivision, by
        Heaton for Shannon &
        Luchs, 165, 166, 167, 215
    See also names of individual resi-
        dences; new towns/satellite
        cities
Howard Johnson restaurants, 43
Hoxie, Vinnie Ream
    Abraham Lincoln statue by, 17
    Washington Monument
        sculpture proposal (1870–78),
        17, 17
Hudnut, Joseph, on John Russell
    Pope, 48
Hughes, Hugh D., 89
Hunt, Gregory, 55
Hunt, Richard H., 176

Jackson, Andrew, 4
Jacobsen, Hugh Newell, 86
Janes, Beebe & Co. (iron foundry),
    78
Janes, Fowler, Kirtland & Co.
    (iron foundry), 78
Jefferson, Thomas
    on enthusiasm for architecture, 58
    founder of Library of Congress,
        vii
    Latrobe, appointment of, 7
    Monticello, alcove bed design,
        11, 232n11
    papers, 89
    President's House: drawings
        commissioned by, 22, 90, 93,
        95, 96, 97, 99; sketch of
        grounds, 89, 90
    U.S. Capitol: conference with
        architects and masons, 66;
        on Hallet's designs, 62;
        Jefferson's plans for (1790),
        60; Turner's plan, 62–63
Jefferson Memorial, 47, 48
John Russell Pope (firm), 47
Johnson, Lyndon B., 108
Julius Garfinckel & Co., 120, 208,
    209
    Spring Valley Store, 140
Justement, Louis, 37, 161

Kaiser Aluminum and Chemical
    Sales, Inc., 43
Kann's (department store), 119
Kennedy, George H., residence in
    Worcester (Mass.), 38, 189
Kennedy, John Fitzgerald, 4, 89
Kevin Roche John Dinkeloo and
    Associates, 53, 196
Keyser, Mary Procter, 18
Kiley, Dan, landscape design,
    50, 160, 161
Kimball, Fiske, 89
King, Robert Jr., map of Wash-
    ington (1818), 63, 64, 65
King's Palace (department store),
    119
Kohlner, August, U.S. Capitol
    west front, engraving, 74
Krosinsky, Marvin, 176–77

Lane, Samuel, 66–67, 73
Langley, John W., 34
Lansburgh's (department store), 119
Latrobe, B. Henry
    appointment by Jefferson, 7, 66
    architectural rival of Thornton, 11
    Bank of Pennsylvania, 11
    domestic buildings: Harvie House (Richmond, Va.), 11; Pennock House (Norfolk, Va.), 11, 231n10; Tayloe house project, 11–12, 13, **185**, 232n13
    Marine Asylum and Hospital proposal, 7, 8, 9, **10**
    National University proposal (1815), 7, 8, **9**, 231n9
    President's House, 22, 90, 93, **96**, **97**, 98, **99**: east front, **207**; looking glass frame, 95, **206**; north entrance stairs, **95**; south front, **207**
    Richmond mixed-use development project (1800), 44
    Riverside House (*near* Bladensburg, Md.), 11
    Surveyor of Public Buildings, 66–67, 70, 73, 93
    temple-form retreat design, **10**, 11
    U.S. Capitol: ceiling plans (1834), 76, **77**; design and building of, 4, 7, 60, 66–67, 69–70, 73; east and north fronts (1806), drawing by, **69**; east front, **204**, **205**; floor plan (ca. 1832–34), 76, **77**; ground floor (1806), **72**, 73; ground floor (1820–25), **72**, 73; House Chamber, rebuilding of, 70; Library of Congress, 7, 8, **9**, 70, **184**; Senate Chamber, magnolia capitals, **70**; Senate Chamber, re-building of, 70; site survey, 70, **71**; south wing sketches, **68**, 69, **201**; west front (1811), **200**, 201

Washington Monument proposal (1799–1800), 7, **13**, 13
Leinster House (Dublin), 89, 102–3, 238n3
L'Enfant, Pierre Charles
    grand fountains proposed, 4
    plan for Federal City, letter to George Washington, 60
    plan for Washington, D.C., 3–4
    principles of reciprocity, 4
    U.S. Capitol designs (unknown), 60–61, 65
Lenthall, John, 69
Lescaze, William, Longfellow Building, designed by, 43
Le Vau, Louis, 62
Library at Alexandria (Egypt), 8
Library of Congress
    access to resources, 220–21
    architectural development, 233n24
    Art Gallery, by Melander, **187**
    burning of (1851), 78
    design competitions (1870s and 1880s), 18
    design proposals: Esty Congressional Library proposal (1880–81), **20**, 21; Latrobe, 7, 8, **9**, **184**; Smithmeyer and Pelz: —precompetition design (1873), **20**, 21; —Victorian Gothic revival proposal (1875), **21**
    interior view, by Thomas U. Walter, **ii**
    iron doors, 81, **82**
    new building, 18, 83
    in U.S. Capitol, 69, 73, 78, **82**
Library of Congress collections
    Architect of the Capitol collection, 81
    Force (Peter) Americana collection, 14
    Gilbert (Cass) collection, 233n37
    Goodman (Charles M.) archive, 44
    Heaton (Arthur B.) archive, 37, 172

Reiss (Winold) drawings, 43
Rudolph (Paul) archive, 50
Urban Design Charrettes Collection, 55–57
Vietnam Veterans Memorial Fund papers, 55
Walter (Thomas U.) drawings, 81
Washingtoniana Project, ix–x, 14, 153, 159, 172
    See also Geography and Map Division; Prints and Photographs Division
Lin, Maya, Vietnam Veterans Memorial competition winner, ix, 54, **174**, **177**, 177, **178**, **216**, **217**
Lincoln, Abraham, statue portrait, by Hoxie, 17
Lincoln Memorial, 13, 27, 233n28
Lippold, Richard, 176
Lipstadt, Hélène, x, 244
Little Tavern restaurants, 43, **110**, 146
Loewy, Raymond, Air Force One design, 108
Longfellow Building, designed by Lescaze, 43
Longstreth, Richard, contributor, 109–50, 245
Longworth House Office Building, 37
Lyndon, Donlyn, 55
Lyon, Frank, 37
Lyon Village development (Arlington, Va.), 37–38, **39**
Lyon Village Shopping Center (Arlington, Va.), 142, **143**, **144**

Madison, James, White House renovations, 93, 95
Madison Memorial Gateway, proposal, 55
Madrillon Restaurant, 41, 43, **193**
Manuscript Division, Vietnam Veterans Memorial Fund records, 179, 243n2
Marin County Civic Center (Calif.), 50

Marine Asylum and Hospital, Latrobe design proposal (1812–16), 7, 8, 9, **10**
Martin Luther King Library, Vietnam Memorial clipping file, 179
Maryland Avenue, Portal site charette designs (1984), 55–56, **56**
Maryland Historical Society, 62, 66, 89, 95, 98, 236n10
Massachusetts Avenue
    Dolphin America Hotel, 56–57, 196, **197**
    elegant residential development, 122
Massachusetts Historical Society, 89
McComb, John Jr., 73, 237n27
McCormick, Harold C., residence designed by Wright, 30
McIntire, Samuel, U.S. Capitol designs, 62
McKim, Mead and White
    Memorial Bridge, design probability, 22
    White House, **92**, 93
McKinley, William, 102
McLachlen Banking Corp., 210
Meigs, Montgomery C., as Superintendent of the Capitol Extension, 60, 78, 81
Melander, Adolph E., Library of Congress, 18, **187**
Memorial Bridge, design proposals, 22, **23**, 27
Meridian Hill Park, **25**, 25, 103, **106**, 107, 233n28
Michelangelo, Piazza de Campidoglio fountain (Rome), 4
Michels, Doug
    Cadillac Ranch (*near* Amarillo, Tex.), 58
    Dolphin America proposal, 56–57, 196, **197**
    Project Bluestar (space station), 58
Miki, Makoto, Stafford Harbor (Va.) ridge clusters proposal, drawings by, 50, **51**, **52**

Miller, Iris, 55
Mills, Robert
    as Architect of New Buildings,
        74
    Patent Office Building, 14, 74
    Post Office Building, 14, 74
    Treasury Department Building,
        14
    U.S. Capitol: alterations to, 74;
        designs for enlarging, 74, 78
    Washington Monument design,
        13, 14, 232n16, 233n22
Monticello (Charlottesville, Va.),
    alcove bed design, 11, 232n11
Morse, Samuel F. B., House of
    Representatives, painting by,
    74
Mother's Day, established by
    Congress (1913), 34
Mothers Memorial, Geddes
    design proposal, 33–34, 35
Motion Picture, Broadcasting, and
    Recorded Sound Division,
    Vietnam Veterans Memorial
    Fund, 179
Mount Airy plantation (Rich-
    mond County, Va.), 11
Mount Falcon (Summer Resi-
    dence for the Presidents), 29,
    29–30
Mullett, Alfred B.
    Baltimore Sun Building, 110,
        116, 117, 239n8
    business buildings, 120
Munger, George, U.S. Capitol,
    ruins (1814), 70, 202
Myers, Denys Peter, x

National Airport, designed by
    Goodman, 44
National Archives, 47, 90, 102
    Vietnam Memorial objects, 179
National Building Museum
    (formerly Pension Building),
    21
National Capital Planning
    Commission (NCPC), 179
National Fisheries Center and
    Aquarium, proposals for,
    53–54, 196, 235n56

National Galleries project, 26,
    26–27, 27
National Gallery of Art, 47–48
National Hall, proposal, 47–48,
    49
National Homes (Lafayette, Ind.,
    44
National Museum of the Amer-
    ican Indian (New York), 34
National Park Service
    dedication of Hart sculpture,
        179
    Vietnam Memorial records, 179
    White House liaison office, 89,
        93, 108
National Permanent Savings Bank
    Building (Langley Park), 147,
    147
National Stadium Project, 36, 37
National University, Latrobe
    design proposal (1815), 7, 8, 9,
    23n9
Natural History Museum
    (London, 1866–81), designed
    by Alfred Waterhouse, 22
neoclassical architecture, 12, 48
Neue Rathaus (Vienna, Austria,
    1872–83), 22
Newton, Sir Isaac, cenotaph
    design by Boullé, 14
new towns/satellite cities, 48, 50
    Columbia (Md.), 48
    Greenbelt (Md.), 48, 171
    Radburn (N.J.), 48
    Reston (Va.), 44, 48
    Stafford Harbor (Va.)
        proposal, 48, 50, 51, 52,
        235n53
New York, N.Y.
    Ford Foundation headquarters
        building, 53
    Grand Central Station, 34
    Guggenheim Museum, 33
    National Museum of the Amer-
        ican Indian, 34
    Riverside Church project, 34
    St. Mark's-in-the-Bouwerie
        Towers, 43
    U.S. Customs House, 34
    Woolworth Building, 34, 233n37

World Trade Center memorial,
    ix
New-York Historical Society, 93
New York World's Fair (1939–40)
    Trylon and Perisphere, 50
    U.S. Government Building, 44
New York World's Fair (1963–64),
    IBM Pavilion, 53
Nivola, Constantino, 176
Nixon, Mrs. Richard (Patricia), 89
N. L. Sansbury Co., 123
Noble, Alfred, memorial fountain
    proposal, 29

Octagon House, 12
Office of the Commissioner of
    Public Buildings, 89
Office of the Curator of the White
    House, 89, 93, 103
Ogle, Ann. See Tayloe, Ann (Ogle)
    Tayloe
O'Gorman, James F., x
Oldenberg, Claes, 55
Olin, Laurie, 55, 56
Olmsted, Frederick Law, U.S.
    Capitol landscaping, 60, 83
Owen, Frederick D., Executive
    Mansion plan (1890), 22, 24,
    25, 102–3, 106, 107
Owen, Robert Dale, 26
Owings, Nathaniel
    National Square proposal, 4, 56
    portrait by Vincent Perez, 4, 5

Palais Royal (department stores),
    120, 240n16
Palmer Shopping Center (Prince
    George's County, Md.), 145
Park and Shop (Cleveland Park),
    139, 239n3
Patent Office Building, designed
    by Mills, 14, 74
Peaslee, Horace W., 37
Peatross, C. Ford, contributor,
    1–58, 245
Pedersen, Brian F., 89
Pei, I. M., 161
Pelz, Paul
    Executive Mansion plan (1898),
    25, 25, 29, 103, 106, 107

Library of Congress plans, 18,
    21, 83
National Galleries of History
    and Art plans, 26
Pennock House (Norfolk, Va.), 11,
    231n10
Pennsylvania Avenue
    Advisory Council on, 4
    department stores, 119
    "National Square" proposal
        (1964), 4, 5, 56
    President's Advisory Council
        on, 4
    revitalization plan, 4
Pension Building, 21
Pentagon, designed by Bergstrom,
    37
Perez, Vincent, portrait of
    Nathaniel Owings, 4, 5
Peter, Martha Parke (Custis), 12
Peter, Robert, 12
Peter family, Tudor Place in
    Georgetown, 12, 186, 187
Piazza de Campidoglio (Rome),
    by Michelangelo, 4
Pierce, Franklin, 98
Plumbe, John
    U.S. Capitol, photo by, 74
    White House, photo by, 93, 94,
    95
Polk, James K., 98
Poor, Alfred Easton
    old Supreme Court chamber
        restoration, 84, 86, 86
    U.S. Capitol extension, 60, 84
    U.S. Capitol west front alter-
        ations proposals, 86
Poor, Swanke, Hayden, Connell,
    and Robert, 86
Pope, John Russell, Lincoln
    Memorial pyramidal study,
    13
Pope, Sadie, 48
population, in U.S. cities, 240n22
Post Office Building, designed by
    Mills, 14
Predock, Antoine, 55
President's Advisory Council on
    Pennsylvania Avenue, 4
President's Park, 14

Prints and Photographs Division, vii, viii, 168
  Online Catalog, vii
  research tools, ix
  Vietnam Veterans Memorial Fund archive, 176, 177
  White House collections, 89, 93, 98, 103, 108
Procter, Thelma G., 18

Ray, George N., 38
  automobile dealerships, 128, 128–29
  bank buildings, 134
  commercial buildings, 110, 111, 112, 113, 113, 120, 123, 124, 125
  daily life of an architect, 110, 113
  housing developments, 162
  retail/shopping centers, 140
  Riggs-Tompkins complex, 134, 134–35, 241n35
  service stations, 130, 131
  "tourist homes," 113, 114
  war housing, 162, 163
Ray, Luther Reason, 38, 40, 43, 193
  Circle Theatre, vitrolite treatment, 194
  porcelain enamel signs by, 110
Reiss, Renate, 43
Reiss, Tjark, 43
Reiss, Winold, 41, 43, 193
Renwick, Aspinwall, and Russell, 26, 27
Renwick, James
  death of, 25
  National Galleries of History and Art, initial plan (1890), 26
  Smithsonian Institution Castle Building, 26
residential development. See housing
Restaurant Crillon, interior design, by Reiss, 41
restaurants
  Blue Bell System, 41, 190, 191, 211
  Howard Johnson, 43
  Little Tavern, 43, 110, 146

  Madrillon Restaurant, 41, 43, 193
  Restaurant Crillon, 41
  White Castle, 41
Reston (Va.)
  new town development, 44, 48
  origin of name, 48
  waterfront houses, designed by C.W. Smith, 50
Rifle Shooting Range, 43, 193
Riggs National Bank Building (Park Road), 134, 240n26, 241n35
Riverside (near Bladensburg, Md.), Latrobe plan, 11
Roberdeau, Isaac, 61
Robert F. Kennedy (RFK) Stadium, 37
Roche, Kevin
  Ford Foundation headquarters building (New York), 53
  national aquarium project, 53, 235n53
  New York World's Fair (1963–64), IBM Pavilion, 53
Rockefeller, John D. Jr., Colonial Williamsburg restoration project, 34
Rococo Revival, 98
Rodier, Gilbert LaCoste, 37
Rogers, Randolph, 17
Roland, Peter, 55
Romanesque Revival, 22
Roosevelt, Franklin D., inaugural reviewing stand, 108
Roosevelt, Theodore, 90, 93
Rosati, James, 176
Rouse, James W., developer for Columbia (Md.), 48
Rudolph, Paul
  Stafford Harbor (Va.) development proposal, 48, 50, 51, 52, 235n53
  Supreme Court relocation proposal, 55

Saarinen, Eero
  death of, 53
  friendship with Charles Eames, 53

San Marcos-in-the Desert Resort project, 43
San Simeon (Calif.), 29
Sasaki, Hideo, 176
Savage, Edward, engraved portrait of George Washington by, 2, 3
Schmidt, Friedrich, 22
Schoenborn, August, U.S. Capitol designs, 78, 81, 84
Scott, Pamela, contribution x, 4, 173–80, 245
Scott, Sir Gilbert Scott, 21, 22
Scruggs, Jan, Vietnam Veterans Memorial competition and, 54–55, 174
Seale, William, contributor, 87–108, 245
Searle, H. R., Washington Monument, proposed design for completion of (1877), 17, 19
Semmes Motor Company Building, 128, 128
Semper, Gottfried, 21
Senate Chamber. See U.S. Capitol, Senate Chamber
service stations, 240–41n27
  Heaton designs, 41, 47, 132, 133, 133, 195, 211
  Hollin Hills development, designs by Goodman, 44, 46, 47
  Ray designs, 130, 131
Shank, Richard Samuel, Vietnam Veterans Memorial design competition, 218
Shannon & Luchs
  housing development, 165, 172, 172
  Wrenwood subdivision, 165, 166, 167, 215
Shannon & Luchs building, 120, 125, 127
shopping centers, 110, 140–47, 212, 241n38, 242n39–49
  Cleveland Park, 138, 139
  Fairway Hills–Glen Echo Shops (Montgomery County, Md.), 146, 146

Lyon Village Shopping Center, 142, 143, 144
Palmer Shopping Center (Prince George's County, Md.), 145
Spring Valley stores, 139, 140
Washington & Lee Shopping Center (Arlington, Va.), 142, 142
Sibour, Jules Henri de, 155
Silver Spring (Md.), commercial development, 141, 242n43
Simon, Robert E., developer of Reston, 48
Sinclair Oil, service station, 195
Skidmore, Owings & Merrill (firm), National Square proposal, 4, 56
Small, John H., 165
Smith, Benjamin Franklin Jr., 14, 187, 232n18
Smith, Chloethiel Woodard
  Southwest Urban Renewal Area, 50–51, 53, 54, 153, 161, 161
  waterfront developments, in other cities, 50
Smith, Franklin Webster, National Galleries project, 26, 26–27, 27
Smith, John Rubens, west front of U.S. Capitol, watercolor by, 74, 204, 205
Smithmeyer, John L., 18, 83
Smithmeyer and Pelz (firm)
  Executive Mansion designs, 25
  Library of Congress design winners, 18, 20, 21, 83
  Memorial Bridge proposals, 22, 23
Smithsonian Institution
  Castle Building, 26
  Mall, National University proposal and, 8
Soane, Sir John, 69
Somma, Thomas, 29
Sonnemann, O., 81, 237n34
Soufflot, Jacques-Gabriel, 62
Spreiregen, Paul, 174, 177
Starrett and VanVleck, 208

Ste. Geneviève church (Paris), 62
Stewart, J. George, as Architect
    of the Capitol, 48, 84,
    234–35n52
Stier, Henri Joseph, 11
Stillman, Damie, contributor,
    59–86, 245
St. Mark's-in-the-Bouwerie
    Towers (New York), 43
St. Pancras Station (London,
    1860s), designed by Sir
    Gilbert Scott, 22
Street, G. E., 21
Strong, Gordon, "automobile
    objective" (Sugarloaf Moun-
    tain, Md.) design, 33, 58, 189,
    233n116
Structural Porcelain Enamel Co.,
    43, 110, 140, 212
Sun Oil Co., service station, 133
Supreme Court Building
    Gilbert design proposals, 34,
        36, 37
    location of, 34, 36, 37, 55
Supreme Court in U.S. Capitol,
    13, 69
Surveyor of Public Buildings,
    66–67, 70

Taliesin (Wis.), home and studio
    of Wright, 30
Taliesin Associates, 50
Tayloe, Ann (Ogle), 12
Tayloe, John III, 11–12
Tayloe house project, 11–12, 185,
    232n13
T. D. Donovan & Associates, 213
Thornton, William
    architectural rival of Latrobe,
        11
    Octagon House, 12
    President's House, drawings
        attributed to, 98, 99
    Tudor Place, 12, 186, 187
    U.S. Capitol designs: east
        front, 204, 205; in the 1790s,
        6, 7, 60–63, 63, 65–66, 67,
        182, 183, 199, 236n24; west
        front, 65–66, 67, 182, 183,
        231n7

U.S. Capitol design winner
    (1793), 65
Washington Monument
    proposals, 13
Thurman, Roy S., developer,
    43–44
Tivoli Theater (movie house), 134,
    241n34
Toledo Porcelain Enamel Co., 43
Torre, Susanna, 55
Transportation Building, designed
    by Wood, Donn & Deming,
    118, 119, 119, 240n12
Treasury Department Building
    designed by Mills, 14, 74
    location of, 4
triumphal arches
    designs by Smithmeyer and
        Pelz: Library of Congress
        entryway, 20, 21; Memorial
        Bridge, 22, 23
    proposals for Washington,
        14, 16, 17
Truman, Harry S., 89, 93
Trumbull, John, 61, 236n10
Tudor Place (Georgetown), 12,
    186, 187
Turnbull, William Jr., 176
Turner, George, 62, 236n10
Tyng, Anne, 176

Union Trust Company Building,
    116, 239n10
University of San Diego library,
    103
University of Virginia, 8
Upman, Frank, 37
U.S. Capitol, ix, 59–86
    British burning of (1814), 8, 70,
        202
    ceiling plans, by Bulfinch and
        Latrobe, 76
    Conference Room: Hallet
        design (1793), 7, 182, 183, 200,
        201; purposes of the, 7
    congressional act establishing,
        60
    design competitions: of 1792,
        for building, 61–62, 65;
        of 1850, for enlarging, 78

designs for enlarging, by Robert
    Mills, 74, 78
dome of the Capitol:
    Bulfinch (study for), 76, 203;
    Brumidi painting, 78;
    peristyle of (1857), 82;
    rebuilding of (1850s), 78, 81;
    Statue of Freedom, 78, 79
east and north fronts (1806),
    drawing by Latrobe, 69
east front: Davis watercolor
    (1834), 74, 204, 205; King Jr.
    engraving (1818), 7, 63, 64;
    Thornton drawing (ca. 1795–
    97), 63, 199
extension projects: nineteenth
    century, 78–86; twentieth
    century, 84, 84, 85, 86
floor plans: by Bulfinch and
    Latrobe, 74, 76; by Latrobe,
    72, 73
foundation and cornerstone
    laid, 66
grand stairway, by Bulfinch, 70
Hallet designs (1790s), 4, 6, 7,
    60–62, 61, 65, 65–66, 198,
    199
House Chamber: glass ceiling
    design, by Bulfinch (1818–22),
    73, 74; Hallet's design (1793),
    65, 65; interior renovations,
    48; Morse painting (1821), 74;
    new (1857), 78; south wing
    construction (1801–3), 66–67
Jefferson design and plans
    (1790s), 60–61
landscape designs, 73, 73, 83
L'Enfant designs (unknown),
    60–61, 65
north wing: entrance, corncob
    capitals, 70, 237n26; Library
    of Congress, 69; Library of
    Congress, Egyptian decora-
    tions, 70
Rotunda and dome cupola
    stairway, Hallet design (1793),
    4, 6, 7
Senate and Supreme Court
    Chambers, restoration of, 84,
    86, 86

Senate Chamber: column
    details, 70; Hallet's design
    (1793), 65, 65; interior renova-
    tions, 48; new (1859), 78;
    rebuilding north wing, 69, 73
site and landscaping plan, by
    Bulfinch, 73, 73
site survey, by Latrobe (1803–6),
    70, 71
south wing: Bulfinch vestibule
    design, 74, 75; Latrobe
    designs (1804–5), 68, 69
Supreme Court chamber, 13, 69
Thornton designs (1790s), 6, 7,
    60–63, 63, 65–66, 67
vaulted ceilings, 69
west front: alterations proposal
    (1963), 48, 49; Bulfinch
    proposal, 86; Kohlner
    engraving (1839), 74; Latrobe
    design (1811), 200, 201;
    Library of Congress
    (1852–53), 73, 78, 81, 83; Poor
    design proposals, 86; Smith
    watercolor, 74, 204, 205;
    Thornton design (1795–97),
    65–66, 67, 182, 183, 231n7
U.S. Customs House (New York),
    34
U.S. embassy (Tokyo, 1914),
    designed by Wright, 30, 31, 33

Van Dorn Street development
    (Alexandria, Va.), 148, 149
Vietnam Generation Project, 179
Vietnam Veterans Memorial,
    173–80
    competition program:
        competitor's designs, 177, 218;
        design requirements, 175; jury
        members, 176; number of
        entries, 176; prize winners,
        176–77; registration booklet,
        174, 176
    monumental helmet and dog
        tag, 55, 196, 197
    winning design, by Maya Lin, ix,
        54, 174, 177, 177, 178, 216, 217
Vietnam Veterans Memorial Fund
    (VVMF), 174

Vietnam Women's Memorial Fund, 179
visionary architecture, 58

Waggaman, Clarke, 38, 110, 112
    hanging sign board, **155**
    war housing, 162, **163**
Waggaman and Ray (firm), 120, 123, 127, 153, 162
Walker, Donald D., 33
Walker, John Brisben, Summer Residence for the Presidents, design commissioned by, **29**, 29–30
Walter, Ida, 81
Walter, Thomas U.
    as Architect of the U.S. Capitol Extension, 60, 78, 81, 83
    Executive Mansion, 22, 98, 100, **102**, **103**, **105**
    Library of Congress: interior view, watercolor by, ii; iron doors, 81, **83**
    U.S. Capitol dome (1859), 78, **80**, 81
Wardman Construction Company Building, 125, **127**
Warner, Olin Levi, 17
Warren & Wetmore (New York), 34
Washington, D.C.
    bird's-eye view perspectives, 4, 7, **28**, **29**, **186**, **187**, 231n7
    design charettes (1982–89), 55–57, **56**
    L'Enfant plan, 3–4, 25
    map of (1818), engraving by Robert King Jr., 63, **64**
    McMillan Commission plan (1901–2), 25, 27, 29, 55
    population in 1930, 240n22
Washington, George
    engraved portrait of, by Savage, **2**, 3
    on executive apartment in U.S. Capitol, 236n11
    Hoxie sculpture proposed, **17**, 17
    See also Washington Monument
Washington, Martha, 12

Washington & Lee Shopping Center, **142**, 142
Washingtoniana Project, ix-x, 14, 153, 159, 172
Washington Loan and Trust Co., 116, 118, **119**, 119
Washington Monument
    design proposals, 232n16
    Force design proposal (1837), 13, 14, **15**
    Hoxie sculpture proposed, **17**, 17
    landscape plan, 29
    Latrobe design proposal (1800), 7, **13**, 13
    Mills designs, 13, 14, 232n16, 233n22
    Searle design, 18, **19**
    Thornton proposals, 13
    view from, 4
Washington National Airport, designed by Goodman, 44
Washington National Monument Society, 13
waterfront developments
    Southwest (D.C.): Capitol Park, 50, 161; Channel Waterfront Bridge proposal, 53, **54**; Harbour Square, 50, 51, 159, **161**, 161
Waterhouse, Alfred, 22
Weese, Harry, 176
White Castle restaurants, 41
White House, 22, 87–108
    architectural history, 89
    Ellipse (*formerly* President's Park), 8, **25**, 25, 107
    Executive Mansion, ix, 22: basement kitchens, 100, **105**; extensions proposed by Mrs. Harrison, **106**, 107; floor plans, **105**; Owen's plan (1890), 22, **24**, 25; Pelz design, commissioned by Mrs. Henderson (1898), **25**, 25, 103, **106**, 107; screen (1853), 102; Walter drawings, 22, 98, 100, **102**, 103
    interior renovations (1940s and 1950s), 48
    north front, **88**, 89, **104**, 105

President's House, ix, 22; design competition (1792), 60–61, 65, 89; Hoban's designs, 65, 89, 95; Latrobe drawings, 22, **90**, 93, **95**, **96**, **97**, 98, **99**, **206**, **207**; north portico, 98, **100**, **101**; site plan (ca. 1804), **90**; south front, Plumbe photo (ca. 1846), 93, **94**, 95
President's Palace, 22
    reconstruction projects, 90, 93
    site plan (1988–92), 90, **91**
    south front, **104**, 105
    South Portico and New Wings (1902), **92**, 93
    State Dining Room (1902), **92**, 93
    West Wing and Oval Office, 90
White House Historical Association, 89, 238n4
Willard Hotel, 4
Williams, William, U.S. Capitol, conference meeting with Jefferson, 66
Williamsburg, Colonial, restoration of, 34
Wilson, Woodrow, 34
Winslow, Lorenzo S., 93
Winterthur Museum, 81
Wisedell, Thomas, 83
Wolanin, Barbara, x
Wolverine Porcelain Enamel Co., 43
Wood, Donn & Deming, 116, 119
Wood, Waddy Butler, 110, 153
    All States Hotel for Women, 162, **163**
    office building, **208**
    Roosevelt inaugural reviewing stand, **108**
    Transportation Building, **118**, **119**, 119, 240n12
    war housing, temporary, 156, **158**, **159**, 159, **160**, 161, 162
Woods, Elliott, as Architect of the Capitol, 83
Woodward & Lothrop, 120
Woolworth Building (New York), 34, 233n37

World Trade Center (New York), memorial design, ix
World War II Memorial, 29
Wright, Frank Lloyd
    Avery Coonley House (Riverside, Ill.), 30
    Cloverleaf project/defense housing (Pittsfield, Mass.), 30, 168
    Como Orchards Summer Colony (Darby, Mont., 30
    Crystal Heights development proposal, 30, **42**, 43–44, 234n49
    Gordon Strong "automobile objective," Sugarloaf Mountain, 30, 33, 58, **189**, 233n116
    Guggenheim Museum (New York), 33
    Imperial Hotel (Tokyo), 30, 33
    Marin County Civic Center (Calif.), 50
    San Marcos-in-the Desert Resort project, 43
    St. Mark's-in-the-Bouwerie Towers (New York), 43
    Taliesin (Spring Green, Wis.), home and studio of, 30
    U.S. embassy (Tokyo), 30, **31**, 33
Wright, Gwendolyn, contributor, 151–72, 245
Wyeth, Nathan C., 37

Younger, Joseph, 124

A Note on the Types

The text of *Capital Drawings* is composed in Adobe Jenson, designed by Robert Slimbach in 1995. Slimbach closely modeled his typeface on that of the 1470 edition of *De Evangelica Præparatione*, a religious tome written by the Christian apologist Eusebius more than a millennium earlier and published in Venice by Nicholas Jenson. This book set the standard for the design of roman type during the *incunabula*, the golden age of classical typography constituting the first half-century of printing with moveable types. The spirit of Jenson's landmark work has been revived in many subsequent type designs of great merit, including the *Golden Type* of William Morris, *Cloister Oldstyle* by Morris Fuller Benton, and *Centaur* by Bruce Rogers. The display type was created by Robert L. Wiser, the designer of this volume, as a companion titling face to Slimbach's Jenson.